East Asian Social Science Monographs

Women and Party Politics in Peninsular Malaysia

Women and Party Politics in Peninsular Malaysia

Virginia H. Dancz

SINGAPORE
OXFORD UNIVERSITY PRESS
OXFORD NEW YORK
1987

Oxford University Press

Oxford   New York   Toronto
Petaling Jaya   Singapore   Hong Kong   Tokyo
Delhi   Bombay   Calcutta   Madras   Karachi
Nairobi   Dar es Salaam   Cape Town
Melbourne   Auckland

and associates in
Beirut   Berlin   Ibadan   Nicosia

OXFORD is a trademark of Oxford University Press

© Oxford University Press Pte. Ltd. 1987

All rights reserved. No part of this publication may be reproduced,
stored in a retrieval system, or transmitted, in any form or by any means,
electronic, mechanical, photocopying, recording or otherwise,
without the prior permission of Oxford University Press

ISBN 0 19 582689 2

HQ 1236.5
M34D36x
1987

Printed in Singapore by Kyodo-Shing Loong Printing Industries Pte. Ltd.
Published by Oxford University Press Pte. Ltd.,
Unit 221, Ubi Avenue 4, Singapore 1440

Preface

THIS book is based on the doctoral dissertation entitled 'Women's Auxiliaries and Party Politics in Western Malaysia' submitted to Brandeis University in June 1980. Research was carried out in West Malaysia from May 1975 until November 1976 and again in April/May 1983.* Because women have often been neglected in more traditional histories of Malaysia, this study actively sought interviews with Malaysian women of all three main races as a major source of information. Interviews were conducted in English or Malay: non-English and non-Malay speaking women were interviewed through a translator. The views of male party leaders were generally taken from abundant party and newspaper sources. Newspaper records from 1945 to 1983 were utilized as well as party records wherever possible. UMNO, the PI and PSRM records, written in Bahasa Malaysia (Malay) were consulted in the original, while thanks need be given to Noraziah Ali who translated UMNO journals which were available only in the Jawi (Arabic) script. The MCA, MIC and the non-communal parties kept their records in English and a communal language.

The government sponsored *Federation of Malaya Daily Press Summary 1958–1964* (from 1965 to 1983, *Intisari Akhbar Harian*) published by the Malaysian Ministry of Information, provided an invaluable source of information on political and party news in all the various parties and on women in parties past and present. For reasons of brevity and clarity it is referred to as *D.P.S.* in all footnotes despite its Malay name change in 1965. Another valuable source of information was provided by the newspaper files of the *New Straits Times* (which included files on *Berita Harian*, a Malay daily). In Chapters 1 to 7, all references to the *Straits Times*, which became the *New Straits Times* in 1972, are presented as *ST* in the footnotes. Chapter 8 uses *NST*, the now familiar abbreviation. The libraries of the Malaysian National Archives, the University of Malaya, Universiti Kebangsaan Malaysia and the University of Singapore also provided valuable information in terms of taped personal histories, party records and personal collections, as well as newspaper clippings and secondary sources. Some Malaysian government publications were also useful.

*Consequently, those developments that occurred prior to 1976 provide the body of the text, while events of the late 1970s and early 1980s are included in the Postscript of Part III.

This book would not have been possible without the help of many people. Thanks need be given to many sources for financial support: my husband, the politics department of Brandeis University, the Universiti Kebangsaan Malaysia for courtesies extended to me and the Sachar Foundation of Brandeis University. Thanks also need be given to my dissertation committee for their aid in guiding the initial study that later became this book. In particular, I am most grateful to Professor Donald Hindley of Brandeis University who spent many hours reading the dissertation cum book. Additionally, I wish to thank a large number of Malaysian women who unselfishly gave of their time and patiently bore with this author's many questions. Such friends are too numerous to name here but to them I give my heartfelt thanks. To one friend in particular, Deputy Minister of Information, Rahmah Othman, I would like to give my special thanks. She tirelessly answered my many questions and took me with her to several Wanita UMNO meetings, efforts I particularly appreciated. To all my Malaysian friends I can only say *terima kasih*.

June 1984　　　　　　　　　　　　　　　　　　VIRGINIA H. DANCZ

Contents

Preface	v
Tables	x
Abbreviations	xi
Introduction	xiii

PART I
WOMEN IN PRE-1945 MALAYAN SOCIETY — 1

1. Malay Women — 3
- Adat — 4
- Islam — 12
- Class — 18
- Women in the Traditional Economy — 20
- The Pre-war Participation of Malay Women in Social Organizations — 23
- The Japanese Occupation and Its Effect on Malay Women — 27

2. Chinese Women — 33
- The First Chinese Women Immigrants to Malaya — 33
- A Wave of Chinese Women Immigrants — 38
- The Economic Role of Chinese Immigrant Women — 40
- Marriage and Chinese Women — 42
- Marital Status and Legal Difficulties of Malayan Chinese Women — 48
- The 1930s—A New Wave of Immigrants — 49
- Chinese Women and the Pre-1945 Political Associations — 49
- The Japanese Occupation and Its Effect on Malayan Chinese Women — 51

3. Indian Women — 56
- The Nature of Indian Immigration to Malaya — 56
- Marriage and Indian Women in Malaya — 60
- The Economic Role of Indian Immigrant Women — 64
- Non-Hindu Indian Women — 67
- Indian Women and the Pre-1945 Political Associations — 69
- The Japanese Occupation and Its Effect on Malayan Indian Women — 70

PART II
THE GROWTH OF WOMEN'S POLITICAL AUXILIARIES 81

4. From War to Independence, 1945–1957 83
Post-war Malaya 83
The Earliest Political Associations of Malay Women 86
The Birth of the Kaum Ibu UMNO 87
The Social and Political Organizations of Non-Malay Women 100
    Chinese Women—The Early Associations 100
    The Malayan Chinese Association (MCA) 102
    Indian Women's Organizations 103
    Non-communal and Other Communal Parties and Women 105
Elections: Women as Candidates and Party Workers 108
Women and Post-1955 Political Developments 112
Conclusion 113

5. Independence to Political Crisis, 1957–1969 122
The Kaum Ibu UMNO 122
The MCA 130
The MIC 132
The Dewan Muslimat of the PMIP 133
Parti Sosialis Rakyat Malaya (PSRM) 135
The Labour Party 136
Other Parties 138
The Emergence of the National Council of Women's Organizations 139
The Importance of Women as Electoral Candidates and Workers—The General Elections of 1959 and 1964 141
Conclusion 146

6. The Kaum Ibu UMNO, 1969–1976 153
Structure and Interests 153
Members and Leaders 164
The Wanita UMNO Leaders (*Ketua-ketua*) 168
Conclusion 175

7. The Growth of Other Women's Political Auxiliaries, 1969–1976 181
The MCA 181
The MIC 189
The Dewan Muslimat PAS 192
The DAP 194
The Gerakan 197
Pekemas 198
Other Parties 199

The Importance of Women as Electoral Candidates and Workers—The General Elections of 1969 and 1974	200
Conclusion	203

PART III
POSTSCRIPT 209

8. A Quarter Century of Independence Fulfilled, 1976–1983 211
Wanita UMNO 212
Wanita MCA 217
Wanita MIC 220
The Opposition—PAS and the DAP 221

9. Conclusions 225
The Political Mobilization of Malaysian Women 225
Party–Auxiliary Relations 231
Auxiliary–Member Relations 233

Appendix 235
Glossary 239
Select Bibliography 241
Index 263

Tables

1.1	Statistics on Malay Marriages, Divorces and Revocations, 1921–1949	16
1.2	Number of Females Employed Outside the Home	21
1.3	Literate Malays per Thousand, 1931	23
2.1	Growth of the Chinese Population, 1840–1922	35
2.2	Growth Pattern of Females per 1,000 Males, 1911–1921	38
2.3	Number of Chinese Women Immigrants per 1,000 Men among the Major Groups	39
2.4	Sex Ratio Disparity among Immigrant Chinese, 1923–1930	39
2.5	Number of Passes Issued by the Mines Department, 1908–1920	41
2.6	Statistics for Married Chinese Men and Women, 1921	43
2.7	Number of Married and Single Chinese per Thousand of the General Population, 1931	44
3.1	Number of Recorded Indian Women Immigrating to Malaya, 1867–1869	57
3.2	Number of Indian Women Employed Outside the Home, 1921	64
3.3	Indian Women in the Agricultural Coolie Class, 1921	65
3.4	Daily Wage Rates of Estate Workers, 1904–1913	65
3.5	Daily Wage Rates of Estate Workers, 1915–1941	66
3.6	Number of Literates per 1,000 of Indian Population by Sex, 1921	67
3.7	Disparate Sex Ratio among Indian Muslims, 1921	68
5.1	Average Size of the Supreme Council, 1957–1967	127
5.2	Number of Sub-committees Served by KI, Various Years	127
5.3	Breakdown of Men and Women Candidates by Party, 1959	143
5.4	Breakdown of Men and Women Candidates by Party, 1964	145
6.1	The Pattern of Representation at the Higher Hierarchy within UMNO, 1967–1976	157
6.2	Number of UMNO Women Candidates, 1959–1974 Elections	162
6.3	Reasons for Joining Wanita UMNO	165
6.4	Background of the Nineteen Members of the 1976 National Executive Committee	167
7.1	State and Federal Electorates by Party, 1969	201
7.2	Results of the Alliance in West Malaysia in the 1959, 1964, 1969 Elections	202
7.3	Breakdown of Candidates by Party and Sex in the 1974 General Election	203

Abbreviations

AMCJA	All-Malaya Council for Joint Action
AWAS	Angkatan Wanita Sedar—Progressive Malay Women's Corps
BN	Barisan Nasional—National Front
CCC	Consultative Committee on the Constitutional Proposals
CIAM	Central Indian Association of Malaya
DAP	Democratic Action Party
DM	Dewan Muslimat—Women's Council (of the Islamic Party)
FMS	Federated Malay States
GRM	Gerakan Rakyat Malaysia—Malaysian Peoples' Movement Party
IIL	Indian Independence League
IMP	Independence of Malaya Party
INA	Indian Nationalist Army
ISA	Internal Security Act
KI	Kaum Ibu—Women's Association (of UMNO)
KMM	Kesatuan Melayu Muda—Union of Malay Youths
KMS	Kesatuan Melayu Singapura—Singapore Malay Union
KMT	Kuomintang
KRIS	Kesatuan Raayat Indonesia Semenanjong—Peninsular Indonesian People's Union
LP	Labour Party
MCA	Malay(si)an Chinese Association
MCP	Malay(si)an Communist Party
MIC	Malay(si)an Indian Congress
MNP	Malay Nationalist Party
MPAJA	Malayan People's Anti-Japanese Army
MPAJU	Malayan People's Anti-Japanese Union
MU	Malayan Union
MWTC	Malay Women's Training College
MWWA	Malay Women's Welfare Association (of Singapore)
NAWIM	National Association of Women's Institutes of Malay(si)a
NCWO	National Council of Women's Organizations
NP	National Party—Parti Negara
Pekemas	Parti Keadilan Masyarakat Malaysia—Malaysian Social Justice Party
PGGPJ	Persekutuan Guru-Guru Perempuan Johor—Union of Johore Women Teachers
PMCJA	Pan-Malayan Council of Joint Action
PMIP	Pan-Malayan Islamic Party (or PAS or PI—Islamic Party of Malay(si)a)

PMLP	Pan-Malayan Labour Party
PMS	Pergerakan Melayu Semenanjong—Movement of Peninsular Malays (Johore)
PPP	People's Progressive Party
PSRM	Parti Sosialis Rakyat Malaya—People's Socialist Party of Malay(si)a
SF	Socialist Front
SIA	Selangor Indian Association
SS	Straits Settlements
UDP	United Democratic Party—Parti Demokratik Bersatu
UMNO	United Malays National Organization
UMS	Unfederated Malay States
WI	Women's Institute

Introduction

Background

POLITICAL scientists have long been interested in political parties, in how they are structured and how they function within different political systems. Little attention, however, has been paid to party auxiliaries,[1] the youth and women's wings, that often function alongside the parties themselves. In particular, the subject of women's political auxiliaries in developing countries has yet to be adequately examined despite a recent surge of interest in the changing social, economic and political roles of women in a variety of societies. Western political scientists, often preoccupied with the democratic parties of Western Europe and North America, have been largely content either to limit their discussions of women's political auxiliaries to a few paragraphs or, when discussing totalitarian parties, to stress the usefulness of the auxiliaries as instruments of party control rather than examining how the auxiliaries serve both the party and its members.[2] Few studies of auxiliaries in developing nations exist despite the plethora of parties and party systems that have emerged since World War II. As early as 1955, Duverger stressed the need to study the nature and scope of female political participation on a multinational level,[3] while Mary Beard has long argued that history is incomplete if it does not include women as historical and political participants.[4] Thus far, little has been written about women as political participants with the exception of a few studies in the 1960s and 1970s, none of which focused on women's political auxiliaries.[5] This book seeks to help fill the gap by examining the nature of women's political participation through the women's political auxiliaries in one developing country, Malaysia. Included in the study is an examination of the relationship that exists between parties and their auxiliaries including the roles that the auxiliaries play both for the parties and for the auxiliary members. Additionally, the contributions Malaysian women have made to the independence effort and to the post-war political parties will become apparent.

Malaysia lent itself to study for its variety of political parties and women's auxiliaries. They varied in size, history, political philosophy and scope of activities. All parties voiced a commitment to encouraging women to enter party activities. All parties were committed, whether in theory or in practice, to organizing women's political auxiliaries as adjuncts to the parties themselves. Malaysia was selected for study due to its diversity of peoples and parties. This offered the chance for comparative study. Peninsular Malaysia itself occupies a position in South-East Asia extending south from the Thai border to the island of Singapore in the South China Sea together with the eastern states of Sabah and Sarawak which lie on the island of Borneo. Lying entirely within the tropic zone, 0° and 7° North, extending from longitude 100° to 119½° East, Malaysia is neighbour to Thailand in the north and the Republics of Indonesia and Singapore in the south. A fourth neighbour, the Philippines, lies just to the north of Sabah. Prior to the 1948 Federation of Malaya Agreement, the term Malaya was used to refer to the nine Malay States of the Malay Peninsula. This consisted of Perlis, Kedah, Kelantan, Trengganu, Perak, Selangor, Pahang, Negri Sembilan and Johore together with the Straits Settlements of Penang, Malacca and Singapore. After 1948, Singapore was administered separately as a British Crown colony and later pursued its own separate path to independence; its political developments have not been included here.

In 1963, efforts were made to increase political stability in the region by joining Malaya, Singapore and the two Borneo states of Sabah and Sarawak. This effort, called Malaysia, lasted until 1965 when Singapore left the coalition. Herein, the term 'Malaysia' designates the country that consists of the 11 Malayan states (the original nine plus Penang and Malacca) together with the eastern Malaysian states of Sabah and Sarawak. Peninsular Malaysia refers to the 11 Malayan states of West Malaysia. The parties of East Malaysia were not included in this study due to the vast historical and cultural differences that exist between the peoples of East and West Malaysia. The term Malaya is used to refer to the nine Malayan states together with Malacca and Penang prior to the formation of Malaysia in 1963. After 1963, the corrected term Malaysia is used in this text though it is used to refer only to events and institutions in West or Peninsular Malaysia. A further note of clarification: Malay is a term used to designate a particular ethnic group in Malaysia while Malayan or Malaysian is used to refer to a citizen of Malaya or Malaysia irrespective of racial or ethnic origin.

At the time of this research, Malaysia was a country of slightly more than 12 million. The Malays represented 55.8 per cent of the population, the Chinese 33.3 per cent and the Indians just under 10.2 per cent. The other races, including aborigines, Europeans, and Eurasians constituted less than 1 per cent of the population. As of 1982, the population within Peninsular Malaysia consisted of:[6]

Malays	6,808,383
Chinese	4,064,963
Indians and Pakistanis	1,241,710
Others	78,500

The Malays, who are discussed in greater depth in Chapter 1, originally came from today's South China and are a predominantly rural people living in villages throughout the Malaysian countryside. Agriculturalists and fishermen, they are the numerically dominant population in the northern and north-eastern states and have not until recently settled in the urban areas.

Malay culture and traditions are governed by two major forces, Islam and one of two types of social organization based on customary law or *adat*—factors which are treated in depth in the first chapter. In addition, the history of the Malays was shaped by the effects of British colonialism which sought to protect the Malay way of life from rapid economic changes but resulted in leaving the Malays economically deprived compared to the Chinese and Indians.

The second major group is the Chinese (discussed in Chapter 2) who came to Malaya in large numbers beginning in the 1850s with the development of the tin and rubber industries and in even larger waves during the early 1900s. Emigrating from South China, these immigrants, largely Buddhists who spoke a number of dialects, concentrated in the west coast states of Malaya, particularly in the towns and urban areas where they quickly came to dominate the economy not controlled by Europeans. Again, colonial policies fostered the position of the Chinese (and to a lesser extent the Indians) as entrepreneurs by encouraging a system of economic *laissez-faire* while excluding them as a political force.

The Indians (discussed in Chapter 3) are the third major ethnic group in Malaysia. The first Indians came to Malaya during the 1800s as recruited labour for the coffee and sugar plantations. Larger waves of male immigrants continued from the late 1800s to the early twentieth century and found employment on the rubber and palm oil estates. Recruited largely from South India, the Indians, mostly Hindus, spoke a variety of languages including, Tamil, Telugu, Hindi and Urdu. In addition, a small number of northern Indians—Sikhs—were recruited by the British for administrative and security work. Always a minority compared to the greater numbers of Malays and Chinese, the Indians lacked the numbers to dominate either the economy or the political system. Instead, one finds that they lie between the Malays and Chinese on the economic spectrum—being generally better off than the Malays but not as well off as the Chinese—while having less political leverage or influence than either the Malays or the Chinese.

A Brief History

The history of the Malaysian party system[7] effectively began in 1946 with the return of the British to their pre-war colony of Malaya. Prior to the war, political parties were non-existent except for branches of the Chinese Kuomintang and the largely Chinese Malayan Communist Party. Nascent nationalism as experienced by the Malays was expressed through a number of Malay associations which first appeared in the 1930s, and which were largely concerned with the spiritual and economic fate of the Malays but did not challenge the colonial status quo. Malaya's two other ethnic groups, the Chinese and Indians, were similarly preoccupied and any strong nationalistic feelings they had were directed towards China or

India rather than towards Malaya. Chinese clan associations were equally strong in Malaya as elsewhere in South-East Asia. Indian men organized themselves into a number of Indian associations, most of which provided social and recreational opportunities for their members though a few did discuss such matters as Indian independence and the role of Indians in Malaya. As will become apparent in Chapters 1 to 3, women played almost no part in these pre-war activities.

World War II and the Japanese Occupation of Malaya had profound political and economic effects on all three races. The British return to Malaya in 1945 brought efforts to unite the Malay Peninsula under a strong central government headed by a British Governor. The Malayan Union, or MU, proposals which would have deprived the Rulers and states of all but nominal authority, sparked the growth of Malay nationalism and prompted the growth of a number of political parties, in particular the Malay Nationalist Party (MNP) and the communal United Malays National Organization (UMNO). The success of the UMNO in mobilizing the Malays to defeat the MU proposals set the dominant pattern that continued: successful parties were communal parties—parties which limited their membership to just one racial or ethnic group. British colonialism, World War II and the Japanese Occupation also stimulated the growth of a number of socialist, communist, anti-colonial and non-communal parties that generally opposed the return of the British as colonial rulers. The outbreak in 1948 of the Malayan communist insurgency, known as the Emergency, resulted in a ban on all parties which the colonial power thought radical or threatening (see Chapter 4). This had a devastating effect on the non-Malay population and greatly inhibited the growth of their political organizations; the success of the UMNO in defeating the MU proposals and the provisions of the 1948 Federation of Malaya Agreement, however, stimulated the growth of parties with its promise of representative government through the introduction of elections. The first municipal elections (1951) were introduced in Penang; other elections followed from 1951 to 1954. By 1951, a number of parties existed to compete for the voter's support: UMNO to represent the Malays, the Malayan Chinese Association (MCA) which sought to appeal to the Chinese, and the Malayan Indian Congress (MIC) which represented moderate Indian interests. The parties that survived and grew during the late 1940s and 1950s were largely pragmatic, moderate parties which, while catering to the specific demands of their respective ethnic groups, were largely free of any political philosophy or ideology. In addition to these three major communal parties, a conservative Malay religious party, the Pan-Malayan Islamic Party (PMIP), which was originally the religious wing of UMNO, and an agrarian socialist party, the People's Socialist Party of Malaya (PSRM), came to compete with UMNO for Malay electoral support. A number of smaller parties seeking to bridge the gap between Malays and non-Malays also attempted to appeal to the populace in general, non-communal terms. The Independence of Malaya Party

(IMP), the National Party (NP), and the Labour Party (LP) were all such attempts while more recently, the Democratic Action Party (DAP), the Malaysian People's Movement Party (Gerakan, or GRM) and the Malaysian Social Justice Party (Pekemas) continued such efforts. These parties have, without exception, largely failed to bridge the communal gap and have either died out or continued to face considerable electoral difficulties.

The 1952 Kuala Lumpur municipal elections prompted an unforseen development which resulted in an electoral arrangement providing Malaya with political stability until 1969; the UMNO and MCA made an electoral pact not to field candidates in the same districts but to direct their efforts against the non-communal parties—in particular, against the Independence of Malaya Party. The electoral success of this *ad hoc* arrangement prompted the formation of the Alliance party, which consisted of the UMNO, the MCA and, after 1954, the MIC. The Alliance solved a seemingly insoluble difficulty—how to aggregate the interests of all communities. Non-communal parties, where politicians of different ethnic groups often could not co-operate with one another, were unsuccessful in appealing to voters. The Alliance arrangement, consisting of separate communal parties linked at the top by the leaders of the respective parties, seemed to guarantee a measure of political stability by establishing government by the élites of Malaysia's three major ethnic groups. These leaders in turn had to convince their respective followers of the wisdom of the compromises they had adopted. As for the parties' rank and file, Goh Cheng-teik noted,

... they remained apart and tended to agitate only for the interests of their race or tribe. The summit leadership acted as a cushion against excessive communal pressure and as a moderator of conflicting demands. This role compelled them to strive for the preservation of a 'balance of power' within the confederation and the prevention of a rise to hegemony by any single constituent.[8]

The Alliance was always dominated by the UMNO. UMNO presidents became Malaya's prime ministers while the majority of cabinet and government positions were held by Malays. In part, this reflected a colonial heritage that favoured the Malays in the realm of government, in part, it was due to the restrictions on citizenship that effectively limited non-Malay political participation until after independence in 1957, and, in part, it was due to UMNO's success in organizing the traditional hierarchy of Malay leadership to mobilize the Malays to defeat the MU proposals. The MCA, on the other hand, was a party governed by prominent members of the Chinese business community. While also serving on the cabinet and in government positions, Chinese and Indians did so in far fewer numbers than the Malays. The appointment of government officials remained with the UMNO leadership, particularly with the UMNO president—the prime minister of Malay(si)a. Though UMNO was the dominant party, a check and balance mechanism worked within the Alliance: any unyielding posture on the part of UMNO would have subjected MCA and MIC leaders to severe criticism from their followers as well as possibly disrupting the peace among the ethnic groups. Such factors prevented UMNO from unchecked dominance within the Alliance.

The 1948 Federation of Malaya Agreement provided for a new constitution, introduced in 1955, which transferred most of the responsibilities of government to the elected representatives of the Malayan people. In the first federal elections to the Malayan Legislative Council, 51 of the 52 elected seats were won by the Alliance and Tunku Abdul Rahman, the President of UMNO, became the Chief Minister. As a result of consultative talks between members of UMNO, the Malay aristocracy and British representatives, independence was achieved on 31 August 1957, when the eleven states of the Federation became an independent monarchy with a federal structure of government, a bicameral legislature and a sovereign selected on a rotating basis from among the sultans.

During the 1950s and 1960s, party politics was dominated by the repeated electoral success of the Alliance party. Though challenged by both communal and non-communal alternative parties, the Alliance never lost control of the federal government and only rarely failed to dominate each of the state governments. The success of the Alliance was in large part due to the ability of UMNO to hold Malay support. UMNO candidates continued to sweep most elections. The Alliance's success was also due to the ability of the Alliance party leaders to work out their differences among themselves and then persuade their respective followers to accept their decisions.

By 1969, however, severe racial disturbances had broken out in Kuala Lumpur following the May general elections. Hundreds of people of all races were killed and the entire Malaysian population was frightened by the depth of violence that was unleashed. Lack of restraint by political candidates and their parties was thought, by members of the government, to be a major cause of the outburst. Consequently, all party and parliamentary activities were suspended and the functions of government were carried out by a 61-member National Operations Council led by Director of Operations, Tun Abdul Razak, and consisting largely of cabinet and Alliance party leaders.

Party activities were resumed in September 1970 while Parliament reconvened in February 1971. However, the nature of the party system had changed: each party had to revise its constitution in order to conform to strict government guidelines as to what constituted suitable party activities. Additionally, restrictions were placed on the types of issues that the parties could advocate. National Operations Council members, believing that the undisciplined speeches of politicians and parliamentarians had sparked the riots, demanded an amendment to the constitution which forbade any discussion or opposition on four sensitive issues: 1) Malay as the national language, 2) the special position of the Malays and other indigenous groups (i.e. quotas in the universities, in special occupations, etc.), 3) the rights and sovereignty of the Malay Rulers and

4) citizenship rights of any ethnic group. Upon passage of this amendment, government by emergency decree ended.

The resounding setback suffered by the MCA in the 1969 general elections prompted a major alteration in the party system. Under the leadership of the new Malaysian Prime Minister, Tun Abdul Razak (1971–6), the Alliance was enlarged to include five parties from West Malaysia and three from East Malaysia. By election day, 24 August 1974, the newly formed Barisan Nasional—BN (National Front) consisted of the UMNO, the MCA, MIC, Parti Islam (PI—previously the PMIP), the Gerakan Rakyat Malaysia (GRM), the People's Progressive Party (PPP), the Sabah Alliance, the Sarawak Alliance and the Sarawak United People's Party. The BN functioned much like the Alliance in that members of the BN did not compete against one another in the same electoral constituencies and all member parties were allocated a measure of representation in the cabinet and parliament. The BN won an overwhelming victory in the 1974 election with the BN in control of the federal as well as every state government. Out of 154 seats in the Dewan Rakyat (House of Representatives), only 19 were then held by members of the opposition. The DAP and the Sarawak National Party had 9 members each while Pekemas had 1. A number of smaller parties were unable to win a single seat; and, more importantly, the UMNO maintained and expanded its dominance of the party system while the MCA, though regaining much of the support it had lost, was now only one of three parties in the BN which sought to speak for the Chinese. A numerical breakdown of the parliamentary seats held by each member of the BN shows clearly UMNO's dominance:[9]

UMNO	61
MCA	20
MIC	4
PI	14
GRM	4
PPP	1
Sabah Alliance	16
Sarawak Alliance	15
	135

The Barisan Nasional continued as the ruling coalition in Malaysia (though Parti Islam has since left and joined the opposition). Although composed of a strange assortment of bedfellows, it managed to preserve political stability in Malaysia, and has avoided repetition of the sad events of 1969.

Women

Malaysian women played a role in the evolution of the party system although they have been excluded from most analyses of Malaysian history and politics. With the exception of one recent study on the Kaum Ibu UMNO,[10] no work has yet focused on the women's auxiliaries attached to Malaysia's political parties. Yet, the women's auxiliaries played an important role both in the history of Malaysia's party system and in the development of electoral politics.

Without question, the history of women's auxiliaries in Malaysia begins with that of the Kaum Ibu UMNO (KI). The Kaum Ibu with its 36-year history and a membership which constituted one-half that of UMNO, nonetheless remained very much underrepresented within the party and government. Research on the KI, however, reveals that Malaysian women, primarily Malay and Chinese, were politically active in a number of organizations immediately following the end of World War II. Later, Malay women continued to remain organized in the two major parties representing the Malays, UMNO and Parti Islam. Non-Malay women, despite a few abortive attempts to start wings in the MCA and MIC, remained largely outside the party system. In light of the organizational and political experience gained by Indian women during the Japanese Occupation (see Chapter 3), this seemed most surprising. Equally enigmatic was the failure of the various non-communal and opposition parties to court women as party members given that the electoral franchise applied equally to men and women. Such phenomena suggest that the auxiliaries need be viewed according to a number of perspectives: the conditions under which they formed, historical development, structure, activities, the composition of their members and leaders, and, most importantly, the major functions that the women's auxiliaries served (for their own members and for the party to which they were affiliated). Further, cultural assumptions concerning a woman's place in society had to be considered as a factor in explaining the development, or lack thereof, of women's political auxiliaries. Rosaldo, for example, theorized[11] that where the public and domestic spheres of activities undertaken by men and women do not overlap the status of women is low. This offers a possible partial explanation for the uneven rise of Malay and non-Malay women's political auxiliaries, as does post-war political development and its effects on the women of each ethnic group. Such explanations helped shape the directions of this work.

The view taken herein is that the political auxiliaries can be understood within the cultural context of Malaysian history and with an understanding of women's place in traditional Malaysian society. This book follows a historical sequence. The first three chapters detail the place of women in Malay, Chinese and Indian societies, respectively, prior to World War II. They examine as well the effects of the Japanese Occupation on women. Chapter 4 traces the emergence of the early women's auxiliaries and the development of the Kaum Ibu from 1946 to 1956, the last year before independence. Chapter 5 continues the history from independence until 1969, the year of the Malaysian racial riots and the suspension of political activities. Because of an increasing volume of information, the developments of the auxiliaries from 1969 to 1976 are dealt with in two chapters. Chapter 6 discusses the continued development of the Kaum Ibu, while Chapter 7 details the activities and histories of the other women's auxiliaries which emerged. Chapter 8 provides a brief update on what changes had occurred within the auxiliaries between 1976 and 1983. One chapter that appears in the original dissertation has been deleted. That chapter focuses on the roles of auxiliaries as pressure groups or lobbies (groups that seek to influence those who govern rather than seek to govern themselves). In the Malaysian case, such efforts would include Kaum Ibu efforts to initiate marriage and divorce reform for Muslims, or to effect equal pay for women; issues that go beyond the domain of any one specific party. Interested readers may refer to the original dissertation, Chapter 8, and to Lenore Manderson's, *Women, Politics, and Change: The Kaum Ibu UMNO, Malaysia, 1945–1972*, Chapter 9, for detailed discussions as to the role of auxiliaries as lobbies. The conclusion summarizes findings and offers some explanations as to the roles and functions of Malaysia's political auxiliaries.

This book, focusing on Malaysia's women's auxiliaries, provides an avenue for investigating one type of political auxiliary. Youth sections, the other common form of political auxiliary found in Malaysia, have yet to be studied. Until such studies are undertaken, the nature of political auxiliaries and parties in Malaysia will only be partially understood.

1. The terms 'auxiliary', 'wing' and 'section' are used interchangeably in this text.

2. For example: D.W. Abbott and E.T. Rogowsky, *Political Parties: Leadership, Organization and Linkage*, Chicago, Rand McNally and Co., 1971; W.J. Crotty, *Political Parties and Political Behavior*, Boston, Allyn and Brown Inc., 1971; W.J. Crotty, *Approaches to the Study of Political Organization*, Boston, Allyn and Brown Inc., 1968; R.A. Dahl (ed.), *Political Opposition in Western Democracies*, New Haven, Yale University Press, 1966; W.N. Chambers and W.D. Burham, *The American Party System*, New York, Oxford University Press, 1967; S. Eldersveld, *Political Parties: A Behavioral Approach*, Chicago, Rand McNally and Co., 1964; Leon D. Epstein, *Political Parties in Western Democracies*, New York, Frederick A. Praeger, 1967; R.C. Macridis (ed.), *Political Parties, Contemporary Trends and Ideas*, New York, Harper and Row, 1967; A.J. Milnor, *Comparative Political Parties*, New York, Thomas Y. Crowell Co., 1969. A notable exception is Duverger who treats the subject of auxiliaries in some depth. Maurice Duverger, *Political Parties*, London, Methuen and Co. Ltd., 1954.

Studies on totalitarian and/or communist parties are too numerous to mention here. An exception to the prevailing trend to examine the auxiliaries as tools of party control, is D. Hindley, *The Communist Party of Indonesia, 1951–63*, Berkeley, University of California Press, 1964.

3. Maurice Duverger, *The Participation of Women in Political Life*, UNESCO, 1955, p. 104.

4. Mary R. Beard, *Woman as Force in History*, New York, Collier Books, 1946, preface.

5. J.S. Coleman, *Political Parties and National Integration in Tropical Africa*, Berkeley, University of California Press, 1964; R. Morgentheau, *Political Parties in French Speaking West Africa*, Oxford, Clarendon Press, 1964; A. Arntsen, 'Women and Social Change in Tunisia', unpublished doctoral dissertation, Georgetown University, 1977; Ian Scott, 'Party Politics in Zambia: A Study of the United National Independence Party', unpublished doctoral dissertation, University of Toronto, 1976; M.J. Blachman, 'Eve in an Adamocracy: The Politics of Women in Brazil', unpublished doctoral dissertation, New York

University, 1976; S. A. Chipp, 'The Role of Women Elites in a Modernizing Country: The All Pakistan Women's Association', unpublished doctoral dissertation, Syracuse University, 1970; E. M. Chaney, 'Women in Latin American Politics: The Case of Peru and Chile', unpublished doctoral dissertation, University of Wisconsin, 1971; M. Dobert, 'Civic and Political Participation of Women in French Speaking West Africa', unpublished doctoral dissertation, The George Washington University, 1970; S. J. Pharr, 'Women in Social and Political Movements in Japan', unpublished doctoral dissertation, Columbia University, 1975; S. R. Maclay, 'Women's Organizations in India: Voluntary Associations in a Developing Society', unpublished doctoral dissertation, University of Virginia, 1969.

6. *Malaysia 1984, Official Year Book*, Kuala Lumpur, Ministry of Information, n.d.

7. The following few pages are a brief outline of the history of party development in Malaysia so as to give the reader a general context with which to read the chapters which follow. Where relevant in the book, the parties and forces acting on them have been discussed in much greater detail though the emphasis will always be on women and their organizations essential to party effectiveness. Additionally, parties declared illegal by the government (e.g. the Malayan Communist Party) have not been included in this book due to the difficulty of obtaining sufficient materials.

8. Goh Cheng-teik, *The May Thirteenth Incident and Democracy in Malaysia*, Kuala Lumpur, Oxford University Press, 1971, p. 5.

9. C. Pillay, *The 1974 General Elections in Malaysia*, Singapore, Institute of Southeast Asian Studies, Occasional Paper No. 25, November 1974, p. 1.

10. L. Manderson, 'The Development of the Pergerakan Kaum Ibu UMNO, 1945-1972', unpublished doctoral dissertation, Australian National University, 1977, later published as *Women, Politics, and Change: The Kaum Ibu UMNO Malaysia, 1945-1972*, Kuala Lumpur, Oxford University Press, 1980.

11. Rosaldo argues that where women's activities are confined to those of the home, for example the domestic sphere, and men perform all activities in the public sphere, for example political, religious, social and most valued economic activities, the status of women is low. Whereas, where there is overlap and women can be found in the public sphere, and some men in the private, the status of women rises. M. Z. Rosaldo, 'Woman, Culture and Society: A Theoretical Overview', in M. Z. Rosaldo and L. Lampere (eds.), *Woman, Culture and Society*, Stanford, Stanford University Press, 1974, p. 36.

Part I
Women in Pre-1945 Malayan Society

1 Malay Women

THE Malays, the most numerous ethnic group to inhabit Malaya, are thought to have migrated from Yunnan, China, down to the Malay Peninsula between 2500 BC and 1500 BC.[1] Settling in the coastal areas of northern Malaya and along the river banks, they displaced the earlier, less numerous, inhabitants of the region, the aboriginal peoples of Negrito and Australoid stocks. By the first or second century AD when South-East Asia was experiencing its earliest contact with Indian culture,[2] the peoples of Malay origin, who inhabit present-day Malaysia and Indonesia, exhibited a well developed culture. That culture included the cultivation of irrigated rice-fields, a mythology imbued with cosmic dualism, and a social structure which emphasized the importance of women and, in some cases, descent by the matrilineal line.[3]

Peninsular Malaya has been subjected to repeated migrations of peoples and ideas. More recent immigrations, beginning in the second century AD, have included the Achinese, Minangkabau, Bugis, Javanese and Siamese.[4] These groups mingled and intermarried with the indigenous Malays. Further, their descendants are now indistinguishable from, and are considered, Malays.[5] During the late nineteenth and early twentieth centuries, a massive influx of Chinese and Indian immigrants to Malaya occurred.[6] In direct contrast to these earlier peoples, Chinese and Indian immigrants have remained racially and culturally distinct. Likewise, Europeans came to the Malay Peninsula beginning with the Portuguese in the sixteenth century. Few in number, the Europeans, as colonialists, have greatly affected the history of Malaya. Even after independence from Great Britain was attained in 1957, the colonial influence continued.

Ideologies, as well as its ethnic origins, have had a profound effect on the course of Malay life and culture. Aspects of Buddhism, Hinduism and most significantly Islam (introduced in the fourteenth century) have been absorbed or adapted into Malay life. For example, Hinduism can still be seen in the Malay wedding ceremony and in the investiture of the sultans. By accommodating and incorporating the earlier animistic beliefs, Islam became the religion of the Malays. The Islamic influence is seen in the religious practices and family law. The school of Islam prevalent in Malaya is the Shafi'i. Shafi'i belongs to the orthodox, or Sunni sect of Islam.[7] Secular concepts of economic, social, and political life were introduced more recently by the Europeans, mostly the British during the colonial period. Parliamentary democracy, with its bicameral legislature, prime minister, political parties and independent judiciary, blended with more traditional features of Malay society: the rule of the sultans and a feudal way of life. The free enterprise economy also reflected the blending of old and new. The village economy based on the cultivation of rice, or fishing, exists side by side with more urban and technological influences brought by the immigrants and the colonialists. It was British policies from the nineteenth to the twentieth centuries which developed Malaya's rubber, tin and oil palm industries. These policies brought to Malaya a large number of immigrants who quickly became a large entrepreneurial community. This also isolated Malay society from the same economic development. Hence, the Malays remained the most economically depressed group in that multiracial society.

Within the Malay social structure, the woman's place traditionally was determined by three factors: *adat*, Islam and class. Each will be discussed in detail.

Adat

Adat is commonly translated as 'custom', but the concept is complex. *Adat* has meant: 1) manners or etiquette, 2) that which is proper or correct, 3) the natural order, 4) law in the sense of rules of law, or 5) law, in the sense of the concept of law, e.g. it is *adat* that law and religion complement each other.[8] *Adat* has also been used by colonial administrators to distinguish between the two existing social systems in Malaya. The matrilineal social organization of Minangkabau descendants in Negri Sembilan is termed *adat perpateh*. The bilateral social form, where equal importance is attached to the mother's and father's kin, *adat temenggong*, exists throughout the rest of the peninsula. *Adat* in this sense, means those traditions, customs and laws which helped determine the structure and organization of Malay society. This latter definition is most useful when examining the role of women in traditional Malay society.

Adat perpateh comprised the traditions, customs and laws of the Malays of Negri Sembilan and a few areas in Malacca. Negri Sembilan Malays are the descendants of Minangkabau immigrants from Sumatra whose main influx to Malaya began in the fourteenth century AD.[9] The Minangkabau brought a social system that exhibited matrilineal descent, had matrilineal clans, practised clan exogamy (marriage outside the clan), conducted vendettas by the entire clan, and practised matrilocal marriage.[10] Tradition had it that the first Minangkabau men intermarried with sakai, or aborigine, women thereby inheriting rights to land in Malaya. According to Wilkinson,[11] not only were sakai women present in Johol, Negri Sembilan, but of four great sakai chiefs, one was a woman. The Minangkabau culture and social structure quickly came to dominate the area. M. G. Swift and P. E. De Josselin De Jong,[12] have provided detailed descriptions of life in matrilineal Negri Sembilan.

In Negri Sembilan, the smallest unit of socio-political organization was the *perut* (meaning womb) or lineage, headed by the *ibu-bapa* (mother-father). The *perut* constituted a lineage which was able to trace its descent from a common ancestress. Related lineages formed a clan or tribe. A clan was an exogamous group where affiliation was determined through the mother, and residence, after marriage, was matrilocal. The clan was often associated with a village, or several villages, and formed the framework for the social, political and economic relations within a district. A clan chief was called a *lembaga*.

Above the clan, structure was based on territory rather than lineage. There were usually four clans (*waris* or *suku*) to a district (*luak*). Of nine *luak* (hence comes the term 'Negri Sembilan' meaning nine states) four were headed by royal chiefs and four by non-royal chiefs. The ninth state was under the control of the *Yang di-Pertuan Besar*, or Ruler, of Negri Sembilan. The selection of the Ruler resided with the four royal chiefs (*undang*) choosing among the eligible princes. The Ruler, however, was symbolic and real power rested with the district chiefs, particularly with the four royal chiefs.[13] In addition, the British introduced an administrative system which did not always correspond to the traditional structure.

Women played a prominent role within Negri Sembilan. The social system was not matriarchal, i.e., women did not rule or occupy formal positions of power—the clan or district chiefships.[14] Yet, it was through women that land was inherited. On the basis of shared descent from a common ancestress clans were formed. Women were the custodians and guardians of *adat*. Girl children, rather than boys, were important to the carrying on of the lineage. Women owned and worked clan land, and it was a wife's social position which determined whether her husband was eligible for clan office. Marriages were matrilocal with the husband being fully subordinate to his wife's lineage. Women, as nowhere else in Malaya, were eligible to select tribal chieftains.

The nuclear family of husband, wife and children was the unit of organization with the husband coming from another clan. Upon marriage, or on the birth of the first child, the couple moved from the wife's family home, to a home of their own on land owned by the woman's kin. The wife's female kin, though in separate dwellings, lived in close proximity to the new couple. Conflict between the wife's husband and her male kin was avoided by the complete subordination of the husband to her kin group.[15] The head of the household was not the husband, but the wife's eldest brother. The husband was a lodger in his wife's house.[16] This did not mean that the wife dominated within the husband–wife relationship. She did not, as the following *adat* saying indicates:

While the Raja rules the country
While the penghulu (village headman) rules the shire,
While the lembaga rules the clan
While the baupak (perut chief) rules the lineage
the husband rules the wife.[17]

The coming of Islam further placed men over women with its recognition of the husband as head of the family. This reinforced the fact that women were not to dominate in the family. Nevertheless, as Swift[18] observed as late as the 1960s, men did not make decisions concerning their families without prior discussion with their wives. In fact, it was not unknown for the wife to be the dominant member.

Within the nuclear family the woman's main role was the daily domestic tasks. In addition to these chores and raising children, women performed the burden of rice cultivation. Women who were good workers were highly respected. Men, too, worked in the rice-fields, though it was not expected that they do so; those who did were regarded as having an extra good quality.[19] Men were responsible for providing the family with the cash income it needed.

Women, while esteemed, were to play little part in the major affairs of Negri Sembilan society.[20] They were expected to be modest and to stay in the background. If publicly active, a woman was first regarded with amusement and then indignation. It was only if a woman was willing to be regarded as mentally unbalanced (*tiga suku*) that she could escape the dictates of modesty. Swift[21] noted that as late as the 1960s, men and women both said that women 'cannot understand affairs'. In fact, peasants regarded female schoolteachers and politically active women with considerable suspicion and hostility. Although women were not to play a public role nor occupy public office,[22] they were concerned with finding the successor to the post of clan chieftain[23]—both men and women being eligible to vote for that office.

Adat vested the woman with customary property, comprising a share of the village land, a piece of rice-land (*sawah*) and a customary house. Hence, the woman was personally identified with the land. It was the duty of the clan chief to see that no female member of his tribe was ever deprived of her customary entail.[24] Thus, a widow or divorcee had a measure of economic security that was hers by right and which was not guaranteed by *adat temenggong*.

Unlike Chinese or Indian traditions, *adat perpateh* was dependent on the birth of females as perpetuators of the lineage. As custodians of the tribal lands, daughters were required for the system to continue. If a family had no natural daughter, a woman could adopt a girl to inherit her property upon her death. The adopted daughter need not have been a member of the close kin, nor was she necessarily Malay. However, the adoption was approved by the clan at a formal ceremony; thereafter, custom dictated that the adopted child inherit the same rights as a natural child. While sons did not inherit customary property, they did marry into families that guaranteed a measure of economic security by providing land, rice-lands and a home. It was also the duty of the mother to provide for her sons until they married and for the mother's kin to provide for a son while he was single (i.e. widowed or divorced).

While girls were valued, the matrilineal system did not differ from patrilineal systems in its raising of girl and boy children. A girl child was taught from an early age to help her mother with domestic chores, to cook, to do laundry and to help take care of the younger children. As she approached puberty, she was required to sit properly among adults, not enter into men's conversations and not to speak to men outside her family, particularly strangers.[25] Boys were allowed greater freedom. After having been circumcised and having undergone religious training, the latter being the most important event in a young man's life,[26] young men were expected to create mischief. Young women most definitely were not. The role differentiation between girl and boy was most clearly illustrated in the following *adat* saying:

The girl is sent to learn to weave and sew,
She completes a mat and pillow
This delights her parents.
The boy is sent to read the Quran
He learns a verse or two to counter gambling
and cockfighting.
When he reaches the age of maturity
If at sea, he is taught to handle the oar
If on land, he learns the art of sword-play.[27]

While *adat* required the parents to see to the welfare and safety of their children, the parents' obligations were greater towards their daughters. It was their duty to see that their daughters married well and obtained their share of clan land. Among the Malays of Negri Sembilan, it was usually female relatives who acted as matchmakers, and it was the female kin who were responsible for a woman if her marriage failed. As in most Malay marriages, marriages in Negri Sembilan were arranged by parents. The young people involved were not expected to have a choice in the matter.

Divorce was frequent among the Negri Sembilan Malays. Swift[28] found that for about every two Malay marriages taking place in Jelebu, Negri Sembilan, between 1950 and 1960, one was ending in divorce.[29] Marriage and divorce procedures in Negri Sembilan, as throughout Malaya, were governed by Muslim law. A man could divorce his wife simply by informing her of the fact. Women could only in rare instances obtain a divorce. Divorce was the prerogative of the male. Often a woman's only tactic was to exasperate her husband into divorcing her. A matrilineal, matrilocal social system did not necessarily give the woman greater freedom within marriage, nor did it necessarily give her any greater latitude in ending a marriage.

One way *adat perpateh* did benefit the woman was in inheritance. Daughters shared equally in the inheritance of their mother's property. Under Islamic law, sons received twice the inheritance of their sisters. (It was assumed that girls would marry and be supported by their husbands.) In this matrilineal system there was no doubt that the husband enjoyed certain rights within the family: according to *adat*, however, he had no final right to his children—they belonged to the mother's lineage.

Adat perpateh also placed a greater emphasis on the death of a woman than a man. The death of a woman called for a customary ceremony. For a man, it was sufficient that he be buried in a manner suitable to his station.[30]

Malay women in Negri Sembilan thus enjoyed a degree of social prominence and economic security that was not found among other women in Malaya. Even though they were prominent members of society, women occupied no formal religious or political positions. Men and women performed separate but complementary roles in society. Women worked through the private sphere of domestic and kinship groups; men dominated the public sphere, filling all religious and political positions. Additionally, the men provided the link between the women and the public sphere by articulating opinions and demands that women were not able to voice in public.

The kinship system of Malays living in states other than Negri Sembilan was bilateral—attaching equal importance to the mother's and father's kin. The terms *adat temenggong*, and *adat kampong*, describe a social system that differed from the matrilineal Malays of Negri Sembilan. In contrast to *adat perpateh*, *adat temenggong* has never achieved the status of law integrated with a centralized political authority.[31] Instead, *adat temenggong* refers to certain fragmentary rules which were a direct result of kinship and pertained to inheritance rules.[32] What is important here is that where *adat temenggong* prevailed: 1) kinship was bilateral with descent traced through both parents, 2) there was no use of surnames and no importance attached to lineage; for instance, among Malays, children were not desired as carriers of the family line, 3) landholding was associated almost equally with females and males,[33] 4) descent as applied to inheritance was determined through the male, 5) political power rested with male groups,[34] and 6) adoption conferred rights to inheritance on the adopted child (not found under Islamic law). While *adat temenggong* differed from *adat perpateh*, there were vestiges of *adat temenggong* in *adat perpateh*. Women enjoyed inheritance rights and there was often a preference for matrilocal marriage, so a woman could rely on her kin in times of trouble. However, differences in the choosing of public office holders and the inheriting of property placed the woman in a less secure and prestigious position than her counterpart in Negri Sembilan.

At birth, both boy and girl children were equally welcomed. There was no lineage requirement for either a son or a daughter.[35] It was common for Malays to adopt either children of relatives or strangers. It was also the Malays who commonly adopted unwanted Chinese female babies. Usually, the adopted child was treated as well as any natural child by the parents. In some cases, girls were preferred to boys because they were considered more reliable in providing security for the parents' old age.[36]

Girls, as well as boys, were permitted to 'run wild' until about the age of five when they began to learn domestic chores.[37] Swettenham[38] wrote in 1906 that:

As a child she does not receive as much attention as a boy, but she is invested with the national garment, a tiny sarong, rather earlier than he is. Whilst the boy is learning to paddle a boat and help his father in any way he can, or is being taught the aliph-ba-ta (Arabic alphabet) and the readings of the Koran, she is mostly in the house, helps her mother to carry water from the river, morning and evening, when all Malays bathe, and assists in the cooking or any other household work.

Girls, particularly from poor families, were expected to share in family tasks:

The girls of poor people share all the women's tasks from an early age, and, in the season they do most of the lighter work in the planting, the reaping, the winnowing, husking and pounding of rice. Many of them find time to learn to read and write nowadays in the FMS,—there are successful schools for Malay girls. A girl sometimes, but very rarely marries at 14; but from 17-20 is much more common. Until she marries she is not supposed to have any conversation with men, and when out of doors (never alone of course) she meets a man she covers her face with extreme ostentation.[39]

Wilson[40] added that, until the age of marriage, a girl's movements were restricted. Any journey, particularly by public transport, had to be undertaken with a chaperon. Djamour[41] noted that unmarried girls were expected to stay at home and become skilled in domestic chores. Hashinah Roose[42] confirmed that traditionally a girl, upon reaching puberty, was usually kept under strict supervision.

Marriage conferred on a girl both status as an adult and greater freedom of movement.[43] Under Muslim tradition, marriage continues to be a contract rather than a sacred tie. Hence, the divorce rate among Malays has always been high; roughly 50 per cent of all marriages ended in divorce. Permanence in marriage was not assumed, yet care was taken in the selection of a future spouse. Under Muslim law, it was the duty of a girl's *wali* (guardian, usually her father or related male kin) to arrange a proper marriage for her. She could marry only a Muslim while a Muslim male was able to marry a Muslim, Christian or Jew. In addition, both Islam and *adat* restricted marriages between certain degrees of kin. It was also preferable to marry within one's cultural, territorial and income group. Marriage within a village and with acceptable kin was preferred.[44]

First marriages for *anak dara* (virgins) were undertaken with great care. It was the duty of the guardian to arrange the most suitable marriage. The guardian of the bride signed the marriage contract with the groom's male relatives in the presence of male witnesses and a *kadi* (a Muslim official who registered Muslim marriages and divorces). A previously unmarried girl could not give herself in marriage. If she had no relative who could act as her guardian, she had the right to appeal to a *kadi* to act as her guardian.

An *anak dara* had little or no choice in the selection of her spouse. Her opinion was seldom consulted and need not be given.[45] It was improper and immodest for a young girl to have any opinions on the subject. Her guardian was supposed to act in her best interests. Djamour[46] noted that among Singapore Malays, the bride's resistance to a marriage could take place only after marriage. Following the wedding ceremonies, she could refuse to consummate the match thus pressuring her husband to divorce her.

Among Malays, girls generally married between the ages of sixteen and nineteen.[47] Child marriages were exceedingly rare; Nathan,[48] at the time of the 1921 census, wrote:

> Infant marriage as practiced in India is unknown among the Malays. In the whole of British Malaya only 234 males and 2,613 females under the age of 15 were returned as married, and all of these were over 10 years of age.... Among females the proportion of married under 15 years of age is highest in Negri Sembilan and lowest in Brunei and Perlis. Over the whole of British Malaya roughly one girl in 100 is married under the age of 15.

Virtually all Malay women married. An unmarried status for both men and women was regarded as somewhat unnatural. Between the ages of 15 and 40, there were 767 married women per 1,000 Malay women throughout British Malaya in 1921. Whereas it was common for men over 40 who had been widowed or divorced to remarry, it was exceedingly difficult for women over 40 to remarry. While only 152 men per 1,000 over 40 remained unmarried, fully 446 women per 1,000 over 40 were unmarried.[49]

Marriages were fragile in Malay society,[50] and little stigma attached to either partner in a divorce. Both men and women frequently remarried. Divorced women (*janda*) had the right to arrange their own marriages; they no longer needed a guardian. Usually they married divorcees or widowers. In general, the festivities attached to the first marriage for a girl were not repeated and the event was much less elaborate.

Islam dictates that the husband be the head of the household and that he be dominant over the wife and children. In general, members of a household were hierarchically arranged according to sex and age. Wilson[51] commented that the female was formally of lower status than the male; but, in a majority of households, the woman dominated all phases of running of the household and the conduct of social relations within it. It was the senior woman of the household who decided what to buy and where, what tasks to complete and whether or not to tap rubber. It was the woman who further undertook the raising and disciplining of the children. Rosemary Firth[52] confirmed this view with her description of the woman's status and position within the family in Kelantan. She added that though women were economically active, kept schools for teaching the Koran, went unveiled and attended special services at the mosque, the real influence of women came from their control of the purse strings. Kelantanese fishermen gave all the money to their wives, for women were in a better position to guard the money while the men fished. Women, as bankers, often decided if a man should buy new boats or nets. Raymond Firth[53] wrote: 'Quite a number of cases came to our notice where men refrained from selling their boats owing to their wives' opinions, and apparently quite sincerely, gave this as the reason to the prospective buyers.' Wilson[54] added that the household income was managed by the senior woman who also spent most of the income. She gave money to her husband and bought goods from the store.[55]

Though women dominated the household, Swift[56] recorded that the division of labour was not rigid. Men did perform domestic work if necessary. Djamour[57] too found that housework and cooking were mostly female chores though a man could be seen tidying the house. There seemed to be less stigma attached to men doing domestic chores among the Malays than among the non-Malays in Malay(si)a. Women, however, retained an inferior position within the family. They stayed in the back of the house, eating after the men had eaten. They displayed obsequiousness before their men and visitors in serving coffee or food. When men discussed business, the women remained in the background. They did, however, offer advice, suggestions and comments.[58] Women's opinions were particularly important for the marriages of children, whether the house would be altered, how money was spent, and even for introducing new methods of rice planting.[59] Thus, the Malay woman had both status and influence within the family, much more so than her Chinese or Indian counterparts. In public, however, women seldom participated. Instead, they conducted their social relations only with other women.

Malay women were not kept in seclusion to the extent of Muslim women in some other countries. Purdah was never accepted, except, perhaps, among the élite of the aristocracy.[60] The use of the veil was very rare. Traditionally women wore either a scarf, or in earlier days a sarong, that could be drawn before the face. Conservative Malay women could cover their faces if they met men, particularly unknown men. In general, women's faces were kept uncovered. In accordance with the Islamic practice that women be fully clothed, Malay women wore a sarong which reached to their ankles and a loose blouse (*baju*) or a tighter fitting blouse-jacket (*kebaya*), both of which reached to the wrist. Malay women remained modestly dressed whether at home or outside until past the child-bearing age when their status would almost equal that of men. At this point women were free to travel alone, visit relatives, speak freely in the company of menfolk, and smoke cigarettes or chew betel in public.[61] These women also made many of the household decisions, indirectly affected village discussions, and determined the household budget.

Within marriage, both husband and wife were expected to perform their allotted roles. Men were expected to provide an income for their families and to treat their wives and children well. Women were expected to run the household efficiently and raise the children. Genuine affection often developed between husband and wife. This, together with Malay customs, allowed the Malay woman greater freedom than her Muslim counterparts elsewhere:

The attitude of the Malay towards his women was not that which is observed in most Muhammadan countries. Married women seem to have always been allowed a very considerable liberty, and the man who tried to exclude his womenfolk from such amusements and social intercourse as was open to them was regarded as a jealous curmudgeon, and whatever happened to him the sympathies of society were with the ladies of the house and not with the master. On all festive occasions—a wedding, ear-piercing, the appointment of offices by the Sultan and so on—it is the invariable practice to give great entertainment to large numbers of people. At these times those who are invited are expected to bring their wives and often their daughters or other near relatives as well.[62]

Winstedt[63] too added that it was difficult to describe Malay women as the inferior sex, citing that Raja Idris, the Sultan of Perak, tried to abolish slavery by releasing his own slaves but had to apologize for being unable to free slaves that were his wife's property.

Islam

In addition to *adat*, Islam (the religion of all Malays) has affected both the status of women and the boundaries of the issues and goals for which they would strive. It is beyond the scope of this book to debate whether or not Islamic teachings do place women in an inferior or subordinate position to men.[64] The fact remains that many Malays, particularly conservative, orthodox Muslims, accept as proof of the exclusion of women from occupying religious or other public offices such Koranic inscriptions as: 'Men stand superior to women in that God hath preferred the one over the other.... Those whose perverseness ye fear, admonish them and remove them into bed-chambers and beat them; but if they submit to you then do not seek a way against them.'[65] And

... (Allah prefers men) in the matter of mental ability and good counsel, and in their power for the performance of duties and for carrying out of (divine) commands. Hence to men have been confined prophecy, religious leadership, saintship, pilgrimage rites, the giving of evidence in law courts, the duties of the holy war, worship in the mosque on the day of assembly (Friday) etc. They also have the privilege of electing chiefs, have a larger share of inheritance and discretion in the matters of divorce.[66]

Prior to World War II, it was unheard of for Malay women to make speeches on public platforms[67] or for Malay women to discuss the matters of marriage, divorce and polygamy. Today it is commonplace, but the women have learned to carefully define their goals. For example, most Malay women have come to oppose early marriage and easy divorce as the choice of men. They are, however, careful never to attack Islamic teachings as the source of their problems. Rather, the focus has always been on interpretation, or the implementation of such teachings as carried out by mortal men. An example is the well-known and oft-quoted Islamic precept that permits a man to take four wives as long as he treats them equally in all respects. Malay women have chosen to argue (following some Islamic scholars) that though polygamy is permissible, in reality, no man can possibly treat his wives equally and hence polygamy should not be practised. If, instead, the women demanded that polygamy be abolished, they run the risk of antagonizing the Malay community which would feel that they were not true to Islam.

While Islam left the question of women's position *vis-à-vis* men open for debate, it provided the framework within which Malay women have defined their goals. In two specific areas Islamic teachings directly affected Malay women's position within Malay society: exclusion from religious leadership and subordination under family law.

Islamic teachings have been so interpreted as to preclude women's participation as religious and, until recently, as public leaders. Islam has no priesthood but the religious officials, the *imam* (prayer leader), *bilal* (caller to prayer in a mosque), *kadi* (Muslim judge) and *mufti* (legal expert), have occupied places of status in society. These positions have been filled only by men. Because women could not occupy these posts, it was often presumed that the women could not debate issues that involved Islamic teachings (e.g. divorce). Equally serious, the *kadi* who hear and register marriages and divorces have often been unsympathetic to women seeking divorces without their husband's consent. The inability of women to act as religious leaders (though they can give religious instruction) also has influenced and reinforced the traditional place of women in the village. The village headman (*ketua kampong*), village elders and the *penghulu* (headman for several villages) as well as district officers have always been men. In fact, in 1976, Malay women urged that women be allowed to become village headmen. Much debate ensued. It was argued that women could not perform such functions because, in addition to the usual arguments about tradition and Islam, 1) they were not strong enough to break up a fight between two men, 2) they would have to go out alone at night, 3) they would not have the respect of the community, and 4) they would not be able to make announcements from the mosque because they might be unclean (menstruating). The question was not taken up by either UMNO or PAS[68] and subsequently died. The issue was not trivial. The village headmen and the *penghulu*, the traditional leaders, form the basis of support for the Malay political parties. They often head the party branches (the lowest level of organization), and later become regional, state and national leaders. These men form a significant segment of the Malay leadership and help determine what issues will be raised within the government. Thus, Malay women have been excluded from a major path to power and access to decision-making within the local community and at the state and national levels. Despite such facts, Malaysia could in 1983 claim two female cabinet ministers and several Malay female Members of Parliament.

The second area in which Islam has had an impact is family law. Islamic law exists in two major groups, following either the Sunni or Shia interpretations of the Koran and the traditions. Each group is further divided into four orthodox schools of law. The Shafi'i school of the Sunni is regarded as the orthodox and authoritative school of law prevailing in Malaysia and Singapore.[69] Based on this school, Muslim laws vary state by state throughout Malay(si)a. Each state is responsible for its own religious enactments.[70] The pre-World War II ordinances of the Straits Settlements (SS), the Federated Malay States (FMS), Johore and Trengganu were mostly concerned with registration or administration rather than with applying Islamic law. Ibrahim[71] wrote that enactments relating to Muslim law dealt mainly with its administration rather than in attempts to modify or codify the law.

In the Straits Settlements following betrothal, Malay women were able to sue for damages in case of a breach of promise to marry. In the Unfederated Malay States (UMS) (except for Kedah and Kelantan), women had no remedy if the marriage contract was broken. In Kedah and Kelantan, through the *Syariah* Courts (Islamic religious courts) Enactment of 1934 and the Moslem Marriage and Divorce Enactment of 1938, the defaulting person paid the value of the *mas kahwin* (bride price) and returned the betrothal gifts.

A Malay woman, of the past or present, could not marry without the consent of her *wali* or guardian. It was not necessary to obtain the direct consent of the bride, though it was 'commendable' to consult her as to her choice of husband.[72] In 1973, only Kelantan and Trengganu required the consent of the bride. In other states, there was no safeguard against marriage by compulsion.[73]

Islamic law states no minimum age for marriage,[74] though the cited statistics show that child marriages were few. Girls were not given to their husbands until they had reached puberty—it was a criminal offence for a man to have sexual intercourse even with his wife if she was under 13.[75]

The *mas kahwin*, or bride price, was paid by the groom to the bride at marriage to give the bride a measure of economic security. Shaikha[76] argued that in Malaysia the practice was only a symbol. While it was meant to deter divorce, the amount was not set by law and, in fact, was usually so low (M$24 in Negri Sembilan in the 1960s)[77] or, alternately, could be deferred, that it did not deter divorce at all.

Once married, however, a Muslim woman partially kept her status as an individual. She did not take her husband's name and she was entitled to retain property she brought to the marriage as well as her earnings and wages earned during marriage. She was permitted to enter into contracts and sue or be sued in her own right. She, and her husband, could obtain damages from a third person for enticement or for negligence in the death of either spouse.[78] While the wife retained certain rights, she could be deemed *nusuz* (recalcitrant) if she refused to obey the lawful wishes or commands of her husband. In such cases, the husband need no longer supply her with a home and maintenance.[79] Examples of *nusuz* offences included leaving the home without the husband's consent, the withholding of sexual favours and refusing to pray.

Divorce was the prerogative of the male though Islam allowed for divorce on the initiative of the wife. Whereas a man might just declare a divorce, a woman had to resort to legal procedure. Four types of divorce were recognized in Malaysia: the *talak* (or *cherai biasa*, ordinary divorce), *ta'alik*, *fasah* and *khula*.

Talak was the most common form of divorce and was begun by the husband. It consisted of a simple repudiation by the husband of his wife. For a *talak* repudiation to be complete, the husband had to pronounce the words of repudiation (*talak*) three times. The husband had the further option to qualify the number of times he repudiated his wife; thus he could announce a one *talak*, a two *talak* or a three *talak* divorce. If he did not state the number of *talak*, it was taken as a one *talak* divorce. If the man pronounced a one or two *talak* divorce, he immediately forfeited any right to his wife's person and he had to maintain her during the *iddah* period. The *iddah* was a period during which a widow or a divorced woman could not remarry. In Malaysia, it was a period of about three months. Its chief function was to show whether or not the woman was pregnant. After a one or two *talak* divorce, a husband could revoke the divorce and resume habitation with his wife. If he chose not to revoke, he could pronounce a second or third *talak* each followed by more *iddah* period(s). After the third *talak* and the *iddah* period, the couple were divorced. If the man wished to remarry his ex-wife, she first had to marry another man, consummate the marriage and be divorced by him. (The husband in a marriage that was undertaken for this purpose was called a *China buta*, or blind Chinese.)

Such restrictions on remarriage were taken to discourage a divorce uttered in anger or drunkenness. While it might be 'ideal' if every husband pronounced a one *talak* followed by an *iddah*, then a second *talak* followed by an *iddah* and so on, in fact, *talak* pronounced in anger or drunkenness or in quick succession were valid. In the SS, FMS and the UMS, tradition did not restrict the husband's right to unilateral divorce.[80] It was not until the post-war period that: 1) the state of Selangor required that a repudiation be pronounced before a *kadi* and with the consent of the wife, 2) the states of Negri Sembilan and Perak decreed that a divorce may be obtained only after an inquiry by the *kadi* and the Registrar of Muslim Marriage and Divorce, and only if no reconciliation was possible, 3) in the state of Perlis, it was decreed that a husband must apply for permission from the *kadi* if he wishes to divorce his wife. Elsewhere in Malaysia, the husband's unilateral right to divorce by repudiation was not restricted.[81]

While the *talak* was the most common divorce, the three other forms existed which women, as well as men, could use to obtain a divorce. The first was *ta'alik* by which a divorce resulted from either spouse breaking a condition made at the time of the marriage contract. If, for example, a man before marriage promised not to take his wife away from her village and later did so, or, failed to maintain her for three months (and it could be proven), then the wife might be granted a *ta'alik* divorce. Like the *talak*, a *ta'alik* was revocable during the wife's *iddah* period.

A wife could also obtain a *fasah* divorce, or judicial dissolution, on the grounds of insanity, lack of maintenance, or impotence. Again, the wife had to be able to prove such charges. While the husband might seek a *fasah* decree, it was more usual for him to use the much simpler form of the *talak*. The last form of divorce was called *khula* (divorce by redemption). The wife would pay the husband a sum of money (so that he would divorce her). Such women 'bought their way out' of bad marriages.

While the husband could by himself declare a *talak*, a woman had to apply to a *kadi* or court for a decree of *ta'alik*, *khula* or *fasah*.[82] Such an act required great courage from illiterate women who seldom knew that they possessed the right of divorce. In addition, the woman had to prove not only that she was married (hopefully she kept a certificate to that effect) but also the validity of her charges. Women unfamiliar with the procedures of the religious courts often had to contend with unsympathetic *kadi* who were unwilling to grant divorces at the woman's request.[83] A woman was indeed fortunate if she could exasperate or nag her husband into divorcing her.

Divorce statistics are hard to obtain; each state maintained its own figures. Figures are available for the post-war period. A sample from Singapore, including years prior to World War II, illustrates the magnitude of the problem. It also shows why Malay women have taken up the marriage and divorce issue as soon as they began to organize in 1946. Table 1.1 shows the data on Malay marriages, divorces and revocations between 1921 and 1949.

For any one year there were at least 50 divorces for every 100 marriages registered. For 1944–5 it rose even higher.[84] As for the types of divorce, Djamour[85] noted that only 5.7 per cent of the divorces were *khula* (redemption); in the late nineteenth and early twentieth centuries, the desertion *ta'alik* was rarely used (though it became more common). It

TABLE 1.1

Statistics on Malay Marriages, Divorces and Revocations, 1921–1949

Year	No. of Marriages	No. of Divorces	No. of Revocations (Rojo)
1921	2,055	1,133	61
1925	2,616	1,311	61
1930	2,307	1,366	78
1935	2,070	1,159	69
1940	2,213	1,249	111
1945	2,982	2,046	193
1949	2,516	1,401	144

Source: Judith Djamour, *Malay Kinship and Marriage in Singapore*, London School of Economics Monograph No. 21, London, Athlone Press, 1965, p. 177. These figures were adapted from her table on p. 117.

would seem that women were starting a few divorces. (It is not possible to say how many *talak* divorces were actually begun by the wife.)

Divorce not only remained in the hands of the husbands, but the right of revocation (*rojo*) also lay with the husband in cases of a one or two *talak* divorce. Only the states of Trengganu, Kelantan and Negri Sembilan require the wife to agree to reconcile. Elsewhere, revocation remains the unique right of the husband.[86]

Maintenance has been closely tied to the question of marriage and divorce. Under Muslim law, a woman was entitled to support from her husband only during marriage and the *iddah* period(s) of a divorce. As early as 1938, Kelantan enforced maintenance orders through the magistrates' courts. Throughout Malaysia, however, a man had to support his wife during marriage and the *iddah* periods only if the divorce was revocable or if the wife's behaviour was not the cause for the divorce. In cases where her behaviour was thought to be at fault, she was not granted support. In such instance, the wife had legal recourse only in the state of Perlis.[87] In recompense, women have had the right to the property they brought to a marriage and to share the property gained during marriage.[88] While Muslim men are required by Islamic law to support their sons until puberty and their daughters until they marry, the reality of the situation up to 1968 was very different. Divorced women were forced into prostitution which created a major social problem because so few received child support. Women who were neither literate nor trained often had no alternative. It was difficult to remarry or find employment. The Ministry of Social Welfare keeps no statistics on prostitutes. The government's concern has been the enticement of young girls into the profession.[89] This problem became so acute that Parliament and the state governments passed maintenance laws in 1968 to provide divorced women with some economic security.

Another related issue in Muslim society has been polygamy. Islamic law permits a man up to four wives at the same time, as long as he treats them equally in every way. Women, however, must be monogamous. Traditionally there were no restrictions on the man's right. In the 1960s and 1970s, activity on the part of the Muslim women had begun to restrict polygamy. By the 1970s, Selangor and Negri Sembilan required a man to declare whether he was indeed already married, when he applied for marriage. If he were married, officials were supposed to investigate if he could afford to support a second (third or fourth) wife.

Polygamy, in fact, has never been widely practised in Malaysia. Unfortunately, no statistics have been kept regarding polygamous marriages. While marriages and divorces must be registered with the *kadi*, prospective grooms have not been required to declare other wives. Neither have the censuses dealt with the issue. Anthropological data in a district of Kelantan in 1938–40 shows only 3 per cent of the men to have more than one wife.[90] In Singapore (1949–50), the incidence of polygamy was given by Djamour[91] who found only two cases of co-residential households out of 572 Malay households. In 1975, Tsubouchi[92] found in a Kelantanese village 5.4 per cent of the men and 7.1 per cent of the Malay women leaders, in interviews, all agreed that polygamy was not widespread—estimates ranged from one to three per cent of all marriages taking place. The practice was limited to the wealthy. Rosemary Firth[93] noted that in Kelantan the low rate seemed to be due to poverty and the chance of domestic trouble among co-wives. It is not therefore surprising that Malay women have not just concentrated their efforts on abolishing polygamy, but also on providing the woman with greater rights within marriage and divorce.

While *adat perpateh* governed inheritance in Negri Sembilan, the rest of West Malaysia followed Islamic law. The distribution of property was modified by *adat*. Under Islamic law the female offspring was entitled to one-half that was due to male offspring. The widow was entitled to one-quarter of the estate of her husband if there was no child (one-eighth if there were children). The rest went to the husband's family. In Malaysia, the widow had a special share in her husband's estate. If they had no children, she could take the whole estate; if there were children, the widow usually obtained one-half of the estate.[94] Thus, widows had a right to property on the death of their husbands, granting them some economic security.

Class

In traditional Malay society, a woman's place was determined by a third factor—class. Society was divided between the ruling, aristocratic class centred around the raja or sultan, and the common peasants. The ruling class led and controlled all aspects of Malay life (military, political, economic and legal). In general, commoners played little or no role in public leadership above the village level.

At the apex of the political system in each Malay state was the sultan. He symbolized and preserved the unity of the state.[95] He was surrounded by princes, officials, advisers and clerks, all male and linked through personal ties. The sultan's function was to serve as the religious head of the Malay community and to symbolize and preserve the state. Within each state, a number of districts were controlled by its own ruling group or lineage. These hereditary lineages selected their own district chiefs who had almost unlimited authority. The chiefs were responsible for levying taxes, maintaining order and defending against outside forces. In essence, each district became the chief's and his lineage's own source of power and wealth. Opposing and competing chiefs and outsiders created the need for the state as a means of defence and also to help trade. The sultans and the ruling class (the royal lineage who claimed their descent from the sultan or the Prophet Mohammed and the non-royal lineages) were interdependent. The chiefs needed a stable state which the sultan could provide. This helped both their defence and their trade. The sultans needed the support of the chiefs and their military aid. Formally, each district chief, though an independent military and political leader, paid obeisance to the sultan and was in fact appointed by the sultan. Thus the sultans depended on the chiefs to preserve their station and the chiefs needed the state (and sultan) as a trading unit and to protect them against attack.[96]

Queens have ruled in parts of the Malay/Indonesian empires. In particular, queens ruled in the states of Patani and Aceh during the 1600s. Within the Malay States, queens ruled in Kelantan from 1610 to 1716.[97] Despite such exceptions, the sultan, district chiefs and the royal and non-royal lineages were male preserves. Women had little direct political power.

Within the sultanate, the royal consort and the lesser wives played no part in government and had no political influence.[98] Neither did they take part in the ceremonies or rituals of the royal house.[99] While the wives and consorts undoubtedly intrigued to gain influence (or to better their son's chances of succession), the sultan's ladies played no part within the public sphere.

Within the ruling class, Malay women exercised little political power. They held no public office, were not members of any political assembly, nor did they take part in the political discussions of their husbands and fathers.[100] Yet, the ruling class was determined by descent; hence, women were important as links between families and as perpetuators of the lineage. Class endogamy for women, i.e. women would marry only within their class while men married whoever they wished, was strictly practised by the ruling class. This preserved the ruling lineages. Though women had to marry within their class, aristocratic males could marry peasant women after taking a first aristocratic wife.

Aristocratic women were influential as links within the descent system and often became personalities within their own right; as Swettenham[101] writing at the turn of this century observed:

Once a woman has married, and so obtained a certain amount of independence, she will, especially if she is of strong character, develop into a considerable power in her household, and often exert her influence in any direction beyond those narrow limits; she may earn a reputation as a good housewife, an excellent manager, a capital hostess and even develop much business capacity. As the wife of an official she takes an interest in State affairs, and does her best to push her husband's claims to preferment and title; in this last ambition she has a special interest, for certain offices and titles held by the husband confer rank and title on his principle wife and that helps greatly to assure her position. It is also the custom to grant offices, titles and salaries to ladies connected to the Court and in these cases, the husband, if there is one, is not concerned. Malay women of the better class, and most of those in the entourage of the Sultan and the leading Rajas, are distinctly intelligent if they cannot be called highly educated. They are usually of a cheerful temperament, capital company, witty and interesting, with a strong sense of humour; a man has to do his best to hold his own in their society.

Aristocratic women were not subject to the rules of purdah and had much freedom of movement within the home. They did not, however, entertain their husbands' guests or travel unescorted. It was common for aristocratic women to control substantial wealth and be mistresses of large households. Aristocratic women also engaged in business activities outside the home. In 1879, there were Malay ladies who owned tin mines, took trade goods on journeys to relatives and who bid for contracts to collect taxes. In Perak in 1878, the two largest investors in debt slavery were women.[102] Even given these freedoms, though, the traditional roles of aristocratic women were quite limited. They were permitted to perform no public function.

At the other end of the social spectrum was the retinue of village women who were obtained by the district chief for concubines and domestic slaves. The women were either bonds-women or slaves and their lot was difficult. This is vividly portrayed in the words of one such woman:

> Our chief works are cooking, nursing, carrying water, splitting firewood, pounding rice and at nights we are to prostitute ourselves giving half of this earning to the Raja and half to supply ourselves with clothing and provisions for the Sultan's house and other slaves. If we fail to get money by prostitution we are punished with thick rattans, and sometimes with canes on our heads and backs. We are prevented from marrying anyone who wishes to offer us in marriage.[103]

These women were kept to satisfy not only the sexual appetites of the ruling class but also the large numbers of young men who formed the chief's and sultan's followers. While the chiefs undoubtedly made raids of their own, the followers also had this right. The only women who escaped from the system were concubines who bore a chief a son, which entitled them to freedom from this practice.[104]

Within the common class, women played almost no public roles. Their activities and influence were largely confined to the home. Village Islam allowed women no public participation. Religious and other public officials (village headmen and *penghulu*) were also men. Women held no office, possessed no executive authority and for many years had no right to enter into contracts, even marriage contracts.[105] It was only the women in Negri Sembilan who enjoyed the right to vote for tribal officers; elsewhere, women held no such right.

Women in the Traditional Economy

Malay women have always played an important role in the economy. This role was vital to operating the peasant society. Tomé Pires,[106] writing on sixteenth-century Malacca noted: 'Malacca had so much (income) a month from the women street-sellers, and this was given to the mandarin.... In Malacca they are on every street.' In 1839, Munshi Abdullah on his trip to Trengganu and Kelantan observed that women hawkers brought to market their garden produce in baskets on their heads.[107] Swettenham[108] added that in certain Malay States a great deal of weaving was done by the women of all classes. In Perak, the women were skilled in mat-making and embroidery. In Kedah, the women wove baskets 'of marvellous fineness' and in Pahang, the women made mats of various colours.

The majority of Malay women employed outside the home did so out of economic need. Recent studies of Malay society have shown that Malay women were essential to the peasant economy. Raymond Firth,[109] writing about the Kelantanese Malays, was impressed with the economic role of the women:

> One of the notable features of the Kelantan peasant life is the freedom of women, especially in economic matters. Not only do they exercise an important influence in the control of the family finances, commonly acting as bankers for their husbands, but they also engage in independent enterprises which increase the family supply of cash. Petty trading in fish and vegetables, the preparation and sale of various forms of snacks and cooked fish, mat-making, spinning and net making, harvesting rice, tile-making, the preparation of coconut oil, the selling of small groceries in shops are some of the occupations followed by women. From the material of our census it was clear that at least 25 per cent of the adult women of this community have some definite occupation which yields regular income and if casual or intermittent work be also taken into consideration—such as selling husband's fish, fish gutting, etc., probably some 50 per cent of the adult women are gainfully employed from time to time.

Rosemary Firth[110] in her study of housekeeping among Kelantanese Malay peasants added that fishermen expected their wives to meet them on the beach after they returned from fishing. The women were to throw the skids for the boats, help sell the fish, distribute the catch allowance to the crew and carry the husband's fishing gear. The women also harvested *padi* for wages, spun thread, made nets and sold snacks, betel and vegetables.[111] Narendran[112] who also wrote on Kelantanese Malays, said that by 1974, 61.8 per cent of the adult women were gainfully employed outside the home. The majority either prepared fish paste, sold fish, cultivated tobacco, made and sold snacks or cultivated rice. Kelantanese Malay women were well known for their industry. In the rest of Malaya,

TABLE 1.2

Number of Females Employed Outside the Home

	Engaged in Agriculture	*Other Occupations*	*Total Occupations*
SS	21,837	7,177	29,014
FMS	75,042	1,142	76,184
Johore	11,409	1,691	13,100
Kedah	47,482	2,435	49,917
Kelantan	61,790	10,651	72,441
Trengganu	18,581	14,209	32,790
Total	236,141	37,305	273,446

Source: J. E. Nathan, *The Census of British Malaya*, London, Waterlow and Sons, 1922, p. 120.

women's activities were not as significant to the economy. However, many Malay women were economically active. In Johore, all members of a family commonly engaged in rubber tapping.[113] In Negri Sembilan, women were the primary cultivators of rice. In Selangor, Wilson[114] noted that in the village he studied the two *bomoh* (village healers) were women. Even the heaviest tasks were being done by women as well as men. In 1921, the total Malay female population was 807,348 (there were 956 females per 1,000 males),[115] the breakdown of those employed outside the home is shown in Table 1.2.

The overwhelming majority of Malay women were engaged in agriculture, primarily as rice planters and agricultural coolies[116] (frequently unpaid family workers). Outside of agriculture, Kelantan and Trengganu women were engaged in petty trading, shopkeeping, weaving and similar occupations. Textile work and the manufacturing of clothes occupied the labour of 1,617 Malay women in the Straits Settlements (SS) and 1,324 Malay women in the Federated Malay States (FMS). Mat-making too was a female occupation as were personal (domestic) services.[117]

Figures for the years 1957–70 indicated little change. The majority of employed Malay women still engaged in agriculture.[118]

Two of the more important explanations of why women were concentrated in the rural occupations are: 1) Malays have been a rural people, not choosing to settle in the urban areas. In 1921, the Malays formed only 16 per cent of the total urban population while the Chinese comprised 66.6 per cent and the Indians 13.8 per cent.[119] Fifty-four years later, in 1975, 82 per cent of all Malays lived in the rural areas.[120] The shift from the rural to the urban areas proceeded very slowly. Many Malays felt that the towns and urban areas (where most non-agricultural opportunities exist) were alien to Malay life and culture. Hence, few women sought economic opportunities in the towns, particularly those with no supporting kin in the urban areas. 2) Education for Malay girls was not encouraged; this limited their occupational possibilities. Malay boys could attend religious schools, government-run vernacular schools, and English-medium primary and secondary schools. Parents were more reluctant to exert 'wasted effort' in educating their daughters. Nevertheless, a Malay girls' school was established in Johore in 1883, while five vernacular schools for Malay girls were established in Singapore.[121] Another opened in Penang[122] in 1884. These schools, like the boys' schools, started as Koranic schools teaching the principal prayers in Arabic. Although some girls acquired such training, most parents saw little point in educating girls. European mission schools often had to take the lead in educating girls. Many parents, afraid of conversion to Christianity, were slow to take advantage of the chance. Also, the mission schools were often located in the towns, access to which was difficult for Malays.

For British Malaya as a whole in 1931, 355 per 1,000 of all males and 76 per 1,000 females of all races were literate in some language.[123] For Malays, census figures in Table 1.3 show that Malay males lagged behind

TABLE 1.3
Literate Malays per Thousand, 1931

	Males		Females	
	All Ages	Over 15	All Ages	Over 15
SS	419	482	71	63
FMS	407	483	84	72
Johore	236	286	31	29
Kedah	185	216	18	19
Kelantan	60	80	4	5
Trengganu	62	79	6	7
Perlis	230	255	25	17

Source: C. A. Vlieland, *British Malaya: A Report on the 1931 Census*, London, Government Printer, 1932, p. 93.

the general population in literacy. Further, the number of literate Malay women fell far behind that of Malay men.

During the British colonial period (1786–1957), English became the language of government and commerce. Progressive parents, of all races, sent their sons to English-medium schools. The Malays, however, were the most reluctant to send their children to such schools. In 1907, the first Malay girl, Sofiah binti Abdullah, entered Bukit Nanas Convent School in Kuala Lumpur; Zain binti Haji Suleiman (Hajjah or Ibu Zain) attended the Rebecca Girls' School in Malacca in 1920.[124] By the 1930s, literacy figures showed that Malay parents were sending their daughters to school, particularly to government assisted primary schools. Figures available for 1938 show that 56,904 Malay children attended government assisted primary schools—40,613 were boys while 16,291 were girls. As was true of the Indians and Chinese, the children of both sexes were most numerous in the earliest school years. The number of girls completing the sixth and final year, however, fell far behind that of boys: in 1938, 479 boys and 24 Malay girls were enrolled in the sixth year.[125] Thus, the rural nature of the majority of Malays, the slow progress made in educating girls, and the cultural traditions of the Malays kept young girls sheltered until married and precluded young women from seeking employment. Hence, Malay women were limited to the agricultural sector of the economy.

The Pre-war Participation of Malay Women in Social Organizations

Malay society precluded the participation of women in religious and public affairs even though it assigned them important roles within the family and economy. Given the limited range of activities and educational opportunities permitted to women, it is not surprising that the earliest stirrings of a women's movement was limited to a few individuals. Further, their goals were strictly limited. The influence of Islam further led Malay men and women to develop separately their social and political goals during the 1920s and 1930s:

> Pre-nationalistic stirrings within the Malay community first arose during the 1920s and 1930s when three separate groups of élites: the Malay-educated intelligentsia, the English-educated bureaucrats drawn from the traditional élite, and the religious reformers educated abroad in Arab schools, began to raise and debate a number of issues. Foremost among these were the questions of Islam and reformism, the increasing economic dominance of the immigrant communities vis-à-vis the Malays, and the future of the Malays in Malaya. Little antagonism was directed towards Britain as a colonial power. Rather, this pre-war pan-Malay consciousness sought to limit what its leaders perceived to be the ever increasing economic and political influence of the immigrants while protecting and preserving the Malay community.[126]

Malay political associations began forming in the 1920s. The first was the Kesatuan Melayu Singapura (KMS, Singapore Malay Union) founded in 1926 by Mohammad Eunos bin Abdullah, the first Malay appointed to the Straits Settlement Legislative Council in 1924. The Union's goals were to encourage Malays to advance in political, social and economic fields, to represent Malay views to the government and to foster higher education among Malays.[127]

The Kesatuan Melayu Singapura (KMS) was the first of many Malay unions and associations that sprang up in Malaya; the KMS, itself, had branches in Malacca, Pahang, Selangor and Negri Sembilan by 1937. Like other associations that followed, the leadership of the KMS was controlled by members of the English-educated civil servants. While mention is made of a women's section of the KMS,[128] details on the organization are lacking.

The KMS led to the formation of other associations. The most important was the Persatuan Melayu Selangor (Selangor Malay Union) founded in June 1938.[129] The Selangor Malay Union had approximately 450 members in September 1938 and its central committee of 15 'tended to be reasonably well-to-do men in their thirties and forties, educated in English and respected as men of substance in the communities from which they came'.[130] Current research indicates women did not play an active role in this association or in others that sprang up in Pahang or Perak. Roff[131] noted that the former was dominated by prominent Malay leaders (males) while the latter was dominated by English-educated middle or lower rank public servants.[132] Only the Negri Sembilan association had informally organized a women's branch[133] but, again, details of the group are lacking.

The associations formed during the 1930s aimed at improving Malay educational and economic opportunities. The associations were not radical. They did not aim at challenging the established political or social order; rather they sought safeguards within the existing political system. Their members were loyal to the sultans and to the British largely because the leadership remained in the hands of the Malay aristocratic élite or with those who held government posts.[134]

It was not until 1937 that a Malay political party was formed that challenged the political and social order. In that year, the Kesatuan Melayu Muda (KMM, the Union of Malay Youths) was formed by Ibrahim bin Yaacob, Hasan Manan, Isa Mohammed and A. Karim Rashid. The KMM was radically nationalist in tone. They condemned the sultans, the traditional élite, and the British, for the influx of non-Malays that resulted in economic domination by Europeans and non-Malays. In contrast to the other associations, the KMM sought independence for Malaya and union with Indonesia. Non-co-operation with the government was to be its main tactic.[135]

The KMM, though limited to a few hundred members,[136] provided the first real focus for Malay nationalism. The British, fearful of the loyalty of KMM members as war approached, banned the party in 1940 and imprisoned its leaders. Later, the KMM members were released by the Japanese though the organization remained banned. The KMM did reorganize and rename itself the Kesatuan Raayat Indonesia Semenanjong (KRIS, Peninsular Indonesian People's Union). When Sukarno, on 17 August 1945, declared an Indonesian Republic that did not include Malaya, the movement failed. The KRIS dissolved itself in that same month. Again, available evidence does not indicate that women played any major part in the KMM history.

A second Malay nationalist organization was formed during the war in 1944. Saberkas, as detailed in Manderson[137] was a left-wing association formed in Kedah by Tunku Abdul Rahman, a member of the ruling family of Kedah and a major post-war nationalist figure. Saberkas, which sought to improve the welfare of the Malays was supported by farmers, students, petty traders and women vernacular schoolteachers as well as housewives.[138] However, the extent to which women were involved and participated in the association's decision-making bodies remains unclear.

While membership in the early Malay associations was limited largely to men, a few Malay women, primarily schoolteachers, were involved with social and economic issues. For these women, the key to the backwardness of the Malays lay in their lack of education and in the reluctance to educate their children.[139] For them, it was the women as well as the men who were to blame for their deteriorating economic position. The women were to blame because they were not educated and did not educate their daughters: 'Every action, every step, everything which contributes to the decline of the status of the Malays, is founded on the weakness of the women, because all behaviour which is praised and honoured derives from the teachings of earliest childhood.'[140]

Education was seen by the women schoolteachers as the key to advancing Malay community. The education problem was acute, particularly for girls. In 1935, there were only 82 Malay-medium girls' schools (primary level) with 5,082 pupils and 227 teachers.[141]

The movement to educate Malay women was led by two groups of women: a small group of well-off, urban English-medium graduates[142] and a larger group of Malay-medium educated teachers (young women who were the daughters of religious teachers, village headmen and prominent landowners).[143] As Halinah Bamadhaj[144] noted, no split developed between the two groups because the women were too few in number and too isolated. Educated Malay women, almost without exception, became teachers.

Prior to 1935, there was no education for girls in the Malay language beyond the primary level. Increased educational opportunities for Malay girls meant attaining greater freedom for Malay women. Greater unity and strength for Malay women teachers proved to be the key to this goal. In 1929, under the leadership of Ibu Zain, women teachers organized the Persekutuan Guru-Guru Perempuan Johor (PGGPJ, the Union of Johore (Malay) Women Teachers). It was the first teachers' union, male or female, in Malaya. The Union soon had members throughout Malaya from all Malay schools: religious, vernacular and afternoon schools. During the 1930s, members numbered about 200 teachers. The women travelled through the villages of Malaya urging parents to educate their girls. In addition, the teachers published *Bulan Melayu (Malay Monthly)*, a journal through which they expressed their views.[145]

The teachers pressed to form a college for Malay girls that offered education beyond the primary level. Such a school, the Malay Women's Training College (MWTC) was established in Malacca in 1935. The MWTC provided two years of schooling beyond the primary level. Its courses concentrated on traditional women's activities: cooking, sewing and the like. This was in contrast to the Sultan Idris Training College for Malay men which furnished a stimulating intellectual environment and indeed was a source of leadership for the Malay nationalist movement. The MWTC, Halinah Bamadhaj[146] observed, served a different function. The intellectual environment was restricted; there were, for example, few textbooks and no library.

In addition to the MWTC, the women teachers also increased the female enrolment within the primary school system. As Asiah binti Abu Samah[147] recorded, the state of Perak alone had 62 Malay girls' schools with 4,000 pupils and 74 teachers by 1939; throughout Malaya and Singapore, there were approximately 40,000 girls in such schools.[148]

The women teachers urged Malay girls to strive and achieve: 'Do whatever you like! Don't be afraid! Don't be shy! Don't take any notice of what people say! As long as whatever you do, or whatever example you follow, will improve you, do it.... Go ahead! Succeed!'[149] However, there was no criticism of Islam and no cry for equality. Women were not inferior to men but they were different: 'They have their separate function which is suited to their soft and gentle nature, and it is natural that they should be dependent on men within marriage.'[150]

After the war, Malay women would struggle for independence, join political parties by the thousands, demand restrictions on polygamy and easy divorce. The pre-war goals were focused on one issue, the education of women. This early movement was led by a few hundred women, the educated élite of the female community. It was the Malay women schoolteachers led by the remarkable Ibu Zain, who foresaw that without education Malay girls would remain in the background of society. Women schoolteachers took the first steps forward in advancing Malay women.

The Japanese Occupation and Its Effect on Malay Women

The Japanese Occupation of Malaya speeded the process by which Malay women increased their role in Malay society.[151] During the first phase of the Occupation there was no policy towards Malay women. Individual Japanese state governors varied in their handling of 'the women's issue'. One might move to equalize the status of men and women, while another might dismiss women in government service to make way for men.[152] Malay women, however, remained committed to the idea of progress for women. When the Women Teachers' Union was dissolved, Ibu Zain formed an informal teachers' group in Johore Baru. Fatimah Harun in Singapore formed a small group called the Pemudi Islam (Daughters of Islam) and in Muar, Johore, Siti Nurani Janain published a journal, *Matahari Memanchar*, which urged women to enter public life and educate their daughters. Other Malay language magazines appeared, such as *Fajar Asia (Asian Dawn)* and *Semangat Asia (Spirit of Asia)*, which urged women to do useful work and help their race and country.[153]

The Japanese by late 1943 were also urging Malay men to enter occupations needed for the war effort. Malay women were encouraged to fill the positions (such as growing cotton and food) which the men vacated. Due to this urging, or more probably due to economic hardship, Malay women by the thousands accepted work outside the home. They worked not only in the fields, but as teachers, clerks, telephone operators and traders.[154]

Malay women leaders agreed that the Occupation was crucial to the progress of women.[155] It forced them to struggle for survival and broke down many restrictions under which Malay women laboured.

While women entered the labour force, they were also organized by the Japanese in 1944–5 into Malay women's organizations.[156] Such groups reportedly were formed in Singapore, Perak, Malacca and Kuala Lumpur.[157] Their functions were to encourage women to work, aid in war relief work, and to co-operate with food cultivation. The effect these associations had on the post-war Malay women's movement cannot be evaluated. Halinah Bamadhaj[158] wrote that the associations were neither active nor popular. Further, none of the women leaders interviewed remembered any such associations (or taking part in them). Whether this is the result of an anti-Japanese attitude (Halinah Bamadhaj[159] suggested that such hatred stemmed from the Japanese damage to female education) or whether the associations were largely ineffectual is unclear. Clearly, no major post-war female nationalists played a role in such associations. It is difficult therefore, to credit these associations with the upsurge of Malay female political and social activities after the war. Neither can be upheaval of the Occupation itself be credited. The Occupation was a time of great upheaval and disruption. All three races, Malay, Chinese and Indian were affected in different ways: yet, broadly speaking, only Malay women became active after the war. While the Occupation forced women out of the home, it was by no means a sufficient condition for post-war developments. If it were a sufficient cause, then the same developments should have taken place among the Chinese and Indian women. The facts do not bear this out.

1. Richard Winstedt, *Malaya and Its History*, London, Hutchinson Ltd., 1948, p. 14.
2. D. G. E. Hall, *A History of Southeast Asia*, London, Macmillan and Co. Ltd., 1964, pp. 12–24. (Experts dispute the date when Indian contacts with Malaya were first made.)
3. Ibid., p. 9.
4. Gordon Means, *Malaysian Politics*, London, University of London Press, 1970, p. 23.
5. Much more recent immigrations of Javanese to Malaya took place during the late nineteenth and early twentieth centuries. For example, in 1901 in the FMS and the SS, there were 22,705 Indonesians out of a total population of 1,452,193. The overwhelming majority of these immigrants were male. Of 17,578 Javanese in Malaya in 1901, roughly, 5,500 were women. In general, prior to 1900, the Indonesian population was under 4,000. By 1911 it totalled 117,600 and by 1957, 242,600. Tunku Shamsul Bahrin, 'The Indonesians in Malaya', unpublished MA thesis, University of Sheffield, 1964, pp. 121–8.
6. See Chapters 2 and 3.
7. Judith Djamour, *The Muslim Matrimonial Court in Singapore*, London, London School of Economics Monograph No. 21, Athlone Press, 1965, p. 10.
8. M. B. Hooker, *The Personal Laws of Malaysia*, Kuala Lumpur, Oxford University Press, 1976, p. 62.
9. P. E. De Josselin De Jong, *Minangkabau and Negri Sembilan*, Djakarta, publisher unknown, 1960, p. 9.
10. Ibid., p. 84.
11. R. J. Wilkinson, *Papers on Malay Subjects (1907–1916)*, Kuala Lumpur, Oxford University Press, 1971, p. 284.
12. M. G. Swift, *Malay Peasant Society in Jelebu*, London, London School of Economics Monograph on Social Anthropology No. 29, Athlone Press, 1965; De Josselin De Jong, op. cit.
13. Swift, *Malay Peasant Society*, p. 12.
14. Bamberger argues that as of yet research has failed to disclose one single undisputed case of matriarchy. Joan Bamberger, 'The Myth of Matriarchy: Why Men Rule in Primitive Society', in M. Z. Rosaldo and L. Lampere (eds.), *Woman, Culture and Society*, Stanford, Stanford University Press, 1975, p. 261.
15. Swift, *Malay Peasant Society*, p. 102.
16. Richard Winstedt, *The Malays: A Cultural History*, London, Routledge & Kegan Paul, Ltd., 1950, p. 59.
17. Mohamed Din bin Ali, 'Malay Customary Law and the Family', *Intisari*, Vol. 2, No. 1, 1965, p. 38.
18. Swift, *Malay Peasant Society*, p. 106.
19. Ibid., p. 105.
20. Ibid.
21. Ibid., p. 106.
22. Wilkinson remarked that the second and third Rulers of Johol were women. The second was named the 'Long Haired' and the third, Setiawan. Wilkinson, op. cit., p. 297.

23. Mohamed Din bin Ali, op. cit., p. 37.
24. Winstedt, *The Malays: A Cultural History*, p. 38; Mohamed Din bin Ali, op. cit., p. 37.
25. Mohamed Din bin Ali, op. cit., p. 35.
26. Girls were circumcised but at a very young age. There were no public celebrations as with boys. Some girls did receive religious instruction but it was usually a less rigorous course than that for boys. Marriage remained the most important event in a young girl's life.
27. Mohamed Din bin Ali, op. cit., p. 34.
28. Swift, *Malay Peasant Society*, p. 120.
29. Ibid, p. 119.
30. Mohamed Din bin Ali, op. cit., p. 41.
31. M. B. Hooker, *Adat Laws in Modern Malaya*, Kuala Lumpur, Oxford University Press, 1972, p. 30.
32. Ibid., pp. 30–1.
33. Ibid., p. 27.
34. Ibid., p. 28.
35. There may have been a slight predisposition favouring boys, as there was a pre-natal ceremony carried out in the seventh month of pregnancy to ensure a boy child.
36. Rosemary Firth, *Housekeeping among Malay Peasants*, London, Athlone Press, 1966, p. 15.
37. Frank Swettenham, *Malay Sketches*, London, John Lane, 1895, p. 6.
38. Frank Swettenham, *British Malaya*, London, George Allen and Unwin Ltd., 1906, revised 1948, p. 150.
39. Ibid., p. 152.
40. P. J. Wilson, *A Malay Village and Malaysia*, New Haven, HRAF Press, 1968, p. 105.
41. Judith Djamour, *Malay Kinship and Marriage in Singapore*, London, London School of Economics Monograph No. 21, Athlone Press, 1965.
42. Hashinah Roose, 'Changes in the Position of Malay Women', in Barbara Ward (ed.), *Women in the New Asia*, Netherlands, UNESCO, 1963, p. 289.
43. Narendran cited a case in 1970 where a girl looked forward to greater freedom with marriage. Vasantha Narendran, 'The Women of Perupuk—An Economic Study', unpublished MA thesis, Universiti Sains Malaysia, 1975, p. 171.
44. Djamour, *Malay Kinship and Marriage*, p. 69.
45. Ibid., p. 72.
46. Ibid.
47. Ibid., p. 71. Rosemary Firth noted that marriages took place soon after a girl reached puberty. Rosemary Firth, op. cit., p. 44. Swift confirmed that women married at a young age, usually around the age of 15. M. G. Swift, 'Men and Women in Malay Society', in Barbara Ward, op. cit., p. 269.
48. J. E. Nathan, *The Census of British Malaya*, London, Waterlow and Sons, 1922, pp. 55–6. Notably, the 1921 Census was the first carried out for all of British Malaya that attempted to answer questions concerning the civil condition of Asians.
49. Ibid., p. 55.
50. Djamour, *Malay Kinship and Marriage*, p. 132. For example, in 1949 the divorce rate in Singapore was 55.7 per cent, whereas for seven other Malay States, excluding Kelantan and Trengganu, the average annual rate during the years 1945–53, ranged from a low of 34 per cent in Selangor to a high of 92.7 per cent in Perlis. Ibid., pp. 136–7.
51. Wilson, op. cit., p. 128.
52. Rosemary Firth, op. cit., pp. 26–8.
53. Raymond Firth, *Malay Fishermen: Their Peasant Economy*, London, Kegan Paul, Trench Trubner and Co., 1946, p. 144.
54. Wilson, op. cit., pp. 90–1.
55. Swift, 'Men and Women in Malay Society', p. 277. Swift argued that traditionally women did not shop. However, at least in Kelantan, not only did women shop, they ran the markets.

56. Ibid., p. 278.
57. Djamour, *Malay Kinship and Marriage*, p. 52.
58. Wilson, op. cit., p. 129.
59. Swift, 'Men and Women in Malay Society', p. 279. Rosemary Firth, op. cit., pp. 26–9.
60. Winstedt, *The Malays: A Cultural History*, p. 44.
61. Wilson, op. cit., pp. 105–6.
62. Swettenham, *British Malaya*, p. 147.
63. Winstedt, *The Malays: A Cultural History*, p. 49.
64. It was the Kaum Ibu/Wanita UMNO members who argued most emphatically that they are not subservient to men. Women members of Parti Islam, the conservative Malay party, argued that there were some activities for which women were not suited (i.e. to be *ketua kampong*).
65. Syed Abdul Latif (trans.), *Al-Quran Rendered into English*, India, The Academy of Islamic Studies, Hyderabad, 1969, Chapter 4, Verse 38. Also reprinted in Reuben Levy, *The Social Structure of Islam*, Cambridge, Cambridge University Press, 1969, p. 98.
66. The thirteenth-century authority Baydawi, in Reuben Levy, op. cit., p. 99.
67. Winstedt, *The Malays: A Cultural History*, p. 46.
68. UMNO, the United Malays National Organization and PAS, Parti Islam (the Islamic Party), were and are the two major Malay political parties.
69. Ahmad Ibrahim, 'Family Law in Malaysia and Singapore', pre-publication copy, Faculty of Law, University of Malaya, 1973. Published under same title, Singapore, *Malayan Law Journal*, 1978, p. 195.
70. Shaikha Zakaria, 'Muslim Women and the Law of Islam in West Malaysia', Canterbury, unpublished MA thesis, University of Kent, 1973, p. 117.
71. Ahmad Ibrahim, 'Family Law', p. 197.
72. Ibid., p. 205.
73. Shaikha Zakaria, op. cit., p. 119.
74. Ahmad Ibrahim, 'Family Law', p. 204.
75. Section 375 of the Penal Code (Cap. 119), in ibid.
76. Shaikha Zakaria, op. cit., p. 120.
77. Ahmad Ibrahim, 'Family Law', p. 226.
78. Ibid., p. 230.
79. Ibid., p. 276.
80. Shaikha Zakaria, op. cit., p. 122.
81. Ibid.
82. Ahmad Ibrahim, 'Family Law', p. 241.
83. Djamour noted that Singaporean Malay women (prior to 1957) would go from *kadi* to *kadi* seeking a divorce. Some *kadi* granted very few *fasah* and *khula* divorces while others granted such divorces much more readily. Djamour, *The Muslim Matrimonial Court*, p. 27.
84. Ibid.
85. Ibid., p. 114.
86. Shaikha Zakaria, op. cit., p. 125.
87. Ibid., p. 124.
88. Ahmad Ibrahim, 'Family Law', p. 284.
89. Interview with Minister of Social Welfare, Aishah Ghani on 1 March 1976.
90. Rosemary Firth, op. cit., p. 48.
91. Djamour, *Malay Kinship and Marriage*, p. 60. The figure does not inlcude those men who may have had additional wives elsewhere on the Peninsula.
92. Yoshiro Tsubouchi, 'Marriage and Divorce among Malay Peasants in Kelantan', *JSEAS*, Vol. 6, No. 2, September 1975.
93. Rosemary Firth, op. cit., p. 48.
94. Ahmad Ibrahim, 'Family Law', p. 326.
95. J.M. Gullick, *Indigenous Political Systems in Western Malaysia*, London, Athlone Press, 1965, p. 44.
96. Ibid., p. 49.

97. Lenore Manderson, 'The Development of the Pergerakan Kaum Ibu UMNO, 1945-1972', unpublished doctoral dissertation, Australian National University, 1977, pp. 27-9.
98. Gullick, op. cit., p. 63.
99. Ibid.
100. Ibid., p. 83.
101. Swettenham, *British Malaya*, p. 155.
102. Gullick, op. cit., p. 85.
103. Ibid., p. 103.
104. Ibid.
105. Winstedt, *The Malays: A Cultural History*, p. 60.
106. Ibid., p. 134.
107. Ibid.
108. Swettenham, *British Malaya*, p. 150.
109. Raymond Firth, op. cit., p. 80.
110. Rosemary Firth, op. cit., p. 26.
111. Ibid., p. 30.
112. Vasantha Narendran, op. cit., p. 127.
113. Swift, 'Men and Women in Malay Society', p. 278.
114. Wilson, op. cit., p. 73.
115. Nathan, op. cit., p. 48.
116. Ibid., Table 36, p. 281.
117. All the above figures were taken from Nathan, ibid., p. 120. Vlieland in the 1931 Census notes the same general trends. See C. A. Vlieland, *British Malaya: A Report on the 1931 Census*, London, Government Printer, 1932, Tables 124 (pp. 262-6), 132 (pp. 288-90), 140 (pp. 312-15).
118. C. Hirschman and Akbar Aghajanian, 'Women's Labour Force Participation and Socio-economic Development in Peninsular Malaysia, 1957-70', *JSEAH*, Vol. 11, No. 1, March 1980, p. 43.
119. Nathan, op. cit., p. 42.
120. C. MacAndrews, 'The Politics of Planning: Malaysia and the New Third Malaysia Plan (1976-80)', *Asian Survey*, Vol. 17, No. 3, March 1977, p. 295.
121. Lenore Manderson, *Women, Politics and Change*, Kuala Lumpur, Oxford University Press, 1980, p. 19.
122. Wong Hoy-kee (Francis) and Gwee Yee-hean, *Perspectives: The Development of Education in Malaysia and Singapore*, Kuala Lumpur, Heinemann Educational Books (Asia) Ltd., 1972, p. 8.
123. The 1931 Census was the first census that took literacy figures for Asians throughout British Malaya. The following figures were taken from Vlieland, op. cit., pp. 91-3.
124. Asiah binti Abu Samah, 'Emancipation of Malay Women, 1945-1957', unpublished BA (Hons.), Graduation Exercise, University of Malaya, 1960, p. 2.
125. Federation of Malaysia, Department of Education, *Educational Statistics, 1938-1967*, Kuala Lumpur, Ministry of Education, 1968, p. 32 (Table 4).
126. W. R. Roff, *The Origins of Malay Nationalism*, Kuala Lumpur, University of Malaya Press, 1974, p. 254.
127. Radin Sunaro, 'Malay Nationalism 1896-1941', *JSEAH*, Vol. 1, March 1960, pp. 11-12.
128. Manderson, 'The Development of the Pergerakan Kaum Ibu UMNO', p. 43.
129. W. R. Roff, 'The Persatuan Melayu Selangor: An Early Malay Political Association', *JSEAH*, Vol. 9, No. 1, March 1968, p. 117.
130. Ibid., p. 129.
131. Ibid., p. 121.
132. Ibid., p. 119.
133. Manderson, 'The Development of the Pergerakan Kaum Ibu UMNO', p. 40.
134. Means, op. cit., p. 137.
135. Radin Sunaro, op. cit., p. 22.

136. Means, op. cit., p. 23.
137. Manderson, 'The Development of the Pergerakan Kaum Ibu UMNO', p. 45.
138. Ibid.
139. So little has been written about the pre-war political activities of Malay women that I have drawn primarily on two sources: Asiah binti Abu Samah, op. cit., pp. 1–8, and Halinah Bamadhaj, 'The Impact of the Japanese Occupation on Malay Society and Politics 1941–45', unpublished MA thesis, University of Auckland, New Zealand, 1975, pp. 39–47. The latter source was particularly valuable.
140. *Bulan Melayu*, August 1930, as quoted in Halinah Bamadhaj, op. cit., p. 45.
141. Ibid., p. 47.
142. Prior to 1920, there were only three such women and over the next two decades only a few more. Asiah binti Abu Samah, op. cit., pp. 2–4. Halinah Bamadhaj, op. cit., p. 40.
143. Halinah Bamadhaj, op. cit.
144. Ibid., p. 41.
145. The above information came from an interview with Ibu Zain conducted by the author on 19 October 1976.
146. Halinah Bamadhaj, op. cit., p. 43.
147. Asiah binti Abu Samah, op. cit., p. 7.
148. *Bulan Melayu*, January 1930, as quoted in Halinah Bamadhaj, op. cit., p. 47.
149. Ibid., p. 46.
150. *Bulan Melayu*, August 1930, as quoted in Halinah Bamadhaj, op. cit., p. 46.
151. There is only one source, Halinah Bamadhaj, ibid., that describes the effects of the Occupation on Malay women. The author is indebted to Halinah Bamadhaj for most of the information contained in the next few pages and for her personal comments concerning the Occupation and Malay women. For greater details, please see pp. 48–58 of her thesis.
152. Ibid., p. 48.
153. Ibid., pp. 48–9.
154. Ibid., p. 51.
155. Ibid., p. 52 and interviews with Malay women leaders.
156. Ibid., p. 54.
157. Ibid.
158. Ibid.
159. Ibid., p. 52.

2 Chinese Women

The First Chinese Women Immigrants to Malaya

THOUGH evidence shows that Chinese contacts with Malaya started as early as the fifth century,[1] settlements of Chinese began with the Portuguese capture of Malacca in 1511. The first Chinese settlements were almost all male. It is not until the middle of the nineteenth century that references are made to the arrival of Chinese females.

When the Dutch captured Malacca in 1641, the number of Chinese was small, numbering no more than 300–400 persons.[2] Over the years, the Malaccan Chinese population grew. By 1860, it totalled 10,039 out of a total population of 67,267 people. Of the Chinese, 3,002 were females.[3]

The second major settlement of Chinese began with the British in Penang (1786). Seeking to form a trading and shipping port, the British encouraged the immigration of Chinese. Chinese were regarded as an industrious people. Eight years after the founding of Penang, Captain Francis Light noted that the Chinese population had grown to 3,000 men, women and children.[4] Penang continued to grow throughout the nineteenth century. In 1812, there were 7,291 Chinese out of a population of 23,418. By 1860, this increased to 28,018 out of 59,956.[5] Figures for two years only are available on Chinese women: in 1851, there was 1 Chinese female for every 4.7 Chinese males and in 1860, there was 1 to 3.3.[6]

The third major settlement of Chinese was founded at Singapore by Sir Thomas Stamford Raffles in 1819. Inhabited by 150 Malay fishermen at the time, a few years later Singapore had a Chinese population of 2,956 males and 361 females (1 Chinese woman for every 8 Chinese men).[7] Records indicating the numbers of Chinese women were not kept until 1850. It was then recorded that 2,239 Chinese females resided in Singapore compared to 25,749 Chinese males (1 female per 12 males).[8] The wives of Chinese were likely counted as Chinese though in fact they may have been of other races. Purcell,[9] quoting Buckley, Newbold and Earl, indicated the number of Chinese women in the Straits Settlements (SS) was small:

> Up to this time [1837], no Chinese woman had come to Singapore from China, and the newspapers said that, in fact, only two genuine Chinese women were, or at any time had been, in the place, and they were two small-footed ladies who had been, some years before, exhibited in England.[10]

... the females were not of course natives of China but all of a Creole or mixed race and mostly from the neighbouring island of Bintang.[11]

From five thousand to eight thousand emigrants arrive annually from China, of whom only forty or fifty are females.[12]

While Chinese could be found in Pahang, Johore, Negri Sembilan, Perak, Selangor and Kelantan, most settled in the Straits Settlements (SS) of Malacca, Penang and Singapore. Having settled in Malaya, the Chinese quickly formed pepper and gambier plantations, fruit and vegetable gardens, performed hard labour tasks (clearing land or pulling rickshaws), and entered many commercial occupations (trading, shopkeeping, shipping, etc.). In Province Wellesley, the Chinese monopolized the sugar industry from 1800 to 1846 when it was taken over by the British. The tin industry, too, was owned and managed by Chinese until the large influx of British capital towards the end of the nineteenth century.

The Chinese who came to Malaya were largely poor peasants from the south-eastern provinces of Kwangtung, Kwangsi and Fukien. While the majority were free workers who paid their passage to the SS, about 27 per cent of the immigrants to Singapore in 1877 were unpaid passengers recruited under the credit-ticket system.[13] Penang, during the 1830s and 1840s, was receiving each year 2,000–3,000 such immigrants.[14] The *sinkeh*, or unpaid passenger, was recruited in China by headmen who offered passage to the SS if expenses could be recovered from employers of the coolies in the SS. The *sinkeh* paid off his passage either by working six months for only food and clothing, or one year for nominal wages.[15] The system, or 'pig trade', was unregulated and open to wide abuse.[16] These credit-ticket and free labour systems provided a steady and ever growing influx of male Chinese to Malaya. During this stage, which predated the tin industry of the 1850s, few Chinese women came to Malaya. Women were not immigrating due largely to three factors: 1) the hope that the stay in Malaya would be short—Chinese men expected to return to their villages to carry out family and religious obligations, 2) the high cost of transporting wives and children to Malaya, and 3) the strictness of Chinese authorities in stopping the emigration of Chinese women. Until the Treaty of Nanking of 1860, Chinese were not free to emigrate; the Chinese government saw little benefit from such emigration. After the Treaty, the flow of male emigrants rose sharply, but the large outflux of Chinese females was still prohibited. Perhaps they hoped that if families remained behind, the men would return.

Immigration figures prior to the twentieth century are often incomplete. They should be read as roughly indicating immigration trends. Massive large-scale immigration of Chinese began in the 1850s[17] with the tin industry. Living conditions in Malaya were hazardous due to a hot and humid climate and the rigours of the mining work.

Many factors contributed to the increase of immigration: deteriorating economic conditions in China, the proximity of South-east China to

TABLE 2.1
Growth of the Chinese Population, 1840–1922

Year	Total No. Arriving	Total No. Departing	No. of Women Arriving
1840	5,063[1]	?	?
1846	9,569[1]	?	?
1850	8,569[1]	?	?
1865	17,439[1]	3,252[1]	655[1]
1881	80,803	?	3,121
1885	111,456	?	4,368
1891	144,264[1]	144,129[1]	7,126
1895	212,776	?	10,650
1901	178,778	?	11,822
1905	173,131	?	13,714
1911	269,854	?	22,738
1915	93,735	?	10,632
1919	70,912	37,590	13,883
1922	132,886	96,869	18,213

Source: Maurice Freedman, *The Chinese Family in Singapore*, London, Colonial Office Research Studies No. 20, 1957, p. 22.
[1] From or to Singapore only.

Malaya, the general industriousness of the people of South-east China, the relative state of peace that existed in the SS and the Malay States due to the British, and the economic possibilities offered by tin, agriculture and the urban areas. Table 2.1 shows the growth of the Chinese population as they arrived in the ports of the SS between 1840 and 1922.

From the figures, it is apparent that the numbers of immigrants rapidly increased. The number of female immigrants prior to 1922 though, never exceeded a small fraction of the total. The sex ratio remained unbalanced, ranging from 1 female to 4 or 5 males in Penang in the 1840s to 1 female per 17 males in the state of Perak in 1891.[18] In the Federated Malay States (FMS), the ratio of Chinese females to males was 100 per 1,000 in 1901. For the whole of Malaya, the ratio was 247 females per 1,000 males.[19] Drunkenness, gambling and prostitution plagued the Chinese; these problems were attributed to an unstable or absent family life.

A small number of the early Chinese immigrants solved the problem by marrying with Malay women to form the *Baba*, or Straits-born Chinese. *Baba* women in turn married only with other *Baba* or with Chinese, to form a new indigenous Chinese group. The *Baba* became the aristocracy of Chinese society. They claimed to be the first Chinese arrivals in Malaya. Intensely proud of being British subjects, the *Baba* kept themselves removed from newer arrivals but preserved many Chinese customs. In *Baba* families, the language was a form of Malay with Chinese syntax. Men wore queues, mandarin clothes and cloth shoes. Children were raised in the Chinese tradition. Boys were often sent to China for education. Unmarried daughters remained at home until married. The life lived by a *nyonya* (female *Baba*) was illustrated in excerpts from a 1913 article by Lee Chou-neo, the first Straits woman to qualify from the local medical school.

> The happiest and merriest period of her life is that spent during her childhood, when no restraint whatever is put upon her actions. She is permitted to associate with boys and roam about the house and streets (there being no nursery) to her heart's content.... Her seclusion dates from the time when she arrives at the age of 13 or 14, and everything considered unladylike is forbidden her. The parents here do not look upon their daughters as being altogether worthless.... No girl is ever sold into slavery. When unwanted, she is usually given away to be adopted into some family, and is there treated as a daughter of the house.
>
> As soon as she is 13 or 14, she ... has to undergo a course in training in cooking and sewing. These two are essential accomplishments to achieve, without which she has scant hope of securing a good match. Education is not yet considered necessary, but her value would be very much enhanced were she able to read and write a little English. The life is indeed lonely and dull.... She is never permitted to venture outside the doors of her abode, unless to pay occasional visits to her closest relations.... She lives in a sphere of her own, quite out of touch with the society of men....
>
> The Chinese girl is seldom provided with an adequate education, the passing of the third and fourth standard being deemed sufficient.... Parents regard it as a waste of money to educate their daughters, who are supposed to be incapable of maintaining the family in time of need, seeing that, according to Chinese customs, it is indecent and disgraceful for girls to work for their living....
>
> A perceptible change has taken place during the last three or four years, and is steadily increasing. Girls are not kept so much cooped up in their houses ... for the parents have now recognized the benefits derived from the little liberty and education which they allow their daughters.
>
> Education is now considered necessary. Even the lower classes ... are helping them by a slight relaxation of the antiquated customs of their ancestors. Girls now obtain as equal an education with boys as their parents' purses can afford.[20]

The early 1900s saw the *Baba* society undergoing great pressures to adapt to changing times. This was shown in the following excerpts from a 1903 article in the *Straits Chinese Magazine*:

> Not many decades ago, the Nyonya was a modest retiring creature, as fearful to be seen of the male sex as a rabbit to be observed by the sportsman.... A change came over our people. With good intentions, certain people relaxed the old rules and gradually the old restrictions became impossible and almost all at once our Nyonyas insisted on their *rights*....
>
> All the evils complained of against the Nyonyas may be traced to the pernicious bondage under which they have been brought up. Gambling will disappear whenever our women learn to make a better use of their time.
>
> Systematic education is the only remedy.... There can be no general improvement in the social condition of the race until the women are refined and elevated

by a sensible education and by the increase in social amenities which only enlightenment can ensure.[21]

Marriage with local women was one way Chinese men overcame the lack of Chinese women. However, most men, due to poverty, were forced to remain celibate or frequent brothels. Prostitution thus became widespread wherever there were Chinese men. For example, the state of Selangor during the 1890s had a sex ratio of roughly 1 Chinese woman per 17 men; the result was widespread brothels. In Kuala Lumpur, the *Kapitan China*, the local Chinese leader recognized by the colonial government and who was expected to keep order within the Chinese community, employed over 300 Chinese prostitutes in 1883. By 1892, Kuala Lumpur with a population of 25,000 had 829 prostitutes, nearly all of whom were Chinese, living in 45 registered brothels.[22] Living and working conditions of the prostitutes were appalling:

The room for each is so small that it is only five feet by five feet and all the women are cramped up without ventilation....
The houses are so soddened with dirt and filth that they are past cleaning ... the rooms in which the poor women live are much worse than pig-styes and so dark that the lamps are in use all day.[23]

Prior to 1927, Chinese prostitutes were permitted to enter the ports of the SS to reside in a brothel, if they did so of their own volition. The Chinese Protectorate, established in 1877 to help bring order to the Chinese community, sought only to prevent the traffic of women and girls, particularly young girls. Raffles himself, had years earlier commented on the prostitution. He noted that while difficult, it was necessary to draw the line between concubinage and prostitution. He felt these women should be treated with compassion, 'every obstacle should be used to prevent the trade as a source of profit to anyone but herself'.[24]

Prostitution, however, was difficult to stop. Officials in Malaya had no way of regulating what type of immigrants they received. Chinese authorities had no system to examine female emigrants. Thus, Malayan officials were faced with having to determine upon arrival if they were entering Malaya under duress. If the authorities suspected duress, the girls could be sent to government girls' homes, the Po Leung Kuks, run by the Secretary of Chinese Affairs. Alternately, the authorities could require the person charged with the girl to enter into a bond. He would forfeit a sum of money if the girl was trained or used for prostitution. The attitude of many prostitutes also prevented the control of the trade. Often, prostitutes (particularly those working off family debts) felt an almost filial obligation to their employers. It thus became difficult to stop a trade which many of the women seemed to accept. The trade further provided a safety valve for the release of tension in a mostly male society. However, the problem became so acute by 1927 that prostitutes were prohibited from entering the SS. After 1930, brothels were no longer permitted to operate openly in the SS, the FMS or elsewhere. While a number of brothels were closed, women continued to be exploited in a different form. Streetwalking increased and coffee-houses and small lodging-houses became the meeting places. Prostitution as a social problem clearly remained.

Prostitutes formed only one segment of the Chinese female population. Though the history of Chinese women has been neglected, one can gain some insights into their lives.

A Wave of Chinese Women Immigrants

By 1921, Chinese women were residing in Malaya by the hundreds of thousands. In that year, British Malaya's population totalled 3,358,054 with 2,061,622 males and 1,296,432 females. The ratio of females to males thus was 628 per 1,000.[25] Among the three major races, the Chinese suffered from the most disparate sex ratio. The total Chinese population was 1,174,767 with only 326,001 women. Though the number of Chinese women had increased over the 1911 census (from 247 females per 1,000 males in 1911), their sex ratio was far less than either the Malays or the Indians (956:1,000 and 405:1,000 respectively). While Chinese men outnumbered Chinese women, the past ten years had seen a sizeable increase in the numbers of female immigrants. Table 2.2 indicates the growth pattern of females per 1,000 males.

Nathan[26] attributed the rapid growth in the last three years to famine and the unsettled state in China. Economic conditions in Malaya further favoured the immigration of women. Malayan rubber estates at the start of this century offered many opportunities for women. Though the rubber industry was dominated by Indian labour, the estates did provide some chance of employment for Chinese women. In 1921, 5,237 Chinese women and 83,518 Chinese men were employed on the estates.[27] Agriculture, too, offered employment possibilities for women. Recovering tin

TABLE 2.2
Growth Pattern of Females per 1,000 Males, 1911–1921

Year	No. of Females
1911	100
1912	113
1913	120
1914	100
1915	138
1916	140
1917	135
1918	216
1919	310
1920	266
1921	384

Source: J. E. Nathan, *The Census of British Malaya*, London, Waterlow and Sons, 1922, p. 48.

from streams was also dominated by Chinese female labour. Chinese women were further sought as personal servants. In short, Chinese female immigration increased because of the poor conditions in China and the improved opportunities in Malaya.

Census figures indicate that Chinese women immigrants were almost all from South-east China. In 1921, the Malaysian Chinese could be divided into five major groups: 1) the Cantonese from Kwangtung (28.3 per cent), 2) the Hokkiens from Fukien (32.8 per cent), 3) the Khehs or Hakkas from several southern provinces (18.6 per cent), 4) the Tie-Chus, from Kwangtung (11.1 per cent) and the Hailams from Hainan (5.8 per cent).[28] Chinese women came from these groups except for the Hailams who refused to allow Hailam women to emigrate prior to 1921. As for the rest, the numbers of women per 1,000 men are shown in Table 2.3.

By 1931 the sex ratio disparity had improved among all five groups of immigrants[29] though Chinese men still outnumbered women by two to one. Table 2.4 shows the increasing numbers of women resulting from continued immigration in slightly higher numbers than in earlier years.

The increase was largely due to a greater tendency for Chinese men to return to China than did Chinese women. Chinese women remained in Malaya for much longer periods than men. Hence the disparate sex ratio began to lessen.[30]

TABLE 2.3

Number of Chinese Women Immigrants per 1,000 Men among the Major Groups

	Groups			
	Hokkiens	Cantonese	Khehs	Tie-Chus
SS	533	717	410	336
FMS	347	378	412	209
Johore	322	259	207	241
Kedah	374	325	267	143

Source: As in Table 2.2, adapted from table on p. 48.

TABLE 2.4

Sex Ratio Disparity among Immigrant Chinese, 1923–1930

Year	Men	Women	Children	Net Increase
1923	32,757	10,024	14,117	56,898
1925	49,700	14,592	26,823	91,115
1927	65,843	29,146	37,222	132,211
1929	59,122	24,644	27,375	111,141
1930	11,427	17,121	22,892	28,586

Source: Freedman, op. cit., p. 23.

The Economic Role of Chinese Immigrant Women

In 1921, out of 326,001 Chinese females (109,271 were under the age of 15), fully 63,498 women were engaged in work outside of the home.[31] In the Straits Settlements, the great majority were engaged in personal service (11,546 out of 19,840 employed women). Others served as agricultural workers, hawkers, seamstresses and managers of businesses. Women professionals, except for temple officials and teachers, were absent.[32]

In the Federated Malay States, Chinese women were engaged in agriculture (15,929 women out of 36,546) primarily as coolies and as fruit and vegetable growers. Other women reared pigs, raised *attap* (a plant used for roofing, etc.), were planters, and a few (375 as opposed to 5,856 men) became estate owners and managers. By 1921 the number of Chinese women engaged in agricultural occupations had doubled from 1911; this indicated an increase of Chinese women in the rural population.[33]

In the FMS, Chinese women were mostly engaged in tin mining. In 1921, 8,116 Chinese women were so employed, primarily as *dulang* washers. *Dulang* washing is notable for its domination by Chinese women. Panning for tin, or *dulang* washing, is a process by which tin is recovered from streams. Each worker laboured under the authority of a pass issued by the Mines Department. Passes were issued only to women and 90 out of every 100 were Chinese. From 1908 to 1920, the number of passes issued is shown in Table 2.5.

Most women worked in Perak where they were independent and self-employed. The work was arduous, as shown by the romanticized comments of the FMS Mines Department in 1909:

> There is no more pleasing sight to be seen in the FMS than the Chinese women washing for tin ore in a stream—up to her waist in water—with a small child strapped to her back above the waist. Of the alien races who live in these states ... there are none to be compared with these women, who for sobriety, morality and honesty are not to be beaten.[34]

Dulang washing is still carried out by Chinese women. In 1963, it accounted for 3 per cent of the total output of tin in Malaysia.[35]

In the Unfederated Malay States, women were also employed in agriculture, primarily as coolies, and rice planters. A few women managed and owned estates. Aside from agriculture, Chinese women were employed as personal servants while a few engaged in commerce, as hawkers and managers of small businesses.[36]

In summary, Chinese women were employed outside the home. The women worked in the low status, poorly paid occupations as personal servants, agricultural coolies, *dulang* washers, seamstresses, hawkers and prostitutes. They were conspicuously absent from the professional and managerial occupations. In any job which needed a trained skill (baking, carpentry, shipbuilding, etc.) women were notable by their absence.

While about 29 per cent of Chinese women over 15 were engaged outside of the home, the other majority of women limited their activities

TABLE 2.5
Number of Passes Issued by the Mines Department, 1908–1920

Year	Number
1908	8,278
1909	9,596
1910	12,257
1911	10,807
1912	12,031
1913	14,155
1914	—
1915	15,859
1916	14,007
1917	13,870
1918	15,774
1919	15,553
1920	12,867

Source: R. N. Jackson, *Immigrant Labour and the Development of Malaya, 1786–1920*, Federation of Malaya, Government Printer, 1961, p. 146.

to the domestic sphere. The main factor which limited women was the Chinese community's traditional view of a woman's place. More so than either the Malays or Indians, Chinese men were reluctant to permit their wives to work outside the home. Freedman[37] noted as late as 1957, that Singaporean Chinese men resisted their wives' occupational pursuits.

Women working outside the home were employed in the lowest job categories. Those women who worked did so out of financial need. In poorer families, economic need overcame traditional views of the woman's place: women worked because of necessity. While statistics were not kept on the basis of class, most likely as one moved up the economic ladder, the number of working women decreased. Society's view that a woman's place was in the home combined with family demands and a lack of education to discourage women from working. Almost all Chinese women married and bore children. This greatly limited their mobility. The formal education of girls also proceeded slowly. Chinese vernacular schools (which first appeared in 1829),[38] English-medium private schools (such as the Penang Free School, 1816, and the Singapore Chinese Girls' School, 1889), as well as the religious and missionary schools, all provided some education for girls. However, the literacy figures of 1931 show that few Chinese girls had taken advantage of these opportunities. In the Straits Settlements (SS), no more than 112 Chinese females per 1,000 were literate as compared to 408 Chinese males.[39] The literacy rate among the Chinese was higher than among the Malays or Indians. The overall literacy rate for women, however, was only 76 per 1,000 as compared to that of 355 per 1,000 for men.[40]

About 94,619 Chinese boys and 36,347 Chinese girls received some education out of a total of 268,007 students attending school in the SS and FMS in 1938.[41] For the Chinese, the majority were in Chinese language schools. A few attended English language schools.[42] As with Malay and Indian girls, Chinese girls enrolled in school rarely completed the sixth and final year: only 565 girls as compared to 1,179 boys completed primary school in 1938.[43] As for secondary schooling, the number of both boys and girls attending assisted Chinese schools was low, only 1,066 girls and 2,149 boys.[44] Figures are not available on the numbers of students in Chinese private secondary schools prior to World War II. Girls were less likely to attend schools than were Chinese boys and girls often failed to stay in school. Even if educated, there was no guarantee that Chinese girls would find suitable employment. English-medium schools were already producing more clerks than British Malaya could absorb. Chinese businesses also did not hire women to do clerical work on a major scale.[45]

Marriage and Chinese Women

Although Chinese women could find employment outside the home, roughly 70 per cent confined themselves to the domestic sphere. Whether employed or not, most women married. The minority who did not marry either became Buddhist nuns or entered 'vegetarian' houses. The latter were women, both immigrant and Malaya-born, who rejected the idea of marriage and instead banded together in sisterhoods.[46] These groups provided unattached women with board and lodging as well as security in their old age. The 'vegetarian' houses were homes for women run along religious lines. Women, young or old, could join by either paying a fee, or, if too poor but able to work, by performing chores within the home. Though run along Buddhist lines, the women were free to live either in the home or outside. If they chose the outside, they returned to the home to celebrate festive occasions. As long as the women lived pious lives, followed vegetarian diet patterns, learned the sutras and attended religious observances, they were free to come and go and live as they pleased. The houses, though found throughout Malaya, were located mostly in the SS and specifically in Singapore. They provided a haven for unmarried women, deserted wives and concubines, actresses, dancing girls and prostitutes. All women who might find themselves alone sometime during their lives, particularly in old age, were welcome.

The vast majority of Chinese women married.[47] When talking about marital status, Nathan[48] noted in 1921 and Vlieland[49] reiterated in 1931, that it was hard to determine marriage and divorce among Chinese. This arose from the uncertainty of the *t'sip* or secondary wife as opposed to the *t'sai* or primary wife. The *t'sip* was not simply a concubine but a second wife. Her children were considered legitimate and could share with the children of the *t'sai* in their father's estate. Because of the linguistic problem in defining marriage, divorce and polygamy, and because Chinese customary marriages (as opposed to Christian marriages) were

TABLE 2.6
Statistics for Married Chinese Men and Women, 1921

	Married Chinese Males	Married Chinese Females	Per cent of Females to Males
SS	123,649	73,530	590
FMS	104,996	61,701	588
UMS	33,625	17,150	510
British Malaya	263,270	152,381	579

Source: C. A. Vlieland, *British Malaya: A Report on the 1931 Census*, London, Government Printer, 1932, p. 56.

not registered in Malaya, data is hard to get. It is not possible to detail with any accuracy the numbers of women who married more than once, or were secondary wives, or were divorced as opposed to widowed. However, as both Nathan and Vlieland noted, the majority of Chinese were monogamous; polygamy was practised only by the wealthier Chinese.

Colouring the entire issue of marriage and family was the fact that men vastly outnumbered women. This is reflected in the 1921 statistics for married Chinese men and women in Table 2.6.

While the ratio of married women to men was lowest in the Unfederated Malay States (UMS) where fewer Chinese settled, it rose much higher in the SS and the FMS. However, even in the most settled areas of Malaya, fully 4 out of every 10 Chinese husbands had left their wives behind in China. This is illustrated by the large seeming discrepancy in the figures of married males and females listed. By 1931, the situation had improved such that there were 756 married Chinese women to 1,000 married Chinese men.[50]

In Malaya, the lack of women discouraged the early marriage of females as well as males. The great demand for wives together with greater prosperity obviated the need of families to rid themselves of girl children at an early age. Table 2.7 shows the numbers of married and single Chinese per thousand of the general population for four different age groups in 1931.

Child marriage was non-existent among males under 15 years and rare among young girls. Almost half of the adult male population was single up to the age of 45, while most women had married by that age. Again, the figures show that older men were marrying younger women. This accounts for the increase in single women over the age of 45. Divorce was virtually unknown in the Chinese community;[51] polygamy made it more or less unnecessary. Most of the single women over 45 were most probably widows.

Traditional Chinese society restricted the freedom of women.[52] The

TABLE 2.7
Number of Married and Single Chinese per Thousand
of the General Population, 1931

Age	Males		Females	
	Married	*Single*	*Married*	*Single*
0–15	–	1,000	5	995
15–35	299	701	715	285
35–45	501	499	836	164
Over 45	537	463	576	424

Source: Vlieland, op. cit., p. 57.

majority of women in China were strictly bound by cultural traditions that governed their position within the family.

The extended joint family, composed of the parents, unmarried children, married sons (and their families) and sometimes a fourth or fifth generation, remained the ideal of Chinese society. Economics, however, forced the family into a stem family, i.e. a husband and a wife, their offspring plus one married son and his family.[53] Regardless of size, the family was structured on the dominance by the parents and distribution of status and functions by sex and age.[54] Families were patrilocal, patrilineal and represented the Confucian state in miniature: 'Inside the smaller doors leading to the inner apartments are to be found all the rules (of government). There is awe for the father, and also for the elder brother. Wife and children, servants and concubines are like the common people, serfs and underlings.'[55] Authority and decision-making rested with the husband/father. He could kill (in the case of adultery), pawn or sell a wife if he desired. (Though illegal, the selling and pawning of wives did indeed take place in China.)[56] He could divorce his wife for any of the seven reasons:[57] 1) if she disobeyed her husband's parents, 2) failed to bear children, 3) committed adultery, 4) exhibited jealousy, 5) had some repulsive disease, 6) was garrulous or 7) stole. However, for women, divorce was not an option. Marriage for the wife signified a bond to a new home, a bond that was meant for life, not to be broken even on the death of the husband. No matter how dissatisfied she became, no matter how cruelly treated, a woman was advised to tolerate her station and preserve the unity of the family. Women were urged to resign themselves to fate: 'When you marry a chicken, stick with the chicken; when you marry a dog, stick with the dog.'[58] If a woman was able to get her husband to divorce her or if she left the family, her chances of remarriage were slim. Further, she forfeited any right to her children. Such women frequently were unable to support themselves. Unattached women had, in essence, stepped out of the bounds of respectable society. Suicide was often the only way out.

For widows, life was hard; they seldom remarried—public opinion would not accept it. They were not able to formally inherit property[59] (women inherited only if no male relative survived). In practice, it was the widow's sons who were responsible for her. If she were widowed while young, her financial position could be and often was precarious.

While financially secure parents rejoiced in the birth of a son or daughter, girls were not always welcomed at birth among the poor. Girls were not members of their fathers' lineages—upon marriage they left the family. They were economically unproductive and a drain on the poor peasant's income. Fathers had the right to sell or otherwise dispose of unwanted girl children. Girls were the main, if not the only victims, of infanticide as practised among the poor.[60] If the girl remained in the family, she was seldom educated but was trained to be an obedient wife and submissive daughter-in-law. In addition, only girl children were subject to the crippling practice of foot-binding, which began in tenth-century China. While the purpose may have been aesthetic, the result was crippled and immobile women unable to leave home. Foot-binding also injured a woman's health by causing her to live an unnatural, sedentary life.[61]

Once a girl was married, a woman's function was to produce male heirs for the continuation of lineage and security in the parents' old age. She was to provide service and comfort to her parents-in-law; her duty was solely to her husband's family. Cruel mothers-in-law and suffering daughters-in-law are a common theme in Chinese literature. There is no doubt that in many families very real tensions existed. Because of the demands of filial piety, a wife could not expect the support of her husband. The husband, out of loyalty, would usually side with his mother. With the death of the mother-in-law, the status of the wife increased, particularly if she had borne a son; in time, she would rule the household as her mother-in-law did before her. The status of the married woman improved throughout the life cycle. In each stage of her life, however, she held an inferior position to the male family members of the same generation and to those generations above her.[62] Whatever power a woman held was derived from that of some man.[63] A mother-in-law dominated the domestic household because she was the wife of the head of the family, the final source of authority. The harshness of the system and the subjugation of the daughter-in-law sought to preserve the family by stopping the young wife and her husband from breaking off into an independent family.[64]

The family changed as it moved from China to Malaya. While the majority of Chinese women remained under the authority of their husbands, certain changes worked to their advantage. The shortage of women meant that some would become more valued. Men needed sons to fulfil filial responsibility and ancestor worship. Men in Malaya were forced to marry late in life. Once a man did obtain a wife, the chances of his selling, pawning or divorcing her were extremely small. (Divorce was almost unknown.) Given that roughly 29 per cent of all Chinese women did earn an income, one would guess that a man would not beat a woman so as to impair her earning ability, thus making the life of the woman somewhat easier. Also, the absence of a mother-in-law in the immigrant group was often a relief for the wife.

Chinese females while not welcomed at birth to the extent of Chinese males, were seldom, if ever, subject to infanticide in Malaya. Nathan noted: 'While there is no suspicion of female infanticide in British Malaya, it is probable that Chinese male children are more carefully nurtured than female children when young.'[65] Poor parents who could not afford to raise girl children could give them to church organizations, to the women of the vegetarian houses, or could sell them to other families desiring children. Sometimes girls were adopted by families who truly wanted a girl. The Malay community often adopted unwanted Chinese girl babies and raised them as their own children. At other times, girls would be adopted by families who were in need of cheap servants or who wanted to obtain a future daughter-in-law at an early age. The former were known as *mui tsai*[66] and numbered 2,749 in 1934 while the number of the latter, *sim pu kia*, or 'little daughters-in-law' remains unclear.[67] Not surprisingly, it was mainly poor families who relieved themselves of the burden. Girls were given up, though, if it was felt that they would bring bad luck to a family. In short, girls were *sih-pun-he*, a Hokkien expression meaning goods on which one loses.[68]

The family as it moved from China to Malaya ceased to function as both an administrative and economic unit. During imperial times, the Chinese household stood at the base of a hierarchy of local units intended to ensure group responsibility towards government.[69] (This collective responsibility was not used by the British in Malaya.) In addition, the family in South China was an economic unit, based on owning and working of land. In Malaya, household members performed very different tasks and derived income from many sources.[70] Family members thus had access to incomes of their own.

The control of capital and family resources, however, rested with the men rather than women and with the older rather than the younger.[71] Thus even if a woman worked, the male head of the family still controlled the finances of the entire family. Freedman[72] noted in 1957 that Chinese men strongly resisted women seeking employment outside the home. Chinese men had not yet adjusted to women operating as free economic agents.

While women did not control family capital, they were vital to religious obligations. The women, usually the senior woman, carried out the daily and monthly ritual acts. Men seldom took a direct interest in religious affairs in the home. Such observances were left to the women.[73] Outside the home, a few women performed as mediums in the major spirit cults. Elliot[74] discovered that women held a monopoly in the practice of soul-raising. In a manner similar to Western mediums, the soul-raiser called upon *Kwan Yin* (the Goddess of Mercy) to locate a deceased person. The soul then spoke through the body of the soul-raiser—answering questions put by the inquiring family. Soul-raising needed great skill and sensitivity by the women involved. This is well illustrated in the following quote by Elliot:

> On whatever powers the soul raiser may depend, it must be admitted that a competent performance requires very great skill. The feelings of the audience must be perfectly judged in order to establish a maximum credulity among all those who are present. Special pains must be taken with those who tend towards disbelief, and the seance must be led forward step by step until a sufficient knowledge of the family's background has been acquired for all pronouncements to be made with the certainty of acceptance. Further, the soul raiser can never deviate from the religious symbolism to which her listeners are familiar, or make mistakes in the manner in which a member of a kinship circle would address his superiors or inferiors. Whatever the psychical content of her performance may be, a good soul raiser at work is a revelation in the skillful use of scoiological knowledge.[75]

For the Malayan Chinese women, marriage remained very much beyond their control. As with their Malay and Indian counterparts, marriages were arranged by go-betweens who negotiated the terms of the marriage between the two families. After the date was set and the festive celebrations completed, the bride moved to the household of her husband. Chinese women were seldom consulted and their consent to the marriage was not necessary. Women were important to maintain the ancestoral line, to raise the children, to perform religious tasks, and, in some cases, to contribute to the family income. While subordinate to their husbands and others, Chinese women were not powerless within the family. Men and women did follow certain norms, for example, it was customary for the women to wait on the men and to keep in the background if there were male guests in the household. They did not, however, efface themselves or avoid all contact with unfamiliar men.[76] Freedman[77] observed that nothing like 'oriental seclusion' existed in Malaya except among some very old families with girls of marriageable age.

The relationship between husband and wife was fixed not only by the division of labour, but also by rules that governed mutual behaviour. While the marriage tradition was marked by the submission of the wife to the husband, in Malaya (as in China) it was not unknown for women to dominate men. If needed, men would share in domestic labour. The management of the household and the raising and disciplining of children remained the primary duties of the woman.

Traditional women were expected to respond promptly and passively to their husband's sexual demands. They could not, though, expect to be the sole object of their husband's sexual attentions. Wives had no right to express jealousy as long as the exploits remained temporary and irregular. 'Eating vinegar', or expressing jealousy was an accepted, if somewhat useless, response to lasting and regular relationships.[78]

Marital Status and Legal Difficulties of Malayan Chinese Women

In Malaya, the lack of legislation governing Chinese marriage and divorce created many problems for the women; the major problem was that marriages were not registered. Upon the death of the husband, there were frequent disputes among his wives and heirs. In contrast to practices in China, secondary wives had by Malayan law the right to inherit a share of their husband's property, while casual concubines could not. Without registration it was difficult to determine who in fact was a secondary wife. In response to these problems and to reformers who wished to abolish polygamy, a Chinese Marriage Committee was appointed in 1926 by the Governor. They investigated the marriage customs and traditions of the Straits Chinese. The aim was to define what constituted a valid marriage and to offer proposals as to how such marriages should be registered. The Committee, composed of all Chinese with the Secretary of Chinese Affairs as Chairman, recommended that all Chinese marriages, including those carried out according to custom, should be registered. However, the Committee could make no recommendations as to what constituted a valid marriage. No basic elements were found common to marriages as carried out in different districts of South China. The Committee did find that divorce legislation ran against the wishes of many residents of the SS—divorce following the Chinese custom of being the sole right of the male. It was further argued, polygamy made divorce unnecessary. Considerations of family, lineage, and face prevented the divorce of first wives. Secondary wives had less status and security. On the other hand, Freedman[79] noted that in 1957 the dissolution of marriages did occur. A signed agreement between spouses marked the end of the relationship. The dissolution of marriages also took place in the FMS between 1899 and 1932. The Secretary for Chinese Affairs had the power to decide matters affecting custody and guardianship as well as divorce and separation.[80] In the SS, Blythe, the Secretary for Chinese Affairs of the Malayan Union (1946–8) noted, as recorded in Purcell,[81] that poor Chinese women did seek divorce by appealing to his office. The greater independence of working Chinese women most likely contributed to their desire to start such proceedings.

Marriage and divorce reform for the Malayan Chinese did not come until after World War II. Women and girls, though, did benefit from one practice unknown in China. The colonial courts ruled that if a man died intestate, all his widows would share one-third of his estate. All their children, girls as well as boys, would have equal rights to the remaining portion.[82] Thus women in Malaya, though they had no right to their children (they belonged to the husband's family) did have a degree of security that was unknown in China.

The 1930s—A New Wave of Immigrants

With the 1930s, the Chinese female population of Malaya soared. The 1933 Alien's Ordinance restricted the number of adult males permitted to enter Malaya. The colonial government alarmed at the ever increasing numbers of unskilled immigrants sought to regulate the admission of aliens. Hence, the number of males was fixed at about 1,000 per month. The result was that shipping companies sought ways to compensate for the limited number of travellers by getting women to emigrate. Ticket brokers at the China ports refused to sell quota tickets unless three or four non-quota tickets were bought by the lodging-houses and ticket agencies. Hence, the lodging-houses and ticket agencies encouraged women to take up the non-quota tickets. The result, from 1933 until 1938 was shiploads of Cantonese women, largely between the ages of 18 and 40 years of age (many claiming to be widows), arriving in Malaya. A quota of 500 females a month was then established. The entire nature of Chinese immigration to Malaya had drastically altered. Blythe[83] observed:

> There can be little doubt that in some cases the old custom of the husband emigrating and sending money back to China for the support of his wife and family was reversed. In the five years 1934–1938, there was a migrational gain to Malaya of over 190,000 female deck passengers. The majority of these women were peasant women—workers who entered the rubber and tin industries, the building industry and factories. They have settled here and many of them have married.

Chinese Women and the Pre-1945 Political Associations

Though greater numbers of Chinese women lived in Malaya by the 1930s, there is no evidence that they played a major role in the traditional clan associations, secret societies or political associations. Such participation was beyond the scope of women's activity. Aside from such women's organizations as the Buddhist nunneries and the vegetarian houses, women did join together either in social welfare organizations or to participate in relief work. One of the earliest examples was the Chinese Ladies Association of Singapore which was active in 1917.[84] The Association had been formed for the general improvement of young ladies. Classes were held in cooking, pastry-making, sewing and embroidery. Its greatest achievement was permitting Chinese women to interact with each other and share common interests.

Malayan Chinese raised funds for China relief projects from 1877 when famine struck Shantung province in North China. Numerous disasters elicited funds from the Malayan Chinese. Whether women were engaged in the earliest days of relief work is not known. By World War I, Chinese women were, however, actively aiding the fund-raising efforts. In 1916, Chinese women launched a campaign to purchase a fighter plane in aid of the British war effort. Singaporean Chinese women alone raised $6,000 towards the purchase of the plane, which was appropriately called the 'Women of Malaya'.[85] Chinese women also helped the war effort by raising funds through children's fêtes and the like.

After World War I, the Chinese continued to raise funds to alleviate natural disasters in China. They also aided the cause of the Chinese Revolution. After the Japanese invasion of China (1937), fund-raising for the China Relief Fund greatly increased. Though women contributed to the Fund, it is unlikely that they played a major role in deciding how funds would be raised or in the actual organizing of most activities. Chinese leaders, whether of clans, guilds, secret societies, or merchant associations, were all men. The Chinese separate spheres of men and women precluded the emergence of women in positions of social prominence.

As women did not play an active part in such organizations, it would be reasonable to assume they played a minor role in political associations of that time. This is, indeed, confirmed by historical accounts of this period. The Chinese did experience nationalistic stirrings directed towards China and not Malaya. Dr Sun Yat-sen's visits to Malaya in 1900, 1906 and 1910, the fall of the Ch'ing dynasty, and China's experiment with republicanism all aroused patriotic interests and emotions. Such interests were channelled through two main organizations both patterned after China: the Kuomintang (KMT) and the Malayan Communist Party (MCP).

In Malaya, the first branch of the KMT was established in Singapore in 1912. The party quickly spread throughout Malaya. Because of its anti-British line, it was suppressed by the government in the 1920s. However, it remained well established among those Chinese who agreed with its anti-British sentiments. The primary function of the KMT was to develop patriotism among the overseas Chinese with the express purpose of obtaining material support for China's revolution. Active membership remained small. By November 1933, the total Malayan Chinese membership was 12,346 persons. On the average, there were fewer than 76 members per 10,000 Chinese in the SS. The figure was lower in the Malay States.[86] Many of the supporters were Hailams,[87] perhaps because they occupied the lowest economic and social positions among the overseas Chinese. Because there were so few Hailam women present in Malaya, one can assume that Hailam women were not taking a visible role in the KMT. The main study of the KMT in Malaya,[88] those studies dealing with pre-war nationalism,[89] and those studies that discuss the history of the Chinese in Malaya,[90] all fail to mention any women active in the movement.

As for the Malayan Communist Party (MCP), it too had few active women members. Prior to the split between the KMT and the Chinese Communist Party (CCP) in China in 1927, the KMT and the MCP had worked together in Malaya. After the split, the Malayan communists established a separate organization in 1930. As Purcell[91] noted, it was largely Hailams who left the KMT to form the MCP and its auxiliary branches. During the pre-war period, the MCP focused its activities on gaining Chinese support. Acting largely through its labour unions and student federations, the MCP did succeed in channelling student and labour discontent.[92] Before the Japanese invasion of China in 1937, the party remained quite small. In 1931, they numbered no more than 1,500 members, about 10,000 organized labourers and supporters, about 50 active women supporters, and 200 affiliates in satellite organizations (such as the Anti-Imperialist League).[93] While acknowledging support among immigrant labourers and Chinese schoolteachers, historians of the MCP fail to discuss women and their participation within the party.[94] After the Japanese invasion of China, the party tightened its organization and established a women's section. Historical accounts, however, do not discuss women within the party. Hence, this aspect of Malayan history remains obscure.

It sometimes seems that the Chinese were apathetic or secretive in their politics prior to World War II. Wang Gungwu[95] has, however, argued that the Chinese were divided into three major groups. Each possessed different orientations towards Malaya and China and each employed different political tactics. Thus, the community failed to act as a cohesive whole. In addition, the Chinese were divided by language, education (Chinese, English or illiterate), occupation (merchants, artisans, clerks, labourers and squatter-farmers), and clan or secret society membership. Such divisions, as well as the perceived temporary nature of their stay in Malaya, all contributed to the failure of the Chinese to unify. This divisiveness extended to the women as well.

Chinese women's political activities were limited prior to the end of World War II. The divisions of the Chinese groups as well as a social structure dominated by the merchant class[96] precluded women from activities outside the home. Lacking education and job opportunities above the lowest levels, women had little chance to gain in status. While research is limited on women in pre-war Malaya, interviews with many prominent Chinese women confirm this view.[97] In fact, no one interviewed could recall *any* Chinese woman in public affairs. The consensus was that the conservative nature of the Chinese community, among both men and women, prevented such developments.

The Japanese Occupation and Its Effect on Malayan Chinese Women

The Japanese Occupation had a profound effect on the Chinese community. The Malayan Chinese suffered greatly under the Japanese who viewed the local Chinese as the same enemy engaged in China.[98] In the early period, the Japanese consolidated their control. It proved to be a particularly brutal time for the Malayan Chinese. Chinese women and men were executed as suspected KMT and MCP supporters. Those who resisted the Japanese advance into Malaya were also killed. Rape by Japanese men was a very real and tragic problem for Chinese and

Eurasian women. There are no figures showing the incidence of rape but it was a widespread problem during the early days of the Occupation.[99]

After the early period of disruption caused by the British retreat and the Japanese Occupation, most Chinese concerned themselves with survival. Survival meant avoiding the Japanese and passively blocking their policies. It also included dealing with the black market which existed throughout Malaya. Women as well as men became adept at making do with substitutes for scarce items. The shortages of goods and the shifting of population caused by people evacuating and later returning to their residences, suggest that Chinese women were forced to lead more active lives. That is, everybody was involved in the struggle to survive.

The Chinese, in contrast to the Malays and Indians, received nothing from the Occupation. They neither gained experience in administrative posts as did the Malays, nor were they helped to organize, as were the Indians in their Indian Independence League. The Chinese remained much the subjugated race during the Occupation. Chinese women, in particular, would gain no organizational experience.

Chinese did join the 2,000 member Malayan People's Anti-Japanese Army (MPAJA) and the 300,000 persons strong civilian volunteers in the Malayan People's Anti-Japanese Union (MPAJU).[100] It is not possible to assess the role women played in the two organizations. Scholars are silent on the subject.

1. Gordon Means, *Malaysian Politics*, London, University of London Press, 1970, p. 26.
2. Victor Purcell, *The Chinese in Malaya*, London, Oxford University Press, 1948, p. 27.
3. Ibid., p. 38.
4. Ibid., p. 40.
5. Ibid., p. 68.
6. Ibid.
7. Ibid., p. 87.
8. Ibid.
9. Ibid.
10. C. B. Buckley, *An Ancedotal History of Old Times in Singapore, 1819–1867*, Kuala Lumpur, University of Malaya Press, 1965, p. 320.
11. T. J. Newbold, *Political and Statistical Account of the British Settlements in the Straits of Malacca*, p. 287, quoted in Purcell, *The Chinese in Malaya*, p. 87.
12. G. W. Earl, *The Eastern Seas*, p. 367, quoted in Purcell, *The Chinese in Malaya*, p. 87.
13. P. C. Campbell, *Chinese Coolie Emigration*, London, P. S. King and Son, 1923, p. 2.
14. Purcell, *The Chinese in Malaya*, p. 60.
15. Campbell, op. cit., p. 5.
16. For example, see Purcell, *The Chinese in Malaya*, Campbell, op. cit., or W. L. Blythe, 'A Historical Sketch of Chinese Labour in Malaya', *Journal of the Malayan Branch of the Royal Asiatic Society (JMBRAS)*, Vol. 20, Part 1, June 1947, pp. 64–114.
17. Blythe, op. cit., p. 1.
18. R. N. Jackson, *Immigrant Labour and the Development of Malaya, 1786–1920*, Federation of Malaya, Government Printer, 1961, p. 51.

19. Purcell, *The Chinese in Malaya*, p. 174.
20. Song Ong-siang, *One Hundred Years' History of the Chinese in Singapore*, Singapore, University of Malaya Press, 1967, pp. 448-50.
21. Ibid., p. 357.
22. Jackson, op. cit., p. 51.
23. Ibid.
24. Buckley, op. cit., p. 113.
25. J. E. Nathan, *The Census of British Malaya*, London, Waterlow and Sons, 1922, p. 46.
26. Ibid.
27. Ibid., p. 140.
28. Ibid., p. 78.
29. C. A. Vlieland, *British Malaya: A Report on the 1931 Census*, London, Government Printer, 1932, p. 180.
30. Ibid., p. 52.
31. Nathan, op. cit., p. 121.
32. Ibid., this figure and the ones which follow on pp. 13 and 14 were derived from Table 37, pp. 289-92, unless otherwise noted. Figures for 1931 were not included but do see Vlieland, op. cit., pp. 269-72 and pp. 294-7 for confirmation of the same pattern in 1931.
33. For example, in 1911 in the FMS, 7,264 women were engaged in agriculture as compared to 15,929 in 1921. Nathan, op. cit., p. 122.
34. Jackson, op. cit., p. 146.
35. Yip Yat-hoong, *The Development of the Tin Mining Industry of Malaya*, Kuala Lumpur, University of Malaya Press, 1969, p. 30.
36. Nathan, op. cit., p. 121.
37. Maurice Freedman, *The Chinese Family in Singapore*, London Colonial Office Research Studies No. 20, 1957, p. 57.
38. Wong Hoy-kee (Francis) and Gwee Yee-hean, *Perspectives: The Development of Education in Malaysia and Singapore*, Kuala Lumpur, Heinemann Educational Books (Asia) Ltd., 1972, p. 8.
39. Vlieland, op. cit., p. 94.
40. Ibid., p. 91.
41. Purcell, *The Chinese in Malaya*, p. 222.
42. Ibid.
43. Federation of Malaysia, *Educational Statistics of Malaysia 1972*, Kuala Lumpur, Ministry of Education, 1975, p. 34. Figures were not available for private schools.
44. Ibid., p. 38.
45. Freedman, op. cit., p. 157.
46. Marjorie Topley, 'Chinese Women's Vegetarian Houses in Singapore', *JMBRAS*, Vol. 27, Part 1, May 1954, pp. 53-4.
47. 'The value of statistics as to marriage in a country like British Malaya is not very great (quoting the 1911 Census): "With regard to the native races in the East ... it is generally admitted that all adult females are either married or living in concubinage."' Nathan, op. cit., p. 57.
48. Ibid., p. 56.
49. Vlieland, op. cit., p. 56.
50. Ibid., p. 57.
51. Nathan, op. cit., p. 57; Vlieland, op. cit., p. 56.
52. Traditional is being used here to describe those patterns of behaviour or activities prevalent in China during the Ch'ing dynasty (1644-1911). M. Levy, *The Family Revolution in Modern China*, Cambridge, Mass., Harvard University Press, 1949, p. 41.
53. Ibid., p. 55.
54. C. K. Yang, *Chinese Communist Society: The Family and the Village*, Cambridge, Mass., M.I.T. Press, 1959, p. 10.
55. Olga Lang, *Chinese Family and Society*, New Haven, Yale University Press, 1946, p. 24.

56. Ibid., p. 45.
57. Ibid., p. 40.
58. Yang, op. cit., p. 64.
59. Lang, op. cit., p. 44.
60. Ibid., p. 43.
61. Ibid., pp. 45–6.
62. Yang, op. cit., p. 106.
63. Levy, op. cit., p. 160.
64. Yang, op. cit., p. 106.
65. Nathan, op. cit., p. 50.
66. '*Mui tsai*' is Cantonese for 'little sister'. Purcell, *The Chinese in Malaya*, p. 183.
67. Freedman, op. cit., p. 65.
68. Ibid.
69. Ibid., pp. 40–1.
70. Ibid.
71. Ibid., p. 43.
72. Ibid.
73. Ibid., p. 45.
74. Alan Elliot, *Chinese Medium Cults in Singapore*, Monograph on Social Anthropology No. 14, London, School of Economics, Department of Anthropology, n.d., pp. 138–9, as quoted in Margery Wolf, 'Chinese Women: Old Skills in a New Context', as cited in M. Z. Rosaldo and L. Lampere (eds.), *Woman, Culture and Society*, Stanford, Stanford University Press, 1974, pp. 165–6.
75. Ibid.
76. In Chinese new villages in Malaysia, Nyce found few cases where the young wife was relegated to an inferior position to that of her husband. Usually a wife's position equalled that of her husband; such equality resulting from the relative economic independence of new village women. Kay Nyce, *Chinese New Villages in Malaya: A Community Study*, Kuala Lumpur, Malaysian Social Research Institute, 1973, pp. 52–3.
77. Freedman, op. cit., p. 45.
78. Ibid., p. 57.
79. Ibid.
80. Purcell, *The Chinese in Malaya*, p. 150.
81. Ibid.
82. Freedman, op. cit., p. 104.
83. Blythe, op. cit., pp. 29–30.
84. Song Ong-siang, op. cit., p. 541.
85. Ibid., p. 534.
86. Png Poh-seng, 'The Kuomintang in Malaya', *Journal of Southeast Asian History*, March 1961, Vol. 2, No. 1, p. 34.
87. Purcell, *The Chinese in Malaya*, p. 214.
88. Png Poh-seng, op. cit.
89. For example, see W. L. Holland (ed.), *Asian Nationalism and the West*, New York, Octagon Books, 1973.
90. See Purcell, *The Chinese in Malaya*.
91. Ibid., p. 215.
92. Holland, op. cit., p. 282.
93. Henry Miller, *Menace in Malaya*, London, George G. Haup and Co., 1954, p. 29; J. M. van der Kroef, *Communism in Malaysia and Singapore*, The Hague, Martinus Nijhoff, 1967, p. 22; Anthony Short, 'Communism in Malaya', in Wang Gungwu (ed.), *Malaysia: A Survey*, New York, Frederick A. Praeger, 1965, p. 58.
94. See Miller, *Menace in Malaya*; Anthony Short, *The Communist Insurrection in Malaya 1948–60*, London, Frederick Muller Ltd., 1975; Lucian Pye, *Guerrilla Communism in Malaya*, Princeton, N. J., Princeton University Press, 1956; J. M. van der Kroef, *Communism in Malaysia and Singapore*, The Hague, Martinus Nijhoff, 1967; Victor Purcell, *Malaya, Communist or Free?*, Stanford, Stanford University Press, 1954.

95. Wang Gungwu, 'Chinese Politics in Malaya', *China Quarterly*, July–September 1970, Vol. 43. p. 1.
96. Wang Gungwu, 'Traditional Leadership in a New Nation', S. T. Alisjahbana, X. T. Wayagam and Wang Gungwu (eds.), *The Cultural Problems of Malaysia in the Context of Southeast Asia*, Kuala Lumpur, University of Malaya, 1965.
97. Including for example: Dr Soo Kim-lan, the first Chinese woman appointed to a national level legislative committee, the Malayan Union Advisory Council (1946–8); Datin Gunn Chit-wha, an early activist in the Malayan Chinese Association as well as the leading woman figure in the party; Mrs Rosemary Chong, the first Chinese woman elected to the Malaysian Parliament (1976) and the current president of the women's wing of the MCA and Mrs Helen Tan, the prominent secretary of the Malaysian YWCA, to mention only a few.
98. For example see Purcell, *Malaya, Communist or Free?*; Chin Kee-onn, *Malaya Upside Down*, Singapore, Jitts and Co., 1946.
99. Chin Kee-onn, op. cit., p. 114.
100. van der Kroef, *Communism in Malaysia and Singapore*, p. 23.

3 Indian Women

The Nature of Indian Immigration to Malaya

INDIAN contacts with South-East Asia existed in the pre-Christian era. Probably as early as the first or second century BC,[1] the Bay of Bengal was the means by which people, goods and ideas were exchanged between South Asia and Malaya. Regardless of the cultural impact of such exchanges, the transmitters of trade and culture were few in number. There is no evidence to suggest that the Indian population in Malaya ever exceeded 20,000 prior to the mid-nineteenth century.[2]

The second wave of Indian immigration, starting in the late eighteenth century and continuing well into the twentieth, was driven purely by economics. The needs of Malayan planters for a cheap and elastic labour supply brought the Indians. Whereas the early contacts with Malaya had been started by the Indians themselves, the second immigration was begun by Europeans. Europeans responded to the planters' need for labour and to the colonial government's need for trained clerks, security officers and servants. Indian immigration was governed by the Malayan demand for labour: it was temporary and consisted largely of men. The immigrants were almost all of South Indian origin. This would greatly affect the development of the Indian community. It would also determine the social and political problems that the Indians would face.

Though some controversy exists as to when Indian labour first appeared in Malaya, there is no doubt Indian labourers arrived in Penang in 1787 at the request of Francis Light.[3] Domestic servants, sepoys (native soldiers in the military service of Europeans), Indian shopkeepers and coolies emigrated from the Coromandel Coast at the rate of 1,000 to 2,000 a year.[4] Between 1790 and 1841, the number of immigrants did not exceed 3,000 a year.[5] Unfortunately, these records do not tell whether the new immigrants were male or female. In fact, one of the first written pieces of evidence that shows Indian women arrived in Malaya, comes from a different source, the records on convict labour: on 18 April 1825, 1 female and 73 male convicts from Madras, arrived in Singapore to serve life sentences.[6] (Singapore, Malacca and Penang served, in part, as penal settlements for the British Empire.) Netto[7] reported that one week later, 122 convicts from Bengal, including one woman, arrived in Singapore. The next year saw the arrival of 80 more males and 3 additional females. Sandhu[8] added that in 1860, 217 out of 4,063 convicts were women, while in 1865, 187 out of 3,339 convicts were women. These and other convicts helped to build the Straits Settlements, constructing roads, reclaiming swamps and erecting buildings and bridges.

Convicts formed only a small minority of the Indians destined for Malaya. While sepoys, clerks and shopkeepers were coming from the late 1780s, labourers headed for the plantations began to enter in the 1830s. Tamil and Telugu workers were recruited in large numbers to work on the coffee and sugar plantations of Penang and Province Wellesley. To meet the demand, employers, or recruiting agents, obtained a major source of labour through the indenture system whereby a person sold his labour to an employer or agent, for five years (three years after 1876). The labour was barter for passage to Malaya, wages and some small savings. The indenture system functioned long before the 1850s and possibly as early as the 1820s.[9] A total of 250,000 indentured Indian labourers arrived in Malaya between 1844 and 1910. The system was then abolished.[10] The system dominated the early period of trafficking in Indian labour; unregulated abuses were common. While theoretically free to return to India (or arrange a new contract) after a period of five (later three) years, the indentured labourer was often kept in bondage to his employer through a system of perpetual indebtedness—wages were not enough for the living conditions.[11] Indian women in particular suffered under this system. In 1879, the sub-collector of Tanjore, a Mr Hathaway, observed that the recruiting involved a 'regularly organized system of kidnapping'. Further, female immigrants were destined to a life of prostitution.[12] Hathaway's successor, Stokes, confirmed that the kidnapping of women and children did take place and that recruitment under duress also occurred.[13] Sandhu[14] also noted: '... women ... who have a passing quarrel with their husbands or parents are seduced away by females employed for the purpose, who bring them on board ship before they know what they have done...'. The Indian Government Emigration Act of 1871 was the first major effort to safeguard the lives of labourers and to check gross abuses.

A second form of immigration recruitment began in the last quarter of the nineteenth century. This was called the *kangany* system of recruited labour. (A foreman from Malaya, himself an Indian immigrant, would be

TABLE 3.1

Number of Recorded Indian Women Immigrating to Malaya, 1867–1869

Year	Indian Women Immigrants	Total Indian Immigrants
1867	264	8,697
1868	225	10,268
1869	188	10,268

Source: K. S. Sandhu, *Indians in Malaya, Immigration and Settlement 1786–1957*, Cambridge, Cambridge University Press, 1969, p. 311.

commissioned to return to his village to recruit labourers for the employer.) This system dominated the immigrant labour supply from 1910 until 1938 when all assisted labour migration from India was stopped. The foreman was provided with funds to pay the passage and expenses of each new recruit. The recruit, in turn, was expected to pay back the loan in a period of two years. While abuses were common under the system, the *kangany* method of recruitment was less brutal than the indentured system that it replaced.

While the number of Indian immigrants to Malaya jumped from 1,500 in 1790 to 10,728 in 1882,[15] the number of women immigrants remained small. Statistics on female immigrants are rare, but for the three years 1867–9, the number of recorded women immigrating to Malaya is shown in Table 3.1.

These figures indicate only those women who were immigrating to Malaya as non-labourers, i.e. women who either served as clerks, teachers, merchants, etc. or came as the dependents of such non-labouring immigrants. It does not include women labourers (plantation workers, servants, etc.), those figures being unavailable. Other information confirms that the number of women immigrants remained limited. The 1891 Census for British Malaya supports this observation. It noted that the Indian female to male ratio was 18 per 1,000[16] while by 1901, this ratio had risen to 171 per 1,000 males.[17]

In 1890, recruiting notices in India appealed to both men and women by offering men $3.60 (Straits Currency) a month and women $2.49 a month for the first year.[18] By 1906, the daily wage for men for indentured labour was, in addition to rations, 20¢ a day for men and 12¢ a day for women.[19] The ratio of 18 females per 1,000 males in 1891 showed, however, that few Indian women took advantage of the chance to emigrate.

Indians migrated to Malaya to help supply European coffee and sugar planters with a large and flexible labour supply. The indigenous Malays were not attracted to plantation life and labour. Owing to the Industrial Revolution in England (and the decline of the Indian handicraft industry), an excessive land tax, repeated Indian famines (1784, 1804, 1837, 1861, 1878 and 1897–1900) and caste which determined occupation, the Malayan plantation system offered the poorer lower-caste Indian peasants a chance for a livelihood and some wealth. Due to changes in the labour needs of the planters, to the nature of the work involved (requiring individual rather than familial labour[20]), to the arduous work and climate, as well as to the short-term nature of the indenture contract, this immigration was regarded by Indians as temporary. The ultimate goal was to return to one's village in India. The immigration was, therefore, undertaken largely by men, aged 15–45. They left their families behind but fully expected to return to them. Sandhu wrote, 'this predominantly male character of the Indian movement was due to the fact that the majority of the Indian immigrants were simply birds of passage, sojourners only in Malaya and preferred to leave their families in India'.[21]

In fact, fully 60 per cent of the Indian immigrants between 1821 and 1924 returned to India while from 1925 to 1957, this figure rose to 80 per cent.[22] The Malayan Census of 1931 commented on the temporary nature of the Indian population: 'the Southern Indian population is subject to even more rapid turnover than the Chinese, the average period of continuous residence in Malaya being only two to three years'.[23]

In addition to the belief that the stay in Malaya would be brief, Indian traditions discouraged female emigration. Women, or minors, were not allowed to leave on their own but rather needed to be accompanied by either husbands or relatives.[24] Further, the Indian joint family system required the presence of women in the home, both as child minders and as a source of domestic labour. In addition to fearing for the women's safety and not wishing to lose their labour, families further guaranteed that the sons would return to India by keeping their wives and children there.

It is likely that some women formed illegal liaisons, or *certtu-k-kolu-tal*, with men in order to emigrate. Possibly women who sought to avoid a life of widowhood, a disastrous marriage, an unhappy love affair, or to escape extreme poverty, would form such unions to circumvent the emigration practices.[25] Data does not show the numbers of these unions. A marriage *tali*, a string or cord worn by the wife to show she was married, was cheap and easy to obtain. However, if the union was not permanent, the single woman could not expect to be treated well by plantation owners and managers. They frequently had a low regard for the Indian women's morals. One planter in 1894 wrote: 'Not more than 6 coolies should be put into each room, but the planter cooly is most philosophical in this respect, a young unmarried woman not objecting in the least to reside with a family or even sharing her quarters, if necessary, with quite a few of the opposite sex.'[26] That attitude was shared by many planters and managers who learned the labourers' language through the 'sleeping dictionary' method.[27] They casually seduced the female Indian labourers.[28] Unattached women were extremely vulnerable.

The 1890s saw the rubber industry, Malaya's major agricultural product, develop and expand. Heavily dependent upon a cheap labour source, the rubber industry caused the numbers of Indian immigrants to soar. By the 1920s the numbers of Indian immigrants had risen to 185,055 in 1926, 167,624 in 1927 and 133,609 in 1929.[29] The demand then dropped due to the world-wide depression. Sandhu[30] adds that female immigrants accounted for 24 per cent of the annual arrivals between 1901 and 1933. Most of these were probably wives travelling with or joining husbands already in Malaya. Children, he noted, were seldom over 10 per cent of the total number of immigrants.[31]

From the 1930s, Indian immigration was sharply curtailed by several factors: the Malayan government's 1933 restriction on the number of male labourers allowed to enter Malaya, the 1938 Indian government's ban on the emigration of assisted (and then free) labour (due to a dispute with the Malayan government over wages and the treatment of labourers), the Japanese Occupation, and the post-war Malayan restrictions on immigration. The Indian population froze at roughly 10 per cent of the total population of Malaya. Thereafter, growth in the Indian community would largely be due to natural increases rather than immigration.

In 1921, a uniform census was performed for all of British Malaya which with the 1931 census, provides a source of information on immigration. Two facts become self-evident: 1) the immigrants were largely men, and 2) most were South Indians of low-caste origins.[32] By 1921, the total Indian population in Malaya was 471,666 of which 136,181 were women.[33] In addition, the immigrants of both sexes were largely South Indians, the Tamils alone constituting 82 per cent of the Indian population, followed by the Telugus (8 per cent), and the Malayalees (4 per cent). There were also Punjabis (3 per cent), Bengalis (1 per cent) and several less numerous groups including the Ceylonese.[34] This dominance by South Indians is not surprising. The Indian government had permitted the recruitment of labourers solely from the state of Madras during the indenture period (1830s–1910). The *kangany* system (1890s–1930s), which depended on kinship and village ties, perpetuated the South Indians ties.

Between 1891 and 1931, the ratio of female to male Indians jumped from 18 per 1,000 to 482 per 1,000 respectively. By 1931, fully 202,981 Indian women were present in Malaya.[35] Though the numbers had improved, the differences resulted in numerous social problems. The enticement of married women away from their husbands was a major concern within the Indian community. Promiscuity in marriage, the rise in *certtu-k-kolu-tal* (illegal unions),[36] as well as drunkenness and brawling were all social problems attributed, in part, to a scarcity of women.

These conditions led the Malayan government to attempt some efforts at reform. The Labour Department did pay extra allowances to married couples and a bonus to each child of a non-recruited immigrant. The Malayan Labour Ordinance of 1923 required that the estates provide paid maternity leave, one month prior to and one month after delivery, as well as providing nursery crèches. It does seem unlikely that employers were eager to encourage the immigration of women, even though the rubber industry offered more chances for female and child employment than had either the sugar or coffee industries. The added costs of maternity, of crèches and schools, of separate housing for single women together with the International Labour Organization's report on plantation labour (which recommended the use of 5 males to 3 females on rubber plantations),[37] all led to a sex ratio disparity. This disparity persisted well into the 1940s and to some extent is still felt today.[38]

Marriage and Indian Women in Malaya

Though men outnumbered women, great numbers of Indian women resided in Malaya by the 1920s. In 1921, out of a total Indian population of 471,666, fully 136,181 were women. In 1931, the corresponding figures were 624,000 and 202,981.[39] Like the men, the majority of the women were Southern Indian Hindus[40] with Tamil women being the most numerous, followed by Telugus, Malayalees, Punjabis and so on.[41]

Most of these women were married.[42] Marriage and the birth of a son was required by the Hindu religious tradition, which saw neither man nor woman being complete until married with male offspring. In 1921, out of 136,181 Indian females, fully 73,119 were married. There were 573 wives to every 1,000 husbands.[43] This shows that many men had left their wives in India. The shortage of women altered the position of Indian women in the immigrant society. Previously, Indian culture and religion greatly limited the freedom of women and subordinated the role of the wife to those of the family and joint family. The most famous illustrations of the place of women are contained in the *Laws of Manu*:

By a girl, by a young woman, or even by an aged one, nothing must be done independently, even in her own house.

In her childhood a female must be subject to her father, in youth to her husband, when her lord is dead to her sons; a woman must never be independent.

(When creating them) Manu allotted to women (a love of their) bed, (of their) seat and (of) ornament, impure desires, wrath, dishonesty, malice and bad conduct.[44]

The transplanted Indian culture and traditions underwent many changes in Malaya. It was no longer possible for the large, extended joint patriarchal family of three generations[45] to exist. Many factors mitigated against such families; most important was the lack of an ancestral family seat and the absence of an economic support base.[46] This is in contrast to India where family wealth was mostly based on the owning of land. In Malaya, the plantations offered housing for the nuclear family and employment for all males and most females. Such employment gave much greater freedom to the young and encouraged nuclear families to develop. In addition, as Rajeswary Ampalavanar[47] observed, the traditional family needed role differentiation and clear lines of authority among the generations. In Malaya, the authority of the father was weakened because the wife often worked for wages; further, it was easy for adult sons to set up separate households. Lastly, most Indians were between the ages of 15 and 50;[48] this reflected the Indian tendency to return to India and re-establish ties with his extended family.

Immigration and the change in the joint family system greatly affected the Indian immigrant women. Aside from becoming a wage earner, immigrant women were seldom, if ever, subjected to the Indian practice of infant marriage; further, some had the chance of divorce, and most could avoid the harsh fate of Indian widows.

In Malaya, infant marriages were practically unknown. In 1911, only 14 girls and 7 boys per 1,000 of each sex between the ages of 0 and 5 were married: by 1921 Nathan[49] wrote that no Indian children were known to be married under the age of 10 years and fewer than a thousand girls between the ages of 10 and 15 were married. By 1931, the census noted that marriage among Indians before the age of puberty was exceedingly rare in either sex. The few cases of married males found under the age of 15 were likely to be the result of either the age or the marriage state being mis-stated.[50] Some child and possibly a few infant marriages did take place and a number of such marriages may have been concealed to avoid disfavour from the authorities. Reports from the Labour Department, however, show that only three or four cases of infant marriages had come to their notice.[51] It is highly unlikely that such marriages occurred with any frequency.

Between the ages of 15 and 40, most Indian women had married. In 1921, fully 842 Indian women per 1,000 over the age of 15 had married.[52] Among men, however, marriage occurred late in life. In 1921, only 404 per 1,000 men were married between the ages of 15 and 40 while 687 per 1,000 of those over 40 had finally married.[53] In contrast, most women married between the ages of 15 and 24 years.[54]

Marriage among Indians took many forms with polygamy being sanctioned by Hindu tradition. The primary marriage, the first for each partner, was arranged by the parents (and, on the estates, with the consent of the estate manager). It was officiated by a non-Brahmin priest, involved the exchange of gifts, the presence of witnesses and usually much celebration and ceremony. While men could marry more than one woman at a time, Indian women were required to remain monogamous. In sharp contrast to Indian custom, widows and divorcees could, however, remarry. Such second unions could be formalized by a simple ceremony, *natu-vitu-tali*, held in the bridegroom's house in the presence of witnesses and a priest. Whether thus formalized or not, such marriages as well as polygamous marriages were recognized according to the rules of marriage. The offspring were all regarded as legitimate in the eyes of society. The Malayan Indian woman, if a widow, was thus able to escape the life that faced women in India—the aesthetic life of virtue and privation with no chance at remarriage and often little chance of survival. The extreme shortage of women in Malaya led to a shortage of acceptable wives. Both divorcees and widows were able to remarry. Because Indian marriages were not registered, it is not possible to estimate the extent to which polygamous marriages took place. However, it is likely that polygamy was largely limited to the upper classes as a means of expressing wealth. The shortage of women (and the concomitant demand for wives), together with the expense of maintaining more than one wife, put polygamous unions beyond the reach of most Indians. For the woman, a monogamous marriage would be preferred, conferring on her greater status and security. Indian women, as well as their Chinese and Malay counterparts, usually did not oppose polygamy in theory; in practice, however, a woman seldom wanted to be a second wife if there was another alternative.[55]

In Malaya, as well as in India, tradition dictated that the woman live with her father, husband or son. In a broken marriage, she would return to her father's house, though this was not always possible. If there was no adult son, she might form a liaison with a man which, if she lived alone or with a widowed mother, might develop into a permanent relationship. The shortage of women indeed made it hard for a woman to remain unattached.

The shortage of women, the temporary nature of the immigration, and the weakening of the extended family, all led to the weakening of the married state. Dissolution and divorce became possible both for men and, to a much lesser extent, for women. The Hindu husband could always divorce his wife: dissolution was easy for the man. Since the Malayan Courts would accept as proof of marriage only the reports of Brahmin priests officiating at a proper Hindu ceremony,[56] and since few Brahmins emigrated to Malaya,[57] few marriages in Malaya could be recognized as legal. This resulted in both the desertion of wives and the abandonment of husbands. The subsequent growth of *certtu-k-kolu-tal*, or illegal unions, also resulted. The Malayan government attempted to remedy the situation by passing the Hindu Registration Act in 1924. As the registration was voluntary, it was also unsuccessful. The Indian Agent estimated that only 74 out of 1,500 marriages were registered in the four years 1924–8.[58]

The formal method of ending a marriage on an estate began with an attempt at reconciliation by the estate manager and the elders. If this failed, the divorce was granted by the return of the *tali* and the return of the bride price by the bride. In addition, divorce announcements were frequently inserted in the Tamil newspapers.[59] Ravindra Jain[60] wrote that either the man or woman could approach the manager who would hold a hearing before the marriage witnesses in his office. This was a sharp change from the Indian practice where divorce was the sole prerogative of the male. However, no studies yet show with what frequency estate women either began a divorce or were granted one. Given that Malaysian women of all races have had a difficult time obtaining a divorce, particularly if the husband objected, it is best to note the phenomenon but not to emphasize it. Off the estates, divorce remained the prerogative of men.

The replacement of the extended family with the nuclear family often freed the Indian woman from the supervision and control of her mother-in-law. She remained, though, subservient to her husband. Devi Sarojini,[61] in her study of Indian women on a Malaysian rubber plantation in 1970, noted that the Indian woman still remained subordinate to her husband in almost all matters. These included the 'economic and politics of family life' and, 'the most outstanding feature of the husband–wife relationship which was very noticeable was the male dominance in all external aspects of the family'.[62]

In short, the immigration to Malaya changed the institutions of marriage and divorce and improved the position of women over that in India. Though marriages were arranged and women married young, infant and child marriages were rare. Immigrant women were also often free from the control of their mothers-in-law, and were sometimes able to dissolve unsuccessful unions. The harsh fate of widows was also mitigated by the conditions in Malaya.[63] Many women became wage labourers which gave them further leverage in the family circle. A man was less willing to divorce or brutalize a partner who was bringing in needed income. That the life of the woman was difficult is not to be denied—she carried both the burdens of employment and the household. Yet, on balance, her chances for a better life improved with migration to Malaya.

The Economic Role of Indian Immigrant Women

The migration to Malaya provided the Indian woman with opportunities for paid employment that did not exist in India. These opportunities helped to make her crucial to the family's financial survival. Indian women were mostly engaged in agricultural work in the FMS and the UMS, where the proportion of married Indian women was much higher than in the SS.[64] The large numbers of Indian women living in the FMS and UMS created opportunities for paid employment not available to Chinese and Malay women. By living in rural areas, though, they were relegated to agricultural jobs that paid low wages and conferred low status.

Indians dominated the estate population. Estate labour was loosely defined as labour wherein the employer had more than 10 resident labourers residing on land in his charge (20 in the SS and Kelantan). This is fully borne out by figures drawn from the 1921 census. At that time, for British Malaya as a whole, 69.3 per cent of estate workers were Indian, 18.9 per cent were Chinese and 10.2 per cent were Malay.[65]

The estates (originally coffee and sugar and later rubber and oil palm) offered the main source of employment for both male and female Indian labour. Rubber tapping could be done by women as well as men, as could the weeding needed for rubber production. Of a total Indian female population of 136,181 in 1921, fully 73,084 were employed

TABLE 3.2
Number of Indian Women Employed Outside the Home, 1921

	No. of Indian Females Employed in Agriculture	No. of Indian Females Employed in Other Callings	Total Number Employed
SS	4,919	1,521	9,440
FMS	47,999	6,198	54,197
Johore	2,920	241	3,161
Kedah	5,749	537	6,386

Source: J.E. Nathan, *The Census of British Malaya*, London, Waterlow and Sons, 1922, p. 122.

TABLE 3.3
Indian Women in the Agricultural Coolie Class, 1921

	Males	Females
SS	21,116	7,783
FMS	105,938	47,508
Johore	9,703	2,910
Kedah	12,312	5,692

Source: Nathan, op. cit., pp. 302-12. These figures were compiled from Table 38.

outside the home. The majority were involved in agriculture as shown in Table 3.2, whereas Table 3.3 shows that in the 'agricultural coolie class' (which included estate labourers) women found their greatest source of employment.

Women were employed on the estates because, prior to the Depression, the rubber industry was constantly expanding. Women on the estates were an ideal source of ready and available labour. The labour required little training and no education and could be undertaken by married women already settled on the estates. Aside from agriculture, Indian women were engaged as government labourers, miners, in personal service, and in some commercial occupations.[66] The vast majority of Indian women found employment within the lowest echelons of the rubber cultivation class, as early census figures show.[67]

The earnings of the wife were vital to the income of the family. Though it never doubled the income, it did greatly increase it. Though the same amount of labour was involved in tapping whether done by man or woman, differences in wages were not abolished until 1953. Prior to that time, women estate workers were consistently paid at a lower rate than men. Table 3.4 shows the daily wage rates from 1904 until 1914; and from 1915 to 1941, the differences were maintained as shown in Table 3.5.

Estate owners did not want to encourage the immigration of single women: costs of maternity leave, crèches, and schools once they married were very high. It did, however, make sense to employ the wives and daughters of estate workers for whom they would still have to pay these expenses whether the women worked or not. By employing these women,

TABLE 3.4
Daily Wage Rates of Estate Workers, 1904-1913 (in ¢)

	With Rations	Without Rations
Women	12	20
Men	20	28

Source: R.N. Jackson, *Immigrant Labour and the Development of Malaya 1786-1920*, Federation of Malaya, Government Printer, 1961, p. 137.

TABLE 3.5
Daily Wage Rates of Estate Workers, 1915–1941 (in ¢)

Years	Men	Women
1915	35–50	25–30
1917	45	40
1920	50	40
1928	50	40
1930	50	40
1937	45	36
1941	60	50

Source: Chew Kee-moi, 'Some Aspects of Women in Employment in West Malaysia with Particular Reference to the Government and Estate Sectors', unpublished BA Graduation Exercise, University of Malaya, 1970, p. 90.

at lower wages, both the estate owners and the Indian estate families benefited. In 1953, laws were passed which equalized the pay of male and female tappers. This tacitly acknowledged that women were a work force competitive with men.

Given that women married at a younger age than men, it is reasonable to assume that many Indian women became the principal bread-winners for their families. Though no such data exists for the pre-war period, Sarojini[68] found in 1970 that out of 140 women in the estate labour force she studied, 22 per cent were the principal bread-winners. The husbands were either retired, transferred or deceased. Further, the other 78 per cent of the families would have been at or below the poverty line without the wife's income. There is no reason to suppose that the pre-war situation was any different. The wife's earnings were vital to the subsistence of the family. In fact, the wages of both husband and wife were paid directly to the husband for many years.

Though the wife contributed her earnings to the support of her family, the responsibility for the home and for raising the children remained with her. Having to rise well before dawn to prepare breakfast and the midday meal, the woman then walked to the trees to be tapped that day. If there was a bicycle in the family, the man rode. She worked from 5 a.m. until 2 p.m., came home, ate, rested, marketed, cleaned house, did the laundry, prepared dinner, saw to the children, sewed and mended clothes, rested or gossiped and went to bed. In these tasks, the wife was helped by the older female children. They looked after the younger children while the mother worked. Men were, in general, spared the domestic chores.

Off the estates, employment for women was scarce. Tied to their families, women could not leave the estates to look for work elsewhere. In addition, estate women were often illiterate and untrained. Though primary schools which used the Tamil language as their medium were common on the estates, it was uncommon for parents to send their girls

TABLE 3.6

Number of Literates per 1,000 of Indian Population by Sex, 1921

Area	Male	Female
Singapore	371	107
Penang	389	103
Malacca	313	105
Kuala Lumpur	519	292
Ipoh	542	258
Taiping	558	249
Kampar	281	92
Klang	371	136
Seremban	489	306
Johore Baharu	415	176
Mersing	484	—
Kota Bharu	620	222

Source: Nathan, op. cit., adapted from the table on p. 109. In 1921, the literacy rate was only calculated for inhabitants of the town.

to such schools. In 1938, of 22,820 children enrolled in Tamil-medium primary schools, only 7,236 were girls. After the first three years, the great majority of students were boys.[69] Sarojini found that, as late as 1970, parents sent their girl children to school only for the lower primary classes. Afterwards, it was common for the older girls to assume responsibility for the younger children.[70] It is not surprising that the literacy of the Indian women lagged behind that of the men as shown in Table 3.6.

The low literacy rate and the reluctance to educate girls reflects a traditional attitude held by many people: it is not worth educating girls because the family loses them and their labour upon marriage. The same census (1921) recorded that literate Indian women were most often found in the urban areas. They were wives and children of clerks and shopkeepers—people who would have some education and know its value.[71] Illiteracy thus prevailed among women in the rural areas.

Non-Hindu Indian Women

A small but significant group within the Indian community consisted of Indian Muslims. In 1921, 41,363 Indian Muslims were identified in the census:[72] of this number, the overwhelming majority were male as shown in Table 3.7.

The majority of Indian Muslims lived in the urban areas where housing was not conducive to maintaining a family. The disparate sex ratio is, however, more adequately explained by the fact that Indian Muslims practised *purdah*—the seclusion of women. A long sea journey, settlement in a society that did not practise seclusion and the temporary nature of the migration, prevented the immigration of Muslim women. Muslim men preferred to leave their wives and families in India.

TABLE 3.7
Disparate Sex Ratio among Indian Muslims, 1921

	Males per Thousand	Females per Thousand
SS	836	164
FMS	871	129
UMS	880	120
British Malaya	855	145

Source: Nathan, op. cit., p. 105.

Another group that merits attention is the (North Indian) Sikh community. Though small in size, its activities and functions include some of the earliest women's organizations in Malaya, the Sikh women's reformist organizations. North Indians prior to 1941 comprised only 7.7 per cent of the total Indian population of Malaya.[73] Of this number, about one-quarter were Sikhs. The North Indians came to Malaya mostly as a non-labourer and unregulated movement. Like South Indians, they immigrated as single people and the female–male ratio was low: in 1921, there were 1,690 females to every 7,617 males.[74] As with the Hindu community, the Sikhs prior to 1930 were riddled with sex-related problems. Fights over women were common and women were often sold from one man to another.[75] If a man died, his brothers or relatives often claimed special rights to the widow—a custom found in religions other than Sikhism as well.

Because they immigrated largely as non-labourers, Sikhs tended to settle in the urban areas. The men became active in the public services, commerce and as petty financiers. Particularly desired for the security forces, they became sought after as private security guards, an occupation they still dominate. The position of Sikh women before World War II was very restricted. Their activities were limited to the temples, to teaching their daughters at home (Sikh boys were sent to English-medium schools), or helping out in the family shop. Hence, many Sikh girls were poorly educated in Punjabi and remained under the control of their mothers. They were groomed to become dutiful and subservient wives.[76] Therefore, it is surprising to find that Sikh women took an active part in one of the first Sikh religious movements—the Sangh Sabha—launched by the Sikh community of Larut, Perak in 1916. This movement was a social–religious reform that aimed at checking the drift of Sikhism towards Hinduism. The movement strove to reduce illiteracy and revive the teachings of the gurus. Though Sikh organizations were an all-male domain, the Sangh Sabha movement was sympathetic to certain issues raised by Sikh women. For example, Sikh women found that upon arriving in Malaya they were subjected to certain practices which no longer existed in India, their major grievance being that in the temples, women were only allowed to sit behind the Sikh Holy Book often in special curtained-off areas. Men sat in front. Arguing that this was reminiscent of purdah, Sikh women gathered at the temples and sought means to improve their position.[77] Under the auspices of the first Sikh women's organization, the Khalsa Diwan Selangor (which formed in 1917 and started a school for Sikh girls), the first conference of Sikh women in Malaya was held in 1933.[78] The outcome of the meeting was the formation of the Isteri Sat Sangh Sabha Sentul (Wives of the Sat Sangh Sabha in Sentul). The organization devoted itself to the service of the community. Pressing for religious reforms, the women were successful in being permitted to sit, with the men, in front of the Sikh Holy Book. The two groups would be separated by an aisle. After the war, the Isteri Sat Sangh Sabha would further expand and take up other issues.

Indian Women and the Pre-1945 Political Associations

The Sikhs were not alone in forming organizations. Wherever educated Indians lived, Indian associations were formed. The first was the Indian Association of Taiping formed in 1906. It was soon followed by associations in Selangor, Perak, Penang and Malacca. The membership and activities of all these groups were very similar. They were dominated by businessmen and professionals who supplied both the leadership and finances.[79] The organizations were also supported by other educated Indians: priests, schoolmasters, government officers and clerks, and officers in private firms and on the plantations. The associations aimed at fulfilling a social need for the Indian community. They concentrated on providing recreational facilities for their members and on celebrating Indian festival days. However, the associations were prone to factionalism and apathy,[80] and were non-political.[81] By 1930, many existed only on paper and the others had a minimal effect. Whether women played any role in these organizations is doubtful. Historians remain unclear on this point. Mrs E. Ramachandran, a founding member and president of the Selangor Indian Association (SIA) in 1976 stated that she did not remember women playing any role in the pre-war associations; she also stressed that it was still difficult to get women to join the SIA. Of approximately 500 members then in the SIA, only 20 were women.[82]

Indians grouped themselves on the basis of caste, regional origin, religion and occupation prior to World War II. Only the Central Indian Association of Malaya (CIAM) carried on political activity as one of its avowed aims. Two other organizations though, had a brief impact: the Young Men's Indian Association (YMIA) formed in 1922 by M. K. Ramachandran, which took an interest in the Indian nationalist movement and later merged into the Indian Independence League; and the Malayan Indian Association formed by G. V. Thaver in 1932 to safeguard the interests of 'Malayan' Indians against immigrant 'Indian' Indians. Neither organization attracted a large following or was able to muster much influence.

The CIAM grew out of the annual joint conferences held by the various Indian associations. The first was held in 1928 following Pandit

Nehru's visit to Malaya.[83] The CIAM was organized in 1937 under the leadership of Dr A. M. Soosay as president. Membership was indirect, the organization was a confederation of 16 existing organizations: 12 Indian associations and 4 Indian Chambers of Commerce and Merchants' Associations. The CIAM wished to promote the status of the Indian community in Malaya. It took up such labour-related issues as toddy (coconut liquor) drinking, Indian land settlement, and the lack of medical and educational facilities on the estates. Labour issues, because they reflected on the dignity of all the Indian community, became the focus. Though the CIAM was the first organization in Malaya set up to foster Indian political opinion, control of CIAM was held by the president and ten leading members.[84] None of these were women. The leaders were middle class, educated men who were ardent Indian nationalists.[85]

The short-term nature of the Indian immigration to Malaya coloured the political orientation of the Indians. From 1925 to 1957, fully 80 per cent of the immigrants returned to India.[86] This situation, together with the division of Malaya into the SS, FMS and UMS, precluded the forming of strong attachments to Malaya. This lack of Malaya-centred thinking and the absence of resistance to colonial rule was found among all three communities, Malay, Chinese and Indian. Nationalism in Malaya was to be a post-war phenomenon. Given that the population was politically acquiescent, it is not surprising that Indian women were not politically involved before the war. This is confirmed by interviews among prominent Malaysians active in the independence movement of the 1940s and 1950s: they could remember no Indian women involved in any pre-war associations. The Japanese Occupation, therefore, had a major effect on the Indian population of Malaya. The political awakening of Indian women was one of the most remarkable results.

The Japanese Occupation and Its Effect on Malayan Indian Women

Prior to World War II, word of the Indian nationalist movement had reached Malaya. News of the Indian Congress and speeches by Indian nationalist leaders had filtered down to all levels of the Indian community. The activities of the CIAM and the visits of Indian leaders to Malaya had laid the groundwork needed for the mobilization of the Malayan Indian community. Since the Malayan social, economic and political order had been divided along ethnic lines, Malayan Indians tended to identify as Indians not as Malayans. One member of the CIAM expressed these feelings as follows: 'Until the local Indians ceased to be aliens and gain the status of the Malayans it is the duty of Indian nationalism to see that the settlers here continue to be true Indians and to counteract any attempts which seek to divide one section of Indians from another.'[87]

The Japanese invasion of Malaya in December 1941 affected all three of Malaya's ethnic groups. Above all, the invasion signalled the end of the old order of unquestioned obedience and loyalty to the European rulers. For the Indians, the Occupation was a time of hardship and deprivation. With the departure of British troops, all British officials and most plantation owners either left the country or were interned. Almost immediately the output of the plantations decreased. Less experienced and less competent Japanese administrators, together with the loss of Allied markets, combined to cause wages to plummet. As the war went on, food became scarce and rice, the Indian workers' staple diet, almost disappeared. Unable to leave Malaya, most labourers survived as best they could. They often existed on a diet of tapioca and millet. Survival was made even more precarious by the Japanese practice of using Indians as forced labour. Thousands of Indian men were conscripted to work on the infamous Siam Railway from Bangkok to Rangoon. Of the many who went, few returned.[88]

The Japanese policy towards the Malayan Indian community was two-sided. On the one hand, forced labour, expropriation of property and dislocation of the economy created severe hardship; on the other hand, the Japanese encouraged Indian nationalist feelings and promised help in freeing India from British rule. The latter policies were well received in Malaya, particularly among the more radical nationalists. India was not viewed as a future part of Japan's Greater East Asia Co-Prosperity Sphere; the country was thought too large to conquer and administer.[89] It was, however, necessary for the Japanese to neutralize the British influence in India. Part of the policy sought to mobilize East Asian Indians for Indian independence. It was hoped that: 1) such a mobilization would favourably dispose Indians in India towards Japan, 2) Indians in Asia (mainly Burma and Malaya) would be easier to rule because they would be sympathetic to Japanese goals, and 3) such a policy would change the sympathies of over 60,000 Indian troops sent to Malaya at the outbreak of the war.[90]

Japanese policy therefore coincided to some extent with the interests of Indian nationalists. This resulted in the forming of the Indian Independence League (IIL). Chosen by the Japanese to head the League was Ras Behari Bose, a radical nationalist leader then residing in Japan. In 1942, Bose was dispatched to Singapore where he was to organize both the military and political wings of the movement. Bose himself was to head the IIL (the political wing) while Colonel Mohan Singh, an officer of the British Indian Army, was to head the Indian Nationalist Army (INA—the military wing). By February 1942, the IIL had branches in Kedah, Perak, Selangor, Negri Sembilan, Penang and Singapore. Membership at this time was estimated at 84,700.[91] By September 1942, Malaya had over 40 state and regional branches and a membership of approximately 120,000 people.[92] As for the INA, the Japanese hoped that a core could be formed from the disaffected Indian army troops in Malaya. In fact, 5,000 did join the INA almost immediately to form its nucleus.[93] By the end of 1942, the INA stood at 16,000 men.[94]

Leadership friction plagued the first organizational phase of the IIL.

The INA was dissolved in December 1942, and the suspension of the political activities of the IIL continued until February 1943. The League up to this point had been mostly concerned with improving the living conditions of Malayan Indians under the Occupation. However, a shift in Japanese policy was to change the make-up and future of the League. In the spring of 1943, the Japanese decided to capture a limited area in North-east India for defence purposes and in doing so to forestall a British invasion of Burma.[95] In order to undermine British Indian forces, the Japanese planned to use the League under the leadership of Subhas Chandra Bose, another radical nationalist and ex-Congress leader, as a fighting force. Undisputedly a charismatic leader, Bose was necessary to the Japanese in order to infuse new vigour into the waning IIL. Bose arrived in Singapore in July 1943, at which time he became President of the IIL and Commander-in-Chief of the INA. In October, he rose to become Prime Minister of the Provincial Government of Free India (Azad Hind). The Azad Hind then declared war on Britain and America and was soon recognized by Japan, Germany and Italy as well as six other countries.[96]

With the arrival of S. C. Bose, the nature of the IIL changed. Indians of both sexes and of all classes and castes were brought out of their political indifference. S. C. Bose had tremendous prestige in Malaya. He was a former president of the Indian Congress, he was a patriot second to none, and he had spent years in British prisons. With his appointment as head of the IIL, Malayan Indians ceased to think of the League as a Japanese inspiration and instead saw in it the main means to an independent India. S. C. Bose was an imposing and dedicated speaker. Wherever he spoke, huge crowds gathered: 'Everywhere he went in Malaya Bose was greeted by enormous crowds, drawn from all sectors of the Indian community. On the occasion of his first public address in Singapore, he drew the largest crowd in the history of the city.'[97] His popularity was all the more intriguing for he spoke only in English or Hindustani. Both languages were foreign to the majority of his audience.

S. C. Bose saw the IIL as a force to free India. He fought to keep control of the League in Indian hands. To this end, it was necessary to mobilize the entire Indian community. The credit for awakening the nationalist spirit of the majority of Malayan Indians, particularly the women, must go to S. C. Bose.

Under R. Behari Bose, the role of women in the IIL had been minor. Under S. C. Bose, they were to play an active role in the movement. S. C. Bose, on assuming command of the League, reorganized it, creating 12 departments for the League and 12 ministries for the government. One department and one ministry were delegated to women's affairs; both were headed by Lt.-Col. Lakshmi Swaminathan, a 30-year-old civilian woman doctor in Singapore.[98] S. C. Bose made a special effort to organize women: he started women's sections in all state and regional branches of the League.[99] Under S. C. Bose, there were 70 Malayan branches with 350,000 members (out of an Indian population of 600,000). The majority of these members were adults.[100] The women's sections drew a great response from Indian women.[101] Most sections raised funds, collected supplies for the INA and taught Hindustani in the 50 'national' schools that were set up in Malaya. It was common for Indian women to strip themselves of their gold jewellery upon hearing Bose speak and donate it to the funds of the IIL.

The most intriguing aspect of the women's involvement in the League was their part in the Rani of Jhansi Brigade, or the women's section of the INA. It is not clear what prompted Bose to organize the women's fighting unit. Ramachandra[102] suggested that Bose intended to use the Brigade in the invasion. He expected British Indian soldiers to refuse to fight Indian women. One of Holland's[103] suggestions is that it was a propaganda stunt. Ghosh[104] too, argued that Bose was sure of the Brigade's propagandistic value. Whatever the motive, the Brigade, in addition to being a possible fighting unit, was successful at mobilizing the support of the women. With the Brigade, the independence movement became real for Indian women, they took part rather than simply being uninformed observers.

S. C. Bose, in preparing to form the Brigade, addressed the women's section of the League in Singapore on 12 July 1943. In the speech, aimed directly at women, Bose urged them to join the Brigade. The words were new to Malayan Indian women and they were exciting:

> To those who say that it will not be proper for our women to carry guns, my only request is that they look into the pages of our history.... It is not important how many guns you can carry or how many cartridges you can fire. It is the spiritual force which will be generated by your heroic example that is important. Indians—both common people and members of the British Indian army—who are on the border areas of India, will, on seeing you march with guns on your shoulders voluntarily come forward to receive guns from you and carry on the struggle started by you.... Therefore, I can say with certainty that the time has come for every Indian—man and woman, boy and girl—to come forward and make great sacrifices for liberating India.
>
> ... in this common task, in this struggle, in this suffering and sacrifice, all of us—without distinction of man and woman, boy or girl, poor or rich, young or old—should stand shoulder to shoulder, should start the final struggle and should hasten the day of India's deliverance.[105]

Bose was successful at that meeting; 2,000 women on the spot declared their intent to join the Brigade.[106]

The Rani of Jhansi Brigade was formed by Bose in October 1943. It was centred in Singapore and in Rangoon. The Singapore centre opened with 100 women.[107] Named after a young Indian heroine,[108] the Brigade sought to inspire, organize and train Indian women. The Brigade consisted of two sections; one trained volunteers as nurses, the other as soldiers. The training of soldiers consisted of a two-month course in drill, physical training (eight-mile hikes with 20-pound packs), the use of arms, and Hindustani. The training for nurses included self-defence. Each day was highly organized and discipline was strict:

In their discipline and training they are in no way inferior to our soldiers, because we have the firm belief in one principle that to be an honourable citizen of the future in a free and ideal India, every Indian, whether man or woman or child must be thoroughly disciplined and trained to defend oneself and one's nation.[109]

The Brigade was open to volunteers over the age of fifteen. Capt. Thaver in her reports noted that young girls ran away from home to join the Brigade.[110] Both the literate and illiterate joined. Mrs Nahappan, a former commandant in the Brigade and a later Malaysian Indian Congress women's section leader, personally recalled over 1,000 women joining, of whom many were educated.[111] Whether or not Bose intended the women to fight is in question; however, the women themselves fully expected to fight to liberate India. The trained Indian women were even sent to Rangoon to prepare for the invasion (which never took place).[112]

Estimating the overall strength of the Brigade is difficult. As of December 1943 M. S. Thaver (now Major), the commanding officer in Singapore, noted that the strength of the Brigade in both camps was 614 of whom 24 were commissioned and 24 were non-commissioned officers.[113] Not satisfied with the Brigade's strength, Major Thaver wrote: 'As we know that wars have their rises and falls, we might have fallen temporarily but we shall rise up again with double strength and determination on another day to avenge the death of those that have fallen and until independence is achieved we shall carry on the fight.'[114] Ramachandra argued[115] that each camp trained about 600 women, Banerjee[116] estimated that 850 women were involved and Ghosh[117] concluded that 500 women were in the Brigade at its peak strength. In all probability, the Rani of Jhansi Brigade contained between 500 to 900 members at its peak.

The Brigade was to be called into action after the fall of Imphal, when Bose thought the morale of British troops would be low. Instead, Imphal never fell and the Brigade was never engaged. However, the significance of the Brigade and the participation of women in the IIL should not be ignored. The extent of their involvement was observed by John Thivy (an active nationalist, member of the League and founder of the Malayan Indian Congress):

They (women) came to realize that the peace and security of their homes could never be guaranteed, until their larger home, India, was swept clean of all foreign control and influence and garnished by those of their own. Once having decided upon their course of action, there was no question of half measures for them. They infiltrated into every possible activity of the movement. Was it Recruitment and Training? They had their camps, and women volunteers came regularly for the combatant services and for medical and nursing services. Was it Finance Revenue and Supplies? At mass rallies where their beloved Netaji Subhas Chandra Bose gave addresses, they marched up to the dais and after garlanding him, showered upon him, for the benefit of the Cause, their jewels and trinkets, removed at the spot from their person.... Beautiful flowing sarees were stripped into bandages, and old clothes were collected, washed and mended and then despatched to the hospital and Relief Homes.... Was it propaganda, education or culture? Women addressed meetings and spoke to the world over the radio, wrote articles in papers and composed, sang and popularised national songs.... They took up posts as teachers in Indian and labour lines and showed the way to better health, cleanliness and sanitation....

Their enthusiasm was a constant inspiration to the League workers and supporters, and a source of embarrassment to the slackers.[118]

For the first time, Malayan Indian women were imbued with a strong nationalistic fervour and were urged to take part in politics. With the League, the horizons of Indian women broadened. They were encouraged to help liberate India by taking up arms against men. This departed radically from their traditionally passive social role. Many Malayan Indian women point with pride to the Rani of Jhansi Brigade and the League. For most Malaysian Indians, the IIL was irrelevant to Malayan politics. Former members of the League, women included, viewed the League as nothing other than a patriotic activity. This view was not shared by all Malaysians, some of whom thought the IIL aided the Japanese. The Occupation and the subsequent development of the League would leave Malaya with a highly politicized sub-group in its Indian population; but, the IIL movement with its emphasis on liberating India and its slogan of *Chalo Delhi* (Let us go to Delhi) would preclude the later activism of Indian women in Malaysian politics. Political awareness and activities for the freeing of India did not carry over to post-war Malaya. Many years would pass before the Indian women would arouse themselves to take part in the politics of Malaya.

* * * * *

The preceding three chapters have sought to provide historical, background information on women in pre-war Malayan society. This background is necessary for understanding the post-war political involvement of Malayan women. The later political involvement of Malay women and the seeming lack of Indian and Chinese women involvement, in part, stems from their positions in the pre-war communities.

For all three groups, culture and tradition placed women in subordinate positions to men. For Chinese and Indian women, the subordination was more complete than for Malay women. Malay customary law (*adat*) allowed Malay women a certain degree of status and security. Islam, however, which was introduced long after *adat* was firmly entrenched, did subordinate women to men. This is most clear in the areas of family law and in preventing women access to religious and public leadership.

Marriage was expected of women in all three groups. The position of married women differed only slightly from one ethnic group to another. Marriages occurred without the consent of the bride; women, but not men, were expected to remain monogamous and men (but not women) had easy access to divorce. Only Malay women were given a measure of security under the customary laws of inheritance. No such provisions existed for non-Malay women.

Economically, all three groups of women were vital to the welfare of their communities. Malay women were indispensable to the Malay peasant economy largely as unpaid family workers, though some controlled the family finances. Chinese and Indian women, particularly the latter, were vital to their families' support. The opportunities available in Malaya altered the position of the woman by making her a wage-earner. Immigrant women, though, seldom, if ever, had any control over the money they earned. Malay, Chinese and Indian women were all concentrated in those jobs which paid the poorest wages, had the lowest status and needed little or no training. A major reason for women being in such fields was the lack of education available to girls during the pre-war era. This resulted from the shared reluctance of all three groups to educate their girl children.

For all three groups, women were denied access to positions of leadership within their communities. Malay women were effectively excluded by Islam from religious and other public posts (e.g. village headman). Chinese and Indian women had little or no access to positions in the merchant, business and propertied classes which led their communities. The cultural assumptions of all three groups placed women clearly in the home. The domestic sphere remained almost exclusively theirs. Men, on the other hand, were not involved in domestic tasks and little involved with child-raising. Regardless of the ethnic group, the roles of women and men were clearly defined and mutually exclusive. For all three groups of women, Rosaldo's[119] hypothesis that the status of women is low where the worlds of men and women do not overlap is appropriate.

The involvement of women in pre-war political and social welfare groups was quite limited. Only a few Malay women, and a small segment of Sikh women, were part of pre-war efforts to improve educational opportunities for girls. Aside from this and a few social welfare activities, there is little evidence of involvement by any group of women. As for the Japanese Occupation, its effect on women differed as to the group. All three races suffered discomfort and dislocation. They were all forced to develop survival tactics such as foraging for food, black market activities, etc. The three communities were, however, treated differently. Malay women moved into occupations freed by Malay men as the men were drawn into the war effort and administrative positions vacated by the British. The Chinese, however, were not brought into the government; their survival depended on accepting an inherently dangerous situation. Indian women lived with deprivation but were allowed to become organized in their branches of the IIL and INA. For Indian women, a few would gain the experience and knowledge of organized politics. This, though, did not carry over into post-war politics.

The most important factor that divided the Malay from the non-Malay women was immigrant status. Both Chinese and Indian women were a minority in their communities and both societies viewed the stay in Malaya as temporary. Pre-war national consciousness that developed was directed towards China and India because most immigrants returned to those countries. Ties to Malaya thus remained weak. In addition, British policies favoured the Malays as the indigenous people. The non-Malays were treated as temporary residents. This reinforced the immigrant groups' thinking on the transient nature of the Indian and Chinese stays in Malaya. The Malays, on the other hand, were treated as the 'true' people of Malaya. Their sultans and upper class signed the treaties, conducted all negotiations, and manned the civil service. All this was to the exclusion of the non-Malays. In return, the non-Malays were left free to follow their economic pursuits—an arrangement accepted by all three groups prior to the end of the Japanese Occupation.

One further factor which affected pre-war women was the homogeneity in Malay society. This was lacking among the non-Malays. Malays were united by religion, custom and language while non-Malays remained divided by these same factors. It was difficult for one group of Chinese (or Indians) to communicate with another in pre-war Malaya. These problems have lessened only recently.

1. Gordon Means, *Malaysian Politics*, London, University of London Press, 1970, p. 36.
2. T. E. Smith, *Population Growth in Malaya*, London, Royal Institute of International Affairs, 1952, p. 83.
3. K. S. Sandhu, *Indians in Malaya: Some Aspects of their Immigration and Settlement (1786-1957)*, Cambridge, Cambridge University Press, 1969, p. 47.
4. Ibid.
5. Ibid., p. 310.
6. George Netto, *Indians in Malaya: Historical Facts and Figures*, Singapore, Netto, George, 1961, p. 16.
7. Ibid.
8. Sandhu, op. cit., p. 135.
9. Ibid., p. 78.
10. Ibid., p. 81.
11. Sinnappah Arasaratnam, *Indians in Malaysia and Singapore*, Kuala Lumpur, Oxford University Press, 1970, p. 14. The average wage in 1869 was 9¢ a day, while in the 1900s it ranged between 16 and 18¢ a day. Sandhu, op. cit., p. 84.
12. C. Kondapi, *Indians Overseas 1838-1949*, Bombay, Oxford University Press, 1951, p. 41.
13. Ibid.
14. Sandhu, op. cit., p. 79. Sandhu is quoting directly from the *Government of Madras Proceedings of 1870*.
15. Ibid., pp. 311-12.
16. Arasaratnam, op. cit., p. 32.
17. Ibid.
18. Netto, op. cit., p. 24.
19. R. N. Jackson, *Immigrant Labour and the Development of Malaya 1786-1920*, Federation of Malaya, Government Printer, 1961, p. 137.
20. Kondapi, op. cit., p. 4.
21. Sandhu, op. cit., p. 8.
22. Ibid., p. 158.
23. C. A. Vlieland, *British Malaya: A Report on the 1931 Census*, London, Government Printer, 1932, p. 53.
24. Sandhu, op. cit., p. 98.

25. Ravindra Jain, *South Indians on the Plantation Frontier in Malaya*, Kuala Lumpur, University of Malaya Press, 1970, p. 273.
26. Jackson, op. cit., p. 104.
27. Ravindra Jain, op. cit., p. 96; P. Ampalavanar, 'Social and Political Developments in the Indian Community of Malaya 1920–41', unpublished MA thesis, University of Malaya, 1969, p. 185.
28. Arasaratnam, op. cit., p. 68.
29. Sandhu, op. cit., pp. 312–13.
30. Ibid., pp. 308–9.
31. Ibid., p. 82.
32. J. E. Nathan, *The Census of British Malaya*, London, Waterlow and Sons, 1922, p. 58.
33. Ibid., p. 190.
34. Ibid. Note that the Ceylonese were counted as Tamils in the 1921 Census and as 'others' in the 1931 Census. Though influential in the postal, rail, accounting and treasury divisions of the government they totalled only 23,000 as late as 1947. Arasaratnam, op. cit., p. 33.
35. Vlieland, op. cit., p. 192.
36. Ampalavanar, op. cit., p. 182.
37. Sandhu, op. cit., p. 99.
38. Sandhu, op. cit., p. 186: *Number of Females per 1,000 Males in Malay(si)a*

1891	1901	1911	1921	1931	1947	1957	1965
18	171	308	406	482	637	692	750

39. Nathan, op. cit.; Vlieland, op. cit.
40. Nathan, op. cit., p. 58. Malaya had over 40,000 Muslims and 20,000 Christians within the Indian population in 1921.
41. Ibid., p. 190; Vlieland, op. cit., p. 193.
42. The 1931 Census noted that as in 1921, no attempt was made to discriminate between married, divorced and widowed people, on the grounds that due to linguistic and cultural differences, the results would be totally unreliable. Vlieland, op. cit., p. 53.
43. Nathan, op. cit., p. 58.
44. Muller, *The Sacred Books of the East (The Laws of Manu)*, Vol. 25, Delhi, Motilal Banarsidas Reprint, 1964, pp. 147–9.
45. S. S. Gupta, *Women in Indian Folklore*, Calcutta, India Publications, 1969, p. xxiii.
46. Ampalavanar, op. cit., p. 163.
47. Ibid.
48. Nathan, op. cit., pp. 209–11.
49. Ibid., p. 59.
50. Vlieland, op. cit., p. 53.
51. Ibid., p. 243.
52. Nathan, op. cit., p. 60.
53. Ibid., p. 59.
54. Vlieland, op. cit., p. 242.
55. Personal interviews with the author.
56. Arasaratnam, op. cit., p. 68.
57. Ibid., p. 67.
58. Ibid., p. 69.
59. Ravindra Jain, op. cit., p. 153.
60. Ibid., p. 272.
61. D. A. Sarojini, 'Socio-Economic Aspects of Women Plantation Workers: A Case Study of the Indian Women Workers of Ladang Tengah', unpublished BA Graduation Exercise, University of Malaya, 1971, p. 33.
62. Ibid., p. 37.
63. The Indian practice of *suttee* whereby a widow committed suicide by throwing herself on her husband's funeral pyre was unknown in Malaya. In India, the practice was banned in 1829. Gupta, op. cit., p. xxx.

64. Nathan, op. cit., p. 58.
65. Ibid., p. 137.
66. Ibid., p. 122.
67. Vlieland, op. cit., Tables 127, 135 and 143 on pp. 273, 298 and 322 respectively.
68. Sarojini, op. cit., p. 25.
69. Federation of Malaysia, *Educational Statistics, 1938–1967*, Kuala Lumpur, Department of Education, Ministry of Education, 1968, p. 35.
70. Sarojini, op. cit., p. 33.
71. Nathan, op. cit., p. 110.
72. Ibid., p. 104.
73. Amarjit Kaur, 'North Indians in Malaya: A Study of their Economic, Social and Political Activities with Special Reference to Selangor, 1870s–1940s', unpublished MA thesis, University of Malaya, 1969, p. 37.
74. Nathan, op. cit., pp. 216–17.
75. Amarjit Kaur, op. cit., p. 255.
76. Ibid., p. 256.
77. Ibid., p. 248.
78. Ibid.
79. Arasaratnam, op. cit., p. 83.
80. Ibid., p. 84.
81. W. L. Holland (ed.), *Asian Nationalism and the West*, New York, Octagon Books, 1973, p. 287.
82. Interview with Mrs E. Ramachandran on 15 July 1976.
83. Usha Mahajani, *The Role of Indian Minorities in Burma and Malaya*, Connecticut, Greenwood Press, 1960, p. 125.
84. G. P. Ramachandra, 'The Indian Independence Movement in Malaya', unpublished MA thesis, University of Malaya, 1970, p. 12.
85. Ibid., p. 13.
86. Sandhu, op. cit., p. 158.
87. Arasaratnam, op. cit., p. 102.
88. Means, op. cit.
89. Ramachandra, op. cit., p. 17.
90. Usha Mahajani, op. cit., p. 146.
91. Ramachandra, op. cit., p. 38.
92. Ibid., pp. 103–4.
93. Usha Mahajani, op. cit., p. 146.
94. Arasaratnam, op. cit., p. 105.
95. Ramachandra, op. cit., p. 191.
96. Arasaratnam, op. cit., p. 105.
97. Ramachandra, op. cit., p. 199.
98. Dr Lakshmi Swaminathan also headed the Rani of Jhansi Brigade. After the collapse of the INA and the disbandment of the Brigade in April 1945, she refused to surrender and was arrested. She was released at a later date. Bejoy Banerjee, *The Indian War of Independence with Special Reference to the INA*, Calcutta, Oriental Agency, 1946, p. 116.
99. Ramachandra, op. cit., p. 205.
100. Ibid., p. 212.
101. Ibid., p. 231.
102. Ibid.
103. Holland, op. cit., p. 297.
104. K. K. Ghosh, *The Indian National Army*, Meerut India, Meenakshi Prakashan, 1969, p. 156.
105. S. A. Aiyer, *Selected Speeches of Subhas Chandra Bose*, India, Ministry of Information and Broadcasting, Publications Division, 1965, pp. 190–1.
106. Netaji Sopan, *Subash Chandra Bose: His Life and Work*, Bombay, Azad Bhandar, 1946, p. 352.

107. Capt. Mrs Thaver, Manuscript No. 83, in John Thivy's *Collected Papers 1938–1948*, University of Malaya Library.
108. Rani Lakshmi Bai of Jhansi commanded an army against British troops during the Mutiny, or Great Revolution, of 1857. Rather than surrender or be defeated, she died by the sword while on horseback leading her troops. Bejoy Banerjee, op. cit., p. 24.
109. Capt. Mrs Thaver, Manuscript No. 82, op. cit.
110. Ibid.
111. Interview with Mrs Nahappan on 13 July 1976.
112. Manuscript No. 82, op. cit. On a personal level, Mrs Nahappan recalled in an interview with the author that she spent her sixteenth birthday in Rangoon while waiting to participate in an armed struggle. Interview with Mrs Nahappan, op. cit.
113. Capt. Mrs Thaver, Manuscript No. 84, op. cit.
114. Ibid.
115. Ramachandra, op. cit., p. 231.
116. Bejoy Banerjee, op. cit, p. 116.
117. Ghosh, op. cit., p. 157.
118. John Thivy, *Collected Papers 1938–1948*, University of Malaya Library, p. 94.
119. See Introduction, fn. 10.

Part II
The Growth of Women's Political Auxiliaries

4 From War to Independence, 1945–1957

THE participation of Malayan women in public life prior to 1945 had been small. A few individuals and women's associations were interested in education and social welfare matters. The majority of women were not involved in matters beyond the home. At the end of World War II, the altered political mood in Malaya caused large numbers of women to enter politics. This was mostly through the organized women's sections of the post-war political parties. Though most parties tacitly espoused the participation of women, the numbers that took part were, in fact, closely linked to the uneven expression of political self-interest among the three ethnic groups. It was Malay women who would play an active role within the emerging party system while Chinese and Indian women would become active only years later, in the 1970s.

Post-war Malaya

With the defeat of the Japanese, the British returned to a Malaya that had altered dramatically from pre-war days. Many non-Malays were permanently domiciled in Malaya. At the same time, the Malays were no longer politically complacent. As Ratnam[1] noted, the Japanese had shown through their harsh treatment of the Chinese and Indians that the immigrants need not be regarded as indispensable to the welfare of Malaya. The outbreak of communal conflicts that took place between members of the largely Chinese Malayan People's Anti-Japanese Army (MPAJA) and the Malay community prior to the British return[2] exacerbated differences. This highlighted the increased communal awareness and sensitivities. The increased awareness also brought a Malay rejection of British supremacy and the right to rule in Malaya. The war and the British return to Malaya sparked the growth of a Malay nationalism. It created a situation in which neither the pre-war colonial structure could be re-established, nor could any new policy be implemented without the participation and support of the Malays. The history of Malay nationalism and events leading to independence in 1957 have been described by many historians.[3] It is, however, less clear what role Malayan women played in creating an independent Malaya and evolving a party system.

Prior to World War II, Britain's need to form a stable and ordered government in Malaya was based on two sometimes conflicting goals: 1) to provide the basis for developing Malaya's natural resources, and 2) to provide for the 'welfare and advancement' of the Malay people within the framework of Malay society.[4] The result was a piecemeal policy that provided Malaya with no less than nine sovereign states, ten sovereign monarchs (nine Malay and one British), ten legislatures and seven judicial, police and civil services.[5] Supreme authority rested with the British official resident in Singapore. He was the Governor of the Straits Settlements (SS) and administered the SS as a Crown Colony directly, in conjunction with an executive council. In the Federated Malay States (FMS) and Unfederated Malay States (UMS), British rule was less direct but still compelling—the Governor of the SS acted as High Commissioner 1) through official Residents in the FMS and 2) through Advisers in the UMS.[6] The 'sovereign' Malay sultans, in fact, seldom acted in matters other than those of Malay religion and culture. Otherwise, they had to consult with their British Residents or Advisers. Though members of the Malay élite participated by sitting on state councils to advise the Residents, direct control of government was exercised by the Residents and to a lesser extent by the Advisers, the Governor of the SS standing behind them as the final source of authority.[7]

Attempts at reform during the 1920s and 1930s by colonial governors (Sir Lawrence Guillemard and Sir Cecil Clementi) were not successful. The existing system was perpetuated until the Japanese Occupation and upheaval of Malayan society.

When the British returned to Malaya in September 1945, they set forth the idea of building a single, united political system. On 22 January 1946, they published a White Paper which presented their proposals for a new Malayan Union (MU). The MU proposals provided for a centralized country which would include the nine peninsular states in addition to Malacca and Penang. (Singapore was to remain separate). The sovereignty of the Malay Rulers was to be replaced by a central government headed by a British Governor. He would be aided by 'broad based and representative' Executive and Legislative Councils.[8] The Malay Rulers, having lost their sovereignty, would function through a Malay Advisory Council which would decide matters that pertained to Malay religion and custom. The individual states were to lose much of their autonomy—they would retain authority over only those matters delegated by the central government.

Beyond these proposals, the British also sought to create a single political body. Citizenship was to be granted to those born within the MU and Singapore, as well as to those who had resided there for ten out of the past fifteen years. They needed only to swear allegiance to Malaya. All would have the rights to both elect and serve in a government that was to become more representative.[9] Thus, once elections were begun, non-Malay voting power would come to rival or surpass that of the Malays. Non-Malays would also have access to posts within the civil service—a hitherto Malay and British service. The MU proposals would thus have drastically altered the pre-war status quo. The MU proposals were seen by the Malays as a threat to their position *vis-à-vis* the non-Malays; a situation which they viewed as intolerable.

Not only the MU proposals but the tactics used by the British to gain their acceptance by the Malay Rulers had incensed the Malay people. In December 1945 Sir Harold MacMichael, representing the British Crown, arrived in Malaya to negotiate new treaties with the Rulers, by which they were to cede their sovereignty to the British Crown. MacMichael was armed with the power to review the conduct of each Ruler during the Japanese Occupation. He was also empowered to depose any Ruler whose conduct he deemed unsatisfactory and name a successor. Consulting each Ruler separately, MacMichael effectively precluded any united action. To no one's surprise, he obtained the signatures of all nine Rulers.

The MU proposals and these tactics used by the British galvanized the Malay community. Convinced that Malaya would cease to be a Malay country and that they faced a major crisis, Malay religious leaders, schoolteachers, and members of the élite mobilized the Malay people to oppose the MU proposals.

MacMichael was met on 15 December 1945, in Kota Baru, Kelantan, by a mass protest demonstration reported to number 10,000.[10] After the MU proposals became public (22 January 1946), Malay opposition crystallized and associations quickly formed in protest. The largest organization was Datuk Onn bin Jaafar's Pergerakan Melayu Semenanjong (Movement of Peninsular Malays). It was established on 10 February 1946, and counted 15,000 Malay members, including 450 women.[11] Ten months later its membership had grown to 24,218. The number of women members was not recorded.[12] Responding to a call by Datuk Onn at the February meeting, 115 representatives from 42 Malay groups met in Kuala Lumpur on 1 March 1946 to form the United Malays National Organization (UMNO).

In response to the outcry of betrayal raised by 'old Malay hands' in the British Press and to the political stirrings of the Malays themselves, the British sent two parliamentary representatives to determine the extent of Malay opposition to the MU proposals. Everywhere Capt. L. D. Gammons and Sir Theodore Adams went, they were met by Malay crowds opposing the MU proposals; it was especially the Malay women who caught their attention (emphasis his):

> In the towns there were demonstrations with 5,000 to 10,000 people standing in front of us. *But the most remarkable thing* of all was the part the women were playing in this great national movement. In the 14 years I lived in Malaya I scarcely ever spoke to a Malay woman. But today they go up on political platforms and make speeches; unmarried girls make speeches through microphones that would not have disgraced anybody in this committee.[13]

Gammons thus witnessed the first stirrings by Malay women—stirrings that differed greatly from their previous public behaviour.

Not only did the women lend their presence to anti-MU rallies, they took an active part in expressing opposition. Zahrah binti Abdullah, a 25-year-old schoolteacher and a member of the Pergerakan Melayu Semenanjong, spoke at a protest rally in Batu Pahat Padang, Johore. She addressed Gammons and Adams in the following words: 'We women were greatly surprised when we were completely ignored by Sir Harold MacMichael. We will not agree to a MU whatever happens. We make our protest strongly. We will work with our men to regain our rights. In short, we don't like the union.'[14]

Several days later, the Raja Perempuan Kelsom Lateh (consort of the Sultan of Perak) and the wife of the Raja di Hilir of Perak, led a procession of several hundred Malay women to protest the MU proposals. Dividing into contingents from various districts, the women assembled before the nine sultans and Gammons shouting, 'Hidup Melayu! (Long Live Malaya!)', 'We don't want the Union'. They also carried banners that urged: 'Save the Rulers'.[15] Similar demonstrations took place in Penang[16] and in Negri Sembilan.[17]

The Earliest Political Associations of Malay Women

Except for three women's service organizations,[18] the earliest women's social (see Appendix) and political associations that formed after the war followed communal lines. Malay women, awakened by the MU proposals, organized a number of groups of which two are of primary significance: the Angkatan Wanita Sedar (AWAS), and the Kaum Ibu UMNO.

The Angkatan Wanita Sedar (AWAS), or the Progressive Malay Women's Corps, was the women's section of the Malay Nationalist Party (MNP). The MNP, a radical party, was dedicated to establishing an Indonesian republic that included Malaya. In addition, the MNP called for independence long before most Malays were ready to make such a demand. In December 1945, at the instigation of the Executive Committee of the MNP under its president, Dr Burhanuddin, the MNP organized its women's wing, AWAS. Dr Burhanuddin had argued that women had a part to play in the struggle for independence and were needed by the party.[19] Ahmad Boestamam (leader of the MNP's youth section (API)) is purported to have argued that women were being brought into the party so as to 'arouse in Malay women the consciousness of equal rights they have with men, to free them from old bonds of tradition and to socialize them'.[20] But there is little evidence to support this claim. No specific appeals were made to women as women and no activities were set up to draw them into the party. The 1946 four-page statement of MNP goals made no mention of women.[21] As Aishah Ghani,[22] the first president of AWAS and later fifth president of the Kaum Ibu UMNO and Minister of Social Welfare, noted: 'The MNP was interested in women for political reasons, to add strength to the party in order to push for independence. Women's issues as such did not exist in 1946.' In reminiscing about AWAS, Aishah Ghani recalled that it was weak and few Malay women joined. At the heyday of its strength, overall membership in the MNP was put at 60,000.[23] Membership in AWAS reached only 2,000 women[24] despite fervent appeals by the women leaders to Malay women.[25] While AWAS held discussions and provided a forum for Indonesian women visitors,[26] it is most remembered for the six-mile walk in Perak where 300 AWAS and API members protested the British prohibition against the use of motorized vehicles in processions. API members at first refused to walk the distance to Kuala Kangsar; they were shamed into going by AWAS women, and in particular by Sakinah Junid (who later became the president of the Dewan Muslimat, or women's section of the Islamic party, Parti Islam). She taunted them with the suggestion that the men and women should change clothes for the women had more spirit.[27] The march took place. AWAS women were also noticed at a mass meeting on 21 February 1947 sponsored by the MNP and API; 200 of them met with 2,000 men to resolve that they would revolt if the Federation plans were forced on them by the British.[28]

Following Aishah Ghani's resignation as president in 1947, the office passed to Shamsiah Fakir, an articulate speaker from Negri Sembilan. She urged that women be allowed to share the same rights as men:

If the women have sufficient amount of grey matter to see and understand the problems of the country and possess the capacity to realize the significance of their responsibility; if men are born with equal rights; if the world is stepping toward a more stable and sound democratic regime; there is no justifiable excuse for the women being denied their rights in determining internal and external policies when the consequences of such decisions are to be shouldered by both....[29]

AWAS existed for two and a half years. With the state of emergency in early 1948, API was banned for violent acts and, by July 1948 AWAS was defunct.[30] Of the first two presidents, the first, Aishah Ghani, went on to become the fifth president of the Kaum Ibu UMNO, a Senator and Minister of Social Welfare. The second, Shamsiah Fakir, pursuing an alternate route, joined the Malayan Communist Party and entered the jungle when the MCP was banned in 1948.[31]

While AWAS was the first Malay women's political group of any size, neither the MNP nor its women's branch ever gained the support of the Malays. It is remarkable that Malay women were active in the MNP to the extent that they were.

The Birth of the Kaum Ibu UMNO

The Kaum Ibu UMNO (KI), the women's section of the United Malays National Organization, did gain the support of the Malays and has continued to play a major role in Malayan politics.

The announcement of the MU proposals caused numerous Malay women's groups to grow and develop throughout Malaya. The women's section of the MNP was created by the executive council of the MNP to strengthen the party. Most of the women's associations that joined together in September 1947 as the Kaum Ibu UMNO, began as independent, nationalist organizations. One of the first was the Kaum Ibu (Women's Association) of Rembau, Negri Sembilan. Formed in March 1946, the association had the Tengku Ampuan (Sultan's consort) as a patron and was led by Halimahton binti Abdul Majid. In 1955, she was to become the first Malay woman elected to the Federal Legislature.[32] The Rembau KI was formed, like many others, to provide a forum for female opposition to the MU proposals. Later, as a branch of the KI UMNO, it became a channel through which women could push for independence. Halimahton, in a personal interview, expressed the depth of feeling from which the KI Rembau emerged: 'It was a hard job organizing the women in the beginning, but the issue was so great that people joined readily. It was simply a matter of survival of our people and country. The women felt it was their duty to join. After all, what was a M$1.00 members' fee when it was to save your people and country?'[33]

By the end of March 1946, other groups had sprung up in Kluang, Muar and Pontian, in Taiping[34] as well as in Kuala Krai and Ulu Langat.[35] In April, organizations had formed in Malacca, Seremban and Kuantan.[36] The Malay Women's Association of Kelantan functioned in August[37] and, in November, the Malay Women's Association of Lower Perak was organized.[38] Selangor women went one step further when they agreed to meet on 15 December 1946 to discuss forming a joint union of Malay women's associations in the state.[39] One of the strongest of the Selangor associations was the Persatuan Kaum Ibu Selangor (Selangor Women's Association). Organized on 17 February 1946, it was led by Saleha binti Mohamed Ali. In a letter dated 29 September 1946, to the secretary-general of UMNO, she explained that her association had about 570 members. The majority were *kampong* (village) women.[40] In stating the reasons for the association, Saleha explained: 'We understood that no women had joined men's organizations. That was why we had established ourselves separately. We cover all aspects of Malay life. We want to be independent, but not apart from men.'[41]

Other women's groups formed as branches of Malay associations. An early example was the Ipoh women's branch of the Persatuan Melayu Perak (Perak Malay Association) which was organized and led by Datin Puteh Mariah binti Rashid. A separate branch for women was needed because those women who joined the association were few in number and very shy. For the most part, they were conservative housewives who were incensed over the MU proposals and wished to help oppose them. They did not, however, feel at ease working directly with men and preferred their own organization.[42]

Not all the associations that later joined the Kaum Ibu UMNO were political in intent. The Kumpulan Ibu Sepakat (United Women's Association, Johore) was organized by Hajjah (Ibu) Zain binti Haji Suleiman in response to a plea by the head of the Religious Affairs in Johore. Fearing that the moral standards of Malay women had fallen due to the war, Ibu Zain was urged to form a self-help group for women. She went from village to village urging the women to join together, help themselves, educate their children and get experience in politics. In short, 'not to leave it all to the men'.[43] Ibu Zain estimated that the organization attracted several thousand members in Johore before it became the women's branch of Datuk Onn's Pergerakan Melayu Semenanjong, Johore (Movement of Peninsular Malays, Johore, or PMS). Ibu Zain brought the Kumpulan Ibu Sepakat into the PMS in May 1946 at the request of Datuk Onn who saw the organization as a means of reaching the women and of using their support to oppose the Malayan Union.[44]

Malay women's association formed from 1946 to 1948. On 25 March 1948, 50 women attended an organizational meeting of the women's section of Pemanas, a Malay political organization in Negri Sembilan, at which Tengku Sharifah Alwijah was elected leader of the women's wing.[45] Meanwhile, on 26 March 1948, Zahariah binti Abdullah Kuang formed the Malay Women's Progressive Party (Persekutuan Wanita Melayu Progresif) of Singapore. Its goals included promoting both the education and social standards of Malay women.[46]

Regardless of their objectives, all the women's associations had similar goals among which were: improving the status of women by aiding those in need, establishing religious classes to increase unity, loyalty and patriotism, finding ways to improve the status of women, reducing illiteracy,[47] and opposing the MU proposals.

The release of the MU proposals in January 1946 resulted in the organizing of Malay opposition. On 1-4 March, the first Pan-Malayan Malay Congress was held to set the guidelines for forming a Pan-Malayan organization. The representatives included one woman, Fatimah binti Musa of the Persatuan KI Selangor. The congress passed a unanimous resolution calling for the various Malay associations to be united into and controlled by a central organization. Thus, the United Malays National Organization, UMNO, was formed as an umbrella organization which contained forty-two autonomous Malay associations.[48]

At the 1946 UMNO (first) general assembly, three women discussed the idea of organizing a women's section of UMNO: Puteh Mariah, representing the Persatuan Melayu Perak, Zainab binti Abdul Rahman, representing the Persatuan Melayu Seberang Prai and Saleha binti Mohamed Ali from the Persatuan Melayu Selangor.[49] The matter was then carried by Puteh Mariah to the UMNO executive council, the Supreme Council, or Majlis Tertinggi, where the women's section was strongly supported by Datuk Onn, the first president of UMNO. Datuk Onn's support was critical to the success of the fledgeling Kaum Ibu. As the single outstanding nationalist leader of the period, his support lent legitimacy to the section and tended to blunt any opposition. Coming out in support of Malay women taking an active part in politics, he condemned those who criticized women in public activities. He argued that,

'Little can be achieved without their cooperation'.[50]

A separate women's branch in UMNO set the pattern that all other Malayan parties were to follow. Puteh Mariah explained that a separate women's section was needed because 'We (women) thought that we could look after our interests better by ourselves. The women at that time were very shy and we [leaders of the women's groups] felt that we could have a greater impact if we were organized.'[51]

On 29 December 1946 the Secretary-General of UMNO offered Puteh Mariah the position of Officer-in-Charge of the Department of Kaum Ibu. Accepting on 4 January 1947, she became the first *Pegawai* (Officer) of the Department of Kaum Ibu,[52] by which she automatically became a member of the UMNO Supreme Council. By 1 September 1947, the first separate women's conference met as a part of the UMNO general assembly; fourteen organizations were affiliated with UMNO; these included women's sections and a female membership which totalled 20,000.[53] (UMNO's total membership at that time was listed at 115,867.)[54] Except for the Persatuan Kaum Ibu Selangor (the Selangor Women's Association), most women's associations were part of a larger party. Within these parties, the women's associations, as auxiliaries, remained distinct. Thus, a woman would be both a member of a women's auxiliary and a larger party. Seventeen representatives from twelve organizations in Johore, Negri Sembilan, Selangor, Perak, Kedah, Perlis and Kelantan attended this first meeting in Johore Baru.[55] Puteh Mariah, addressing the women, stressed that the meeting was to provide them with a chance to talk and exchange ideas. She urged them not to isolate themselves from the men and not to limit their activities except in the sphere of religion.[56] The delegates were concerned with several issues at this first meeting. Their first concern was organizing the various women's groups into a united group affiliated to UMNO. While retaining their identities as distinct associations, they agreed that a KI branch should be set up in each state. With this meeting, the KI began its long campaign against early marriage and divorce as the prerogative of the male. What disturbed the women most was the practice of marrying young girls of fourteen or fifteen to older men of fifty and sixty.[57]

After the failed attempt of the Malayan Union (from 1 April 1946 until 31 January 1948) and in response to the intense Malay opposition, the British introduced a new policy in February 1948. This was known as the Federation of Malaya Agreement.[58] The Federation Agreement provided that the nine peninsular states plus Penang and Malacca be confederated; Singapore was to remain separate. The Malay Rulers were to become constitutional monarchs within each state, while, at the federal level they were to act through a council, the Conference of Rulers. The council would oversee matters of Malay custom and religion and have certain powers of review. These included any proposed changes in the immigration laws, salary changes for public officers, or any government reorganization plans. Executive authority lay with the High Commissioner aided by a Federal Executive Council made up of three official and a number of unofficial members. (Official members held an office of emolument under the Federation government or the Crown). A Legislative Council, consisting of 76 members (11 officials, 15 ex-officials and 50 unofficial appointees representing various community and economic interests) would serve to draft and/or vote on all legislation. The High Commissioner, though, would have the power to override any action of this Council or make enactments without the consent of the Council.

The states were to administer the schools, local authorities, land laws, Malay reservations, agriculture, forestries and aborigines. The federal government, however, could exercise its authority if it cared to do so. At the lower levels of government, state and settlement councils and town councils were created to perform functions like those of the Legislative Council.

Citizenship provided under the Federation Agreement was restricted compared to the MU scheme. The Federation Agreement granted citizenship to the Malays (and a few others) and provided a legal means whereby non-Malays could receive citizenship; however, the restrictions, in fact, set severe limits on political participation by non-Malays. In 1951, amendments were added which allowed non-Malays to apply for citizenship under more relaxed birth and residence requirements. Progress towards self-government was to be made by introducing municipal elections in 1951–2 and elections to state and federal legislative bodies in 1955.

The Federation Agreement was developed largely by British officials and members of the Malay élite—the latter being either the sultans or important members of UMNO. Non-Malays and all women remained peripheral to the decision-making process. In an attempt to assure Malay support for the plan, Governor Gent on 25 July 1946, created a 12-member committee, known as the Working Committee, to oversee the drafting of the new constitution. The Committee's members comprised 6 British members, 4 Malay Rulers and 2 representatives from UMNO.[59] None were women. Two and a half months later the Committee presented its recommendations for a Federation of Malaya. In the meantime, non-Malay opposition to the unrepresentative nature of the Working Committee resulted in the non-Malay Consultative Committee on the Constitutional Proposals (CCC) forming. This group included 'influential members of the non-Malay communities'.[60] The organization of the CCC promptly resulted in still another organization, the All-Malaya Council for Joint Action (AMCJA). AMCJA, formed on 22 December 1946 was an umbrella organization that included as members such groups as the Pan-Malayan Federation of Trade Unions, the Malayan Democratic Union, the Malayan Indian Congress, the Selangor and Singapore branches of the Women's Federation and the Malay Nationalist Party. All these groups were opposed to the return of colonial rule, the specifics of the Federation of Malaya Agreement, and what they viewed as the unrepresentative form of the CCC. AMCJA boycotted the CCC by refusing to recognize the Working Committee's report (completed March

1947) as the basis for a Federation Agreement. Thus, the CCC which came to represent only a segment of the non-Malay community, i.e. the moderates. The Working Committee then reconvened and adopted some of the CCC recommendations. They drew up the final constitutional draft which was ratified by the British on 24 July 1947, signed by the Malay Rulers in January 1948 and implemented on 1 February 1948. While non-Malays had a limited voice in the final form of the Federation Agreement, women were rarely consulted by the Federation Agreement's creators. The only KI contribution seems to have taken place at a closed Supreme Council meeting of UMNO, attended by two KI members, in November 1947. It was decided that one seat in the proposed Federal Legislative Council should be reserved for a woman.[61] Of the eighty-one memos and letters submitted to the Advisory Council of the Malayan Union regarding the Federal Legislative Council, none were submitted by women or their organizations.[62] Further, no women were appointed as members of the Working Committee or to the 9-member non-Malay Consultative Council.[63] The issue of women's suffrage came up at one of the meetings of the Working Committee. Through Puteh Mariah's presence and the firm support of Datuk Onn and several other members, women were granted the vote over notable reluctance. Puteh Mariah recalled that several men had argued that women needed a period of 'tutelege and education' before they could become enfranchised.[64]

While women did protest the MU proposals and thus became prominent, progress towards bringing women into the decision-making bodies proceeded slowly. One of the first calls to grant women a role in government bodies came from the president of the Selangor Ladies Association, Wong Chin. In January 1946, she urged that a woman be appointed to the newly-formed Selangor Advisory Council.[65] Halimahton binti Abdul Majid (an active member of the KI in Negri Sembilan and later president of the KI Selangor and the first woman elected to the Federal Council in 1955), also took a step forward when she attended a dinner in honour of UMNO at Balai Besar in Alor Star on 12 January 1947. It was the first time a Malay woman had attended such a function. She used the chance to urge that women be included on councils and other public bodies.[66] It was ironic, given the emerging prominence of Malay women at the time, that the first two public appointments of women were Chinese: Mrs Cheah Inn-kiong to the Penang Advisory Council in October 1946[67] and Dr Soo Kim-lan to the short-lived 15-member Malayan Union Advisory Council.[68] Dr Soo was the only woman appointed to the Advisory Council. This fact was not lost on her when the composition of the proposed Federal Legislative Council was debated by the Advisory Council:

> In addition, if I am not mistaken, I have noticed that no allowance has been given to women to play their role in the proposed Federal Legislative Council, except in one instance. If it is not too late, Sir, I should like to insert my proposal now, that women should be allocated, at least eight seats in the proposed council, namely two official and six as unofficial members.[69]

Dr Soo Kim-lan, like the women who were to follow her in the Federal Council and later in the Dewan Rakyat (House of Representatives) was an eloquent speaker who partook fully in the matters of the Council. She was not content to speak on those matters which were of direct concern solely to women during the 25 August 1947 session. She condemned the Revised Constitutional Proposals (the Federation Agreement) arguing that unity could never be attained while one-half of the people (the non-Malays) remained without political power.[70]

The birth of the Federation saw women start to hold public office. The first two such women were Hajjah Zain binti Suleiman and Azizah binti Jaafar. Both were appointed as unofficial members to the Johore State Council on 13 January 1948.[71] During the same month, Puteh Mariah was appointed to both the Perak State Council and to the Federal Legislative Council.[72] She was joined on the latter by Mrs B. H. Oon of Penang, Malaya's first and only practising woman lawyer at that time.[73] All of these women were well-known members of their communities: Ibu Zain had long been active in seeking to improve the lot of Malay women, while Azizah was the daughter of the *Mentri Besar* (Chief Minister) of Johore, Datuk Jaafar bin Mohammed. She was also Johore's first Domestic Science Mistress in the Education Department (1938) and, in 1941, organized the Johore Malay Women's Association, a self-help improvement association for Malay women.[74] Puteh Mariah was *Ketua* (Leader) of the KI UMNO, while Mrs B. H. Oon was a prominent lawyer and later became the first woman to create a political party (the Province Wellesley Labour Party). These appointments were the first of a series which, by 1951, saw Malayan women join the state councils of Negri Sembilan, Selangor and Perak.[75] The appointment of Tengku Azizah binti Tengku Petra to the Negri Sembilan state council in April 1949, was clearly a response to complaints by women that they were not represented in public positions. The Chief Minister, in welcoming her, noted: 'It has been complained that the requirements of women have not been sufficiently represented in the past. I hope that the appointment of Tengku Azizah will help obviate the complaints and that she, though the first, will be by no means the last of the women's reps.'[76]

This limited progress was far from satisfactory to the members of KI UMNO. Halimahton binti Abdul Majid in her presidential address to the second annual meeting of the Selangor KI in March 1948, declared the KI's dissatisfaction with the progress made by women in attaining public office:

> But although we took our full share in the struggle, we, the KI of Selangor are sorry to see that we have been left out of several matters of importance. For instance, in the discussions proceeding the forming of the Selangor State Constitution, only the men were invited to attend while no offer was made to the Kaum Ibu to participate in them. Again, in the choice of members to the State Legislative Council not one seat has been offered to the Kaum Ibu. In other states such as Johore and Perak members of the KI have been appointed as Councillors but here it looks as if none of the members of KI is considered by the authorities

fit enough to occupy such a position. We of the KI are not at all satisfied with the present state of affairs.[77]

Not until three years later, in March 1951, did the Sultan of Selangor finally appoint a woman to the Selangor State Council: Saleha binti Mohamed Ali, an active KI member.[78]

The KI UMNO was unable to do more than voice their dissatisfaction with the progress women were making in the emerging political system. The organization, in 1948, was still a loose confederation of women's associations just as UMNO remained an 'umbrella' organization of autonomous Malay associations. Not until August 1949, was it decided to make UMNO more cohesive. Its associations were merged and reformed into divisions. With the UMNO executive decision, 200 KI members met at the twelfth UMNO general assembly on 26 August 1949. (The KI and Pemuda sections held their assemblies the day before that of UMNO.) They chose to reorganize the KI into a single auxiliary body affiliated to UMNO, the Pergerakan Kaum Ibu. This replaced the unwieldy, 14 original associations.[79] It was at this meeting that UMNO, the KI and the Pemuda, adopted the hierarchical structure which is retained today.

The basic unit for all three became the branch, followed by the division, state and national levels. Control and communication would run vertically in all sections. There was little contact horizontally, i.e. one KI branch would have little to do with another KI branch. The KI and Pemuda remained distinct organizations; they seldom interacted with each other. The parent body, 'Bapa UMNO' (Father of UMNO), would be represented at all levels within the Pemuda and KI; and they, in turn, would be represented at all levels within the party proper. Prior to this reorganization, KI women were poorly represented within UMNO. Few women attended the UMNO general assemblies, as opposed to their separate KI assemblies. Women simply were not chosen as delegates by the early UMNO affiliates. For example, the Alor Star general assembly in January 1949 chose only 3 women delegates out of 65.[80] The members realized there was a problem with the lack of female representation. They passed a resolution (No. 23) that KI members be selected to serve on UMNO committees at all levels.[81] The need for such representation was clear; at the 27 August 1948 general assembly, all 40 delegates from the UMNO affiliates were men.[82] The reorganization, however, guaranteed that the KI and Pemuda would have 2 delegates at the general assembly.[83] Recognizing the importance of the KI to UMNO and to assure the support of the women, Datuk Onn bin Jaafar (the first president of UMNO) at the 1949 meeting stressed that the role of the KI was important both within UMNO and for the future of the Malays. Addressing the KI general assembly he stated:

The shape of the administration desired by the people of the country will be established when the time comes, when every citizen has the right to elect his own representative ... so the KI will have the right to elect their own representatives. When we compare the number of KI with the men, we find that they are almost the same. Therefore, the voice of the KI is as powerful as that of the man.... The voice of both will determine the shape of the administration of the country.[84]

The primary purpose of the KI, however, was clearly delineated by Datuk Onn:

> I hope before the end of the year the KI will work together with one aim, that is to strengthen its position in UMNO beside the men. If the KI did not strengthen its position, when the time comes for election of members to the various councils, the KI will be left behind, which means the Malays will be left behind....[85]

Following the speech, the KI assembly elected as leader of their auxiliary, Puteh Mariah. Under the reorganization, the position of Secretary of Women and Welfare Affairs was abolished, the president of the women's section was henceforth a vice-president of the party.[86]

The efforts of the KI during its early years centred on increasing its membership and strengthening its organization within UMNO. Patriotic appeals were made by KI leaders to attract new members to the party. The various cooking, sewing, and religious classes conducted by the KI also helped. In addition, talks and lectures on health, childcare, and politics were given by the KI to attract new members. Such activities, plus the appeal to patriotism, attracted village women who had few diversions. The KI undertook another major function for UMNO which has never abated—party fund-raiser. During these early years the KI began staging fun fairs (at which food and handicrafts were sold and games played), also cooking contests, and it began selling handkerchiefs, flags, etc. all to raise money to aid the independence effort. The theme of party fund-raiser extends throughout the history of UMNO. The party came to rely on its women's wing for some of its needed operating expenses. As one (male) UMNO official put it, UMNO could 'rely' on the KI: they were much more 'stable' than the Pemuda.

KI women also began to define and discuss those issues of direct concern to women. Following the first KI assembly in 1947, they again debated the issues of higher education for girls and the protection of women within marriage at the KI conference in Arau, Perlis, on 27 January 1949. They passed two resolutions urging: 1) the government to provide higher education for Malay girls, and 2) the authorities in every state set procedures for the issuance of *nusuz*—a decree that declared a woman recalcitrant (declaring that she received no support from her husband, see Chapter 1).[87]

Beyond such activities, the major task of the KI emerged with the municipal elections in 1951–2. Malay women proved numerous and dependable voters. Thus they became indispensable to UMNO's electoral success. It quickly became the task of the KI to help guarantee that not only would Malay women support UMNO but that all Malays would support the party. The KI became entrusted with the task of conducting pre-election activities (canvassing, setting up polling booths, getting voters to the polls, etc.). The repeated UMNO Alliance victories attest to the success of the KI.

Aside from these matters, the KI faced many problems during its first decade. The increased public role of the women sometimes wrought opposition from more conservative circles, at times from within UMNO itself.

A potentially damaging matter arose in September 1952. The Council of Ulamas—Council of (Islamic) Religious Teachers, banned Malay women from taking part in politics.[88] They argued that increased activities would lead to excessive mixing of the sexes and this would be contrary to Islam.[89] Malay women leaders responded promptly. Zahara binti Mohamed Noor of the Singapore Malay Women's Association urged the Council to look at more serious matters.[90] The president of the KI (Ibu Zain) argued: 'If women take part in politics, men will be inspired to work hard.'[91] Tunku Abdul Rahman, the president of UMNO, gave the KI his full support: '*Kaum Ibu UMNO* is doing very well, either in its political or in its social contributions to Malay society, and it never crosses my mind to dissolve this prosperous organization.'[92] The Council's decision had little if any effect on the fortunes of the KI for, in December 1952, yet another branch was created in Singapore. Tunku Abdul Rahman, in addressing the first meeting, praised the women for their 'bold step'.[93]

The largest dispute to occur between the KI and the UMNO was the issue of the expulsion of the third KI president, Khadijah binti Mohamed Sidek in 1956. The subject of the expulsion is important for it shows the degree of control that the party had over an auxiliary whose members were crucial to the party's well-being.

On 11 October 1953, the UMNO Supreme Council met in Kuala Lumpur and created the Pejabat bagi Hal Ehwal Kaum Ibu (Office of Women's Affairs).[94] The position of head of the women's section was at that time vacant. Puteh Mariah had been replaced as *Ketua* in 1950 by Ibu Zain who resigned in 1953 for reasons of health.[95] After the position of Setiausaha Pejabat bagi Hal Ehwal (Secretary for the Office of KI Affairs) was offered to the Raja Perempuan of Perlis, Tengku Budariah,[96] the UMNO Supreme Council then offered the position to Khadijah Sidek to start on 17 October 1953. She accepted.[97] The appointment of Khadijah Sidek was an interesting choice given her background; later, her appointment would lead to internal tensions within the party. Ultimately, she was the only KI leader ever to be expelled from UMNO.

Khadijah Sidek was an ex-Indonesian nationalist from Sumatra who in flight from Dutch police action, settled in Singapore in 1947. Marrying a Malayan citizen, she opened a home economics school for girls and started the All Indonesian Women's Association in 1947. The Association's aims were apolitical and attracted a following of 200–300 women. Its main goal was, 'to let Malayans know what Indonesian women were doing'.[98] Khadijah Sidek, however, had contacts with many of the Malay associations as well as with several Chinese women's groups. She was also quite vocal in seeking independence for Malaya. With the outbreak of the Emergency in 1948, she was jailed without trial for two years in Singapore (1948-50) where she gave birth to a daughter. After her release, she remained under a ten-year detention order to remain in Johore Baru. In 1953, she joined UMNO (being eligible as the wife of a Malayan citizen) having been asked to join by Ibu Zain. Khadijah Sidek, at once, became involved in party politicking. While attending a party congress meeting in 1953, she urged the UMNO to be fair to the KI, noting that, while 500 men attended the conference, the KI and Pemuda had only four delegates each. She further suggested that the women would be better off forming a separate party; the idea was rejected by KI leaders.[99] The UMNO general assembly also rejected the idea of forming a separate women's youth section. Khadijah Sidek further urged UMNO officials to appoint more women to the Supreme Council, UMNO's highest body. She argued, it was the women who worked hard and raised funds for UMNO.[100] Tunku Abdul Rahman's response was to appoint her as Secretary of the Office of KI Affairs to the Supreme Council. As an executive council member, she was able to go to the *kampong* and speak to the women though still under a ban not to travel outside of Johore Baru. UMNO records leave no doubt that Khadijah Sidek travelled throughout Malaya establishing KI branches in Pontian, Ayer Balai, Telok Kerang, Kota Tinggi, Tanjong Buai, Tanjong Surang, and Kengkong to mention only a few.[101]

In October 1954, Khadijah Sidek was elected *Ketua* of the Kaum Ibu and two weeks later was expelled from the UMNO Johore Baru division on the grounds that she breached party discipline—she divulged Supreme Council matters to the general assembly.[102] The accusation stemmed from her charge at the party general assembly that women had been deliberately excluded from the Johore state election lists. Taking other delegates with her, Khadijah Sidek walked out of the general assembly in protest and thus threatened party unity. The expulsion order, however, did not stand; Tunku Abdul Rahman maintained that there was not enough evidence to expel her.[103] There were also some, within UMNO, who did not want her expelled but only to be given a 'severe warning'.[104]

Khadijah Sidek remained a focal point for controversy. KI members, active party workers during elections, launched a campaign to urge UMNO to select KI members as electoral candidates. With the forming of the Federal Legislative Council in 1955, Tunku Abdul Rahman, the Chief Minister as well as President of UMNO, was urged to appoint Khadijah Sidek to one of the five reserve seats on the new Federal Council. The only woman to be elected to one of the 52 elective seats was Halimahton binti Abdul Majid from the Ulu Selangor district. The Selangor KI urged the Tunku to appoint Khadijah Sidek, and threatened to boycott the Alliance in the state elections in September 1955 if he did not.[105] He replied that the demand for a Malay woman Federal Legislative Councillor had been met by the election of Halimahton: 'I have never promised to nominate a woman to the Council. I said there would be a woman councilor and there is. In any case, Khadijah Sidek would not be the right person to sit on the Council as she is under a bond of good conduct.'[106] One week later, on 11 August 1955 the women's section of the Bukit Mertajam section of UMNO met to discuss boycotting the town council elections in protest. Che Bee Noor, president of the KI section, voiced the dissatisfaction of the women: 'We feel that the big part played by UMNO women in the July 27th Federal elections has been overlooked.'[107] By 17 August the Alliance announced it would put up more women in town and municipal elections. Said the spokesman: 'We have asked our branches to tell the women that they should start from town or municipal councils and then work their way up. The Alliance policy to increase women's participation in councils is a recognition of their contributions in the recent Federal elections.'[108]

The male leadership, though, claimed a problem existed in finding capable women to stand as candidates. The Alliance did promise that it would soon pick and train UMNO, MCA and MIC women as party candidates.[109] This proved to be an empty promise.

Khadijah Sidek was not appointed to the Federal Council and was not chosen as a party candidate. In October 1956 the subject of her expulsion was again in the Press. In September 1956, she had been expelled by the Johore Baru UMNO division. The UMNO Supreme Council which heard all expulsion matters upheld the branch decision. They maintained she was no longer suitable as the KI *Ketua* (Leader) and a member of the Supreme Council. The reasons for her expulsion included: 1) she acted contrary to the rules and conduct of UMNO, 2) her conduct was detrimental to the interests and well-being of UMNO and, as such, 'the KI throughout Malaya would be in danger', 3) her public speeches were at times faulty and injurious, and 4) she had not been co-operative and was likely to cause dissension among members of UMNO.[110] Though many KI members threatened a mass protest against the expulsion, Tunku Abdul Rahman appealed to them and the crisis abated.[111] Khadijah Sidek, however, fought back. Challenging the UMNO Supreme Council to bring her case to a public hearing, she argued that the Council could not expel her as she was selected by the UMNO general assembly. The Council declined by claiming they had the right to decide the matter. Many KI sections held emergency meetings to discuss the crisis.[112] UMNO spokesmen urged the KI members not to get excited over the expulsion.[113] In fact, it appears that the KI was ordered not to protest the expulsion as is shown by a statement by UMNO Secretary-General, Senu Abdul Rahman: 'But this does not mean that they are going to protest, as a matter of fact they cannot do that now in view of the directive headquarters had sent them.'[114] Both the Perak and Pahang KI branches had been told by UMNO to postpone meeting until the Supreme Council had made a decision.[115] Confusion reigned as to the real reason for the expulsion. UMNO spokesmen maintained: 'Why we expelled her is not meant for the newspapers to publicize.'[116] On 12

November 1956 the Supreme Council made its final decision; they upheld the expulsion of Khadijah Sidek from UMNO and named Fatimah Hashim (leader of the Perak section) as temporary leader of the KI.[117] UMNO had succeeded in checking a challenge to party discipline by a KI member. Khadijah Sidek then joined the Pan-Malayan Islamic Party (PMIP) and became the leader of its women's section, the Dewan Muslimat. In 1972, she once again joined UMNO though she did not regain a major role in the party.

Khadijah Sidek's combative style differed from that of her predecessors. Her early life in Indonesia, her part in the nationalist movement there, her internment in Singapore, and her personal frustration over the role women played in UMNO all resulted in her unique style. That style, though, quickly alienated her from the UMNO male leadership and led to her expulsion. Though she had a charismatic quality and was a great orator, she was seen as a disruptive force within UMNO. The KI members were uneasy about the situation, but tight party discipline required the KI to agree to her expulsion.

These difficulties were only one problem that the KI faced. In addition to the party turmoil that would recur periodically in 1956 and 1960, the KI faced major membership and leadership problems. Early KI membership was largely limited to village women who were illiterate and had little or no leadership experience. In 1951, Ibu Zain, the second president of the KI, wrote in the party paper, *Suara UMNO* (*Voice of UMNO*), that of the 100,000 UMNO members only 10,000 were women. She went on to explain that many women failed to join the party because they were given no encouragement by their husbands who were themselves UMNO members.[118] In order to combat the problem, KI leaders by 1950 were making many trips to the villages to encourage the growth of KI branches. These visits, which helped to explain the goals and the objectives of the KI, most likely resulted in the rise of KI membership from 10,486 in 1949 to 12,898 in 1950.[119] (This was down from the 20,000 estimated members in 1947. The drop was due to the MU plan no longer being an issue.) Literacy among the women, however, remained a problem. Ibu Zain estimated that of the women who joined the KI only 50 per cent were literate; that number included 2,000 teachers.[120] The high illiteracy rate explains the heavy emphasis the KI placed on forming literacy classes and its interest in education for Malay girls and women. It also explains why the KI has had to rely so heavily on the support of schoolteachers and the wives of UMNO officials. UMNO women themselves point out that it was the wives of 'political' UMNO men who led the movement in its early years.[121] Of equal importance were the aristocratic Malay women who were willing to lend their support to the KI. During these early years, one finds in the UMNO records many titles preceding the names of KI leaders. While the KI was able to find enough women with literacy and leadership skills to guide the section at the national and state levels, it was difficult to find capable women to head and guide the divisions and branches.

The KI women also had little or no experience in public affairs. The first public prominence attained by Malay women after the war was in large, mass efforts, such as protests against the Malayan Union. Very few women had any public speaking or organizing experience aside from these spontaneous mass efforts. In addition to these structural problems that hindered the KI, there was a split in the goals of the sections at the time. The KI's primary objective was to strengthen UMNO as a Malay party, to oppose the Malayan Union, and, afterwards, to push for an independent Malaya that would maintain the Malay domination in political life. As such, the other goals (marriage and divorce reform, higher education for girls, getting women to participate in politics) remained secondary. As will be shown, the KI has never been willing to challenge UMNO on the position of women in the party and government except through the passage of annual resolutions. The conservatism of the women in the late 1940s and 1950s was a strong factor, setting the direction the KI would take. KI leaders maintained that during these years most KI members, while wishing to improve their lot, were only just becoming accustomed to political activity. They were not ready for any drastic changes in their roles as homemakers. It should also be remembered that Malaya was still a colony with no history of representative government. Further, Islam did not encourage such activity by women. Yet, despite the problems the KI faced, the auxiliary continued to grow and play a major role within the Malayan party system.

The Social and Political Organizations of Non-Malay Women

Chinese Women—The Early Associations

There was an early post-war growth of organizations of Chinese women just as with the Malay women. One of the first was the Penang Women's Association founded on 11 January 1946. It sought to improve the education of women by forming a night school for girls.[122] Another example was the Selangor Ladies Association (SLA). It's president, Wong Chin, urged that women be represented on the Advisory Council then being formed in Selangor. There was no further word on the functions of the SLA.[123] In April 1946, 36 leading Chinese women met in Kuala Lumpur to form the Selangor Women's Relief Association, who sought to provide free education for women and relief for all unemployed Chinese women in Selangor.[124] The Chinese Press also mentioned the upcoming inauguration on 1 January 1947 of the Perak Chinese Women's League.[125] These organizations were devoted to social welfare matters, but by 1946 Chinese women began to organize an association with definite political goals, the Women's Federation.

The Women's Federation was organized by Miss Lee Kiu, its first president;[126] and, by May 1946 it consisted of twelve branches.[127] Ideologically linked to the Women's International Democratic Federation,[128] a communist group, the Federation consisted largely of non-English-speaking Chinese women and girls. It numbered about 20,000 throughout all of Malaya.[129] The Singapore branch alone claimed 3,000 members and was able to collect $12,000 to finance a campaign to teach dressmaking skills to about 1,000 destitute women. The branch also offered evening classes for those wishing to learn Mandarin and conducted a campaign to dissuade housewives from using the black market.[130] In January 1947 the Federation became involved in controversy over the MU proposals. Meeting in Kuala Lumpur, the members of the various branches passed resolutions which demanded suffrage for women in Malaya. It also supported the principles of the Council of Joint Action which opposed the constitutional proposals.[131] In fact, the Selangor and Singapore branches of the Women's Federation were among the original members of the AMCJA (All-Malaya Council for Joint Action). Thompson[132] suggested that the Federation was believed to be a communist or communist front as were the New Democratic Youth League and the Malayan Peoples' Anti-Japanese Ex-Servicemen's Association. Regardless of the truth of this claim, one finds no further mention of the Federation once AMCJA disbanded in the spring of 1948.

In June 1948, the communist rebellion began. Its effect on the political involvement of the non-Malays, particularly the Chinese, cannot be overemphasized. The insurgency, whose main support came from the Chinese, resulted in firm measures being adopted by the colonial government. The Emergency, as the twelve-year insurgency was called, produced mass deportation to Kuomintang China for suspected and proven rebels. Others were detained or imprisoned in Malaya. To cut supply sources to the rebels, large numbers of rural Chinese dwellers were rounded up and placed in 'new villages'—camps which indeed succeeded in denying the rebels new recruits and supplies. A ban was also placed on all political parties and organizations (such as trade unions, youth groups, etc.) which were thought to be leftist oriented or opposed to the British role in Malaya. API (the youth wing of the Malay Nationalist Party), the Malayan Communist Party, the New Democratic Youth League, and numerous other groups were banned. The Women's Federation was the main Chinese women's organization affected by the ban. After declaring the Emergency in June 1948, one finds no mention of the Federation again. The Emergency lasted twelve years. In 1960, the fighting was down to a low level. It cost many lives, huge financial expenditure, and imposed restrictions on the freedom of speech and assembly. The psychological effect on the Chinese population must also be mentioned: Since the rebels were largely Malayan Chinese and government measures were directed largely against Chinese organizations and Chinese rural dwellers, the Chinese attitude towards government was reinforced. It was wise and safer not to be involved in politics. Instead, Chinese interests continued to be expressed through groups such as the clans, the Chinese Chambers of Commerce, and the Straits Chinese British Association—groups which appeared to have little access to or influence upon the colonial government.[133] The Kuomintang (KMT) in Malaya, while still functioning, kept a low profile. Little mention is made of the Ladies Committee of the KMT in Malaya after the war, though in 1946 it appears that they did raise M$20,640 to erect a girls' school in commemoration of Chiang Kai-shek's sixtieth birthday.[134]

The Malayan Chinese Association (MCA)

It was not until 1949 and the birth of the Malayan Chinese Association (the MCA) that Chinese interests became the formal focus of a moderate political party. The MCA began as a social welfare organization to aid Chinese families displaced as a result of the Emergency. Encouraged by the British who sought to reduce the appeal and support of the MCP, the MCA quickly became the main spokesbody of moderate and conservative Chinese interests. By 1952 the MCA contested the new municipal elections; it functioned as a political party.

Prior to Independence in 1957, the leadership of the MCA was dominated by members of the Chinese business and merchant community. In particular, the party was led by its founder president Sir Tan Cheng-lock, a Straits-born Chinese and Datuk Sir (Henry) Lee Hau-shik, who was responsible for initiating the UMNO–MCA alliance in 1953, and who was subsequently ousted from the party in 1956. It was during these years that the party acquired its image of a party for the Chinese business and merchant class—an image it has had difficulty altering. By 1958, however, Tan Cheng-lock and other MCA leaders were challenged by a younger faction, led by Dr Lim Chong-eu, who sought to revitalize the party by promoting younger people to positions of leadership. Lim and his group also urged that the MCA take a stronger stand *vis-à-vis* UMNO to safeguard and promote what they saw as Chinese interests. Successful in his challenge to Tan Cheng-lock, Lim Chong-eu took over the presidency of the MCA and one year later was himself challenged and defeated by Tan Cheng-lock's son, Tan Siew-sin. Similar leadership difficulties have continued to plague the MCA at repeated intervals and, where relevant, the details have been included. For present purposes, however, it is important to note that up until the late 1950s the MCA remained a party dominated by its national élite and poorly organized at the local or mass level. Until 1959 the MCA constitution did not provide for local and district level bodies. It maintained itself largely at the state and national level (unlike the UMNO which was grassroots and up: branch, district (division), state, and national levels). During these early years, the MCA made little attempt to broaden its support base. Hence, Chinese women played little part in the early party. Leaders, both men and women agreed that women played no part in the birth of the MCA. The MCA's first set of rules passed on 12 June 1949, made no mention of women or youth sections; the General Committee (the top executives of the party) were empowered to appoint any sub-committees to deal with special matters.[135] By 1951, the MCA had 8 sub-committees with women included in the 'Women and Youth' sub-committee. Tan Cheng-lock, the first president, readily admitted though that the sub-committees were not working well due to the MCA being 'still in its infancy' and 'owing to a lack of funds'.[136]

The first indication that women in the MCA had begun organizing a section was in November 1953. This was the women's section of the Johore Baru district branch of the MCA.[137] Lim Swee-sim led the section but little is known of her. Within a week, a liaison meeting was held with members of the KI UMNO Johore Baru branch.[138] The two women's branches agreed to co-operate in social welfare work, to co-ordinate election efforts, and to support UMNO–MCA policy. However, the Johore Baru branch remained the only functioning women's section until September 1954, when the party announced that it would form women's sections throughout Malaya. The major goal of the women's section was: 'To improve the objects, programs, and policies of the MCA and to provide for its members opportunities and facilities for meetings and physical or intellectual pursuits.'[139] However, tight control by the party over the women's section was evident in the party guidelines:

> The general committee of the MCA, or CWC [Central Working Committee] shall through the Chairman of the Political, Youth and Women sub-committee have full power of control over the State and Settlement committees regarding the formation, organization, management, control, discipline and finance of the two sections [i.e. Women and Youth], their aims and policies, and may issue to the State and Settlement Committees such direction or directives as it may think fit and proper and the State or Settlement Committee shall put the same into effect.[140]

The directive had little effect. Women's sections failed to develop even though by 1 December 1954 a women's section functioned for a time in Selangor.[141] Though the Johore branch of the MCA made an effort in 1955 to form youth and women's sections, and Mrs Ten Yoon-fong, head of the women's section, was given a seat on the Johore State Executive Committee,[142] progress in drawing women to the MCA proceeded slowly. Those who did join, however, were praised by the party for their efforts in the 1955 state and federal council elections.[143]

In 1956, newspapers began to refer to Gunn Chit-wha, a well-known attorney and the first Chinese woman elected to the Selangor State Council (1957), as the chairwoman of the Women's Committee of the MCA.[144] However, the MCA women's section did not exist except for the Johore branch. Pleas to Chinese women to put aside their differences and fight for equality had little effect.[145]

Indian Women's Organizations

The actions of Indian women in the Rani of Jhansi Brigade of the INA during the war would suggest that Indian women might be in the foreground of the women's groups to form after the war. This did not happen. Two pre-war Sikh women's groups re-emerged, the Isteri Sat

Sangh Sabha and the Isteri Milap. The latter group was the women's section of the Selangor Sikh Union—a socio-religious organization. The two women's groups merged in 1949 and confined their efforts to culture and religion, drama, singing, and seminars on the Sikh religion. They pushed to educate Punjabi girls (in the Punjabi language), and published two magazines, the *Milap* and *Isteri Sansar*—neither endured.[146] Aside from these two groups, one finds two Indian women's associations, one in Negri Sembilan and one in Selangor, that functioned in 1946.[147] Mrs S. M. Thevar, president of the Indian Women's Association of Negri Sembilan, urged Indian women to come out of the home. She asserted that political, social, and military affairs were also important to women.[148] Such urgings had little effect. In Malaya as a whole, the public participation of Indian women remained low.

In August 1946, 500 Indians from all walks of life joined in the Malayan Indian Congress (MIC). The party was founded to press Indian interests in Malaya. For a brief time, the MIC was a member of the All-Malaya Council for Joint Action (AMCJA). Many MIC members also supported the Independence of Malaya Party which sought to build a multiracial party. In 1954, the MIC became the third member of the Alliance. Since that time, it expended its efforts on its original purpose—to preserve Indian interests, largely through its UMNO and MCA partners. The significance of the MIC as a party stemmed from being a member of the Alliance or Barisan Nasional (BN). As a member, its strength is in part due to the support that Chinese and Malay voters give MIC candidates on the Alliance ticket. Indians did not form a majority in any constituency.

Like the MCA, the MIC was beset with major internal problems among those seeking to lead the party. These problems were due to the MIC obtaining only a small number of the Alliance nominations; competition for these slots was thus severe.

Among those who created the MIC were a handful of women. They included Janaky Thevar Nahappan and Mrs Lobo from Singapore.[149] The MIC constitution, drafted in 1946, did not mandate a national women's section (one was not formed until 1975). It did provide that women serve on the local and state executive committees of the party; the number was to be fixed by the strength in party membership. The regional committee was to include two women regardless of the number of women in the party. Power to form a women's section was left to the local committee. It was to set up those sub-committees that its members saw fit.[150] Though the first president of the party, John A. Thivy (1946-7) encouraged women to join,[151] and though women were urged to attend a meeting on Congress work in Kuala Lumpur on 21 November 1946,[152] women still did not involve themselves in MIC activities. They were not included on the first Executive Council of the MIC.[153]

The first attempt to create a women's section occurred on 19 June 1955 at Jalan Brickfields in Kuala Lumpur. Seventy women attended the first meeting of the Wanita MIC Selangor.[154] The idea for the section was a joint effort between Mrs Devaki Krishnan, the first woman candidate elected in Malaya (1952), and the Selangor MIC Regional Committee; Mrs Devaki Krishnan was appointed as president of the section. The women's section seems to have been approved by the Selangor regional MIC as a means to gain support. As one MIC official[155] commented: 'To be frank, women were only encouraged to join in the 1950s and 1960s because they were voters and because they were useful in elections.' During 1955, 11 branches of the women's section sprang up in sections of Kuala Lumpur, where most, if not all, of the Wanita MIC members lived. Members tended to be uneducated, and the wives of MIC members.[156] The women's section led a precarious life and was more or less defunct by 1959. One of its problems was rapid changes in leadership. The Selangor Regional MIC Committee seems responsible for the problem. It appointed Mrs Devaki Krishnan as leader in 1955, Mrs Koruthi in late 1955, Mrs James Nathan in 1958, and, in turn, Mrs Devaki Krishnan in 1959. While activities, such as sewing, cooking, and literacy classes were held to draw women into the party, the Selangor Wanita MIC section did not serve as a spur to forming other state women's branches. Instead it remained the only women's section in the MIC until the 1960s.

Non-communal and Other Communal Parties and Women

While the UMNO, MCA and MIC were the main sponsors of communal interests in Malaya, other parties played a part in forming Malaya's party system. Within the other communal parties, women played a very limited role. Foremost among these have been the Pan-Malayan Islamic Party (PMIP) and the People's Socialist Party of Malaya (PSRM) both composed of Malays.

The Pan-Malayan Islamic Party (PMIP, later known as PAS and still later as the PI) was the spiritual Muslim Malay party. It was formed as the religious wing, or auxiliary, of UMNO. Later the PMIP became UMNO's chief rival for Malay support. The PMIP launched its women's section, the Dewan Muslimat (Muslim Women's Council), in 1956, under Zubaidah Ali at the party's fifth annual assembly. The Dewan Muslimat, led by women religious teachers saw the section's role to support the party.[157] It retained a very low profile and remained under the firm control of the central party leaders.

The Parti Sosialis Rakyat Malaya (the People's Socialist Party of Malaya—PSRM) was launched by Ahmad Boestamam (former leader of the Youth section, API, of the MNP) on 10 November 1955.[158] In January 1957 the party announced a plan to set up women's sections, called Wanita Rakyat, at the state and settlement level throughout Malaya. The first section was in Kelantan in February 1957. The idea was approved at the PSRM's second annual conference in Ipoh, Perak, in 1956. Spokesmen for the party announced the future Wanita Rakyat: 'Already more than 200 Malay women in Kelantan, many of them girls, are clamouring to join the Wanita Ra'ayat. This is a great step forward in the political struggle particularly in bringing greater political consciousness to the women fold in the kampongs.'[159] In August 1958, the Wanita Rakyat president, Zainab binti Ahmad, addressed the first meeting and urged the delegates to make the section strong and active. She called on them to be prepared to fight and struggle for the defence of Malaya.[160] The PSRM during the 1950s remained a small party with a largely Malay membership. (It numbered about 5,000 in 1956, though the number of women members is unrecorded.)[161] PSRM women would play a vocal but minor role within the party during the next two decades.

Malaya's first try at non-communal parties occurred when Datuk Onn bin Jaafar launched the Independence of Malaya Party (IMP) on 16 September 1951.[162] This was after he failed to open UMNO to non-Malay members and then stepped down from the presidency of UMNO. He was supported by an impressive array of Malayans—the organizing committee of the IMP included: Datuk Onn, Datuk Tan Cheng-lock, R. Ramani, Khoo Teck-ee (Treasurer of the MCA), P. P. Narayanan (President of the Malayan Trade Union Congress) and Saleha binti Mohamed Ali (one of the founders of the KI UMNO).[163] The IMP sought independence for Malaya within ten years, Malayanization of the civil service, and the 'well-being and advancement of the people based on equality of opportunity and of political, social and economic rights and obligations.'[164] While the MIC supported the IMP, the new party was unable to attract the rank and file members of either the UMNO or the MCA. In May 1952, the Kuala Lumpur branch of the IMP, which contained the core of the party, counted only 1,229 members.[165] Malays stayed out of the IMP because membership meant expulsion from UMNO—a fact which was not anticipated by either Datuk Onn or Puteh Mariah, a staunch supporter of Datuk Onn. Tunku Abdul Rahman, Datuk Onn's successor as president of UMNO, declared on 17 September 1951, that members who joined the IMP would be expelled from UMNO.[166] To ensure the KI's support for UMNO, the Tunku also gave thanks to the KI women for their strong support of the party. He praised the women with the oft-quoted phrase of: 'Remember, the hand that rocks the cradle rules the world.'[167] Most Malays were not ready to give up their membership in UMNO for a non-communal experiment, though two prominent Malay women, Puteh Mariah and Saleha binti Mohamed Ali, gave their full support to the new party. Saleha went so far as to be the first person to formally resign from UMNO arguing that 'Malaya for the Malays is no slogan for UMNO in 1951'.[168]

Datuk Onn believed in a women's section within the IMP.[169] Women were to be represented at every party level. The 15 September 1951 policy statement of the party included point three: 'The IMP will work for equality of opportunity and rewards, irrespective of sex, the emancipation of women and free and equal opportunity of physical and mental development for the young.'[170] However, the failure of the IMP to develop as a party meant that the women's section was never started. The

IMP still continued to function through its Kuala Lumpur branch. The active women in the IMP were just a few prominent women. Six women in particular were active as leaders in the Kuala Lumpur branch: Saleha binti Mohamed Ali, Mrs E. Ramachandran, Rahmah binti Salleh, Mrs Nair, Loke Soh-lip and Mrs Lloyd Williams.[171] Puteh Mariah also worked for the new party and became Secretary-General[172]—the first woman to hold a top-level post not reserved for a woman.

The failure of the IMP in the 1952 municipal elections, the break between Datuk Onn and Datuk Tan Cheng-lock, and the reluctance of the Chinese and Malays to support the IMP all added to its decline. By 17 July 1953, Datuk Onn announced that the IMP was almost dead due to the interest its members retained in communal parties.[173] After giving up on the IMP and after failing to form any national party coalition,[174] Datuk Onn launched Parti Negara (the National Party) in February 1954. Parti Negara became a Malay party that proved unable to compete with UMNO. Puteh Mariah, in support of Datuk Onn, joined in and helped organize the new party. Women were among the 500 people present when the new party was launched on 1 March 1954.[175] It was not until 4 April 1955, however, that the women's section of the Kuala Lumpur branch was formed. Mrs K. V. Thaver, wife of a Federal Councillor, was elected chairperson of the newly formed section. It was hoped that the branch would bring in other Parti Negara women to start their own sections.[176] Datuk Onn based his hopes for a political come-back on a strengthened women's section. He organized Putri Negara (Daughters of the Country) in August 1955.[177] Putri Negara was to be organized in Johore Baru—a separate body with its own officials though Datuk Onn himself planned to supervise the task.[178] Unlike the KI UMNO, the women's section in Parti Negara was to exist separately only at the branch level; there was no intent to form state or national level organizations. In the words of Puteh Mariah: 'We felt it was time to do away with all such distinctions.'[179] Parti Negara, like the IMP, did not succeed in gaining the support of Malay women (or men). This was in spite of the 23 May 1954 statement of party policy which included equal pay for equal work, equal opportunity and rewards, and the emancipation of women.[180] In January 1959, the party made a last attempt to gain the support of women for the 1959 federal elections. A party spokesman announced that women were crucial to the party for they were one-half of the electorate.[181] This is the last reference to women in the Parti Negara. The party fortunes further declined and it was, in essence, defunct by the 1964 elections.

Besides the IMP, Malaya's other major experiment with non-communal parties was the Pan-Malayan Labour Party formed on 26 June 1952. The PMLP was a loose grouping of many state labour parties that had sprung up as early as 11 May 1951. While at least 71 delegates and observers helped form the PMLP, only 2 observers were women (Mrs S. E. Chia from the Selangor Labour Party and Rahmah binti Salleh from the Operators Union).[182] The Labour Party, so renamed in June 1954, was open to 'all labour and socialist organizations of democratic composition which accept the constitution of the party'.[183] The party, however, had few women members. As the leading opposition party to the UMNO–MCA–MIC Alliance, the LP simply could not woo women away from the communal parties, though the LP would in later years urge the government to: 1) provide equal pay for equal work,[184] 2) enact a Women's Charter to guarantee women's equality in work and marriage,[185] 3) declare International Women's Day a public holiday,[186] and 4) support monogamy for all non-Muslims; such policies were not enough to attract women members. The 1954 change to the party rules, which allowed individuals rather than associations to join, had no effect. As Vasil[187] noted, the bulk of the party support came from the states of Penang, Selangor and Perak. The members were either Indians or English-educated Chinese, white collar workers. In short, the party lacked a mass support base.[188] There seems to have been few attempts to draw in women as members even though the 1954 draft rules had provided for a National Women's Executive Committee. The Committee was to represent women at all levels in the party.[189] Despite the urgings of a few LP leaders who saw housewives as ready-made members of the Labour Party,[190] women still eschewed party membership.

One consequence of the Labour Party was the birth of the Province Wellesley Labour Party on 8 September 1953. This was the first time that a party was organized by a woman, Mrs B. H. Oon—one of the first two women Federal Councillors and the first and only woman elected chairperson of a political party.[191] The Province Wellesley Labour Party never joined the PMLP and failed to play a major role in Malayan politics.

The last non-communal party to be discussed is the Perak Progressive Party (PPP). It was organized by the Seenivasagam brothers in January 1953. While professing to be non-communal, the PPP was, in fact, a party made up largely of Chinese and Indian members who rallied to the personal appeal of the Seenivasagams. During the 1950s, the party made no attempt to form a women's section and no women were included on the party's Central Executive Committee.[192] The PPP claimed 20,000 members in April 1958, though it is not possible to say how many were women.[193] The role of women in the PPP was most likely quite slight given the lack of women participating in the other parties.

Elections: Women as Candidates and Party Workers

Prior to the first municipal elections in 1951, the function of the KI UMNO and the other women's sections had been to strengthen their own organizations and to increase party membership. With the advent of Malayan municipal elections in 1951 and 1952, the importance of women to party fortunes became clear. It was in these first elections that a pattern was set: women would campaign, provide the labour needed to conduct an election, and vote. Only a few would be chosen as party candidates.

The first woman to campaign for elective office was Mrs Malathi Pillai who ran against fourteen men for one of six elective seats on the Singapore Legislative Council in May 1948.[194] She was not successful.

In Malaya, the first city election was held in Georgetown, Penang Island on 1 December 1951. Elections in Penang turned on local issues and personalities. They were of limited national interest.[195] The Kuala Lumpur city elections of February 1952, did attract national attention. The non-communal Independence of Malaya Party (IMP) was opposed by an *ad hoc* alliance between Malaya's two chief communal parties, the UMNO and the MCA. Of the 32 candidates for 12 seats on the council, only 4 were women. Three non-Malay women were fielded by the IMP while an Indian woman was fielded by the UMNO–MCA. None of the women were Malays, for candidates were chosen to appeal to the greatest number of voters. These constituencies were urban and largely non-Malay. Loke Soh-lip, President of the Selangor Women's Athletic Association, Mrs E. Ramachandran, co-founder of the Selangor Indian Association, and Mrs Devaki Krishnan, a teacher and later president of the MIC women's section, were the three IMP candidates. Mrs. L. C. Somasundram, active in the Women's Service League and in the YWCA, was supported by the UMNO–MCA in the Bangsar ward.[196] Only Mrs Devaki Krishnan won; she obtained 53 more votes than the UMNO candidates in her district.[197] Mrs Devaki Krishnan promised to fulfil the election promises of the IMP and further promised that, 'I will interest myself particularly in the lot of women in Kuala Lumpur and in extending the programs of social work already carried out by the municipality'.[198]

Though only four women ran as candidates in the Kuala Lumpur municipal elections, the role of women in the electoral success of party candidates was one of its most prominent features. Malayan women were eager voters. Of the 20 per cent of qualified voters in Kuala Lumpur[199] many of those who voted were women:

> In sari, cheongsam and sarong, they went to the polling stations with dignity and confidence, as though they had been doing it for years and their mothers before them.... The general impression was that the women's minds were clear not only as to the procedure of voting but also as to the way in which they wished to vote.... At Kampong Baru stations crowds of women came early, mostly on foot on their way to market.... Many women of all races took an active part in the various parties last minute efforts to win votes.... Staid Malay women, who seldom appear in public life, sat at tables under party banners and gave out information and literature. Young Chinese girls, looking excited and efficient, checked off voter's names on lists, drove cars and exchanged backchat with rivals....[200]

By December 1952, six other municipal elections had been held in Malacca, Johore Baru, Batu Pahat, Muar, Singapore and again in Kuala Lumpur and Georgetown. Again, women showed a desire to compete for electoral office: of 99 candidates for 37 seats, 9 were women and 6 were elected. Mrs Devaki Krishnan was re-elected to the Kuala Lumpur council, while Mrs Amy Joseph, running on the Labour Party ticket, won in Malacca. Mrs Robert Eu and Mrs Amy Laycock were successful Progressive Party candidates in Singapore. Two UMNO women, Fatimah binti Haji Yunos and Zahara binti Mohamed Talib were elected in Muar and Batu Pahat, respectively. Among the unsuccessful candidates were two Malay women running on the IMP ticket and an Indian woman running on the Indian Socialist Party ticket in Singapore.[201] (She was defeated by Mrs Robert Eu.) Again the turnout by the women was a feature of the elections:

> The most striking feature of the elections yesterday was the way the women of Malaya turned up at the polls. In the six Federation towns of Penang, K.L., Malacca, Batu Pahat, Muar, Johore Bahru and Singapore, they went in the thousands to choose their representatives to the three municipalities, three town councils and city councils.
>
> In Penang, despite the rain, the women cast their votes on the way to do the day's marketing. In Johore Bahru, they defied their husbands and exercised their rights as citizens to have a say in the running of their towns....[202]

Women ran as candidates in local and state elections from 1952 to 1954.[203] The first federal election to the Legislative Council in 1955 clearly set the pattern for future elections: women would campaign, vote and even be successful candidates. None of the parties, though, were willing to put forth female candidates in line with their voting strength. This was understandable from the viewpoint of the non-Malay parties, Chinese male electors outnumbering Chinese females by 2 to 1, and Indian male electors outnumbering Indian females by 4 to 1.[204] This was due mainly to the disparate sex ratio of men to women among the non-Malays as well as to citizenship requirements which prevented many non-Malay women from voting. This was less understandable from the Malay parties' point of view, for Malay male and female electors were equal in number.[205] The reluctance of the UMNO and other Malay parties to put forth Malay women was due to many factors: 1) the party officials did not see Malay women as being proper candidates, 2) competition was severe among the men themselves for each seat and 3) the parties were so sure that Malay women would vote for a Malay or other Alliance candidate that they felt no need to put forth women candidates. While there were no facts to show that women preferred women candidates, it is interesting that the issue did not even arise. Of the 129 candidates seeking the 52 seats on the Federal Legislative Council,[206] only 1 was a woman. Halimahton binti Abdul Majid, president of the KI Selangor and a prominent UMNO member, ran on the Alliance ticket. In her Ulu Selangor district, she polled 5,430 votes against Abdul Rahman bin Haji Maulana (1,160 votes) of Parti Negara.[207]

Women fared only slightly better in the state level elections held from October 1954 to November 1955. UMNO selected three women candidates, two of whom ran uncontested in Kedah: Bibi Aishah binti Hamid Don in Kulim Utara, and Normah binti Kamaruddin in Sik-Gurun.

Ramlah binti Dahlan ran against a PMIP candidate and won easily in Temerloh Selatan, Pahang. The only other woman candidate was an independent, Madam Oei Soie-nio, who was defeated by Dr Lim Chong-eu of the MCA in Kelawai, Penang.[208]

T. E. Smith, writing the official report on the elections, noted that women were 'very active'[209] and presented photographs that showed women canvassing, lining up to vote, and running the information booths.[210] As Asiah[211] noted, it was the KI women who conducted house-to-house campaigns in the villages and encouraged Malay women to vote; it was also the KI who saw to it that voters were transported to the polls. Again, Malay women stood out as eager voters:

> UMNO women played a part in the Alliance campaign. In the fishing village of Kuala Kedah, Kaum Ibu members came out by the hundreds and formed long queues at the polling stations.... Polling in Malacca was very keen, especially among Malay women, both young and old ... while in Penang UMNO women as usual stood out among the voters. Carloads of KI members entered the polling stations.... From an early hour, in Province Wellesley rural areas, hundreds of KI members waited patiently by the roadside for transport to the polling stations. Apart from the eagerness of UMNO women, there was no excitement....[212]

> It was a women's election all right. In brilliant sarongs and headdresses they stood 6 deep cramming the entrances to general offices waiting to cast their votes. There were only two men in the queue.... In Pahang ... polling day was women's day.... They beat the men and often outnumbered them as much as fifty to one in the first hours of voting....[213]

The Alliance swept the election with 80 per cent of the vote in the 51 constituencies and 51 out of 52 seats to the Federal Legislative Council.[214] As Ratnam and Milne noted: 'The outstanding feature of the 1955 election had been the overwhelming victory of the votes cast for UMNO.'[215] Much of the credit must go to the Kaum Ibu and its ability to mobilize female voters. The activities and appeals of its branches as well as to its well-organized electoral efforts (going house-to-house in the Malay villages and bringing voters to the polls) all helped.

The role of the KI in UMNO's electoral successes had always been pointed out by the KI. Repeatedly they have pressed the UMNO leaders to select more KI as party candidates. The question of picking women to serve on elected bodies had first been raised by the KI, in 1949, over the issue of the membership in the Federal Legislative Council.[216] This issue was again, in 1954, at the KI general assembly. KI members called for the setting aside of 5 seats to the KI in the 1955 Federal Legislative Council. Aishah Ghani, a leading KI member, urged UMNO to allow UMNO women to take a more active role in Malayan politics.[217] Following their request for more seats, the KI threatened to boycott the elections if they were not allowed to stand. They were 'fed up with being merely voters every time'.[218] While the 1954 UMNO general assembly passed a resolution which allowed KI members to contest elections,[219] the only woman candidate selected was Halimahton binti Abdul Majid, though three KI were selected as state-level candidates. KI members remained disappointed with having only one woman on the Federal Legislative Council and although they had threatened to boycott the state elections, the KI did not carry out its threat. The KI were, first and foremost, stalwart UMNO supporters and hence did not wish to jeopardize UMNO by such a measure. By having threatened to boycott the state elections and then having declined to do so, the KI by the mid-1950s had shown that as an organization it remained obedient to the party and was not likely to resist party directives.

Women and Post-1955 Political Developments

The 1955 election campaign of the Alliance focused on self-government for Malaya within two years and a commission to draft a constitution for independence within four years. From 18 January to 8 February 1956, an eight-member Malayan delegation was composed from 4 representatives of the Rulers and 4 from the Alliance government. They met with the British High Commissioner, the Colonial Secretary and the Minister of State for the United Kingdom, to discuss the steps to attain independence. There were few points of contention[220] with self-government. It was to be effected upon closure of the conference on 8 February 1956. The British advisers to the Rulers were withdrawn and all functions of government, aside from Malaya's external security were passed to the Malayans. On 31 August 1957, Malaya became independent.

The government retained a federal form with the rights of the states clearly subordinate to the federal government. A parliamentary system was chosen with an elected lower house (Dewan Rakyat—104 seats) and a partially elected upper house (Dewan Negara—38 seats: 2 elected by each of the 11 state assemblies, and 16 appointed by the King). The Dewan Rakyat was stronger with full legislative powers over justice, external affairs, finance and defence. The Dewan Negara, modelled after the British House of Lords, lacked the power to veto lower house legislation. The sultans and chief ministers of Penang and Malacca now comprised the Conference of Rulers. Once every five years, they would choose a king from among themselves. The Rulers remained heads of Islam in their states and, through the Conference of Rulers, were permitted to discuss matters of national policy (for example, immigration) and to agree or disagree with the change of any religious acts.[221] The king became the head of state (as a constitutional monarch) and his powers included the appointing of the prime minister, withholding consent to a request for dissolving Parliament, and setting meetings of the Conference of Rulers.[222] The third arm of government, the judiciary, was independent; judges were subject to removal only under the most serious circumstances.

The issue of liberties raised the most problems. The so-called Malay privileges introduced by the British were retained under Article 153 of the constitution. The privileges included quotas for public scholarships, the licensing of certain businesses, posts in the public services, and Malay reservation lands (lands that cannot be sold to non-Malays). While privileges were retained, citizenship was also extended. Non-Malays could apply for and obtain citizenship. Further, all persons born in Malaya after 1957 would be natural citizens.

Women had little to do with writing the constitution. Negotiations within the Alliance and between the Malayans and the British were done solely by the élites of both groups. These élites excluded women since women did not occupy high positions within the parties or government. Women were largely party members giving tacit support to male party leaders. KI leaders lent their support by garnering Malay support for UMNO. Khadijah Sidek, for instance, exhorted KI women at the 29 January 1955 KI meeting in Malacca. She stressed the importance of the 1955 federal elections to independence.[223]

Women did not object to the constitution and did not protest the lack of guarantees for equality of the sexes. In fact, it was an editorial in the Malay language paper, *Utusan Melayu*, that queried the omission.[224] Article 8 Clause(2) prohibits discrimination on the basis of religion, race, descent, or place of birth; it omits the basis of sex.[225] The omission continues to this day. Women leaders explained their position on Article 8 by saying, 'Yes, it should be changed', but it is not a major point. There are 'few cases' of sex discrimination. Women leaders approved the constitution; one woman on the Federal Legislative Council, Halimahton binti Abdul Majid, even gave her support during the Legislative Council debates held from July to August 1957.[226]

Conclusion

The first decade after World War II saw the birth of many women's social and political associations, but only a few of these have survived. Several of the welfare associations, such as the Women's Institutes and the YWCA still exist. These have pushed for an improved status for Malayan women. Other organizations, especially those with political goals, simply vanished. Only the KI UMNO grew and took an active part in the politics of the 1950s.

A number of points can be concluded from the early women's political organizations: 1) The participation of women, aside from voting and holding appointive office, was through activities of the party auxiliaries. Women unattached to an auxiliary, did not play a role in the politics of the 1940s and 1950s. The major women figures, Puteh Mariah, Ibu Zain, Aishah Ghani, Mrs Devaki Krishnan and others, all were involved with one political organization or another. 2) Without a separate auxiliary, women had only a minor part in party affairs. A women's auxiliary seemed to encourage female party membership. 3) Women's groups formed largely along communal lines as did the parties. Of these, only the KI UMNO successfully mobilized women as party members and voters. Yet, the KI played a limited party role and was subject to party discipline.

The KI was the main example of the power women could wield and the limits put on that power. KI members campaigned and voted in large numbers but were rarely chosen as party candidates or sat on important party committees. Despite such limitations, the KI organized Malay women into an indispensable section of the major Malay political party.

The KI success in organizing Malay women mostly stemmed from the impetus to Malay nationalism. After the war, the colonial government faced a legitimacy crisis.[227] The MU proposals were the colonial government's response; they, though, were perceived by the Malay community as a threat to its very survival. UMNO, a party born of the crisis was a tool to mobilize a mass nationalist movement to oppose the MU proposals and press for independence. The KI emerged because the threat was perceived to be so great as to almost demand the expanded public role of women. Malay nationalists saw the KI as vital to their efforts. To challenge the colonial government, Malay leaders had to prove that they did indeed represent the Malay people. As Rupert Emerson[228] noted:

> Their legitimacy in the eyes of their imperial opponents, and no doubt, in their own as well, rested in very considerable part on their ability to demonstrate that they had the mass of their people behind them. If it could be established that they spoke for a nation with the blessing of its people, their moral claim to take over approached the irrefutable. To this moral aspect of their struggle must be added the hard political fact that if they were to represent enough of a political force to have a serious impact on the imperial power whose position they contested, they must be able to enlist the masses in battle behind them.

Women were 50 per cent of the 'masses' to be so enlisted. The success of the Malay opposition to the MU proposals opened the way for an active women's section within, but subordinate to, UMNO. The KI, in turn, gained from the support and encouragement they received from leaders such as Datuk Onn and Tunku Abdul Rahman. Such support legitimatized the KI and made the wing acceptable to Malay society. Not only was it patriotic for women to join the KI, it was also accepted socially.

By the 1950s, the KI proved to be vital to UMNO–Alliance fortunes, both as election workers and voters. Neither fact was lost on party leaders who gave much verbal support to the KI. Another factor leading to KI success was the core of educated Malay women who provided the section with dedicated and capable leaders. Puteh Mariah, Ibu Zain, Halimahton, and Khadijah Sidek, to name just a few, provided the leadership needed for the KI's growth. In sum, the KI was both vital to the nationalist effort and to the fortunes of the party.

In contrast, an effective Chinese women's political wing during the 1950s was prevented by a number of factors: 1) The post-war political crisis faced by the Chinese was different from that experienced by the Malays. The Emergency, and the measures taken to curb it (the deportations, detentions, creation of 'new villages' and the ban on numerous organizations) all served to dissuade the Chinese from taking part in political activity. For Chinese men and women, the Emergency simply reinforced beliefs that politics were best avoided. 2) For many Chinese, there was still little allegiance to Malaya. Loyalty was directed towards China, the land to which many hoped to return. Thus a certain amount of indifference towards Malayan politics retarded the growth of Chinese political organizations. 3) Chinese male leaders did little to bring women into party politics during the late 1940s and 1950s. Such encouragement was vital not only to motivate the women to become involved, but also to legitimatize their involvement. 4) The lack of homogeneity among the Chinese was a problem. The Chinese were divided by clan, language, education and membership in associations. The problem existed for women as well as men. 5) Cultural assumptions about a woman's place kept most Chinese women firmly in the home and out of politics. During the post-war years, Chinese women were denied access to important posts within the business and merchant classes. Chinese male leaders emerged from these classes. It is no surprise that one finds little evidence of activities by Chinese women; there were simply too many obstacles.

Few Indian women took part in politics during the decade following World War II. Indian women shared the same problems as Chinese women. Indian women, despite their experience in the Indian Independent League, became depoliticized after the war. In part, this reflected a desire to return to normal day-to-day living; in part, it also reflected a fear of politics once colonial rule was re-established. The climate created by the Emergency and the later government crackdowns made politics a risky business. Indian women who had been active in the INA feared British reaction to their wartime activities. As with the Chinese, the Emergency was viewed as a political crisis; neither Indian men nor women saw a reason for expanding the traditional domestic roles. Lastly, Indian women were given little encouragement by male leaders. The MIC has been, in the words of a MIC official, very much a 'leader-led' party. The members closely followed the guidance of its leader. While it is agreed that John Thivy, the first president, encouraged women to join, his successor, Sardar Budh Singh (1947–50) and later leaders, did little to encourage women. Until Manickavasagam became president of the party in 1973, little was done to bring women into the party.

The history of women and politics during the first decade to follow World War II was dominated by the activities of Malay women in the Kaum Ibu UMNO. Non-Malay women, despite a few efforts, remained outside the political system. The next chapter takes up the history of the Kaum Ibu and other women's groups which emerged from 1957 to 1969; the years that led from independence to crisis.

1. K. J. Ratnam, *Communalism and the Political Process in Malaya*, Singapore, University of Malaya Press, 1965, p. 43.
2. Halinah Bamadhaj, 'The Impact of the Japanese Occupation of Malaya on Malay Society and Politics 1941–45', unpublished MA thesis, University of Auckland, 1975, pp. 185–223.
3. See, Gordon Means, *Malaysian Politics*, London, University of London Press, 1970; R. S. Milne, *Government and Politics in Malaysia*, Boston, Houghton Mifflin Co., 1967; Mohamed Noordin Sopiee, *From Malayan Union to Singapore Separation 1945–65*, Kuala Lumpur, University of Malaya Press, 1974.
4. W. R. Roff, *The Origins of Malay Nationalism*, Kuala Lumpur, University of Malaya Press, 1974, p. 12.
5. Mohamed Noordin Sopiee, op. cit., p. 13.
6. In 1824, Britain united the three territories of Malacca, Singapore and Penang into the Straits Settlements (SS). In 1896, the Federated Malay States (FMS) of Pahang, Perak, Selangor and Negri Sembilan was formed. Those states remaining outside of these unions, namely Kelantan, Kedah, Johore, Perlis and Trengganu became known as the Unfederated Malay States (UMS).
7. W. R. Roff, *Malay Nationalism*, p. 16.
8. K. Von Vorys, *Democracy Without Consensus*, Princeton, Princeton University Press, 1975, p. 65.
9. For details on the Malayan Union proposals see Ratnam, op. cit.; Mohamed Noordin Sopiee, op. cit.; and J. Allen, *The Malayan Union*, New Haven, Yale University, South East Asian Studies Monograph Series No. 10, Yale University Press, 1967.
10. Mohamed Noordin Sopiee, op. cit., p. 25.
11. Ibid.
12. *UMNO/SG 49/47*, Senarai-senarai Fail-fail, Kuala Lumpur, 1946–62.
13. *British Malaya*, August 1946, Vol. 21, No. 4, p. 53.
14. *Straits Times (ST)*, 25 May 1946.
15. *ST*, 30 May 1946.
16. *ST*, 3 June 1946.
17. Interview with Halimahton binti Abdul Majid on 16 September 1976.
18. The Malayan Women's Service League, the National Association of Women's Institutes, and the Young Women's Christian Association, each of which has been briefly described in the Appendix.
19. Interview with Aishah Ghani on 1 March 1976.
20. Asiah binti Abu Samah, 'Emancipation of Malay Women 1945–57', unpublished BA (Hons.) thesis, University of Malaya, 1960, p. 13.
21. *UMNO/SG 94/96*, the Malay Nationalist Party.
22. Interview with Aishah Ghani, 1 March 1976.
23. *Malaya Tribune (MT)*, 3 April 1946.
24. Asiah binti Abu Samah, op. cit., p. 15.
25. *MT*, 18 April 1946.
26. Asiah binti Abu Samah, op. cit., p. 14.
27. Ahmad Boestamam, *Merintis Jalan Ke Punchak (Shortcut to the Top)*, Kuala Lumpur, Penerbitan Pustaka Kejora, 1972, pp. 74–5.
28. *MT*, 21 February 1947.
29. *MT*, 26 July 1947.
30. *MT*, 24 July 1948.
31. Asiah binti Abu Samah, op. cit., p. 14.
32. Ibid., p. 25.
33. Interview with Halimahton binti Abdul Majid, 16 September 1976. She estimates that by 1947 there were 4,000–5,000 members of the Kaum Ibu in Negri Sembilan.
34. Asiah binti Abu Samah, op. cit., p. 25.
35. 'Majlis', 12 March 1946, in *Summaries of the Vernacular Press*, Malayan Union Files 1099/46, subsequently to be referred to as *S.V.P.* 1946.
36. Asiah binti Abu Samah, op. cit., p. 25.

37. *Utusan Melayu*, 18 November 1946, *S.V.P.* 1946.
38. 'Majlis', 28 November 1946, *S.V.P.* 1946.
39. 'Majlis', 5 December 1946, *S.V.P.* 1946.
40. *UMNO/SG 83/1946*.
41. *UMNO/SG 47/1946*, No. 28.
42. Interview with Puteh Mariah on 30 August 1976.
43. Interview with Ibu Zain on 19 October 1976.
44. Interview with Ibu Zain on 19 October 1976.
45. *ST*, 25 March 1948.
46. *Information Department Malaya Files 1945–1948*, 347/48, Kuala Lumpur, Arkib Negara.
47. Asiah binti Abu Samah, op. cit., p. 26.
48. *UMNO/ED 4/46*.
49. *Buku Cenderamata Jubli Perak Wanita UMNO Malaysia pada 25hb Ogos 1974*, Utusan Melayu Berhad, Kuala Lumpur, 1974.
50. *ST*, 5 December 1946.
51. Interview with Puteh Mariah, 30 August 1976.
52. *UMNO/F 30/47*.
53. *UMNO/SG 161/47*. Kaum Ibu Secretaries Annual Report from 1 January 1947. The 14 organizations were: the Pergerakan Melayu Semenanjong Johore, the Persatuan Melayu Kluang, the Pergerakan Melayu Semenanjong Melaka, the Pergerakan Kebangsaan Melayu Selangor, the Persekutuan Melayu Negri Sembilan, the Darul Ihsan Club Jeram, the Persatuan Kaum Ibu Selangor, the Persatuan Melayu Daerah Sabak Bernam, the Persatuan Melayu Pahang, the Persekutuan Melayu Ulu Selangor, the Perikatan Melayu Perak, the Kesatuan Melayu Kedah, Saberkas Kedah and the Persatuan Melayu Perlis, *UMNO/SG 161/194*.
54. *UMNO/SG 62/48/4*.
55. *UMNO/GA 24/47*.
56. Asiah binti Abu Samah, op. cit., p. 29.
57. *UMNO/SG 161/1947*.
58. For details on the Federation of Malaya Agreement, see Means, *Malaysian Politics*, pp. 55–6.
59. Mohamed Nordin Sopiee, op. cit., p. 39.
60. George M. Kahin, *Government and Politics of Southeast Asia*, Ithaca, NY, Cornell University Press, 1969, p. 292.
61. *Malay Mail*, 1 December 1947.
62. Government of Malayan Union, *Proceedings of the Advisory Council of the Malayan Union, July 1946–48*, Kuala Lumpur, Government Printer, 1948, p. 288.
63. *UMNO/SG 32/47*, *Report of the Consultative Committee: together with the Proceedings of six Public Meetings, a Summary of Representations made and Letters and Memorandam considered by the Committee*, Malayan Union. Government Printer. Also see, *MT*, 24 December 1946.
64. Interview with Puteh Mariah, 30 August 1976.
65. *ST*, 24 January 1946.
66. *ST*, 15 April 1948.
67. *ST*, 16 October 1946.
68. Dr Soo Kim-lan was one of the first women doctors in Malaya. In addition to serving on the Advisory Council, she was responsible for establishing the first Chinese maternity hospital in Kuala Lumpur, a hospital which still functions. Interview with Dr Soo Kim-lan on 12 July 1976.
69. *Proceedings of the Advisory Council of the Malayan Union, July 1946–48*, p. 67.
70. Ibid., pp. 179–80.
71. *ST*, 13 January 1948.
72. *ST*, 31 January 1948. Interview with Puteh Mariah, 30 August 1976.
73. *Malay Mail*, 9 February 1948.
74. *ST*, 13 January 1948.

75. *Malay Mail*, 16 March 1951.
76. *MT*, 22 April 1949.
77. *MT*, 23 March 1948.
78. *Malay Mail*, 16 March 1951.
79. *UMNO/KL 3/49*.
80. *UMNO/SG 123/49*.
81. *UMNO/SG 123/49*.
82. *UMNO/SG 123/49*.
83. *UMNO/SG 123/49*.
84. *UMNO/KL 3/49*.
85. *UMNO/KL 3/49*.
86. *UMNO/KL 3/49*.
87. *MT*, 1 June 1949 and *UMNO/SG 13/49*.
88. *Utusan Melayu*, 18 September 1952 in *Daily Highlights of the Malay, Chinese and Tamil Press, September 1952–December 1957*, subsequently to be referred to as *D.H.P.*
89. Asiah binti Abu Samah, op. cit., p. 32.
90. *Utusan Melayu*, 23 September 1952, *D.H.P.*
91. *Utusan Melayu*, 23 September 1952, *D.H.P.*
92. *Utusan Melayu*, 19 September 1952, *D.H.P.* and Asiah binti Abu Samah, op. cit., p. 32.
93. Asiah binti Abu Samah, op. cit., p. 33.
94. *UMNO/SG 138/53*.
95. *UMNO/SG 10/50/19*.
96. *UMNO/SG 67/53*.
97. *UMNO/SG 138/53*.
98. Interview with Khadijah Sidek on 26 July 1976 and Ardjasni (Sidek), 'Communalism in Malaya', part 7 of 'Riwayat Hidup Saya: My Life', *Eastern Horizon*, July 1962, Vol. 2, No. 7, p. 56.
99. *Melayu Raya*, Editorial, 8 April 1953, *D.H.P.*, and interview with Khadijah Sidek, 26 July 1976.
100. Interview with Khadijah Sidek, 26 July 1976.
101. *UMNO/SG 178/53*.
102. *ST*, 3 August 1955.
103. *Utusan Melayu*, 12 November 1954, *D.H.P.*
104. *Utusan Melayu*, 12 November 1954, *D.H.P.*
105. *ST*, 5 August 1955.
106. *ST*, 5 August 1955.
107. *ST*, 11 August 1955.
108. *ST*, 17 August 1955.
109. *ST*, 17 August 1955.
110. *ST*, 12 October 1956.
111. *ST*, 12 October 1956.
112. *Malay Mail*, 18 October 1956.
113. *ST*, 15 October 1956 and *ST*, 23 October 1956.
114. *ST*, 15 October 1956 and *ST*, 23 October 1956.
115. *Malay Mail*, 22 October 1956.
116. *Malay Mail*, 22 October 1956.
117. *ST*, 12 November 1956.
118. *Suara UMNO* (*Voice of UMNO*), 15 May 1951, p. 9.
119. Asiah binti Abu Samah, op. cit., p. 35. It might be argued that a KI membership of 13,000 as compared to roughly 90,000 male members was a small or insignificant membership. It should be remembered that the KI represented one of the first attempts at political organization by Malay women—women who had had no previous political experience and more importantly, who traditionally had been subordinate to men in all areas of activity. KI members viewed from the perspective of political pioneers and in terms of the activities they performed for the party, were a significant number and were vital to UMNO.

120. *Suara UMNO*, 15 May 1951, p. 9.
121. *Buku Cenderamata Jubli Perak Wanita UMNO Malaysia pada 25hb Ogos 1974*, p. 8.
122. *ST*, 14 January 1946.
123. *ST*, 24 January 1946. Note no woman was appointed.
124. *MT*, 27 April 1946 and *MT*, 28 April 1946.
125. *Kin Kwok*, 20 November 1946, *S.V.P.* 1946.
126. V. Thompson and R. Adloff, *The Leftwing in Southeast Asia*, New York, William Sloane Associates, 1950, p. 146.
127. *ST*, 23 October 1947.
128. *MT*, 12 March 1947.
129. *MT*, 12 February 1947.
130. *MT*, 23 October 1946.
131. *MT*, 12 March 1947.
132. Thompson and Adloff, op. cit., p. 146.
133. Margaret Roff, 'The Malayan Chinese Association 1948-65', *JSEAH*, September 1965, Vol. 6, No. 2, p. 41.
134. *China Press*, 12 June 1946, *S.V.P.* 1946.
135. MCA, *1st Set of Rules of the MCA, Passed June 12, 1949*, Clause 17(1), *Private Papers of Tan Cheng-lock*, Arkib Negara Malaysia.
136. MCA, *Presidential Address of Annual Meeting of (the) Central General Committee of (the) MCA, 21 April 1951* and *Sunday Standard*, 22 April 1951; *Private Papers of Tan Cheng-lock*.
137. *Malayan Mirror*, Vol. 11, 15 November 1953.
138. *Malayan Mirror*, Vol. 11, 15 November 1953.
139. *Malayan Mirror*, Vol. 2, No. 16, 1 September 1954.
140. *Malayan Mirror*, Vol. 2, No. 16, 1 September 1954.
141. *Malayan Mirror*, Vol. 2, No. 16, 1 September 1954.
142. *Malayan Mirror*, Vol. 2, No. 22, 1 December 1954.
143. *Malayan Mirror*, Vol. 2, No. 22, 1 December 1954.
144. *Malayan Mirror*, Vol. 21, 4 November 1955.
145. *ST*, 2 July 1956. Note Gunn Chit-wha does not recall being appointed Chairwoman of a MCA's women section. Interview with author on 7 September 1976.
146. Amarjit Kaur, 'North Indians in Malaya: A Study of their Economic, Social and Political Activities with Special Reference to Selangor 1870s-1940s', unpublished MA thesis, University of Malaya, 1973, p. 249.
147. *MT*, 29 April 1946.
148. *MT*, 29 April 1946.
149. Interview with Janaky Nahappan on 23 September 1976.
150. MIC, *Constitution of the MIC, 1946*, Paragraphs 10a, 10g and 12d. Collected Papers of John Thivy, Kuala Lumpur, University of Malaya Library.
151. Nahappan distinctly remembers his urging women to join. Interview with author on 23 September 1976.
152. *Tamil Nesan*, 20 November 1946, *S.V.P.* 1946.
153. MIC, *MIC Ulangtahun Ketiga-puluh 1946-1976 (MIC Thirty Year Yearbook 1946-1976)*, Kuala Lumpur, MIC, n.d., p. 33. Mrs Lobo, a representative from Singapore was the first woman to join the Council in 1948.
154. Interview with Mrs Devaki Krishnan, Secretary of the Wanita MIC and historian for the Wanita MIC, 6 July 1976.
155. Prefers not to be mentioned by name.
156. Interview with Mrs Devaki Krishnan on 6 July 1976. Note there are no official membership figures for this period.
157. *Malay Mail*, 28 December 1956.
158. *Malay Mail*, 11 November 1955.
159. *ST*, 29 January 1957.
160. *ST*, 23 August 1958.
161. *Malay Mail*, 6 August 1956.

162. *ST*, 17 September 1951.
163. R. K. Vasil, *Politics in a Plural Society*, Kuala Lumpur, Oxford University Press, 1971, p. 50.
164. *ST*, 23 June 1951.
165. Vasil, op. cit., p. 55.
166. Ibid., p. 51 and interview with Puteh Mariah, 30 August 1976.
167. *UMNO/SG 137/51*.
168. *ST*, 3 September 1951.
169. *ST*, 7 September 1951.
170. *Misc. Publication of the IMP*, 6 September 1951.
171. *ST*, 28 October 1951.
172. *Tamil Murasu*, 6 January 1956, *D.H.P.*
173. *ST*, 17 July 1952.
174. Vasil, op. cit., pp. 74-82.
175. *ST*, 1 March 1954.
176. *ST*, 4 April 1955.
177. *ST*, 10 August 1955.
178. *ST*, 10 August 1955.
179. Interview with Puteh Mariah, 30 August 1976.
180. Parti Negara, 'Statement of Party Negara Policy, 23 May 1954', Objective 5, sections 3, 5, and 7, mimeograph, Kuala Lumpur, PN, NST Library.
181. *Malay Mail*, 3 January 1959.
182. Labour Party, *Report on the Foundation of the Pan-Malayan Labour Party, 26 June 1952*, Kuala Lumpur, LP, NST Library.
183. Quoted in Vasil, op. cit., p. 101.
184. Labour Party, *1955 Election Manifesto of the Labour Party*.
185. Labour Party, *Report of the 10th Annual Party Conference, August 18-19 1962*, Malaya, LP, NST Library.
186. Labour Party, *The 1959 Annual Report of the Labour Party*, Malaya, LP, NST Library.
187. Vasil, op. cit., p. 110.
188. Ibid., p. 141.
189. *Malay Mail*, 21 February 1954.
190. *ST*, 7 August 1955.
191. *ST*, 8 September 1953 and *ST*, 22 September 1953.
192. *ST*, 16 March 1956.
193. *Sunday Standard*, 8 April 1958.
194. *MT*, 29 January 1948; *ST*, 20 March 1948 and *ST*, 22 May 1948.
195. Means, *Malaysian Politics*, p. 132.
196. *Malay Mail*, 15 February 1952.
197. *Malay Mail*, 17 February 1952.
198. *Malay Mail*, 15 February 1952.
199. One-tenth of the adult population in Kuala Lumpur. *ST*, 15 February 1952.
200. *ST*, 17 February 1952.
201. *Malay Mail*, 7 December 1952.
202. *ST*, 7 December 1952.
203. *Malay Mail*, 23 June 1953, 13 August 1953. Mrs Wong Nook-ying was elected to the Perak State Council in June 1953 and Tengku Asiah binti Tengku Muda Chik was elected in 1953 to her second term in the Negri Sembilan State Council.
204. T. E. Smith, *Report on the 1st Election of Members to the Legislative Council of the Federation of Malaya, 1955*, Kuala Lumpur, Government Printer, 1955, p. 11.
205. Ibid.
206. Fifty-two of the 99 seats were elective.
207. Smith, op. cit., p. 66.
208. L. Manderson, 'The Development of the Pergerakan Kaum Ibu UMNO

1945-1972', unpublished doctoral dissertation, Australian National University, 1977, p. 196.
209. Smith, op. cit., p. 26.
210. Ibid., pp. 20, 21 and 25.
211. Asiah binti Abu Samah, op. cit., p. 30.
212. *ST*, 28 July 1955.
213. *ST*, 28 July 1955.
214. Smith, op. cit., p. 30.
215. R. J. Ratnam and R. S. Milne, *The Malayan Parliamentary Election of 1964*, Kuala Lumpur, University of Malaya Press, 1969, p. 13.
216. UMNO, *Minutes of the Kaum Ibu, Arau, May 1949*, p. 6.
217. *ST*, 16 October 1954.
218. *ST*, 18 October 1954.
219. *UMNO/KL 7/55* (Motions Passed at the UMNO General Assembly Pulau Pinang, 16-17 October 1954).
220. Means, *Malaysian Politics*, p. 171.
221. Mohamed Suffian bin Hashim, *An Introduction to the Constitution of Malaysia*, Kuala Lumpur, Government Printer, 1976, p. 46.
222. Ibid., p. 22.
223. *Suara UMNO*, 1 February 1955.
224. *Utusan Melayu*, 18 July 1957, *D.H.P.*
225. Mohamed Suffian bin Hashim, op. cit., pp. 214-15.
226. *Legislative Council Debates Official Report of the 2nd Legislative Council and Session, October 1956-August 1957* in *Proceedings of the Federal Legislative Council, 1948-1959*, Kuala Lumpur, Government Printer, pp. 2997-8.
227. J. La Palombara and M. Weiner (eds.), *Political Parties and Political Development*, Princeton, N. J., Princeton University Press, 1966, p. 16.
228. Rupert Emerson, 'Nationalism and Political Development', *Journal of Politics*, February 1960, Vol. 22, p. 16.

5 Independence to Political Crisis, 1957–1969

FROM Malayan Independence, in 1957 until the racial riots of 1969, a number of women's political associations grew. It was also a period of further growth for the KI UMNO. In part, the KI's success lay in the nature of the Malayan party system—a one-party dominant system with UMNO being the major party. Credit need also be given to the efforts of the KI women themselves who built the organization that laboured long and hard in support of the UMNO. Though vital to UMNO's fortunes, the KI had little power or leverage within the party that depended so much upon it. Party constraints and the Malay culture acted through the power élite in UMNO to render the KI weak.

While the KI was the key women's association at this time, it was by no means the only one. Other women's groups would also form and grow. Though smaller than the KI, these associations were also wings of political parties. They raised issues of concern to Malayan women and shared similar problems with the KI. For the most part, these women's wings belonged to Malaya's opposition parties—both those with an all-Malay base and those composed of non-Malays. As for the MCA and MIC, their efforts during these years remained minimal: women played almost no role within those parties. Yet, the history of these auxiliaries is needed to understand the nature of women's political participation in Malaysia. What emerges is a major political role for Malay women and a limited involvement for non-Malay women. During this period, a related development was the forming of the National Council of Women's Organizations (NCWO). The NCWO was an umbrella organization of both political and non-political women's groups. It even succeeded in bridging communal differences. As the women's political wings provided the bulk of the NCWO membership, the question remained: could this body provide the means by which women could find their common interests and solve their common problems?

The Kaum Ibu UMNO

In 1949, those groups which comprised UMNO merged as one organization. With this move, the structure adopted by the party was copied by its youth and women's wings. Except for minor changes, the KI would remain the same from 1949 to the present. A study of this structure reveals that the KI, in spite of numerical strength and importance to party fortunes, remained subject to the needs and authority of the parent party. Changes in UMNO's constitution in 1956 and 1960, while having an impact on the KI, made little difference to the section's stance *vis-à-vis* the party. Women within UMNO had little power beyond those matters which related to the KI.

UMNO, the Pemuda and the Kaum Ibu were formed as a hierarchy in which communications and control ran vertically through the levels: from the national level through the states, divisions, and to the branches. In each of the three parallel organizations, the branch (*cawangan*) was the lowest level. KI branches could be formed where there was an UMNO branch.[1] Women sixteen years of age and older could join. Prior to the 1956 UMNO constitution, a woman who joined the KI also became an UMNO member. She remained ineligible for UMNO party offices (as opposed to all KI offices), though. After 1956, a woman who joined UMNO would become a member of the KI. From that year, KI members could stand for elective office at all levels within both the KI and UMNO. They could also attend either KI or UMNO branch meetings though the women seldom attended the branch meetings. KI members at their branch annual assemblies elected their branch executive committee, a leader (*ketua*), deputy leader (*naib ketua*), secretary (*setiausaha*), treasurer (*bendahari*) and from three to five committee members.[2] The women also elected two members to represent their branch at the next higher level, the KI division (*bahagian*). It was the branch that held the literacy, sewing and cooking classes which attracted women to join UMNO, and it was the branches which would be set in motion for the elections. Members of one KI branch seldom had contact with members of other KI branches; horizontal contact at all levels within UMNO was minimal. Each KI branch had to account to its UMNO branch committee; the KI branch *ketua* was an automatic member of that committee. UMNO oversaw its wing's activities at the branch level by having the UMNO branch chairperson act as chair of the KI branch assembly.

Above the branch was the KI division or *bahagian*. Though the ratio of KI to UMNO members changed, the combined numbers in an UMNO division was about 500. KI executive committees consisted of four officers and a number of members elected by the women at the division's yearly assembly. The division executive committee would oversee the affairs of the branches. They also co-ordinated the party's political work, i.e. election activities, party training courses, etc. The division's annual assembly was attended by 2 women from each branch, members of the incumbent division committee, and up to 3 non-voting members from the parallel UMNO division committee. The KI division delegates elected 3 members to the parallel UMNO division committee. The KI division members also elected 3 women to the parallel UMNO division assembly and 2 women to the KI national general assembly.[3] Under the 1956 rules of the KI (which were in effect from 1956 to 1960), the division assemblies elected not more than 3 members each to the state level KI general assembly.[4] It was here at the division assembly that the delegates: 1) worked to elect KI electoral candidates, 2) decided on the resolutions to be forwarded to the national level of the KI, and 3) relayed party information from the state and national levels back to the branches. At the division level, the way the KI related to UMNO paralleled the branch with one change: party control was maintained by the UMNO division secretary serving as the KI secretary. This pattern was repeated at the national level. As KI women stressed, the secretary almost always left all responsibility to the KI assistant secretary. In fact, he had little to do with the affairs of the KI division.

Through the years (except 1956–60), power in UMNO was controlled by the UMNO division 'chairman'. All UMNO national leaders had, as a base for their power, the support and control of at least one division. It was the division chairpersons, almost always men, who held the top posts in UMNO and who served on UMNO's most important committees. The fear of a rival base of power prevented division leaders from encouraging the growth of KI divisions despite the KI's support for the party. During the 1950s and early 1960s, KI divisions numbered about one-half those of UMNO. (In 1955–6, UMNO had 76 divisions while the KI had 38.)[5] UMNO sources claim this disparity lay with the fear of UMNO division leaders to form KI sections which would cleave UMNO and thus weaken the party.[6] This view is ironic given that the KI had yet to prove any real threat to any UMNO division. Instead, it was a fairly compliant and stable section.

Prior to 1956, the UMNO constitution placed KI divisions under the control of the related UMNO divisions which in turn were under the direct control of party headquarters (the Supreme Council of UMNO). State liaison committees existed to co-ordinate the affairs of the divisions and relay party policy to the party members. Largely to strengthen party control over the section,[7] a new party constitution was adopted in 1956. The provisions which applied to the KI were: 1) women joined the party first as UMNO members and so became KI members, and 2) the divisions were to report to state executive committees which were to oversee their affairs. The KI state executive committees and annual assemblies were structured to parallel the divisions and branches. The executive committee was elected at an annual assembly attended by two members from each KI division in the state, the outgoing state executive committee, and leaders of the divisions. These state level organizations existed for only four years (1956–60). They were then replaced by the resurrected state liaison committees.[8] These committees lacked decision-making powers—their main function was to pass information and to act as a go-between for the KI divisions and the KI national executive committee. The state executive committees were aided from 1957 to 1964 by regional leaders, Malaya being divided into north, south, east and central sections.[9]

Above the state liaison committees lay the KI national assembly and the KI National Executive Committee. The KI assembly met annually (just before the UMNO general assembly). It was attended by one to three delegates from each division (which included the KI division leader), the incumbent executive committee, and not more than three, non-voting, members from the UMNO Supreme Council.[10] Supreme authority for the KI was supposed to rest with the general assembly; in fact, it lay with the KI Executive Committee whose members were elected at the annual assemblies. Those women with the most influence at the division level were elected to the KI Executive Committee. The most powerful woman becoming the *Ketua*, or Leader, of the KI. The *Ketua*, after 1951, was aided by 4 assistants whom she appointed.[11] This committee expanded and became the executive committee of the KI. Aside from the eight women on the committee, the UMNO secretary-general was also a member as the official KI secretary.[12] When queried as to the need of his presence on that body, some KI women replied that it was needed at first because of their lack of experience in running a section. Others replied that it was one way that the party 'kept its eye' on their section. In fact, the secretary-general has always delegated almost all his power to the KI assistant secretary. He was present at KI meetings largely as a party spokesperson—there to present the party's policies and views. As at other levels, the KI national assembly was chaired by an UMNO representative until 1967 when the KI elected their own chairperson.

At all levels, the KI's role within UMNO was limited. Prior to the 1956 constitution, the KI general assembly elected 2 delegates to the UMNO general assembly. With the 1956 constitution, the nature of the KI and Pemuda representation was altered. The Pemuda was given 24 seats[13] and the KI was given 1 seat for every 750 members.[14] At the branch and division levels, women were able to compete for any office within the party. The change in the constitution, while it did not produce any action on the part of the KI, did cause UMNO women concern over losing what they saw as their rights. The UMNO secretary-general released a letter to all KI assistant secretaries which explained the change. In the letter, he argued that the change was not an attempt to weaken their organization but rather was an effort to 'give the KI a greater opportunity to participate in the UMNO body proper'.[15] While uneasy, the KI, submitted to party authority and accepted the change.

The revoking of the 1956 UMNO constitution and its replacement in 1960 by a new constitution resulted in little change for the KI. The UMNO national leaders attempted to stop the concentrating of power in the hands of the members of the state executive committees. They abolished these committees as decision-making bodies with the 1960 constitution. Once again, the state level performed as liaison bodies while the division again became the main decision-making body. Delegates to the UMNO general assembly would be appointed by the divisions and not at the state level.[16] For the KI and Pemuda, the change meant once again a fixed representation within the party. Each section was given 3 seats in the general assembly while UMNO men were allowed 1 seat per division for the first 500 members and an extra seat for each added 750 members.[17] Except for the Selangor, Malacca, and Trengganu KI organizations, the KI supported the UMNO decision to revoke the 1956 constitution. Any split within the auxiliary was healed at the KI general assembly where KI *Ketua* Fatimah Hashim calmed KI fears.[18] Changes in the party constitution, however, had little real effect on the role of the KI in UMNO.

Study of party records, shows that the role of women within UMNO remained small. In 1956, 43 UMNO divisions which filed reports had no women as chairpersons or secretaries.[19] Other party records for 1957, 1958, 1961 and 1963 to 1967, show that only 2 women have ever headed UMNO divisions. In fact, Aishah Ghani led the Kuala Lumpur Bandar division for 18 years (1964–82).[20] After 1956, KI women could run for any UMNO office. Party records, though, show that KI members were very seldom elected to party posts.[21] During these years UMNO division committees had at least 20 members and never averaged more than 2 or 3 KI.[22] Except for 3 divisions which had KI treasurers, the KI remained grossly underrepresented at the division level. At the state level, the state committees consisted of about 14–20 members. Only once was a woman a deputy leader; while only 2 women ever served on state committees.[23] From 1960 to 1970 when UMNO had formed regional level committees, no women ever sat on the 4 five-member committees.[24] KI members were seldom chosen as UMNO representatives to the state and national level Alliance co-ordinating committees. At most, one well-known woman would be selected. During the 1960s, this woman was Halimahton binti Abdul Majid and during the 1960s, it was Fatimah Hashim. At the national level, the KI took little part in party affairs. Within UMNO, the apex of party power was the Supreme Council, or Majlis Tertinggi. After 1956, when women could stand in the UMNO general assembly for the Supreme Council, the number of KI candidates remained small. This occurred in spite of the UMNO president's power to appoint 6 people to the Council to correct any inequities.

Table 5.1 shows the average size of the Council over the years and the number of women present on it. The column which shows the numbers include the KI *Ketua* who sat as an ex-officio deputy leader.

Women as UMNO members were free to stand for elected posts on the Supreme Council. The presence of 2 or 3 women on the Council shows that a few women were present but does not indicate whether they did indeed stand for election or were appointed. Competition among all UMNO members for a post on the Supreme Council was fierce—only leaders with at least the full support of their divisions could hope to be elected. Usually, a Supreme Council member also led an UMNO division. KI members, since they never became UMNO division heads,

TABLE 5.1
Average Size of the Supreme Council, 1957–1967

Year	No. of Members	No. of KI
1957	32	3
1958	22	3
1961	30	2
1963	29	2
1964	29	2
1965	30	2
1966	30	2
1967	38	3

Source: UMNO, *UMNO Annual Reports 1957–67*, UMNO, Kuala Lumpur, 1958–68.

lacked the support needed to get elected by the members of the general assembly. For example, of 57 candidates competing for a spot on the Supreme Council in 1963, only 4 were women. Of these, only Aishah Ghani was elected.[25] In 1964, 50 members ran for 15 posts on the Council; again, only 4 were women and only 1 succeeded.[26]

As in Malaysia's other major parties, UMNO formed a number of sub-committees to deal with matters ranging from labour to finance to politics and elections. Influential party members, e.g. the chairpersons of the UMNO divisions, sat on these committees. Women were once again conspicuous by their absence as shown in Table 5.2.

KI members had little role in the major policy committees because they were poorly represented at the party's annual assemblies. That was where major policies were debated and where elections to party offices took place. A fixed number of posts, 2 prior to 1956 and 3 after 1960, did not provide for equal representation. However, neither the 1956 nor 1960

TABLE 5.2
Number of Sub-committees Served by KI, Various Years

Year	No. of Sub-committees	No. of Sub-committees Served by KI
1953–4	4	0
1956	9	2
1957	9	2
1958	9	2
1961	7	4
1963	7	3
1964	8	2
1965	6	2
1966	6	2
1967	6	4*

Source: UMNO, *UMNO Annual Reports, 1953–67*.
*One woman served on three committees and three women served on one committee.

constitutions precluded women from serving as party, rather than as KI, delegates to the UMNO general assemblies. Party records show that women were selected as delegates at the UMNO division assemblies only on a limited scale. At the 1957 UMNO general assembly, only 2 women were included among the state level delegates; at the June 1958 annual assembly, each state sent 1 to 3 women. (Trengganu, Perlis and Malacca had none.)[27] With the 1960 constitution, the presence of women decreased. Of 166 official delegates and officers to the May 1961 UMNO general assembly, only 11 were women: 3 official KI delegates, 2 members on the Supreme Council, and 6 from the divisions.[28] Two years later, the numbers increased but the pattern remained the same: 2 women on the Supreme Council, and 3 KI delegates. Of about 600 delegates, no more than 20 per cent were women.[29] It is not a surprise therefore that the KI as an auxiliary lacked the needed presence on the major policy-making bodies of the party. Thus, it failed to enter fully into party affairs.

Another factor which reduced the power of the KI was party finances. The KI had little control over their 'own' money. KI members upon joining UMNO paid a M$1 fee which was levied again each year. Of this dollar, 25¢ was retained by the UMNO branch, 50¢ went to the UMNO division and 25¢ was forwarded to UMNO headquarters. The KI, while able to request funds from the UMNO branch or division, had no guarantee that the funds would come. Hence, the section had to rely on donations and fund-raising to finance their local activities. The fact that the KI received little party money prompted a 1962 party decision which gave the local KI branch 10¢ and the KI division 5¢ of every dollar.[30] Such funds though, were not enough for the running of the section. The KI at the local level still had to rely on local KI fund-raising events—hence one often reads of KI fun fairs, the selling of handicrafts, etc. The KI also financed such efforts as the baking and sending of *Hari Raya* cakes to Malaysian troops during the Confrontation with Indonesia (1963-5), sponsored flood relief projects, and conducted literacy campaigns. Even with all this, the auxiliary had to rely on personal donations (*derma*) to cover much of its operating costs. The 1975 budget for the KI shows that of an income of M$57,263.47, only M$18,000 came from UMNO, $13,000 came from two major contributors and the rest came through fund-raising and reserved KI funds.[31] The dues forwarded to the party added to UMNO coffers. These were needed for the party's functions; yet, since the KI had no control over those dues and since they were so poorly represented on most UMNO bodies, their funding did not become a tool for increased power.

The nature of the KI's relations with UMNO precluded the section from having much impact on policy-making. KI women were concerned though, with a wide range of matters during years which saw only limited growth of other women's political groups. The KI studied a number of issues that went beyond the traditional concerns, i.e. marriage and divorce reform, more job opportunities for women, etc. These would remain among their key interests. On other issues raised by the party, such as Indonesia's confrontation with Malaysia, South African apartheid, and nuclear testing, the KI supported UMNO. As a rule, the section's views supported the party.

The accepted tactic used by the KI to express its views to the party élite has been by passing resolutions at the KI general assemblies. The resolutions would start at the division assemblies and were then forwarded to the KI secretary (prior to 1959, to the UMNO secretary-general). He then forwarded the resolution to the proper government department for action, reserved it for debate at the annual assembly, or answered and/or explained the party's stand on the resolution. Those to be debated and agreed upon at the KI assembly were first reviewed by the UMNO secretary-general. He also had the right of veto.[32] The resolutions debated and agreed upon at the KI assembly were then forwarded to the UMNO Supreme Council who chose resolutions to be debated at the UMNO general assembly. Passage at the UMNO assembly would result in the resolutions being referred to the proper governmental agency and be incorporated into government policy.[33]

A sample of the resolutions passed by the KI between 1957–9 shows their variety, they: 1) condemned the irresponsibility of Malay men in marriage ((1958),[34] 2) opposed South African apartheid (1960),[35] 3) urged that women be selected to the post of *ketua kampong* (1960),[36] 4) organized drives to increase UMNO efficiency and to raise the status of the KI (1962),[37] 5) supported the forming of Malaysia (1963)[38] and registering women for national service (1964).[39] Some other resolutions included: 1) urging a woman cabinet member be selected and that one-quarter of all parliamentary and state assembly seats by reserved for women (1964),[40] 2) urging a campaign be started to raise the economic standards of Malay women by forming co-operatives (1966)[41] and 3) supporting Gerakan Mei 11, an UMNO campaign to expand UMNO and to discourage those Malay customs (i.e. great spending at Malay weddings) leading to Malay poverty (1967).[42] Although as Manderson noted,[43] it was common for KI resolutions to be overshadowed by other UMNO resolutions. The resolution that recurs in later years shows that the passing of resolutions did not always lead to their implementation. Aside from exhortations by KI leaders and the repeated submission of resolutions, there is nothing to show that the KI took any other steps to bring about implementation.

By 1967, a change in emphasis in the KI could be noted. The KI began to focus on special issues that were of direct concern to women. The emphasis was quite unspecific at that time: 'up-lifting the status of women'—which for Malay women meant greater educational, economic, and political opportunities. It also meant equality for women within Muslim family law—a long-time KI interest. At the same time, there was a conservative element whose wish was that Malay women not lose contact with their traditions and 'Malayness'. Hence one also finds calls to ban swim-suits in beauty contests. Always the stress was on change that was in accord with the teachings of Islam and Malaysia's national culture.

The MCA

MCA efforts to expand the role of women in the party were few during the years which followed independence. Party records for the 1960s show that women held no leadership positions within the MCA. Women had yet to play a major role in party affairs.

Given that the MCA was controlled by the personalities of its first presidents, Tan Cheng-lock, Lim Chong-eu and Tan Siew-sin, it has been described as a 'cadre-patron party' without a mass membership base.[44] However, it strove to attract a mass following and structured the party to this end.[45] After 1959, the smallest unit of the party was the ward which consisted of about 50 members and corresponded to either a city, municipality, or a town. Above the ward were the district and state level organizations. Each level elected its own officers which included the chairpeople for at least 10 sub-committees. This included a women's sub-committee at every level.[46] Co-ordinating the state activities was the annual Central General Assembly, which in turn, elected the Central Working Committee (CWC)—the most important body of the party. The CWC consisted of the key party posts: president, 3 vice-presidents, secretary-general, treasurer, chairs of the political, labour, youth and alliance relations committees, plus 1 delegate from each state. Section IV, Article 23 of the MCA Constitution also provided that the General Assembly elect the chairpeople of the standing committees. These were to include one woman. According to Article 24, that chairwoman would also sit on the CWC. This was changed by a 1967 amendment which provided that a women's delegates conference would be held to elect the woman to the CWC.[47] As Chan[48] noted, the CWC formed party policy and contained all the major leaders. Thus, it became the most important body within the party. In 1961, newly elected president Tan Siew-sin, formed the President's Committee which in effect became a select inner circle of policy makers. Members of the committee were the CWC without the state delegates. The president was also allowed to appoint 5 to 9 members.[49] Tan Siew-sin also formed a Council of Elders, in 1963, whose function was 'to tender advice to the president in matters of vital importance to the Association'.[50] Members consisted of older party figures who were being 'kicked upstairs'[51] by the top party leaders.

As in other parties, the many subjects vital to party welfare brought about a number of sub-committees at the national level. There were at least 12 of these committees. They provided much of the information and policy recommendations later adopted by the CWC and the President's Committee. The subject matter covered by the committees included labour, youth, education, welfare, finance, and women. Positions on these committees, as well as on the CWC and the President's Committee, was held by the MCA's most influential members. Women were conspicuous by their absence. Party records for 1961[52] show that none of the 12 sub-committees, each with 4 to 32 members, included a woman.[53] Neither were women included on two MCA delegations to Sarawak, Brunei, and North Borneo.[54] This pattern continued throughout the 1960s. In the 1962/3 report, the 31-member CWC included no women (the woman's post was vacant). All members of the other committees were men except for Lee Choo-lan of the Reorganized Working Committee of the Singapore MCA.[55] The Council of Elders and the President's Committee were also all men.[56] The year 1964 saw a break in the pattern: the CWC (consisting of 29 members) included 1 woman: Lim Swee-sim, the chair of the sub-committee on women.[57] Four other women served on her sub-committee. These four members stayed on after her death in 1965. The leadership post though remained vacant. By 1967, the committee can be presumed to have been defunct; it merited no mention in the 1967 annual report.

In 1966, party President Tan Siew-sin seemed to realize that the party had neglected women. He gave an encouraging speech to MCA women at the International Women's Day celebration on 25 August 1966. He urged Chinese women to wake up to the fact that women in other communities were ahead of them. It was their duty to catch up and share the duties of free citizens in a free country.[58] Tan Siew-sin went on to say that they were living in an era of change; what was accepted in 1956, might not be accepted in 1966, and everyone must adjust accordingly.[59] The editorial of *The Guardian*, the MCA party paper, endorsed his speech. It even went one step further and urged Chinese women to exert their influence on their husbands to persuade them to partake in public affairs.[60] However, the 1967 annual report shows that there were no changes made in the party. An amendment to the constitution stating that a women's section should be set up at all levels in the party was not implemented.[61]

Half-hearted efforts to bring women into the MCA began in 1967 and 1968. In August 1967, a women's section of the Perak branch, led by Suit Sai-mooi, was purported to number 2,000 members;[62] it appears to have been the only working women's section at that time. During the same year, the party secretary-general, Kam Wooh-wah, issued a directive to all MCA division leaders to set up women's sections by the end of the year. This was to be part of the party's preparations for the 1969 general elections. Kam urged that the wives and women relatives of the MCA MPs, state assemblymen, councillors, and party officers could be the base for the sections.[63] Kam's directive appears to have resulted from the election commission's report that the number of Chinese women voters had increased greatly; this move was to have a major impact upon the coming general elections.[64]

Deputy leader Lee San-choon also saw the need to encourage women members. Speaking in October 1968 on party membership, he noted: 'Generally, our women's section should be given greater encouragement to develop'.[65] Party President Tan Siew-sin confirmed that to date the women's role in the party had been limited:

One [of] our greatest regret is that we have never had a strong women's movement in our party... it indicates that efforts to attract women to our cause have not been determined and concerted enough.... I, therefore, propose to launch a Women's Assembly some time next year as a first step to strengthening our women's section. UMNO, for example, has an exceptionally strong KI and I am convinced that if we work hard enough, we can emulate the example and standard of UMNO.[66]

Membership figures for 1968 show that the party had met some success in attracting women. In that year, one-third of the 52,146 new members were women. The overall male and female membership of the MCA was purported to total 224,000.[67] Regarding these figures, it should be noted that the number 224,000 is probably highly inflated. In 1962/3, party sources gave a figure of 32,745 dues-paying members. An increase to 224,000 by 1968 would be most unlikely. Rather, the 107,845 member figure as of December 1968, reported by the MCA to the Registrar of Societies, would be a better estimate of party strength.[68] Of this number, one cannot say what the number of women members were as MCA records do not distinguish between the sexes.

Party records show that women played little part in the internal affairs of the party. The MCA annual report for 1968 shows that no women sat on the 39-member Central Working Committee, none were on the President's Committee of 13 members, none were on the 11-member National Council of the Alliance party, and none were officers of the ward branches. Even the post of a woman's delegate to the CWC was vacant. Not until the 1970s would Chinese women begin to play a major role in the MCA.

The MIC

Like the MCA, the MIC made little progress in increasing the role of women in the party during the first years which followed independence. The Johore State MIC had planned to launch a women's section in 1963;[69] one year later only the Selangor Wanita MIC section, headed by Mrs Devaki Krishnan, functioned. Secretary-General of the party, S. S. Murugesu, citing the state of women's section in the party's 1964 annual report, urged the branches to enrol more women. Murugesu,[70] noting that a women's section at headquarters was not forming, entreated all branch officials to go all out to enlist female members—a plea that went largely unheeded.

The lack of influence exerted by women was shown by their absence on the major policy-making organ of the party, the Supreme Council. From 1957 to 1967, there were 10 councils of about 30 members each; only Mrs Devaki Krishnan was elected by the MIC General Assembly to the Council (1960–2) during the period.[71] Further, V. T. Sambanthan, President of the party from 1953 to 1973, declined to appoint a national women's section leader, though the 1966 party constitution permitted him to do so.[72] Underrepresented on the Council and without national leaders, women were also absent from the party's annual general assemblies. Mrs Devaki Krishnan noted that from 1955 to 1964 she was the only woman delegate present at those assemblies: 'Every year, year in and year out, I am the only woman delegate and I don't see any other women and I am sick of it.'[73] Her plea for women delegates did not go unheeded. Later, she noted,[74] two or three women (Mrs Jayaraj, Mrs Fernandez and herself) attended the meetings. On the other hand, there was no attempt by the party to discourage women delegates. In fact, where a male delegate had to be a member of the branch he represented, there was no such provision for women delegates because there were so few of them.[75]

It is not possible to establish the number of women members in the MIC during this period. The party estimated that it had 55,000 members in 1967.[76] The figure is probably inflated. Given that MIC members, both men and women, when asked about female membership would reply 'they weren't many', 'only a few' etc., such membership clearly remained only a small fraction of the total.

To conclude, the years 1957 to 1969 saw no improvement or increase in the role of women within the party. In 1975, this would change but only in a limited way.

The Dewan Muslimat of the PMIP

Following independence, there was also a slow growth of the Dewan Muslimat (DM), or women's section of the PMIA, the Pan-Malayan Islamic Association. (This body would later be known as the PMIP, still later the PAS, and then the PI.) Numbering 700–800 members in 1958,[77] the section's activities included religious, sewing, and cooking classes and electoral campaign tasks. During its early years, the DM had several changes in its leaders. The first *Ketua*, Zubaidah binti Haji Ali, was followed by Zaharah Othman, who, in turn, was succeeded by Khadijah Sidek and then by Sakinah Junid. The *Ketua*, though elected by the women themselves, did not automatically sit on the Supreme Council of the party. Khadijah Sidek was the first such woman council member appointed in 1958 by Dr Burhanuddin, President of the party. She sat on the council as a PMIP member and not as a representative of the DM.[78]

PMIP women members were governed by their own by-laws until the party's 1971 constitution. The section's dedication to Islam was clearly shown in its goals:

1) to unite Muslim women into one organization to carry out Allah's and the Prophet's struggle,
2) to make the soul and spirit of the true faith of Islam become the theory and guiding hand in the lives of ordinary women,
3) to improve the livelihood of Muslim women, and
4) to work with other PAS members to carry out [the party's] aspirations and goals.[79]

The DM's organization on paper paralleled that of the party. DM branches were to be set up at the state level or wherever there were 25 members.[80] Above the branch, the national body was made up of the annual general assembly and the DM Executive Committee. While members elected their own officials at both the branch and national levels, the section remained under the complete authority of the party. Section 18 of the PMIP constitution provided that the section be subject to the authority of the party; further, the election of the DM Executive Committee was subject to the approval of the party's Supreme Council.[81] Within the DM, the most powerful body was the Majlis Mesyuarat Agong DM, or the General Assembly of the DM, which met each year prior to the PMIP General Assembly. Those eligible to attend were the members of the DM Executive Committee and representatives (and leaders) from each branch. However, the general assembly was once again 'under the view and responsible to the Jawatankuasa Agong PAS' (Supreme Council).[82] Overall, the organization of the DM was weak with many areas being without women's sections and many branches remaining inactive. (The party was strongest in the mostly Malay states of Trengganu and Kelantan). Like the party organization which itself remained weak according to PMIP leaders,[83] this was not a serious shortcoming. The PMIP depended more on popular appeal than on the strength of its organization.[84] Stimulation of grassroots enthusiasm rested largely with the religious leaders who gave their support to the party.

DM leaders, mostly religious teachers, spoke out on a number of issues and gave staunch support to what they saw to be Malay causes. DM *Ketua*, Zubaidah binti Haji Ali, in 1957, addressed over 600 people in Alor Star, Kedah. She chided Malaya's political leaders for 'selling the country and nation just for a plate of rice', and causing the 'loss of national rights of the native people'.[85] This referred to the 1957 independence provisions. Similarly, the secretary of the DM Pasir Mas branch, Wan Aminah binti Yusoff, likened the Malay Peninsula of 1958 to 'a big and well-furnished home that is rented out while the owner lives in a little hut at the back'.[86] This was in reference to the Malay/non-Malay situation. Zaharah Othman, speaking in Trengganu, said that there were no 'visible results of Merdeka (Independence) after one year'.[87] DM leaders also decried practices which, in their eyes, went against Islamic teachings, such as the promoting by Muslims of beauty contests among Muslim women.[88] DM leaders were also vocal in support of the party's electoral candidates; Salmah Sheikh Hussein, head of the DM in Penang and the only PMIP woman senator, addressed one such rally in 1959. She said that the Alliance was striving only for the interests of the capitalists and neglected the Malay poor.[89]

From 1963 to 1966, Khadijah Sidek was president of the DM. By the end of this period, the auxiliary claimed 3,000 members; the male membership of the PMIP reached 40,000.[90] DM members were mostly rural women, often uneducated, but committed to Islam and 'Malay rights'.

Despite the section's growth, the women were castigated at the 1964 PMIP general assembly. Secretary-General of the party, Abdullah Zawawi, addressed the meeting and lamented the lack of activity by PMIP women. This criticism was put forth in spite of the PMIP electoral success in Kelantan which was largely due to the role played by PMIP women.[91] Sakinah Junid, in her response before the same assembly, regretted that the party had no female representatives in the House of Representatives[92]—a speech that recalled the 1962 address to the DM by the Deputy President of the party. Zulkifli Mohammed had said that the party might put up 20 women candidates in the 1964 federal elections.[93] This was never done. Ultimately, the section remained under the firm control of the party. It was perceived by neither the PMIP nor the DM as an autonomous body.

Parti Sosialis Rakyat Malaya (PSRM)

While the KI UMNO and the DM PMIP grew during the 1950s and early 1960s, the Wanita Rakyat, or women's section of the PSRM, remained in a fledgeling state. The section came to life only during elections. In 1957, the party leaders announced the forming of a 'Wanita Rakyat'[94] and selected Zainab binti Ahmad the first *Ketua* in 1958. However, the auxiliary remained poorly organized and sections formed at the branch and state level only in Pahang, Kedah, Trengganu,[95] and Selangor.[96]

Though weak when compared to the much larger KI UMNO (the PSRM numbered between 5,000 and 10,000 members in this period),[97] PSRM women leaders spoke out on a number of issues. By 1959, the women's section of the Selangor Wanita Rakyat had called on the government to: 1) check cultural infiltration by the West, 2) build more schools in the rural areas, and 3) protect women and children from the impact of immoral foreign culture.[98] The women further chose to fight for the political, educational, and economic rights of women as well as for the equal treatment of workers of either sex;[99] they repeated these calls six months later.[100] The section planned to send a delegation to Deputy Prime Minister Tun Razak to clarify the recent arrests of several of its members detained as communist sympathizers.[101]

In 1961, Sharifah Mahani binti Syed Hamzah emerged as a colourful spokesperson in the PSRM. Sharifah was the wife of the famous (or infamous) Hamid Tuah. (He was once detained for opening up state land to squatters.) Sharifah was elected leader of the PSRM's branch at Tanjong Karang, Selangor.[102] She led repeated protests urging the release of Hamid Tuah. After her unexplained expulsion from the party in 1961,[103] there is little news of the Wanita Rakyat until March 1962 when an attempt was made to enlarge the women's section. In July, Zaidah binti Hashim, the *Ketua* of the Wanita Rakyat, urged all party branches to form women's sections.[104] The following November party headquarters announced that the Wanita Rakyat was launching a large-scale membership drive. It targeted the rural areas for the 1964 elections.[105] This attempt would have little effect on the party's electoral fortunes.

In February 1963, the PSRM suffered a severe set-back with the arrest of the party president, Ahmad Boestamam under the ISA.[106] Umi Kalthum Ahmad, secretary of the women's section, issued a directive from the Wanita Rakyat urging all its divisions and branches to keep calm and strengthen their organization.[107] Additionally, Umi Kalthum Ahmad led a team of 50 women in a house-to-house campaign to ensure Ahmad Boestamam's re-election to his parliamentary seat in the 1964 elections.[108] That year the Wanita Rakyat reaffirmed its position in favour of equal pay for women and urged that women should be accorded the same rights as men in all spheres of activity.[109]

It is hard to evaluate the role women played within a party that was both limited in membership and whose members were subject to government surveillance and detention. The Wanita Rakyat issued a number of declarations and its leaders were outspoken on a number of topics. However, while outspoken, the section as a whole remained weak. One cannot estimate the number of women members in the PSRM during this time—the party did not state its membership figures by sex. Probably the number of women remained only a small fraction of the 5,000–10,000 party membership, if examples provided by other opposition parties apply. The Press also does not mention the Wanita Rakyat holding any activities during this period—information which is routinely reported on all the parties if such events take place. A party spokesman confirmed that the wing had been loosely formed and functioned largely as an electoral aid to the party.[110] The Wanita Rakyat remained a small, weakly organized group of socialist Malay women, with only a few women standing out in this period.

The Labour Party

The Labour Party (LP), much like the PSRM, had little success in organizing women during the years which followed independence. As early as 1959, the LP had put forth its Women's Charter which provided for equal pay for equal work, monogamy for non-Muslims, and International Women's Day as a public holiday.[111] Despite the Charter, the organizing of women members proceeded on a limited basis; 'ad hoc' women's committees formed with 'some success' in Johore and Malacca.[112] In 1961, the LP Annual Report noted that it could not organize women's committees in each district and that 'ad hoc' committees in Selangor, Johore and Malacca had more success.[113] One year later, the party appraised its women's section and found it wanting. Sections existed only in Johore, Malacca, Pahang and Selangor. The party noted that there was 'a great need to strengthen this section by clarifying the programme and demands of [the] women of Malaysia to serve as a call for the unity of one womanhood. But most important of all is the fact that this section is Chinese based and has no awareness of

Muslim problems.'[114] Despite its limits, a new woman's section would sometimes form: in 1963, a Penang section joined those which functioned in Johore, Malacca, Pahang and Selangor.[115]

The women who joined the Labour Party were few in number—no more than 300 of the roughly 3,000 party members in 1965.[116] The women were all Chinese and most were either rubber tappers, labourers, domestic workers or seamstresses. Only a very few were housewives and almost no one was a professional.[117] Party records for 1966 show that women often sat on the party committees at the branch level though seldom did they number more than 3 on a committee which averaged 11–18 members.

Limited leadership was provided by Miss P. G. Lim, a successful lawyer, electoral candidate and later ambassador to Yugoslavia; Tan Siew-eng, a clerk who led the LP women's section in 1963 and led the Socialist Front's women section in Johore in 1960;[118] and Ganga Nayar, an Indian woman who would later become an MP and a major opposition figure. In talking about the LP, Ganga Nayar[119] noted that those women who did join took little part in party activities and seldom sat on any major committee or attended the party general assemblies. Noting that the LP was an opposition party and one viewed by most of the public with distrust, she explained that it was very hard for the LP to attract any women members.

Though few in number, the LP women were outspoken on issues such as equal pay[120] and women's rights within marriage.[121] They were highly visible to the public. In March 1962, LP women with a few women from the PSRM protested discrimination against women workers at a Socialist Front rally in Kuala Lumpur. The Socialist Front (SF) was an alliance between the LP and PSRM in 1957. One week later, the SF women met in Kuala Lumpur to celebrate International Women's Week in Chinwoo Stadium. Again they urged the government to grant equal pay and to pass laws against bigamy.[122] In October 1963, Labour Party women in Perak resolved to press for a system of equal pay, to declare 8 March Women's Day, and to enact monogamy laws.[123]

Between 1965 and 1966 there was increased activity on the part of LP women. In 1965, the Selangor women's branch met and passed resolutions which supported the SF central committee's decision to withdraw support from the central government over its National Emergency programme. It also urged the celebration of Women's Day on 8 March.[124] In February, women from all sections in the party met and resolved to: 1) support the LP's 5-point plan for a Malaysia–Indonesia settlement, 2) condemn the dispatch of foreign troops to Malaysia, 3) appeal to all women of the world to unite and defend world peace and oppose American and British imperialism and all forms of colonialism, 4) condemn the arrest of party leaders and members, 5) oppose high taxes, 6) demand a review of educational policy, 7) support the SF's move to stage a peaceful procession in February and 8) request that 8 March be declared International Women's Day and 1 May, Labour Day.[125] Two days later, on 19 February, the women's section announced that it would mobilize more than 500 women to take part in the 13 February march. (This march protested the arrest of certain SF leaders.)[126] The march turned riot.[127] It was one of the causes leading to the government's ban of the SF. A later mass demonstration occurred in Penang where 1,000 LP members (both sexes) marched in October 1966.[128] Another occurred in Kuala Lumpur.[129] These led to the arrests of many LP members. Such protests prompted the ban on the LP in 1967. Thereafter, the activities of LP women were confined to individual actions. In September 1967, 10 LP women detained in the Taiping jail held a hunger strike.[130] In January 1969, the most important LP woman leader, Tan Siew-eng, was released from the Batu Gajah detention camp.[131] At once she joined with other LP women, notably Chan Sow-ying and Siow See-lian, to launch a campaign for the release of political detainees. Thereafter, they agreed to support the LP's boycott of the 1969 general elections.[132] With the detention of many members, the loss of other members to other parties, and its stand which opposed the forming of Malaysia, the LP had largely ceased to function by 1967 when it was banned. In 1972, the party was dissolved.

Other Parties

The other parties of this time showed little electoral strength. Discussion of women party members will, therefore, be brief.[133] In August 1957, the LP and the PSRM formed an alliance, called the Socialist Front (SF). Their objectives included: 1) to organize and maintain a united front of all socialist political groups in Malaya, and 2) to strive for a democratic socialist state which would secure for the peasants and workers the full fruits of their industry.[134] In 1964, a third party, the National Convention Party (NCP), founded in 1963 by Abdul Aziz bin Ishak, joined the SF. The NCP remained a minor party and was defunct soon after the 1964 elections. The forming of the SF, though, failed to strengthen the role of women within the front. For example, the 1958 Central Executive Committee of the SF consisted of 12 men and no women.[135] Occasionally, one finds mention of election rallies or joint meetings between PSRM and LP women;[136] but these were rare—the few women in each party tended to act on their own.

In April 1962, a new party, the Parti Demokratik Bersatu (United Democratic Party, UDP) was launched by Dr Lim Chong-eu and other dissidents from the MCA.[137] Though non-communal,[138] the party sought to promote harmony among capital, labour and management.[139] There is nothing to show that women played any role within the party. For example, the 24-member Executive Committee, was male as was almost all division committee officials.[140] Nine women sat on the division committees and all were Chinese (four were housewives, two were clerks, two were dressmakers, and one was a medical assistant).[141] The only mention made by the Press of UDP women was a reference to Mrs Lim

Chong-eu. She addressed a UDP rally in Penang in 1964—she spoke in Mandarin, her husband spoke in English.[142] Even the party's resolutions passed at its 1964 general assembly, made no mention of equal pay or marriage and divorce reform.[143] These issues were of concern to non-Malay women during this period. The UDP remained a small party which was poorly developed. The number of party members did not exceed 2,600 members.[144] In 1968, the UDP became defunct, although it did pledge its full support to a new party, the Gerakan. The Gerakan founder–leader would also be Dr Lim Chong-eu.

The People's Progressive Party (PPP), founded in 1953, also made little progress in bringing women to its doors. It was ten years later, in April 1963, that the PPP started its first women's section in Sungei Rokam (Ipoh, Perak). This section, the party hoped, would consist of Malays who would be grouped with 4 other Malay branches. Together they would form a Kinta division of the Wanita PPP Malaya. Vice-president of the Party, Samsuddin bin Harun explained that it was a bid to woo women into the party: '[it] is part of the strategy for the municipal elections next month and the state elections in 1964'.[145] The PPP, however, remained a one-state party (Perak). The limited support it enjoyed (membership estimates for 1963–76 range from 115 to 314)[146] was based on the personal appeal of its founders, the Seenivasagam brothers.

Like the PPP, Parti Negara was a one-state party. It confined most of its activities to Trengganu. The party's fortunes declined as it suffered set-backs in the 1955 elections. It won only Datuk Onn's seat in the 1959 parliamentary elections. By the 1964 elections, Parti Negara was defunct.

Lastly, two other parties were formed prior to the 1969 general elections: the Democratic Action Party (DAP) and the People's Movement Party (Gerakan or GRM). These parties will be discussed in the next chapter. Both parties remained weak and poorly organized prior to the elections. Afterwards, both parties developed more fully.

The Emergence of the National Council of Women's Organizations

In August 1960, the YWCA began a campaign to draw the non-political women's groups into one body. The next December, delegates from eight women's groups, which represented 35,000 women,[147] met to discuss the forming of a single, advisory and consultative body. Mrs Rasamma Bhupalan led the pro tem committee elected by the delegates. From 7–12 August 1961, the pro tem committee held a workshop at which they drafted a constitution for the new Women's Council. Mrs Bhupalan explained the purpose of the new council: 'The new Council of Women's Organizations will act as a spearhead group initiating action for [the] betterment of women. Our whole idea is to work in unity. We feel that women of Malaya can play a vital part in the life of the country if they will unite themselves.'[148]

Meanwhile, the KI UMNO, in April 1962, called for a meeting of all women's organizations. This was to organize a Women's Day (*Hari Wanita*) to honour the women of Malaya. The first *Hari Wanita* committee, chaired by Fatimah binti Hashim, the *Ketua* of the KI, represented 16 groups.[149] Women's Day was first celebrated on 25 August 1962, in Kuala Lumpur. Following a mass rally and an address by Fatimah binti Hashim,[150] 350 delegates met to discuss four working papers—all on the subject of women. Resolutions were then forwarded to the proper government bodies in order to raise the status of women. Women's Day was seen as a major goal by the women's groups in order to: 1) mark the role women played in their nation's history, 2) unite women so as to improve their lot, and 3) make women feel they had a major role to play in developing the country.[151]

The success of *Hari Wanita* prompted Fatimah binti Hashim to contact Mrs Bhupalan in order to discuss merging the two groups. On 2 March 1963, members of both groups met and agreed to form one organization. Subsequently, the National Council of Women's Organizations (NCWO) was formed to represent all the women of Malaya. It would co-ordinate the efforts of the many women's groups both political and non-political. The Council was to consult and advise but was to have no control over the internal affairs of its affiliates. Declaring itself to be non-political, non-religious and non-communal, the NCWO announced its purpose: 1) to bring all the women's organizations together, and 2) to raise the status of women and work for the welfare of women and children.[152] Specifically, the NCWO sought to improve the lot of women. It included among its aims: 3) to study the laws affecting women and children; 4) to work towards the advancement of the status of women through the improvement of their legal, political, social, economic, moral and educational status, and 5) to encourage an informed and intelligent participation of women in the development and growth of the nation.[153]

On 25 August 1965, the NCWO held its first conference. At that time, the NCWO had 12 affiliates.[154] It lost the representatives from the PSRM and the PMIP. The activities of the NCWO in its first two years consisted of two efforts: celebrating *Hari Wanita* and recommending that a Women's Bureau be formed. At a seminar attended by 160 delegates on 24 August 1964 (*Hari Wanita*), the women urged that the Bureau include these functions: 1) to implement fair terms of service for women and equal opportunity for all, 2) to assist in major programmes for urban and rural women to meet changing demands, 3) to put forth policies which would promote the welfare of women, 4) to review standards of qualifications, training and terms of service (of working women), 5) to provide legal aid for women who had problems over compensation, wages, work contracts, maintenance, divorce, property and inheritance.[155] The women also urged that compulsory education for girls be introduced. This was to ensure that rural girls attend school. Further, they urged kindergartens be started and that a department of home economics be formed at the University of Malaya.[156]

The efforts to form a Women's Bureau continued throughout 1966. In November, the NCWO once again recommended that a Women's Bureau be formed within the Department of Labour. Further, it called for a National Advisory Board of the Women's Bureau. It was to consist of 1 representative from each of the 12 ministries. Also to be included was 1 member from the University of Malaya, 2 from the trade union movement, 6 from the NCWO, 1 from the Chamber of Commerce and 4 from the public sector.[157] The struggle for a Women's Bureau would take many years and take the sustained efforts of the NCWO. The NCWO would play a major role in the effort to improve the status of women.

The Importance of Women as Electoral Candidates and Workers—The General Elections of 1959 and 1964

It was expected that women party members would contribute to the success of the Alliance in the 1959 state and federal elections as in the 1955 elections. Women played a major part not only as voters but also as contestants; the political parties were 'seriously' going to put forth women.[158] Both the UMNO ('There is no doubt about it. We are going to put up women candidates.') and the Socialist Front ('We have decided to field at least 60 candidates in the next parliamentary elections. Of these at least 10 will be women.') announced they would present women candidates. Parti Negara and the PMIP were 'considering' it but had yet made no decision.[159] All this intent, though, did not lead to more women candidates.

The UMNO success in 1955 had depended in part on Malay women voters. They had turned out in large numbers to vote. This was not lost on the KI who had strongly pressed the UMNO leaders to select more KI members as candidates. This issue had first been raised by the KI in 1949 over female membership in the Federal Legislative Council.[160] Later, in 1955, it was also raised over the exclusion of their *Ketua*, Khadijah Sidek, from candidacy in the 1955 elections. At the 1958 KI general assembly, the KI warned UMNO that it might adopt an 'unco-operative attitude' if the KI was not given the chance to contest elections at all levels.[161] This issue had also been often raised by the KI sections in Penang, Selangor and Negri Sembilan.[162] In February 1959, Fatimah Hashim, the KI *Ketua*, had been assured from the UMNO Supreme Council that more seats would be given to the women in the 1959 elections.[163] The 1959 conference of the KI Selangor was a harbinger of what lay ahead of KI candidates: the women were shocked to learn that no women had been chosen to stand in any of the state's fourteen districts. Halimahton binti Abdul Majid, the state *Ketua*, urged them not to think of it as an insult. They were asked to abide by the decision for the sake of party unity. In a show of party loyalty, the KI assembly unanimously passed a resolution pledging to work hard in the elections even if no women were selected.[164]

The process used to select party candidates sought separate lists of potential candidates from the parent party and the wings. Several months before an election, selection committees were set up at every level within UMNO. Branches would forward their lists of candidates to the divisions. The divisions then made a selection. They forwarded the culled list to the national level UMNO selection committee. The KI and the Pemuda wings also selected their candidates in this way. The final list then came before the UMNO national committee. It was not unknown, however, for the selection committee to bypass the lists and select their own nominees.[165]

Because the KI was a separate wing, UMNO seemed to leave the selecting of women candidates to it. It was rare for an UMNO division to put forth the name of a KI member on its own. However, the most likely reason for the failure was that KI members held few posts of power within the party proper. Only two women had ever led an UMNO division. It must also be mentioned that competition among UMNO members for an electoral seat was fierce. The party was also very concerned with its electoral success. It was therefore prudent, if perhaps unfair to the KI, for the party to rely on those who could show the strongest support.

To increase both the electoral efficiency and the status of the KI, the UMNO Supreme Council, in September 1958, established the office of a full-time paid secretary of the KI. The new secretary was to be a 'superwoman to make the KI a real political force'. Not only must she be willing to travel throughout Malaya, be a good public speaker and organizer, but she was also to have a working knowledge of English.[166] Her primary task, however, would be to woo Malay women to vote for the Alliance.[167]

Rahimah binti Abdul Rahman, a 25-year-old KI member was appointed. Educated at Malay primary and religious schools, she had joined the party in 1953 and had taken part in the 1955 election campaign, aiding Khadijah Sidek. Soon after her appointment, Rahimah binti Abdul Rahman embarked on her mission to ensure the Alliance success. She attempted 'to rally all the Malay women voters on the side of UMNO'.[168] Since most of UMNO voters in the 1959 elections (like those in 1955) would be Malay women, she toured Malaya to ensure their votes. While she urged UMNO not to be complacent, she believed that at least 80 per cent of Malay women were behind UMNO and it was important that UMNO obtained their votes.[169]

The Alliance was not alone in its reliance on women. Though Parti Negara had made no recent attempt to woo women to join the party and its number of women members remained small, women were still expected to play an important role. The party, in its belief that women were the best campaigners, was 'solely depending on women to do house to house campaigning.... We are leaving the matter to the women. Over a *sireh* session [betel chewing] they can do much more than men.'[170]

In May and June 1959, state elections were held throughout Malaya. Federal elections followed on 19 August. At the state level, 282 seats

TABLE 5.3
Breakdown of Men and Women Candidates by Party, 1959

	State		Federal	
	Male	Female	Male	Female
Alliance	271	11	101	3
PMIP	199	1	57	1
SF	122	2	38	0
PN	78	1	9	0
PPP	39	0	19	0
Malayan Party	6	0	2	0
Independent	76	0	28	1
Total	791	15	254	5

Source: Compiled by the author from the *Report on the Parliamentary and State Elections 1959*, Federation of Malaya, Government Publication, Malaya, 1960.

were contested by 806 candidates of whom 15 were women; at the federal level, 5 women competed with 254 men for 104 seats in the national parliament. The promise of the parties to present women candidates was hollow indeed. Table 5.3 shows the breakdown of men and women candidates by party.

Of the 15 women at the state level, 6 (all UMNO/Alliance) were successful. Only 2 of the defeated women were non-Malays (Lew Siat-yee of the SF and Mrs Devaki Krishnan of the MIC/Alliance).

At the federal level, 3 women won seats in the Dewan Rakyat and 2 were defeated. Of the Alliance winners, Ibu Zain and Fatimah binti Hashim were both influential KI members. Khadijah Sidek was elected for the PMIP. A future KI *Ketua*, Aishah Ghani, lost to the President of the SF and Parti Rakyat, Ahmad Boestamam, in a district that was largely non-Malay. The last woman candidate was Mrs B.H. Oon, founder of the Province Wellesley Labour Party. She ran as an independent and was narrowly defeated by an Alliance (MCA) candidate (3,945 votes to 3,782 votes).

The Alliance carried the election as it had in 1955. The 1959 results were not so remarkable—the Alliance majority was reduced. At the federal level, the Alliance won 74 out of 104 seats (including 4 uncontested seats). At the state level, the Alliance was successful in 207 of the 282 seats (again 4 uncontested seats were filled by Alliance candidates).[171] Furthermore, the Alliance won 51.8 per cent of the vote.[172] As Ratnam and Milne[173] noted, the division of the opposition among many parties and regional areas, together with single member constituencies, permitted the Alliance to win its large number of seats.

Women, as in 1955, helped bring about this victory by voting. Thus, they did not fail party hopes. In fact, the election greatly resembled the 1955 general elections: In the Rembau area of Negri Sembilan, the number of women going to the polls exceeded men five to one while in

Dungun, Trengganu '70% of the electorate had voted and most of them were women. People driving from Kuala Trengganu to Dungun passed hundreds of Malay women, some of them carrying babies, walking along the road to the nearest polling station.'[174] Elsewhere on the East Coast, Malay women were expected to turn out in large numbers and thus make a big difference: 'Smartly dressed office girls on their way to work mingled with mothers carrying shopping baskets and children at polling stations.'[175] In Kuala Lumpur, it was reported that: 'It was a day for women according to the turnout this morning, most of them dressed in their best.'[176] In Pahang:

... women voters overwhelmingly outnumber men and they went to the polls early with shopping baskets. Malay women lent colour to the scene in their bright Hari Raya [a major Muslim holiday] clothes and in six constituencies, women were out in greater numbers than their menfolk who either had gone to sea or were out tapping.[177]

In 'Province Wellesley, after a sluggish start, polling stepped up as hundreds of UMNO women emerged from the kampongs to await transport at the main roads'.[178]

The effort to increase the number of Malay, and particularly Malay women, voters was stepped up in 1960. In September, UMNO began its first course to train KI members to become better and more efficient leaders. Its purpose was to 'enable them to work harder at future elections'. Four hundred KI members attended this first session.[179] Meanwhile, party leaders praised the KI and stressed its importance to party fortunes. UMNO Secretary-General, Hussein Noordin (1961) commented:

In the Federation, the UMNO gives its women's section, KI, equality of status with the men's section. The most important work of Malay women is and will continue to be [in the] field of politics. In fact, in the last parliamentary election, the KI played a big part. . . . We found the majority of voters in most constituencies were women ... this clearly shows KI leaders are doing valuable work in enlightening their rural sisters about politics.[180]

The failure of parties, particularly UMNO, to select women to stand in 1955 and 1959, prompted the KI to demand yet again that UMNO select KI members as candidates. At the 1962 KI general assembly, the women passed three resolutions which urged that: 1) the number of women selected as candidates be increased, 2) that more seats be set aside for women in the Dewan Rakyat and Dewan Negara, and 3) that at least one woman in each state be selected to stand in the next federal elections.[181]

The KI was the only organization to protest the paucity of women candidates; the women sections of the other parties were either non-existent or did not take up the issue. Even though the KI was the largest women's group, the request went unheeded; the election pattern set earlier was to be repeated in 1964.

As had been the case, pre-election press coverage expected that the KI would play a major role in the 1964 elections. *Berita Harian* on 29 March

1964, noted that the success of the Alliance had in the past depended on the help of the KI. In fact, the KI had become the 'backbone of the Alliance success'. The efforts of the KI on the East Coast had not been sufficient to guarantee an Alliance victory. In an effort to 'win back' the PMIP-controlled states of Kelantan and Trengganu, KI secretary, Rahimah binti Abdul Rahman, was put in charge of streamlining the KI[182]—an act which prompted the PMIP to issue a directive to all its state commissioners and branch secretaries:

> As we know, our women's section is still behind that of the opposition parties, particularly the UMNO. Therefore, it is imperative for us to make an immediate effort to rectify our backwardness.... The duty of the members of the women's sections during the elections will be to explain things to the voters, particularly through house to house canvassing, until they are able to attract the womenfolk in each constituency to support PMIP candidates.[183]

These tributes to women party members and what they could do for party electoral changes were, once again, not matched by their being selected as candidates. On 25 April 1964, state and federal elections were held. At the federal level, 281 candidates contested 104 seats to the Dewan Rakyat. Of these 6 were women. At the state level, 16 women competed against 753 men for 282 seats in the state legislatures. Table 5.4 shows the breakdown by party.

The 1964 election was a set-back for women. They achieved no increase in their numbers on electoral bodies. Of the 6 parliamentary candidates, only 2 won: KI *Ketua*, Fatimah Hashim (Kedah), and Fatimah binti Abdul Majid (Johore), another prominent KI member. Khadijah Sidek who ran on the PMIP ticket was defeated as were Tan

TABLE 5.4

Breakdown of Men and Women Candidates by Party, 1964

	State		Federal	
	Male	Female	Male	Female
Alliance	274	8	102	2
PMIP	155	3	52	2
SF	165	2	62	1
PPP	26	0	8	0
PN	17	0	4	0
UDP	63	2	27	0
(PAP)	15	0	13	0
Malayan Party	—	—	—	—
Independent	38	1	7	1
Total	753	16	275	6

Source: *Report on the Parliamentary and State Legislative Assembly General Elections, 1964 of the States of Malaya*, Kuala Lumpur, Government Printer, 1965, p. 13.

Ah-gogh, secretary of the women's section of the Labour Party, Salmah binti Sheikh Hussein of the PMIP and independent N. Saraswathi Devi. In Johore Baru Timor, Fatimah binti Abdul Majid (UMNO) defeated Tan Ah-gogh of the Socialist Front 12,600 to 5,343.[184]

At the state level, all eight Alliance women won. All other women candidates lost. Two of the PMIP women, Khadijah Sidek and Salmah binti Sheikh Hussein had stood for both parliamentary and state elective seats. They were doubly unlucky, both times losing. Of the Alliance victors, all were KI members—neither the MCA nor the MIC stood any women candidates. All three female PMIP candidates were Malays as was the independent. The two UDP women were non-Malays. Of the SF's two female candidates, one was a Malay woman while the other was a prominent Chinese lawyer, Miss P. G. Lim. In one case, the Alliance candidate, Hasnah binti Ahmad (UMNO), defeated her PMIP rival, Khadijah Sidek 6,601 to 687.[185]

The Alliance victory in 1964 exceeded that of 1959, winning 89 out of 104 parliamentary seats (74 in 1959) and 58.3 per cent (51.8 per cent) of the vote. The Alliance also won 240 seats out of 282 seats in the state elections compared to 207 in 1959. The Alliance crushed the SF. The PMIP remained the only real threat to the Alliance having won 21 out of 30 state seats in Kelantan.[186]

Once again, women voters took their task seriously and turned out in large numbers. In the 1964 election, about one-half to one million out of two million voters were women.[187] Once again, women were often the first voters—the majority of early morning voters in Kuala Lumpur, Johore, Penang, Perak and Negri Sembilan.[188] The turnout by the women was all the more remarkable when it is noted that the parties made no direct appeal to women voters. (The party manifestos were general statements which avoided any direct appeal to women.)[189] The Alliance, for instance, avoided the then current issue of equal pay for equal work. It promised to ensure that 'labour is adequately rewarded' and that the salary wage structure would be reviewed.[190] Only the SF took a firm stand and declared that: 'We uphold the principle of "equal pay for equal work" and shall take steps to abolish discrimination against women.'[191] The UDP pledged to provide free legal aid to all destitute wives to ensure their legal rights against deserting spouses.[192] Except for these, the parties avoided the issues of equal pay and marriage and divorce reform. In general, the parties seemed to feel that there was little need to appeal to women voters.

Conclusion

For women in politics, the first years of independence were dominated by the activities of one group, the Kaum Ibu UMNO. The KI's growth in its scope of activities and in its electoral efforts was not accompanied by an increase of power within UMNO itself. Excluded from a role in the party's major policy-making bodies, the KI had little impact upon

UMNO decisions. It was during these years that the role of the subordinate wing evolved. First set in the early 1950s, this role became firmly set. Efforts to improve the position of KI women within UMNO had no success. The section placed support and loyalty to UMNO above its own interests. This was not always the case with the all-male youth wing, the Pemuda.

Aside from the KI, women in the PMIP, PSRM and the Labour Party had a limited role in their parties. For the Dewan Muslimat PMIP, the years which followed independence saw the pattern set for the complete subordination to the party leadership. For those few women active in the PSRM and the Labour Party, the politics of this first decade were directed towards agitation against the government. Little was done to encourage more women either to become party members or to become involved in party affairs. Those few women involved in the MCA and MIC remained in the background. There was no concerted effort to draw women into the two parties. Most likely their leaders did not perceive a need to use women as a base for increased party support (even though MCA dissidents would split from the party and form the UDP in 1962, leaving the MCA in a greatly weakened state). The party leaders still did not feel a need to court women for increased party support. Equally, one finds no outstanding MCA or MIC spokeswomen at this time who might have been the key to increasing the women's role within their parties. The fact remains that non-Malay women, who were more urban and better educated than their Malay counterparts, abstained from political activity in direct contrast to Malay women. While the next chapter takes up this issue in greater depth, one can consider a number of reasons for this disparity: 1) among non-Malays, politics was still perceived as a male activity with little scope for women, 2) non-Malay women saw no reason to work in the parties, since the parties made no direct appeals to them and it was not clear how membership would benefit them, and 3) fear of political involvement among non-Malays, in general, was much stronger than among Malays, hence non-Malays took part in politics in much smaller numbers. Because they did not join the parties, it was not surprising that so few non-Malay women were chosen as either party officials or electoral candidates.

These years also saw the NCWO emerge. The NCWO was a united front of Malaysian women of all races and politics. The NCWO would become the main spokesbody for female interests in Malaysia because of the strength and nature of its membership. It would aid women where the more parochial interests of the member groups might fail.

1. UMNO, *Peratoran Pergerakan Pemuda dan Kaum Ibu UMNO 1956 (Rules of the Pemuda and Kaum Ibu UMNO 1956)* (approved by the UMNO Supreme Council, 13 March 1961), Kuala Lumpur, UMNO, 1961.
2. *UMNO/SG 178/53*.
3. Lenore Manderson, 'The Development of the Pergerakan Kaum Ibu UMNO, 1945–1972', unpublished doctoral dissertation, Australian National University, 1977, p. 77.
4. UMNO, *Peratoran Pergerakan Kaum Ibu UMNO 1956*, Kuala Lumpur, UMNO, 1956, Clause 9.
5. UMNO, *Annual Report of the Pergerakan Kaum Ibu UMNO, 1956*, Kuala Lumpur, p. 79.
6. Ibid., and *Buku Cenderamata Jubli Perak Wanita UMNO Malaysia pada 25hb Ogos 1974*, Utusan Melayu Berhad, Kuala Lumpur, 1974, p. 9.
7. Manderson, op. cit., p. 85, and *Times of Malaya*, 19 October 1955.
8. Manderson, op. cit., p. 78.
9. UMNO, *UMNO Annual Reports 1957–64*, Kuala Lumpur, 1958–65.
10. Manderson, op. cit., p. 79.
11. *UMNO/SG 176/51/1* and *UMNO/SG 8/52*.
12. UMNO, *UMNO Annual Report 1956*, p. 70.
13. Manderson, op. cit., p. 81.
14. *ST*, 28 December 1955.
15. *UMNO/SG/KI 7/55*.
16. Manderson, op. cit., p. 87.
17. Ibid., p. 81.
18. *ST*, 14 February 1960. Also see Fatimah Hashim's speech to the KI annual assembly of 1959/60. *Annual Report of the Pergerakan KI UMNO 1959/60*, p. 102.
19. UMNO, *UMNO Annual Report 1957*. UMNO had a total of 83 divisions at this time.
20. UMNO, *UMNO Annual Reports for 1957, 1958, 1961, and 1963–1966*.
21. Ibid.
22. Ibid.
23. Ibid.
24. Ibid.
25. UMNO, *UMNO Annual Report 1963*, p. 77.
26. UMNO, *UMNO Annual Report 1964*, p. 82–3.
27. UMNO, *UMNO Annual Report 1958*.
28. UMNO, *UMNO Annual Report 1961*.
29. UMNO, *UMNO Annual Report 1963*.
30. Interview with Rahmah Othman, Secretary of the KI on 22 and 23 April 1976. (Confirms Manderson, op. cit.)
31. *Kertas Persidangan Bil. 3/25/76 Kenyataan Kira-kira Pergerakan Wanita UMNO 1975/76*.
32. Manderson, op. cit., p. 213.
33. Interview with Rahmah Othman on 22 and 23 April 1976.
34. *Malay Mail*, 20 May 1958 and *Suara Merdeka*, 16 May 1958.
35. *ST*, 16 April 1960.
36. *Utusan Melayu*, 14 March 1960 and *Utusan Melayu*, 6 March 1960. These references and all others which refer to the vernacular press, i.e. the Chinese, Malay and Tamil dailies, with the exception of *Berita Harian* comments on the Dewan Muslimat PAS, are contained in the government publication, *Daily Press Summaries—Vernacular Press 1958–1976*, henceforth to be referred to as *D.P.S.*
37. *Malay Mail*, 2 December 1962.
38. *Utusan Melayu*, 19 February 1963, *D.P.S.*
39. *Malay Mail*, 12 March 1964.
40. *ST*, 16 September 1964 and *1964 KI Annual Report*, p. 23.
41. *ST*, 21 February 1966.
42. *Malay Mail*, 29 December 1967.

43. Manderson, op. cit., p. 214.

44. Chan Heng-chee, 'The Malayan Chinese Association', unpublished MA thesis, University of Singapore, 1965, p. 118. According to Chan, quoting from Aziz and Silcock, neither the MCA nor the UMNO was a 'democratic body with a mass membership and in both, the (executive) committee consists largely of established community leaders'. See T. H. Silcock and Ungku Abdul Aziz, 'Nationalism in Malaya', in William L. Holland (ed.), *Asian Nationalism and the West*, N. Y., Macmillan, 1953, p. 326. The author concurs to the extent that it is only in the 1970s that the MCA sought a widely based membership. Prior to this time, party membership, leadership and finances were dominated by members of the business and commercial communities. For the UMNO however, this view is too simple. While organized and led by members of the Malay élite, UMNO reached out to include as many rural Malays in the party as possible. Additionally, if one of the functions of a 'mass' party is to politically educate the masses (Chan Heng-chee, op. cit., p. 116), UMNO fulfilled this function by rallying Malays behind what the UMNO leadership defined as Malay causes.

45. MCA records indicate that total membership figures in the party in 1962–3 totalled 32,745 people out of a Chinese electorate of 990,000. Chan Heng-chee, op. cit., p. 129.

46. MCA, *The First Constitution of the MCA adopted and approved by the General Committee of the MCA, March 22, 1959, Amended 1963*, Section III, Art. 1, 2 and 3.

47. Ibid., Section IV, Art. 24, 3a.

48. Chan Heng-chee, op. cit., p. 78.

49. MCA, *The First Constitution of the MCA*, Section V, Art. 25.

50. Ibid., Section VI, Art. 25 and Chan Heng-Chee, op. cit., p. 80.

51. Chan Heng-chee, op. cit., p. 81.

52. Though Chan Heng-chee mentions in 1953 and 1956 annual reports on p. 127 of her thesis, an MCA spokesman denies that these records currently exist.

53. MCA, *Annual Report of the MCA, 1961–2*, Kuala Lumpur, MCA, 1962, p. 4.

54. Ibid., p. 13.

55. MCA, *Annual Report of the MCA, 1962–3*, Kuala Lumpur, MCA, Appendix 1.

56. Ibid., Appendices 2–6.

57. MCA, *Annual Report of the MCA, 1963–4*, Kuala Lumpur, MCA, Appendix 2.

58. *The Guardian*, November 1966, Vol. 1, No. 5, p. 3.

59. *The Guardian*, November 1966, Vol. 1, No. 5, p. 3.

60. *The Guardian*, November 1966, Vol. 1, No. 5, p. 3.

61. MCA, *Constitution of the MCA Incorporating all Amendments up to 1967*, Kuala Lumpur, MCA, 1967, Section 7a, Art. 28a.

62. *ST*, 26 August 1967.

63. *The Guardian*, October 1967, Vol. 1, No. 2, p. 3.

64. *The Guardian*, October 1967, Vol. 1, No. 2, p. 3.

65. *The Guardian*, October 1968, Vol. 2, No. 10, p. 6.

66. *The Guardian*, December 1968–January 1969, Vol. 2, No. 10, p. 5, and *Malay Mail*, 16 December 1968.

67. *The Guardian*, December 1968–January 1969, Vol. 2, No. 12, p. 5.

68. *Registrar of Societies Report on the MCA*, Kuala Lumpur, Registrar of Societies, 1968.

69. *Malayan Times*, 10 December 1963, *D.P.S.*

70. MIC, *MIC 18th Annual Report, 1964*, Petaling Jaya, Victory Press, p. 17.

71. MIC *Ulangtahun Ketigapuluh 1946–1976*, Kuala Lumpur, MIC, n.d., pp. 33–41.

72. MIC, *Constitution of the Malaysian Indian Congress, 1966*, Kuala Lumpur, Registrar of Societies, Section 8, Art. 14b.

73. *Tamil Nesan*, 26 November 1963.

74. Interview with Mrs Devaki Krishnan on 6 July 1976.

75. Ibid.

76. *Registrar of Societies 1967 Report on the MIC*.

77. Interview with Khadijah Sidek on 26 July 1976.

78. Ibid.

79. PAS, *Peratoran Dewan Muslimat PAS, 1966*, Tujuan Bab Kedua 1–4 (*Rules of the Dewan Muslimat PAS, 1966*, Goals Second Section, points 1–4).
80. Ibid., Section 8.
81. Ibid., Section 4 and PAS, *Undang-undang Tuboh Persatuan Islam Sa-Tanah Melayu, 1966*, Bab Kelapan (*1966 Constitution of Party Islam*, Section 8).
82. PAS, *Constitution of Party Islam, 1966*, Section 8, Art. 5.
83. K. J. Ratnam and R. S. Milne, *The Malayan Parliamentary Election of 1964*, Kuala Lumpur, University of Malaya Press, 1969, p. 50.
84. Ibid.
85. *Warta Negara*, 30 December 1957, *D.P.S.*
86. *Utusan Melayu*, 25 March 1958, *D.P.S.*
87. *Utusan Melayu*, 24 September 1958, *D.P.S.*
88. *Utusan Melayu*, 26 November 1958, *D.P.S.*
89. *Warta Negara*, 7 August 1958, *D.P.S.*
90. Interview with Khadijah Sidek on 26 July 1976 and *Berita Harian* (*BH*), 16 April 1965.
91. *BH*, 22 August 1964.
92. *BH*, 22 August 1964.
93. *Utusan Melayu*, 4 January 1962, *D.P.S.*
94. See Chapter 4.
95. Interview with A. Razak Khalifah, State Secretary of the Selangor PSRM on 17 October 1976.
96. *Malay Mail*, 14 March 1959.
97. Interview with A. Razak Khalifah, 17 October 1976.
98. *Malay Mail*, 14 March 1959.
99. Ibid.
100. *Utusan Melayu*, 12 October 1959, *D.P.S.*
101. Ibid.
102. *Utusan Melayu*, 4 February 1961, *D.P.S.*
103. Ibid., 31 August 1961, *D.P.S.*
104. *BH*, 16 July 1962.
105. *Utusan Melayu*, 22 November 1962, *D.P.S.*
106. *Malay Mail*, 15 February 1963.
107. *Malay Mail*, 15 February 1963 and *ST*, 16 February 1963.
108. *ST*, 9 April 1964.
109. *ST*, 7 November 1963.
110. Interview with A. Razak Khalifah, 17 October 1976.
111. LP, *The 1959 Annual Report of the Labour Party*, the Labour Party, Malaya, n.d., Resolutions 12 and 13.
112. LP, *The 1959 Annual Report of the Labour Party*.
113. LP, *The 1961 Annual Report of the Labour Party*, the Labour Party, Malaya, n.d.
114. LP, *The 10th Annual Party Conference, August 18–19, 1962, Yearly Report of the Labour Party*, Malaya, the Labour Party, n.d.
115. *ST*, 11 March 1963.
116. Interview with Ganga Nayar on 24 May 1976. Note membership figures are inconsistent. Party records for example, estimate that as of 24 October 1963 the LP had 26,000 members while by December 1963 the same source listed 4,500 members. See the Registrar of Societies file on the Labour Party.
117. *1966 LP Report to the Registrar of Societies*.
118. Labour Party press release, 15 September 1963.
119. Interview with Ganga Nayar, 24 May 1976.
120. *Tiger Press*, 26 January 1960, *D.P.S.*
121. *Sin Chew Jit Poh*, 10 March 1960, *D.P.S.*
122. *Sin Chew Jit Poh*, 15 March 1962, *D.P.S.*
123. *Sin Chew Jit Poh*, 1 October 1963, *D.P.S.*
124. *Sin Chew Jit Poh*, 26 January 1965, *D.P.S.*

125. *China Press*, 8 February 1965, *D.P.S.*
126. *Sin Chew Jit Poh*, 10 February 1965, *D.P.S.*
127. *BH*, 15 February 1965.
128. *Sing Pin Jih Pao*, 31 October 1966, *D.P.S.*
129. *Min Mao*, 31 October 1966, *D.P.S.*
130. *Kwong Wah Yit Poh*, 5 September 1967, *D.P.S.*
131. *Malayan Thung Pau*, 15 January 1969, *D.P.S.*
132. *China Press*, 14 April 1969, *D.P.S.*; *Nanyang Siang Pau*, 12 April 1969, *D.P.S.*; *China Press*, 5 May 1969, *D.P.S.*; *Sin Chew Jit Poh*, 2 April 1969, *D.P.S.*

133. No discussion of women in the Peoples' Action Party (PAP) is included. Though the PAP contested several seats in the 1964 elections, it had practically no formal organization in Malaya at the time of the elections, and had no time to develop one prior to the withdrawal of Singapore from Malaysia in 1965. See Ratnam and Milne, op. cit., p. 53.

134. *Malay Mail*, 24 January 1958, *D.P.S.*
135. *Malay Mail*, 31 October 1958, *D.P.S.*
136. *Sin Chew Jit Poh*, 9 March 1965, *D.P.S.*
137. *Malay Mail*, 19 April 1962, *D.P.S.*
138. *Malay Mail*, 19 April 1962, *D.P.S.*
139. UDP, 'United Democratic Party, UDP Constitution', Kuala Lumpur, mimeograph, Section 3, Art. 1-4.
140. *ST*, 22 April 1962.
141. UDP, Report of the UDP to the Registrar of Societies, 1962, Kuala Lumpur, Registrar of Societies.
142. *Malay Mail*, 23 April 1964.
143. UDP, Resolutions Passed at the Central General Assembly of the UDP, 12 January 1964, Kuala Lumpur. Miscellaneous speeches and press releases of the UDP, New Straits Times Library.
144. UDP, Report of the UDP to the Registrar of Societies, 1962.
145. *ST*, 28 April 1963.
146. PPP, *Registrar of Societies Report on the Peoples' Progressive Party*, Kuala Lumpur, Registrar of Societies.
147. The eight were: the YWCA, the Pan-Pacific South-East Asian Women's Association, the National Association of Women's Institutes, the Malayan Trained Nurses Association, the Girl Guides of Malaya, the Women's International Club, the Women Teachers' Union and the Muslim Women's Welfare Council. *ST*, 5 June 1961.
148. *ST*, 5 June 1961.
149. The 16 included: the National Association of Women's Institutes, the Women Police, the Malayan Trained Nurses Association, the YWCA, the Kaum Ibu UMNO, the Lai Chee Women's Association, the Indian Association's women's section, the Women's International Club, the Dewan Muslimat PMIP, the Young Women's Indian Association, the Women Teachers' Union, the St. John's Ambulance Brigade, Parti Rakyat Women's Section, the Wanita MIC, and the Pan-Pacific South-East Asian Women's Association. *ST*, 25 August 1962.
150. *ST*, 25 August 1962 and, Report of Women's Day, 25 August 1962, Kuala Lumpur. Miscellaneous Papers of the NCWO 1962-1983, NCWO.
151. Report of the NCWO 1st Biennial Conference, 25 August 1965.
152. The NCWO Malaya: Rules and Constitution, Kuala Lumpur, NCWO, n.d., Art. 2.
153. Ibid., Art. 3.
154. The 12 were: the National Association of Women's Institutes, the Women Teachers' Union, the Wanita MCA, the KI UMNO, the St. John's Ambulance Brigade, the University Women's Association, the Selangor Indian Association women's section, the PPSEAWA, the Wanita MIC, the YWCA, the Lai Chee Women's Association, and the Women's International Club. *NCWO 1st Biennial Conference 25 August 1965*, Miscellaneous Papers 1962-1983, Kuala Lumpur, NCWO Office.
155. *ST*, 26 August 1964.

156. *ST*, 26 August 1964.
157. NCWO, Report of the NCWO 2nd Biennial Conference, 25 August 1976, Miscellaneous Papers 1962–1983, Kuala Lumpur, NCWO Office.
158. *Malay Mail*, 18 September 1958.
159. *Malay Mail*, 18 September 1958.
160. Minutes of the KI UMNO General Assembly, Arau, May 1949, p. 6.
161. *ST*, 7 June 1958.
162. *Malay Mail*, 20 March 1959; *ST*, 2 June 1958; *Malay Mail*, 26 May 1958; Manderson, op. cit., p. 198 and Daniel E. Moore, 'The UMNO and the 1959 Malayan Elections: A Study of a Political Party in Action in a Newly Independent, Plural Society', unpublished doctoral dissertation, University of California, Berkeley, 1960, p. 53.
163. Moore, op. cit., p. 53.
164. *Malay Mail*, 19 April 1959.
165. Interview with KI Secretary Rahmah Othman on 22 and 23 April 1976.
166. Moore, op. cit., p. 53 and *ST*, 24 September 1958.
167. *Malay Mail*, 20 January 1959.
168. *Malay Mail*, 18 February 1959.
169. *Malay Mail*, 18 February 1959.
170. *ST*, 15 August 1959.
171. *Report on the Parliamentary and State Elections 1959, Federation of Malaya*, Government Publication, Malaya, 1960, Appendix A.
172. Ibid.
173. Ratnam and Milne, op. cit., p. 13.
174. *Malay Mail*, 20 September 1959.
175. *ST*, 19 August 1959.
176. *ST*, 19 August 1959.
177. *ST*, 19 August 1959.
178. *Malay Mail*, 20 August 1959.
179. *Malay Mail*, 20 September 1960.
180. *Malay Mail*, 5 February 1961.
181. Manderson, op. cit., p. 200.
182. *Malay Mail*, 6 August 1960.
183. Ratnam and Milne, op. cit., p. 168.
184. *BH*, 28 April 1964.
185. *BH*, 28 April 1964.
186. *Report on the Parliamentary and State Legislative Assembly General Elections, 1964 of the States of Malaya*, p. 18.
187. *BH*, 28 April 1964.
188. *ST*, 26 April 1964.
189. Party Election Manifestos, *1964 State and Parliamentary Elections Manifestos*, Jabatan Penerangan Malaysia, April 1964. Manifestos from the following parties were included: the Alliance, PAP, PMIP, UDP, SF, PPP and Parti Negara.
190. *Alliance Manifesto*, p. 6.
191. *Socialist Front (SF) Manifesto*, point 8 (c).
192. *United Democratic Party (UDP) Manifesto*, p. 39.

6 The Kaum Ibu UMNO, 1969–1976

THE Kaum Ibu UMNO, renamed the Wanita UMNO in 1971, dominated the women's political groups through (and beyond) 1976. The seven years witnessed both a concern for old causes (such as Muslim marriage and divorce reform), as well as new causes (the launching of the Wanita UMNO Economic Foundation 'Dermajaya Wanita'). Yet, the ways of the KI remained the same: slow incremental change, lack of power within the party, and the pursuit of limited goals. While the auxiliary favoured equal pay for women and urged that the status of women be uplifted, these goals were pursued through traditional, passive means. They passed resolutions and had individual KI leaders press UMNO leaders. In pursuing its goals, the section did not challenge its position *vis-à-vis* UMNO.

By 1976, some KI women were becoming more aware of the special problems faced by women. This caused them to re-examine the auxiliary's goals. Notably, a few KI began to assess the section's strengths and weaknesses—particularly the control of the section by older rural women who some accused of limited vision. This conflict between 'old and new blood' had little effect on the power structure of the KI. The number of younger, better educated women was limited. The inability to attract such women led to charges by UMNO that the KI had failed to produce acceptable women leaders (i.e. well-educated, politically experienced, articulate women leaders). Hence, the number of KI members in parliament and in government service remained low. The public image of the KI was of older, rural and unsophisticated women. Nonetheless, the KI increased its membership and broadened its areas of interest. Both the KI's structure and the issues addressed by the KI help to show both the continuity and change that had taken place. By examining both the members and the leaders of the KI, the evolution of the KI can be better understood.

Structure and Interests

By far the most major event effecting Malaysia in the 1960s and 1970s was the 1969 post-election riots. Breaking out just after the May 1969 general election, the riots shook Malaysia to its core. It further challenged the Alliance assumption of political accommodation. Politically, the riots resulted in a ban on all party politics from May 1969 until September 1970. During this time, a state of national emergency was called and Malaysia was governed through emergency decrees by the National Operations Council. By February 1971, parliamentary democracy was restored with qualifications. Regarding political parties and wings, each was required to examine its goals and co-ordinate them with new government guidelines. These guidelines were made to reduce future racial strife. In keeping with this self-examination, UMNO, with its KI and Pemuda wings, adopted a new party constitution in 1971. New by-laws for the KI were also approved by the Supreme Council in January 1972.[1] The basic structure of the KI and its roles within UMNO remained unchanged.

The major goals of the KI remained: to encourage its members to become active in the fields of politics, religion, education, economics, law and women's rights, social welfare, the arts and culture.[2] To help achieve these goals, leadership and training courses were implemented.[3]

As for structure, changes in KI by-laws were minor. The branch remained the basic unit for both UMNO and the KI. There were two changes at the branch level for the women's section: 1) the expansion of the branch executive committee from three to five elected members to about ten elected members, and 2) the appointment of the KI secretary, treasurer and up to five members of the branch committee by the KI branch leader with the approval of the committee.[4] A similar change was adopted at the division level with the same expansion of the division executive committee.[5] The UMNO division secretary and treasurer remained the secretary and treasurer of the KI division. The KI division leader, though, now appointed the previously elected assistant secretary and treasurer.[6]

Under the 1972 by-laws, the main task of the KI state liaison body was to administer the affairs of the division.[7] The liaison body, which was to meet every two months, consisted of a chairperson, assistant chair, secretary, assistant secretary, treasurer and the leader (or representative) of each division in the state.[8] The chair and vice-chair were to be appointed by the national KI leader after consulting with the KI division leaders. The UMNO secretary was to function as the KI secretary.[9] The newly appointed chairwoman was then to appoint the body's assistant secretary and assistant treasurer.[10]

Changes at the national level mirrored those of the branch and division. The expanded national executive committee now provided for the KI delegates at their annual assembly to elect up to ten members and the elected national leader to appoint up to seven members.[11] The secretary general and treasurer of UMNO remained the secretary and treasurer of the KI wing. The *Ketua* appointed the assistant secretary and assistant treasurer. At the national level, the composition of the executive committee was subject to the approval of the Majlis Tertinggi UMNO (Supreme Council)—an approval which was not required at the lower levels.[12] The subordinate role of the KI and Pemuda was shown by the fact that each section was allowed to select only five delegates (previously three) to the UMNO general assembly.[13] Though the women's wing was a large component of the UMNO membership by the 1970s, with over 200,000 KI UMNO members by 1976,[14] the women remained clearly underrepresented. The continued presence of the UMNO secretary and treasurer as KI officers also served to remind the women's wing that it was subject to party control.

Though KI leaders had often lobbied for an increase in their members as electoral candidates and as government appointees, little effort had been made by the women to increase their role within UMNO itself. The pattern of underrepresentation, which had developed earlier, had not changed. Party records show that women members remained on the periphery of party decision-making.

By 1976, UMNO's membership numbered 517,000, of whom half or 257,000 were women.[15] The division remained the basic unit of power within the party. As of 1976, there were 114 UMNO divisions corresponding to parliamentary constituencies. Each division had a parallel KI and Pemuda division. Of the 114 UMNO divisions, only one was headed by a woman, Aishah Ghani—the fifth national leader of the KI section, who had led the division since 1962. Of UMNO's 5,000 branches, fewer than 20 were headed by women.[16] KI members had been unable to build support based on control of a branch and then a division which UMNO leaders required for upward mobility in the party. The failure of women to partake of the affairs in the party branch was a problem recognized by the women themselves. This was shown by Rogers in his study of a rural Malay community: 'During the annual meetings of the local UMNO branch, it is the men who nominate the required number of women as members of the local executive committee. The few women present do not participate.'[17]

Women leaders on the National Executive Committee were very much aware of this problem. They felt it must be tackled by the women themselves and must be aimed at the local level:

> ... even if women go to the branch [general] meeting, they never nominate women for leadership positions at the branch level—and certainly the men won't. So they are handicapped at the beginning. You must work your way up for it is the leader of the division that is the key position. If you are a division head then you have a strong base of support. UMNO demands of its men and hence its women, that they have a strong base of local support before one gets to the Majlis Tertinggi or gets to run for election. It is very difficult for anyone, let alone a woman, to get on the electoral lists. (Aishah Ghani, Wanita UMNO Ketua, 1/3/76 interview.)

> Women are very numerous in the branches but they do not understand that they should attend the UMNO branch meetings as well as the Wanita; hence, they aren't there to elect general branch and division leaders and remain weak. (Rahmah Othman, Wanita UMNO Secretary, 16/2/76 interview.)

> What is lacking is an awareness by the women of the power they could wield. Many times there are more women than men in an UMNO branch and they could elect a *ketua cawangan* [branch leader], but they don't. Yet, they don't

realize their rights under the [UMNO] constitution and they don't nominate and elect women to positions of influence in the party. (Zaleha Ismail, Parliamentary Secretary and Wanita UMNO Executive Council member, 14/7/76 interview.)

Women leaders maintained that they were trying to tackle this problem through political education. On their many visits to the KI divisions, members of the National Executive Committee emphasized the rights that women enjoyed under the UMNO constitution. Yet most KI members preferred to stay within the confines of the women's wing. This reflected the greater comfort the women felt in all-women groups. While women have been accepted as party members, some women leaders felt that UMNO men were waiting for UMNO women to 'prove themselves'—an opinion which was reinforced by the fact that women were seldom appointed or elected to UMNO division committees. In 1967, the average UMNO division executive committee numbered 22 members. There were never more than four women (which included the KI division leader who, due to her office, sat on the committee as a vice-chairperson). The average committee contained only two women. Of 114 divisions, three women held the position of treasurer while one was a division secretary. Aishah Ghani remained the only woman to head a UMNO division.[18] The 1968–70 *UMNO Yearbook* presents the same picture as do the later annual reports of 1971/2, 1973/4, 1974/5 and 1975/6. Of the latter three reports, only the officers were listed. Of these, only one woman was an officer (a vice-president) in addition to the KI division leader. Zaharah binti Abdul Majid briefly headed a division in Johore while five other women sat as officers on division committees in 1973/4.[19]

Above the division, the pattern of underrepresentation continued, as shown in Table 6.1. UMNO records show that women have played a minor role at higher levels within the party. On UMNO's major policy-making body, the Supreme Council, women have never numbered more than three on a committee that averaged 38 members. On the party's advisory bureaus, women have played a small role. The leader of the KI section served on many bureaus. Other able KI members have not been chosen. At the state level, the pattern was the same as at the division: over the years state committees have had 11–30 members, though only one or two KI members have served. None of the women have been chosen as an officer.[20] The data of 1976 showed little change. There were still only three women out of 37 people on the Supreme Council. The state committees averaged two women each but with no women as officers. Further, no women have served as UMNO representatives on the National Front Executive Committee, the body that co-ordinated the affairs of the Alliance.[21] A few more women had been appointed to the party bureaus but the change was slight; again, the KI *Ketua* was the main party choice for such bureau work (e.g. in 1976, Aishah Ghani served on four out of seven bureaus).[22]

When parliamentary democracy returned in 1971, the party's self-evaluation changed the KI's emphasis. Still loyal to UMNO, the KI began to take a greater part in the economy and in the legal system.

TABLE 6.1
The Pattern of Representation at the Higher Hierarchy
within UMNO, 1967-1976

Year	Alliance Working Committee	Western Malaysia Alliance Committee	Malaysia Alliance	National Front Executive Committee	Supreme Council	Party Bureaus	Headquarters' Committee	State Level Committee	Regional Committee
1967	5/0[a]	—	15/1[a]	—	35/3[a]	4/1[b]	2/0[c]	10/1[d]	4/5/0[e]
1968-70	—	—	—	—	34/3	6/1[f]	2/0	8/1[g]	4/5/0
1971-2	5/0	14/2[a]	10/1	—	34/3	6/3	3/0	9/1[h]	—
1973-4	5/0	15/1	11/1	—	36/2	7/5	4/1	11/2-3	—
1975	**No Longer Exists**			5/0[a]	39/2	Data Incomplete		7/0	—
1976				5/0	34/3	7/5[i]	Data Incomplete	11/1-3	—

Source: Compiled from UMNO, *UMNO Annual Reports, 1967-76.*

[a] '5/0' denotes 5 men and 0 women.
[b] '4/1' denotes 4 bureaus (committees) with 1 woman each. Committee sizes varied from 6 to 15 members.
[c] '2/0' denotes 2 committees with no women members in toto.
[d] '10/1' denotes 10 committees with one woman on each state committee. State committees averaged 10-25 members. In 1967, Selangor had 2 women.
[e] '4/5/0' denotes 4 committees of 5 members each with no women.
[f] The one woman served on 3 bureaus.
[g] Perak had no women, Malacca 2, Selangor 3.
[h] Johore had 2 women, Selangor 3.
[i] 2 women served on 5 committees.

Women's rights and leadership training for women were to receive increased attention.[23] Five new committees were created: 1) education and welfare, headed by Fatimah binti Hashim, 2) economic affairs led by Aishah Ghani, 3) religious affairs headed by Aishahton binti Mohd. Fadhullah Suhaimi, 4) laws and women's rights, Marina Yusof, and 5) finance, Saadiah Sardon.

A women's foundation was set up by the KI economic bureau.[24] Its purpose was to encourage Malay women to take part in commerce and industry. It also provided loans to Malay women who wanted to start businesses.[25] Capital came from the M$1 donation from each member.[26] Later, an employment agency was formed together with a training and advisory bureau. In the short term, the foundation sponsored branch courses in commercial tailoring, catering and co-operatives.[27] Deputy Leader Aishah Ghani, explained the KI view, 'You can only raise your standard of living if you are forward looking and always aim high.... Rural women must take part in economic projects, no matter how small, if a better life is to be achieved.'[28] In 1972, KI (now known as Wanita UMNO) sections opened a co-operative tailoring shop[29] and set aside educational funds for members' children.[30] The Perak section formed a business enterprise, Sharikat Sendikit Sri Wanita, which included transport, light industries, mining and sundries.[31] Further, a group of 20 Wanita members were selected to attend the Mara Institute of Technology for a three-month tailoring course—a prelude to women attending the institute.[32] In 1972, the Wanita UMNO company, Syarikat Dermajaya, was formed with a M$40,000 operating fund. It sought to aid Malay women in starting their own businesses.[33]

Aishah Ghani emphasized the importance of Malay women being involved in the economy. She stressed that Malay women should emulate their non-Malay counterparts.[34] By October 1974, a six-member Wanita UMNO committee drafted plans to set up the section's first major co-operative, Koperasi Dermajaya Wanita. The co-operative served many purposes: to build shops for rent, to acquire truck and taxi licences for UMNO members, and to engage in logging and agricultural enterprises.[35] The most notable achievement of the co-operative was the opening of a department store in Kuala Lumpur in 1976. (It was jointly owned by the co-operative and a Singapore firm.)

Political activities which began again in September 1970, saw a challenge to the leadership of Fatimah binti Hashim. Aishah Ghani called for the old leaders to make way for younger, better educated women; she also proposed that the section be reorganized.[36] However, she declined to openly challenge Fatimah binti Hashim who was re-elected as *Ketua* at the KI General Assembly.[37]

In 1971, Fatimah binti Hashim urged a new image for the KI. In keeping with the new emphasis and the section's desire to attract younger urban women, Fatimah binti Hashim appointed five intellectuals (*kaum intelek*) to sit on the five sub-committees.[38] She also brought a number of younger, better educated women into the party. KI secretary at that time, Rahmah Othman, herself one of the younger members, explained the situation that faced the section: 'Since its inception in 1949, the KI has only been able to attract Malay women in the rural areas—who form the bulk of the organization—and women whose husbands are in UMNO or the government.'[39] The desire for better educated women members reflected a growing need to widen the base from which future leaders would come. It also coincided with a call for new ideas and restructuring that was being heralded by UMNO, the MCA and the MIC. At this time, the KI membership was more than 150,000, nearly two-thirds of the party.[40] The bid to woo younger women to the party was shown by the section's name change from Pergerakan Kaum Ibu UMNO to Pergerakan Wanita UMNO. The change was approved 141 to 96 by the 1971 KI General Assembly.[41] 'Ibu' meaning 'mother' was replaced by 'wanita' which simply meant 'woman' and thus applied to women of all ages. Wanita UMNO leaders explaining the changes argued:

Fatimah Hashim, 'The Pergerakan Wanita must move ahead and play a more meaningful role not only in the party but also the government.... Members must be prepared to encourage more Malay women intellectuals to join the movement to face another twenty-five years of struggle.' Dasimah Dasir said, 'These new members can lead the older group with ideas on national issues.'[42]

The bid to woo urban women also appealed to younger rural women to join the section. Aishah Ghani, at a division annual assembly in March 1972, urged younger rural women to join. They could help speed up the change in the thinking of the older women. These younger women could also provide the leadership needed at the local levels: 'We still lack leadership at the local level and these girls are the answer—they can be trained, not only in politics but in economics and business as well.... We can send our rural girls or women for specialized courses and they can return to lead the others.'[43] The same view was expressed by Fatimah binti Sulaiman, secretary of a Kuala Lumpur division. This is shown when she discussed the division's goals and the role women could play in nation-building:

We are out to prove that rural women can be a potential force of change and reconstruction.... If the men are the pillars of the nation, the women are the foundation without which the section would collapse.... The main thing to do is to change their [rural women's] attitude and outlook, this is no easy job.... We must first win their trust and build up their confidence through words and deeds. We must show them we are sincere in our efforts to encourage them to come forward.... There has been a good response generally and I think this is a good sign.... It shows that our women folk are awakening and realizing their potentiality.[44]

The appeal to younger women was in accord with party policy. Tun Ismail in opening the combined 1972 Wanita–Pemuda General Assembly[45] assessed the section's major weakness:

Your feelings and actions should be limited within the framework of policy and strategy of the party.... I do not wish to belittle the success achieved by UMNO Wanita and its ability to tackle national issues but I would like to suggest here that it put forward more leaders who are acceptable to our multiracial society.... UMNO Wanita leaders in recent years belong to an older generation. With the changes around us, I hope there will be a merger between them and the younger people, particularly intellectuals and professional groups, so that it can become stronger.[46]

The advice was heeded: Aishah Ghani replaced Fatimah Hashim (191 votes to 123) as *Ketua*. Two new members, both younger and well educated, were elected to the Wanita UMNO National Executive Committee (Marina Yusof, legal adviser to Bank Bumiputra and Rafidah Aziz, economics lecturer at the University of Malaya). Aishah Ghani pledged to bring the women's section down to the grassroots level:

In the past, there was a tendency for Wanita UMNO to produce leaders at the national level. The usual practice was to centralize some of them for political and leadership training courses once or twice a year at a particular town. At the practical level, the district leaders know little of the Second Malaysia Plan and the new economic policy. They ask many questions but do not know how to implement these schemes.[47]

In keeping with the newer, more assertive image, Wanita Chairperson, Normah Kamaruddin, called on Prime Minister, Tun Razak to implement all of the Wanita proposals, 'We can prove it to the men; we are no more Kaum Ibu and this change in name to Wanita makes us more dynamic and brave, like young men.... We are even prepared to picket in front of the Tun's house if our resolutions are not given serious attention.'[48]

An issue on which the Wanita UMNO focused during the 1970s was marriage and divorce reform for Muslims. Thwarted efforts to reform Muslim marriage and divorce procedures in the past led to impatience among Wanita UMNO members. In March 1973, Aishah Ghani announced that the Wanita would study the issue of the minimum age for Muslim women to marry. It would later recommend to the Religious Council and the government that girls under the age of 16 not be allowed to marry.[49] Two days later, Aishah Ghani announced that the Wanita should carry out a campaign to educate Muslim women on their constitutional rights[50]—a campaign urging the National Islamic Council to regulate Muslim marriage and divorce laws: 'At present, the laws differ from one state to another. This has brought about a raw deal for women. It has prevented problems arising from divorce and polygamy to be effectively tackled.'[51] She argued, the status of women would be uplifted by standardizing the law.[52] Throughout 1974, the pressure to bring about Muslim marriage and divorce reform was maintained largely by the efforts of the section's leader, Aishah Ghani. Addressing 300 Wanita UMNO members in Penang, she criticized the *ulama* (religious scholars) as unfair to women when interpreting the laws of the Koran on marriage and divorce, 'There have been a great deal of interpretations of these laws and most of them, I am sorry to say have been unfair to women because they tend to deviate from the basic facts of the laws.'[53] Islamic marriage and divorce laws were still a 'thorn in the flesh' to Muslim women.[54] Aishah Ghani's 'thorn in the flesh' remark led to a public outcry. This prompted her to explain that while Islamic laws were just and fair to women, they were interpreted and enforced according to the whims of men. This, she said, resulted in unfairness to women.[55] Aishah Ghani, in an interview with the author in 1976, explained that the Wanita had been largely unsuccessful in tightening and unifying Muslim family laws (laws varied from state to state). One of the biggest fears of Muslim men, she elaborated, was that Wanita UMNO sought to eliminate polygamy. She felt it was best to avoid the term polygamy as it was fraught with emotive content. The older, more traditional Muslim men felt that a basic right granted to them by the Koran might be taken away. Nonetheless, she maintained, the Wanita UMNO's struggle would continue. The struggle would include her call to Wanita members to form work camps. Members could then discuss social, political and economic issues at these camps. She also called on the Wanita to safeguard the interests of women by forming close ties with the *Kadi*'s offices. Lastly, she urged that state level discussions be held within the Wanita on implementing Islamic family law.[56] The lack of women electoral candidates as well as the problems women faced to obtain appointments to government office led to corrective actions by the Wanita.

In March 1974, the section began to gear its members for the August general elections. Aishah Ghani spoke at a delegates conference in Klang and announced that the Wanita would try to field at least one candidate in each state. She noted that currently Malacca and Perlis had no women at all in their state assemblies. UMNO President, Tun Razak, who was also Prime Minister (1971–6), she went on, had been informed of the Wanita's intent to field more candidates.[57] By 28 June, when the Wanita General Assembly was held, dissatisfaction with the lack of opportunity to stand for election was clear. Aishah Ghani addressed the 400 delegates from 114 divisions and noted, 'No less than 15 divisions have asked for the number of seats for women to be increased in the coming elections in line with (the) services and sacrifices made by Wanita UMNO.'[58] As if he expected the auxiliary's dissatisfaction, Deputy Prime Minister Hussein Onn outlined a 50-point plan to create a leadership of 'noble quality' in the two wings; this included: 'Keep strictly to the aims of the policies of the party.' He stressed that the sections were subordinate to the party: 'We also do not wish to see UMNO youth and Wanita UMNO become pressure groups in order to achieve their goals.'[59] Hussein Onn thus acknowledged that the two sections could be both a danger to party unity and lobbies for special interests. In view of the Wanita's past history, there was, though, little real cause for alarm. The party did little to temper the

TABLE 6.2
Number of UMNO Women Candidates, 1959–1974 Elections

Year	Combined State and Federal KI Candidates
1959	14
1964	10
1969	16
1974	16

Source: Compiled from reports on the General Elections of 1959, 1964, 1969 and 1974.

Wanita grievances: in the general elections of August 1974, once again only 16 Wanita members would be chosen as party electoral candidates.

Contrary to earlier pledges, Wanita members were not selected to stand in all states. No women were put forward as federal or state candidates in Penang, Perlis or Trengganu. A total of 16 UMNO women did stand and all won—the first time in 25 years that all Wanita candidates were successful. This showed, according to Aishah Ghani, 'that women politicians have received the trust and support of the voters'.[60] The number of UMNO women candidates, though, remained the same from one election to the next as shown in Table 6.2.

Of the parliamentary candidates in the 1974 elections, all were long-time Wanita division leaders. Their names had appeared in Wanita UMNO literature since the early days of the KI. As for the state level, women were also less prominent than at the parliamentary level. For example, Wanita UMNO candidates were not selected to stand in Penang—not because there were no suitable candidates, but probably because of the largely non-Malay population. In Perlis and Trengganu, where once again there were no women candidates, the reason is less clear. Strong male competition, combined with few popular female candidates at the state level resulted in almost all male candidates. Clearly, the constant demand by the women for more candidates had not been met.

In January 1976, the Wanita addressed the problem involving women at the local level. At that time, the Perak Wanita UMNO again raised the issue of the lack of women village leaders. The Wanita called on the Perak State Government to appoint women as *ketua kampong* (village leader) and *penghulu* (leader of several villages). They were once again thwarted by religious leaders who argued that such appointments would be in conflict with Islamic teachings. The Perak *Mufti*, Dato Haji Abu Hassan Ashaari, argued that though women had been appointed as *penghulu* at Batu Kurau and Kampong Deu, it was no longer 'appropriate'.[61] While the Perak Wanita was not successful in its plea, women in Negri Sembilan praised their state government for appointing two women as *ketua kampung*[62]—a decision which was supported by editorials in the *Malay Mail*[63] and the *Star*.[64] Further support came from Rafidah Aziz, an UMNO Supreme Council member, who argued that women qualified to be *ketua kampong* should be given the chance to prove their worth.[65]

Opposition to women as *ketua kampong* and *penghulu* quickly mounted in February and March 1976. The Negri Sembilan Islamic Fatwa (Ruling) Council (an advisory body to the Sultan) decided that such appointments would be contrary to Islamic law. The Association of *Ketua Kampong* in Johore and the Association of *Penghulu* in Selangor also came out against women appointees. They argued that 'the rural community still could not accept women as their leaders'.[66] Women, too, were divided on the issue. Salmah Sheikh Hussein, the Deputy Leader of the Dewan Muslimat PAS, spoke out against such appointments; she argued that women were not suitable for such appointments.[67] In the face of this opposition, the Negri Sembilan government backed down and rejected the call for women appointees.[68] If a woman could not become *ketua kampong*, at least one Wanita had succeeded in becoming the leader of an UMNO branch in 1976. More remarkably, Wan Teh Aminah binti Wan Yusof defeated the former Chief Minister of Perak for the post of *Ketua* of the Kota Lama Kiri Hilir Perak UMNO branch in Kuala Kangsar, Perak. Most of the UMNO members who attended the branch's annual assembly were women (62 women and 14 men). (It was the women who carried the election—proof that if UMNO women used their power as voters at UMNO general meetings then, 'we might witness a great change in the leadership of the party'.)[69]

Frustration over the lack of women appointed to political posts resulted in a memorandum being presented to the Prime Minister. The decision to draft the memorandum was made by the Wanita UMNO Executive Committee.[70] The memorandum was, in part, a response to the general lack of women in the administrative and diplomatic services as well as in political posts.[71] In part, it was also a response to the cabinet named by the new Prime Minister, Datuk Hussein Onn in March 1976. There was only one woman minister, Aishah Ghani, Minister of Welfare Services, and one woman parliamentary secretary, Rafidah Aziz. All other cabinet positions, deputy ministers, assistants, etc. were held by men.[72]

The Wanita UMNO was frustrated over its long-time underrepresentation in the party and government. Changes in the party constitution did not change the composure of the party's decision-making bodies. The 1970s saw no change in the Wanita's relation to UMNO despite the adoption of the 1971 constitution.

The lack of Wanita members on party committees was one basic problem that faced the Wanita section. Leadership was another major problem; that is, the failure to attract younger, better, educated women to the party. Without such members, the section was accused of not leading the Malay female community and not tackling issues that were important to Malay women (e.g. poverty of Malay women). In reply, Wanita UMNO leaders argued that such comments were unfair: the Wanita was first and foremost a wing of UMNO and not a separate party of women. The Wanita operated within the constraint of what Malaysia's multiracial society and its older members would accept. The questions then arise: who were the women who joined UMNO? Did they differ (and if so how) from the Wanita leaders?

Members and Leaders

Without exception, Wanita UMNO leaders agreed that most of the section's members were older married women from the rural areas. These women were often described by the party as the 'backbone of the Wanita'.[73] Often they were illiterate and women of little means for whom the Wanita provided a diversion from village life. M. L. Rogers's 1968 study of a rural Malay community provided the first profile based on survey data of the political involvement of the rural Malay woman, the main Wanita UMNO recruit.[74] Beginning with a sample of 55 women and 79 men in Kampong Sungai Raya, Johore, Rogers found that roughly one-half of the women supported UMNO, and one-tenth were active UMNO members. Among the village women, the illiteracy rate was high: 21 per cent of the women were literate as compared to 70 per cent of the men. Ninety-six per cent of the women over 41 were illiterate as compared to 53 per cent of the men. The level of political awareness among the women was not high. Most had a very vague concept of what UMNO was but looked for the party to protect Malay rights.[75] Rogers gave a somewhat bleak picture of the political role of the village women in Sungai Raya:

> Women in Sungai Raya generally do not participate in politics in any way other than voting. Three-fourths of the women who were old enough voted in the 1964 election. Most voted because they were asked to do so by the kampong political leaders or by prominent illiterate village women who worked with the local UMNO committee on election day. Just over a tenth of the women in Sungai Raya are members of UMNO. Almost all of these live in Sungai Raya; most are illiterate and are married or related to prominent men with average incomes. Only four of the wives of the ten kampong political leaders are UMNO members. The most common explanations women give for not joining a political party are: 'I'm stupid', 'I'm uneducated', 'I don't know anything', or 'People didn't ask me'. Women are not invited to join UMNO because the men feel that politics is not a concern of women, and that one membership per family is enough. Moreover, the men are confident that the women will vote as instructed.[76]

Rogers's findings are also confirmed in Abdul Hamid bin Ahmad Khan's 1969 study that examined the role of the KI as an organization.[77] Focusing on the 115 members of the rural Kluang Utara division the image of the middle-aged, married, rural picture of the average Wanita woman was accurate. Of the 115 women, 105 were married, 15 were 26–30 years old, 57 were 31–40 years old and 40 were over 40 years of age.[78] Forty per cent of the women were educated in Malay primary schools, 20 per cent had a post-primary education, 40 per cent had no education. All of the office-holders had completed English secondary schools.[79] Most of the women's husbands belonged to UMNO (83). All the married women said their husbands consented to their joining the Wanita.[80]

In Table 6.3, Hamid's findings are like those of Rogers's in showing that women joined for a variety of reasons.

Malay women were slightly less sophisticated than Malay men (see Rogers). Factors that shape this image of the somewhat naïve and apolitical Wanita member were: 1) few Malay women were educated—there were few schools in the rural areas and the Malay culture underplayed educating girls, and 2) men have had greater access to political information. Newspapers, radios, and television are available in coffee shops, the 'meeting' place of Malay men but not of Malay women. As more radios, televisions and newspapers make their way into the home, women will be able to become better informed. However, as young women become educated and are exposed to influences outside the village, it may become more difficult to attract them to the Wanita. As Rogers found,[81] teenage girls supported UMNO not simply because others liked it but because they approved of its policies: almost all felt UMNO protected Malay rights.

If the average Wanita member was older and lacked education, the same cannot be said of the women who led the section. At the branch level, survey data is lacking but interviews with Wanita leaders show that teachers, UMNO officials' wives, and the wives of village leaders often led the Wanita branch. Literacy was required to lead the branch so that records could be kept, announcements made, etc.

Manderson provided data on some 33 out of 113 Wanita UMNO division leaders.[82] Wanita division leaders were usually married, with children, had received either religious or some formal vernacular education and often worked in paid employment outside the home (as teachers in Malay schools, adult education or religious classes).[83] Division leaders

TABLE 6.3
Reasons for Joining Wanita UMNO

Factor	No. of Women
Interested in politics	20
Encouragement from husbands	17
Persuaded by friends	19
To serve the country	7
Interested to know more people	31
Not sure	16
Don't know	5
Total	115

Source: Abdul Hamid bin Ahmad Khan, 'An Analysis of the Kaum Ibu as a Women's Political Organization', unpublished Graduation Exercise, University of Malaya, 1969, p. 61.

were also apt to read extensively (all read at least one newspaper a day, two-thirds read two or more daily).[84] More than 90 per cent of the leaders also belonged to other organizations—Women's Institutes, Girl Guides, social-welfare organizations, etc. Only 3 out of 33 had no family involvement with UMNO. (Most had husbands, parents or siblings who were members.) The women stressed, though, that they joined because of their own political views either to work for independence or to improve the status of the Malays.[85] Division leaders were well-educated, motivated women who used sources of information available and possessed the skills needed to run the wing.

Manderson's data also supported the general trend that Wanita division leaders retained power for many years. This substantiates the charge that there was little vertical mobility in the section. At the division level, the mean time required from joining UMNO until first gaining a position on the division committee was nine years. The mean time to become a division leader was slightly more than 11 years.[86] Division leaders also tended to retain their posts for years at a time (20 per cent of the women served less than five years, 15 per cent for fifteen years or longer while the mean was eight years).[87] Division leaders were often appointed and elected (one-third of the division leaders) to state or national level Wanita committees. Only three had not yet served at the state or national level and did not aspire to do so.[88]

Women at the state and national level followed the pattern of the division leaders: married with children, often middle-aged, and having enough wealth that they could afford household help to free themselves for political work. Often they were the wives or daughters of activists or government servants from the Malay aristocracy or the English-educated élite. Taking a sample of 20 women active in the Wanita at the national level, Manderson found that 8 of the women had post-primary schooling in Malay/English, 5 in English schools, 4 in Malay primary schools, 1 in Malay/Arabic, 1 in Indonesian/Dutch and only 1 had no formal education.[89] Seven of the 20 were schoolteachers, 4 were professionals, and 9 were housewives.[90]

Table 6.4 shows the background of the 19 members of the 1976 National Executive Committee, many of whom had held division and state office. It coincides with Manderson's profile. The national leaders were married, middle-aged women, much like the mass membership. The difference was that the leader had often had post-primary or post-secondary schooling and had been employed outside the home.

While it was common for the husbands of national women leaders to be UMNO members or government civil servants,[91] one cannot conclude that the women were active in the Wanita because of their husbands. The time and effort required to run the section, to organize and direct the party's electoral campaigns, and to run for political office made them activists in their own right. Several women explained that if they were looking for a hobby or something to do they would have found something else. Politics, they explained, was often frustrating, not rewarding, and

TABLE 6.4
Background of the Nineteen Members of the
1976 National Executive Committee

Factor	n = 19
Age of National Executive Members	
0–30 years	0
31–40 years	3
41–50 years	7
50+ years	9
Marital Status	
Married	15
Widowed or divorced	4
Never married	0
Types of Education	
No formal education	2
Arabic/Malay	3
Malay school only	4
English education	4
Malay/English	3
University	3
Profession	
Supervisors of adult education classes	2
Businesswomen	3
Information Officer for pilgrims in organization	1
Arabic school teacher	1
Housewives	6
Paid secretary for Wanita UMNO	1
University lecturer	1
Member of Parliament	1
Parliamentary secretary	1
Welfare Worker	1
Journalist/Senator/Cabinet Minister	1

Source: Compiled from interviews with the author.

not financially lucrative. It is also notable that the wives of the top UMNO officials (Datuk Onn Jaafar, Tunku Abdul Rahman, Tun Razak, Datuk Hussein Onn and Mahathir bin Mohamad) have been plain party members. They have not occupied major posts within the Wanita section; further, they have not served on the Wanita National Executive Committee. Suhaila Hussein, wife of former Prime Minister Datuk Hussein Onn, explained that the responsibilities imposed on her as Prime Minister's wife precluded her active involvement in the Wanita. She added that because her husband held such high office, 'it was better to let others [women] have a chance'[92]—feelings that are probably shared by other cabinet officials' wives. (Rather than too much involvement by high officials' wives, the Wanita has complained that they do not get their adequate support.)[93]

Continuity of leadership was present in the Wanita at the national, state and division level. The best example was the 16-year term of the fourth Wanita leader, Fatimah binti Hashim. She served from 1956 to 1972. While extreme, her example was not atypical. Manderson again provided data to support the hypothesis that turnover in the state and national élite has been low. Surveying the members of the National Executive Committee of the Wanita from 1956/7 to 1971/2, she noted that of eight women in 1956, four remained in 1962/3. Two or three remained on the committee until 1970 (committee size expanded from eight in 1956/7 to nineteen by 1971/2). The pattern was repeated for the three women who first joined the committee in 1957/8; at least one and at times all three new members were on the committee from 1957 to 1972. The pattern was the same year after year. Previous members rejoined the committee at various intervals.[94] Manderson provided more evidence that state level leaders remained in office for long periods of time. From this data, it becomes clear that in many states the same women held power for many years. For example, the state leader of Penang (Dasimah Dasir) led the section from 1956 until 1971 except for one brief term (1962/3– 1963/4). The Selangor section had two leaders over the same period, Perak three, Trengganu three, Malacca four, Johore three and Kedah, with the greatest turnover, seven.[95]

A review of more recent party records confirms that the national and state leadership has changed little. Averaging 21 members on the National Executive Committee as of 1976, 11 have remained on the committee since 1973. Four joined in 1974 (and were still serving in 1976), and only three who were on the committee in 1973 were no longer present in 1976. The presence of younger women on the committee continued with Rafidah Aziz, Zaleha Ismail and Rahmah Othman. The resignation of Marina Yusof (1975), in part due to her progressive attitude towards women's rights, halted the practice of selecting younger women as national Wanita committee members. As for leadership at the state level, the chairmanship changed hands in only two states (Trengganu and Perlis with Malacca records being incomplete) between 1971/2 and 1976.[96] In short, those who held office continued to do so. Mobility within the ranks was restricted by the lack of openings in the upper echelons.

The Wanita UMNO Leaders (Ketua-ketua)

In the 30-year history of the Wanita UMNO (1946–76), the key post of *Ketua* (Leader) changed hands five times. Only once had an incumbent leader been challenged and defeated by a rival (Fatimah binti Hashim by Aishah Ghani in 1972). Otherwise, two of the leaders resigned and one was expelled from UMNO—also an unusual event. The fifth *Ketua*,

Aishah Ghani, retained her post. She, in particular, provided the Wanita with a stable, continuous leadership at all levels. Comparing leadership styles[97] shows that the office of *Ketua* was relatively free from risk. Once selected, a leader could retain her post as long as she desired. She only had to project the modest beliefs and values of the Wanita woman member. The Wanita leaders, politically aware and educated women, have appealed to the older, village women, the bulk of the Wanita membership.

The first *Ketua* of the section, Puteh Mariah binti Ibrahim Rashid of Perak,[98] was a Western-oriented Malay, a member of the élite that led Malaya to independence and came to govern the country. Born in 1924, the daughter of an English-educated civil servant, Puteh Mariah attended English-medium schools. She married a member of the British Military Administration and District Officer, Zainal Abidin, who became the second Secretary-General of UMNO.

In 1945, the spasmodic outbreaks of racial violence together with the rising wave of Malay nationalist sentiment prompted Puteh Mariah to join the Persatuan Melayu Perak and the Citizen's Advisory Bureau in Ipoh. The Persatuan Melayu Perak was one of many Malay associations that sprang up to oppose British post-war plans. Puteh Mariah quickly became the leader of the women's wing. Though few in number, the women were opposed to any change in the pre-war arrangements which had favoured the Malays.

As a leader of the Persatuan Melayu Perak, Puteh Mariah attended the first UMNO General Assembly of 1946. Together with two other women, she conceived a women's section of UMNO. In January 1947, Puteh Mariah became the Officer in Charge of Women's Affairs in UMNO. This was, in effect, the first Kaum Ibu *Ketua*—she held the post for two and a half years. Datuk Onn Jaafar, the first President of UMNO and the leading post-war nationalist, actively encouraged the UMNO women. Like many others, Puteh Mariah was profoundly influenced by Datuk Onn Jaafar and his ideas. It was her good working relationship with Datuk Onn Jaafar and her ability to 'fit' into the new Malay élite, that led her to become the only woman involved in the pre-Federation consultative meeting. (That is, the 12-member, all-male Working Committee, composed of British administrators, four Sultans and two representatives from UMNO. The committee was called for by Governor Gent to assure Malay support for the proposed Federation of Malaya Agreement in July 1946.) She, with the support of Datuk Onn Jaafar, insisted on female suffrage.

It was largely Puteh Mariah's skill in organizing and managing women's groups that saw their consolidation into one UMNO body in 1949. As the leader of a group that by 1950 numbered about 10,000,[99] she had become the major woman leader of the period. She was appointed to both the Perak and the Federal Legislative Councils in 1948.

Upon Puteh Mariah's resignation as *Ketua* in August 1950, the post passed to Hajjah Zain binti Suleiman, commonly known as Ibu Zain. Born in Malacca in 1903,[100] Ibu Zain, like Puteh Mariah, was the daughter of an English-educated civil servant (schoolteacher). He sent all eight of his children to English schools—expecting them to pick careers that would serve the cause of independence.[101] Imbued with the 'Hidup Berkerja' ('Live to Work') spirit, Ibu Zain was the only Malay girl in the Methodist Girls' School in Malacca. Having studied Malay, English, Arabic and religious affairs, Ibu Zain went on to become an innovator in education. She founded the first teachers' union in Malaya, established the journals *Guru* (*Teacher*) and *Bulan Melayu* (*Malay Monthly*) which argued for monogamy, modern childbearing methods and careers for women as well as men, and opened and supervised government schools throughout Johore. Additionally, Ibu Zain was married and the mother of three children. In 1945, she was widowed at the age of 42.

Following the Japanese Occupation, Ibu Zain formed a Malay women's self-help organization, the Kumpulan Ibu Sepakat, KIS (United Women's Association) of Johore. Later, at Datuk Onn Jaafar's request, the KIS became the women's branch of the Pergerakan Melayu Semenanjong (Movement of Peninsular Malays). This nationalist group was later to become part of UMNO.

In leading the Kaum Ibu, Ibu Zain relied on her working relationships with Datuk Onn Jaafar and then Tunku Abdul Rahman (the second President of UMNO). The UMNO crisis of 1950–1 greatly weakened the party when Datuk Onn Jaafar withdrew and took many of his supporters with him to form the Independence of Malaya Party, the IMP. It was the task of Ibu Zain to build up the women's section in support of UMNO. Ibu Zain saw the KI as a form of support for the party structure. She likened UMNO to a 'crippled bird' without its KI wing.[102] For her, the main issue for the KI (as well as UMNO) had to be independence. Women's issues (i.e. marriage and divorce reform, higher education for girls, etc.) had lesser importance. In the independence struggle, Ibu Zain believed the main KI task to be that of party fund-raiser.[103] For Ibu Zain, greater educational opportunities for Malay women followed closely on the independence issue. The high numbers of illiterate KI women helps explain her call for a campaign to wipe out illiteracy. This resulted in the KI anti-illiteracy campaigns of the 1950s.

Ibu Zain resigned for reasons of ill-health as *Ketua* in 1953. She was followed by Khadijah Sidek. Khadijah Sidek led the Kaum Ibu for three years (1953–6) until her expulsion. Her approach to leading the KI differed greatly from that of other KI leaders. Khadijah Sidek was a fiery orator who confronted UMNO over the issue of women and their role in the party. Challenging UMNO to increase the role of KI women, she created discord within the party and threatened to split it. Such behaviour was unacceptable to both the party leaders and some KI members. She was expelled from the party. Fiery speeches aside, Khadijah Sidek greatly aided the growth of the KI. It was Khadijah Sidek who firmly established the practice of the KI leaders visiting the divisions and branches.[104] Such visits, which were used to explain UMNO and KI policies, hear grievances and increase the membership of a branch or division, became an important duty of the KI *Ketua*. The majority of KI were illiterate and the link between leaders and led, assumed major importance. Following her expulsion from UMNO in 1956, Khadijah Sidek joined the Dewan Muslimat PAS. Serving as its *Ketua* from 1963–1966, she resigned from PAS in 1967. Five years later she rejoined UMNO, but played little role within the party.

Khadijah Sidek, in turn, was followed by the Supreme Council's appointment of Fatimah binti Hashim. This appointment was approved by the 1957 KI General Assembly.[105] Fatimah binti Hashim, who later was to become the first woman honoured with the title 'Tan Sri' and the first woman cabinet minister, differed markedly from Khadijah Sidek. Far less combative, she was convinced that the KI was a supportive wing of UMNO. She led the KI for 16 years and oversaw its dramatic growth from a minor group of 15,000 members to a section which numbered about 200,000 in 1972.

Fatimah binti Hashim more clearly typified the KI women she led. Born in 1924 and educated in Malay and religious schools, she was married (to the future Attorney-General of Malaysia, Tan Sri Abdul Kadir bin Yusof). She was a homemaker and the mother of six children when she joined the Johore branch of UMNO in 1947. By 1955, she headed the Ipoh division and Perak state KI organizations. In 1956, she took over as national leader, from Khadijah Sidek.

Fatimah binti Hashim continued the practice of travelling extensively throughout Malaya. By 1959, she was aided in these efforts by Rahimah binti Abdul Rahman, the new Assistant Secretary of the KI. Her duty, in particular, was to aid in the expansion and re-organization of the section. Personal contact between national, division and branch leaders, and the KI members, was most important. The wing had to rely heavily on oral communications.

KI *ketua* visits were gala events: they not only informed village women as to political issues such as independence and marriage and divorce reform, they were also a form of entertainment. They also helped reinforce UMNO's image of 'Bapa UMNO' the 'Father of UMNO', which (aided by its KI wing) would safeguard the interests of the Malays. UMNO records resound with requests from KI branches and divisions for visits by members of the KI National Executive Committee. The *Ketua* was always in the greatest demand followed by other publicly prominent members and then local members involved at the national level.

The visits by the national leaders, fun fairs, cooking contests, and such activities became important KI methods to increase membership. Fatimah binti Hashim stressed the need for these functions. They were a means to attract women to the party. Once involved in some party activity or exposed to UMNO speakers, it was then possible to educate the women in politics and recruit them as new members.[106] These activities, together with UMNO's prominence as a champion of Malay rights, led to the rapid growth in KI membership. At the end of her tenure in 1972, the KI membership equalled that of UMNO men.

The 'style' of Fatimah binti Hashim gave the section a stability and continuity it had lacked hitherto. She, much like Puteh Mariah and Ibu Zain, relied heavily on her personal relationship with the UMNO male élite, particularly Tunku Abdul Rahman. Unlike Khadijah Sidek, Fatimah binti Hashim did not publicly challenge party leaders nor did she use the KI General Assembly as a forum to express dissatisfaction with party policies—a tactic sometimes used by PAS women leaders.[107]

Fatimah binti Hashim used her position as MP to support legislation aiding women (equal pay for equal work) and, as an individual, she would advocate Muslim marriage and divorce reform. Her view as the KI leader, though, remained in loyal support of UMNO: she felt the KI, as a central part of UMNO, should never jeopardize the welfare of the party for its own interests. 'UMNO is one party. It does not belong solely to the Pemuda or the Wanita. Both are wings of the party. Both must help the party. UMNO is for the Malays—all the Malays.'[108]

However, the view of Fatimah binti Hashim of the KI as a loyal party wing did not blind her to the special needs of the section. Though she did not have a higher education herself, she was aware of the section's need to attract urban, educated members as well as its rural following. Realizing that younger educated women would not wait for the usual advancement in the section, which was quite slow, she brought what was called '*kaum intelek*' into the party in the early 1970s; they were appointed to the National Executive Committee. Rafidah Aziz (who was asked to join the KI by Fatimah binti Hashim), Marina Yusof (a young attorney and outspoken advocate of women's rights), and Rahmah Othman (Assistant Secretary of the Wanita UMNO) were the major examples of the younger, more 'progressive leadership'. Such appointments were supported by those KI who wished to revitalize the section. Other members, however, resented this technique to bypass the traditional section structure. Such tensions contributed to the resignation of Marina Yusof from the National Executive Committee in 1975. Marina Yusof's progressive, liberal and ardent views which supported 'women's rights' (marriage and divorce reform and economic rights for women), and opposed more conservative KI stands (such as requiring that all schoolgirls wear 'Malay' dress), antagonized the more conservative KI members. A wide chasm existed between her and most KI members.

During her 16 years as section leader, Fatimah binti Hashim was challenged as *Ketua* three times by her deputy leader, Aishah Ghani. Failing in her bids in 1960 and 1968, Aishah Ghani unseated Fatimah binti Hashim in 1972 by a margin of 191–123.[109] The reasons for the defeat of Fatimah binti Hashim were that after 16 years, the section was ready for a new leader and she did not wage as vigorous a campaign as Aishah Ghani. With her defeat, Fatimah binti Hashim also resigned as Minister of Social Welfare. She then directed most of her energies to the

National Council of Women's Organization—the group she helped start and continued to lead.

Aishah Ghani was the same age as Fatimah binti Hashim and Puteh Mariah (all born in 1924). She shared with Khadijah Sidek (also born in the 1920s) a more aggressive approach to leading the KI. She, though, never challenged the UMNO élite to the extent of Khadijah Sidek.

Aishah Ghani, in contrast to Puteh Mariah and Ibu Zain, was not sent to missionary schools as a child. Afraid that their child might be converted to Christianity, her parents sent her to the Islamic College in Padang, Sumatra. She spent eight years there prior to World War II. The rising nationalist sentiments of the Indonesian against the Dutch influenced the young Aishah Ghani. In reminiscing, she said they were all fired with the idea of independence. On return to Malaya in 1943 at the height of the Japanese Occupation, she joined Dr Burhanuddin's Malay Nationalist Party, MNP (Parti Kebangsaan Melayu). This radical party advocated independence for a unified Indonesian/Malayan republic. Aishah Ghani became the first President of the women's wing of the MNP, the AWAS (Angkatan Wanita Sedar—the Progressive Malay Women's Corps).[110] Her stewardship was brief; she resigned from the party in 1946. She said she was unsure of the direction the party was taking.[111] Eschewing any political party for three years, she married Abdul Aziz bin Abu Hassan, head of Radio Malaya, Malay Service, and an UMNO member.[112] She began her career as a journalist and became the first woman announcer for Radio Malaya.

Aishah Ghani's career in UMNO began in 1949 when she joined the Kampong Baru branch in Kuala Lumpur. The following year she was chosen as one of the KI delegates to the UMNO General Assembly. She retained that post until 1954. A brief hiatus in her political career occurred from 1955 to 1959; she resided in Great Britain and the United States while she pursued her education as a journalist. Upon her return to Malaya, she joined the staff of the Straits Times News Association working as a journalist for *Berita Harian*, a Malay daily paper.

Upon her return, Aishah Ghani rejoined UMNO and one year later, in 1960, she was elected *Naib Ketua* (Assistant Leader) of the KI UMNO. She held that post until 1972 when she became the *Ketua*. Aishah Ghani not only influenced the KI but also was the only KI member who maintained an important post within UMNO. From 1962, she led the influential UMNO division of Bukit Bintang in Kuala Lumpur. Appointed a federal senator by the King in 1962, elected national *Ketua* of the Wanita in 1972, appointed Minister of Social Welfare in 1973, and elected an MP in 1974, Aishah Ghani clearly belied the myth that political acumen is a trait of the male.

Aishah Ghani brought to the KI leadership a style that again differed from her predecessors. As a professional woman, well-educated in both Malay and English, a proven nationalist, and an astute politician, she enjoyed the respect of the UMNO élite and the Prime Minister. These good working relations were needed by her as the KI *Ketua*. Issues of party politics in Malaysia were decided by a small group of the top party leaders in the UMNO, MCA and MIC. One finds in her public and private statements, an impatience with the pace of change on matters that affect the Wanita. On the issue of Muslim marriage and divorce reform, she showed a frustration over the slow rate of progress the Wanita had made.[113] The frustration, however, remained muted. Like most of her predecessors, she saw the main function of the KI as a loyal party supporter. However, she also viewed the KI as a defender of women's rights—an emphasis that has increased in the section over the years.[114]

The KI under Aishah Ghani had two major goals:

The first goal focused on the homemaker. She stressed the need to educate women not only to become better homemakers (i.e. cooking, sewing, health and childrearing classes), but to be better citizens. The hope was for homemakers to realize the many and varied roles that they could play in society.

The second goal reaffirmed the KI's commitment to UMNO. The Wanita continued its efforts to strengthen the party and the government.[115] In her speech to the 1973 KI General Assembly she acknowledged the contributions made by the KI to the party; Aishah Ghani also pointed out to KI members the section's basic weakness: 'Although enormous praise is due, the Wanita UMNO still faces important problems—especially the lack of effort at the branch level... there are still UMNO branches without Wanita sections.'[116] This shortcoming was to be remedied. It was the women, she noted, who could be the 'tap root' (*akar tunjang*) of the party. It was the women who could listen to and speak for the people.[117]

Aishah Ghani represented a 'younger', more progressive approach to leadership than Fatimah binti Hashim. She did not however directly challenge the accepted assumptions by which the KI UMNO functioned. She recognized that the section was mostly one of older rural women. There was no spate of appointments of urban, educated women to the section's national committees as was the case of Fatimah binti Hashim. Aishah Ghani stressed that the section was a party of rural poor women and that the issue of educated women joining, or not joining UMNO, should not be pressed.[118]

In short, Aishah Ghani was not the dynamic leader hoped for by the section's younger minority. On the other hand, she did not alienate the bulk of her supporters, the rural Malay wives and mothers, who formed the base of the wing's support.

The five KI *Ketua*, with the possible exception of Khadijah Sidek, shared a common view as to the major function of the KI. The KI's main role was to loyally support UMNO over their own specific interests. Additionally, each leader relied on a similar political style. That is, each generally relied on a close working relationship with the UMNO national élite as a means to present the wing's interests. None, with the possible exception of Khadijah Sidek, used the auxiliary as a base of power with which to confront UMNO leaders for specific KI interests; this was a sharp change from the tactics employed by the Pemuda. The KI was to be a loyal wing of the party and a strong supporter of the Malay cause. The only *Ketua* to challenge this assumption and to pursue a more aggressive political 'style' was expelled from the party. Clearly, the supportive role of the KI corresponded to the wishes of KI members themselves and their leaders as well as to those of UMNO male party members and leaders. For the KI, the auxiliary grew steadily in membership among rural women but not among the urban and better educated women. The bulk of the KI membership continued to be composed of rural, older women who viewed women in a supportive role. It is, therefore, doubtful that any other leadership would have been acceptable to either the KI members themselves or to UMNO male members; a fact not lost on any of the KI *Ketua*.

Conclusion

The years between 1969 and 1976 saw a shift in emphasis within the KI UMNO. During its previous history, the section had always been concerned with issues that affected Malay women, i.e. Muslim marriage and divorce reform, the lack of female electoral candidates and greater educational opportunities for Malay girls and women. In addition, they remained firm supporters of party decisions and policies.

While still loyal to UMNO in the 1970s, the section was becoming aware of and involved in so-called 'women's issues'—issues that were of concern to Malay women. Foremost among these were two, marriage and divorce reform for Muslims and Malay women's role in the economy. The former was pursued in the traditional way through resolutions, the submission of memoranda and public appeals. The latter was actively pursued by expanded skills-training courses for Malay women, the creation of economic funds to finance small businesses run by Malay women, and co-operatives. Such endeavours reflected the view held by many division, state and national leaders that the KI had to become actively involved in aiding women; the passage of resolutions was simply not enough.

National KI leaders, Fatimah binti Hashim, Aishah Ghani, Rafidah Aziz, Zaleha Ismail and Rahmah Othman, all agreed that the section had become more aware of and involved with the problems Malay women faced. In addition, the leaders stressed to their members that Malay women, as in the past, had a great role to play in nation-building. The members were said to be integral to the future economic and political success (political stability) of Malaysia. Such an increased awareness stemmed in part from the 1960s and 1970s world-wide renewed interest in women often reported in the Malaysian Press. There was also some spirit of competition with non-Malay women who were often employed in small businesses. In addition, the KI have been repeatedly exhorted by the UMNO leadership 'not to remain backward', 'to put forth acceptable leaders', and 'strengthen the party'.

These factors caused the KI leaders to examine the section for its weaknesses. In an effort to 'modernize' the KI, national leaders saw the major problem to be a failure of the KI to attract urban, educated women. The failure to attract such women stemmed from: 1) UMNO was a party based in the rural areas. Few attempts had been made to attract the small numbers of Malays living in the urban areas of UMNO's doors. 2) Most KI members joined because of the social opportunities and activities the section provided. Urban women had other interests and groups competing for their time, such as employment opportunities outside of the home. 3) The section was controlled by older rural women. There was limited access to positions of influence. The long upward climb through the ranks to such positions held little appeal to ambitious women who could direct their energies elsewhere. 4) Until comparatively recently (the KI's economic thrust of the 1970s), the section was often seen as being unable to address the main issue that affected all Malays, Malay impoverishment.

A second problem was the failure of KI members to take part in the general affairs of the party. KI women still failed to attend UMNO branch meetings and still failed to elect their own members to posts of party importance: UMNO branch and division officers, delegates to various level assemblies, etc. By 1976, the section had begun to tackle this problem. The section repeatedly extorted KI women as to their rights as UMNO members and held training classes for leaders at the grassroots level. The effect of such efforts would become apparent in the 1980s.

The personal effort of Fatimah binti Hashim to bring in younger women, the economic funds and co-operatives, the increasing dissatisfaction over the lack of KI in the party and government posts, and the name change from Kaum Ibu to Wanita UMNO, all reflected a change in the KI. However, it is important to emphasize that the section still held much in common with its past.

The bulk, or 'backbone' of the membership remained the older, rural, conservative women. Their emphasis on 'women's issues' often differed from that of many of the leaders and younger members. It was the rural conservative women who directed KI affairs at the grassroots level and many of them occupied posts of importance at all levels within the KI. These women had much at stake in maintaining the status quo. Longtime KI members moved up 'through the ranks'. It is no wonder that they disapproved of 'leap-frogging' younger, newer members to posts of state or national prominence.

The KI was caught in a quandary. On the one hand, it was urged by the party and its own more impatient leaders to be 'relevant' and to produce quality leaders for the party and government. On the other hand, it had to define goals and institute activities and practices that were acceptable to the bulk of its members.

This has proven an arduous task. Aishah Ghani's leadership typified this problem. While often impatient with the slow rate of progress, she was careful not to antagonize the bulk of the membership to whom she often appealed. While some differences existed between the members and their leaders, the sheer numbers of members and the political acumen of the leaders (who wished a future in the party) prevented any major splits.

With its own internal problems, the KI faced a reluctance by the party to include them in party affairs. UMNO leaders pressed for more and better KI leaders, yet had given capable KI members few chances to 'prove themselves'. The pattern of the 1950s and 1960s, of underrepresentation in party affairs, continued. Denied access to positions of authority, women were denied the political experience needed to become party and national leaders. While urged to improve itself, the auxiliary was often reminded, that it was subordinate to party authority. UMNO had little to fear that the KI would become a disruptive force. Loyalty by KI UMNO remained strong despite the fact that the auxiliary, with over half the membership of UMNO, could be a major disruptive force to the party.

1. UMNO, *Peraturan Pergerakan Wanita (Rules of the Women's Section) (approved by UMNO Supreme Council)*; 15 January 1972, Kuala Lumpur, Utusan Melayu Berhad, 1972.
2. Ibid., Clause 3. The *UMNO Constitution*, Chapter 10, Clause 22, 1971, states the functions of the Youth and Women's sections clearly:
1. The Youth and Women movement at all states of UMNO shall be established with the following aims:
   (a) to encourage youths and women in the field of politic(s), economic(s), culture, arts, sports, religion and social welfare;
   (b) to co-operate with other bodies as approved by the Supreme Council.
2. To achieve the objective in 1(a) and (b) above the Supreme Council shall have the authority to make regulations from time to time consistent with the UMNO constitution. UMNO, *Perlembagaan UMNO (UMNO Constitution) passed by UMNO Special Assembly, May 8–9, 1971*; Utusan Melayu Berhad, Kuala Lumpur, 1971, Chapter 10, Clause 22.
3. UMNO, *Rules of the Women's Section*, Clause 3, Sections a, b and c.
4. Ibid., Clause 17.1, 17.2 and 17.3.
5. Ibid., Clause 12.3 and 12.7.
6. Ibid., Clause 12.7.
7. Ibid., Clause 11.1.
8. Ibid., Clause 11.3.
9. Ibid., Clause 11.5.
10. Ibid., Clause 11.6.
11. Ibid., Clause 6.1.
12. Ibid., Clause 6.6.
13. Ibid., Clause 10.4b.
14. Interview with Rahmah Othman, Secretary of the Wanita UMNO on 22, 23 April 1976.
15. Interview with Rahmah Othman, 22, 23 April 1976. Membership figures are difficult to ascertain. The Wanita UMNO office is only able to provide estimates of overall membership. Records dating back over the years have at times been destroyed and at other times, not kept. What records do exist must be considered with latitude as branches and divisions differ as to how they define 'member'. Members may include those who have not paid their dues in years. Therefore, any membership figures are estimates and only estimates of party size.

16. Interview with Aishah Ghani on 1 March 1976.
17. M. Rogers, 'Political Involvement in a Rural Malay Community', unpublished doctoral dissertation, University of California, Berkeley, 1968, p. 223.
18. UMNO, *1967 UMNO Annual Report*, Kuala Lumpur, UMNO, 1967.
19. UMNO, *1973/4 UMNO Annual Report*, Kuala Lumpur, UMNO, 1974.
20. See UMNO, *UMNO Annual Reports, 1967–1976*, Kuala Lumpur, UMNO, 1968–76.
21. UMNO, *1976 UMNO Annual Report*, Kuala Lumpur, UMNO, 1976.
22. Ibid.
23. *Malay Mail*, 21 March 1971.
24. *ST*, 8 May 1971.
25. *Malay Mail*, 17 April 1971.
26. *ST*, 27 March 1972.
27. *Malay Mail*, 17 April 1971.
28. *Malay Mail*, 17 March 1972.
29. *ST*, 12 July 1972.
30. *ST*, 15 July 1972.
31. *ST*, 5 August 1972.
32. *ST*, 17 November 1972.
33. *Malay Mail*, 28 February 1972.
34. *ST*, 13 May 1973 and *ST*, 4 June 1973.
35. *Malay Mail*, 25 October 1974.
36. *ST*, 18 January 1971.
37. *ST*, 23 January 1971.
38. *ST*, 23 March 1971.
39. Interview with Rahmah Othman, 22, 23 April 1976.
40. *Malay Mail*, 3 March 1971.
41. *ST*, 10 May 1971.
42. *ST*, 16 May 1971.
43. *ST*, 13 March 1972.
44. *Malay Mail*, 22 March 1972.
45. *Malay Mail*, 23 June 1972.
46. *ST*, 24 June 1972. Also see *Pelopor*, 6 June 1972, Bil. 6, pp. 9–10.
47. *Malay Mail*, 24 June 1972 and *ST*, 24 June 1972.
48. *ST*, 26 June 1972.
49. *ST*, 12 March 1973.
50. *ST*, 14 March 1973.
51. *ST*, 6 April 1973.
52. *ST*, 6 April 1973.
53. *ST*, 19 February 1974.
54. *ST*, 30 December 1974.
55. *ST*, 10 January 1975.
56. *Malay Mail*, 13 March 1975.
57. *ST*, 18 March 1974.
58. *Malay Mail*, 29 June 1974.
59. *Malay Mail*, 28 June 1974.
60. *ST*, 26 August 1974.
61. *ST*, 27 January 1976.
62. *ST*, 13 February 1976.
63. *Malay Mail*, 8 February 1976.
64. *The Star*, 16 February 1976, *D.P.S.*
65. *The Star*, 16 February 1976, *D.P.S.*
66. *Malay Mail*, 27 March 1976.
67. *BH*, 26 February 1976, *D.P.S.*
68. *Malay Mail*, 27 March 1976.
69. *Malay Mail*, 21 March 1976.

70. *ST*, 13 August 1976.
71. *ST*, 15 August 1976 (Editorial).
72. *ST*, 16 March 1976.
73. UMNO, *Buku Cenderamata Jubli Perak Wanita UMNO Malaysia pada 25hb Ogos 1974*, Kuala Lumpur, Utusan Melayu Berhad, 1974, p. 14.
74. Rogers, 'Political Involvement', p. 223.
75. Ibid., p. 423.
76. Ibid., pp. 465-6.
77. Abdul Hamid bin Ahmad Khan, 'An Analysis of the UMNO Kaum Ibu as a Women's Political Organization', unpublished Graduation Exercise, University of Malaya, 1969, p. 47.
78. Ibid.
79. Ibid.
80. Ibid., p. 50.
81. Rogers, 'Political Involvement', p. 428.
82. Lenore Manderson, 'The Development of the Pergerakan Kaum Ibu UMNO, 1945-1972', unpublished doctoral dissertation, Australian National University, 1977, p. vii.
83. Ibid., p. 151.
84. Ibid., p. 160.
85. Ibid., p. 162.
86. Ibid., p. 154.
87. Ibid.
88. Ibid., p. 155.
89. Ibid., p. 148.
90. Ibid.
91. Interviews with KI leaders.
92. Interview with Datin Suhaila Hussein on 1 July 1976.
93. Note, rather than too much involvement by high officials' wives, the KI have complained that they do not get enough involvement from them. *ST*, 29 April 1958 and *ST*, 2 May 1958.
94. Manderson, 'The Development of the Pergerakan', Table 6.2, p. 150.
95. Ibid., Table 6.3, p. 152.
96. See UMNO, *UMNO Annual Reports 1971-1976*.
97. Also see, Lenore Manderson, *Women, Politics, and Change: The Kaum Ibu UMNO, Malaysia, 1945-1972*, Kuala Lumpur, Oxford University Press, 1980, pp. 109-15.
98. The data for this section was taken from various *Who's Who in Malaysia*, interviews with the subjects, archival materials, newspaper clippings, as well as from the *Buku Cenderamata Jubli Perak Wanita UMNO Malaysia pada 25hb Ogos 1974*.
99. Interview with Puteh Mariah, 30 August 1976.
100. See footnote 98.
101. *ST*, 17 June 1975.
102. Interview with Ibu Zain on 19 October 1976.
103. Interview with Ibu Zain on 19 October 1976.
104. See Chapter 4.
105. Interview with Puteh Mariah, 30 August 1976.
106. Interview with Fatimah binti Hashim on 7 October 1976.
107. See Chapter 7 on PAS women.
108. Interview with Fatimah binti Hashim, 7 October 1976.
109. See footnote 98.
110. See Chapter 4 for details on AWAS.
111. Interview with Aishah Ghani on 1 March 1976.
112. Her husband is an ordinary UMNO member but holds no party office. Interview with Aishah Ghani on 1 March 1976.
113. Aishah Ghani noted in an interview that if marriage and divorce reform were not a religious matter dealt with state by state, she would have brought it before the Cabinet. Interview with Aishah Ghani on 1 March 1976.

114. Interviews with Fatimah binti Hashim, 7 October 1976, and Aishah Ghani, 1 March 1976.
115. Speech by Aishah Ghani at the Wanita UMNO General Assembly on 29 June 1973, UMNO, *1973/4 UMNO Annual Report*, p. 150.
116. *Pelopor*, Bil. 6, June 1973, p. 10.
117. Ibid.
118. Interview with Aishah Ghani, 1 March 1976.

7 The Growth of Other Women's Political Auxiliaries, 1969–1976

SINCE 1969, women's branches of other political parties have come into being. Of these, the Wanita MCA and the Wanita MIC had the potential to become major forces for non-Malay women's interests in Malaysia. As of 1976, these branches were mostly concerned with problems of organization and the definition of goals. In these early years, the nature of auxiliary–party relations became more apparent.

Besides the Wanita MCA and Wanita MIC, the Dewan Muslimat of the PMIP (now PAS) also functioned and DM leaders began to challenge party leaders over the role of the DM. The role of women in the PSRM and the PPP remained the same. Three new parties (the DAP, the Gerakan and Pekemas) also emerged to compete with the Alliance. All voiced a wish to represent and organize women.

The MCA

The 1969 general elections were a severe set-back for the MCA and its special relation with UMNO was threatened. The MCA's claim that it was the main spokesbody of Chinese interests was in doubt. In its effort to broaden its base of support, the MCA began to mobilize Chinese women.

With the 1969 elections and the state of martial law that followed, the MCA adopted a new constitution (1970). The leaders hoped this would make the party stronger and more dynamic. One feature allowed for the establishment of both youth and women's bureaus.[1] The constitution did not, though, provide for specifically placing women on any party committee.[2] In July 1972 the first state level women's section was formed. Chow Poh-kheng, widely known as Mrs Rosemary Chong, was appointed by Tan Siew-sin as the Selangor state women's leader.[3] This was in keeping with the revitalization efforts of the MCA. A new image was sought—one that had the interests of the 'masses' at heart rather than the business community and middle class (its traditional base of support). In this attempt to broaden its base, the MCA showed, by dissolving an MCA task force in Perak (1972), that it would accept very limited initiative or independence.[4] This was an ill omen for reform in the party. The Selangor state Wanita MCA organized a celebration for Women's Day for 25 August to promote the political consciousness of Chinese women.[5] Over 1,000 women attended the event which was addressed by MCA president Tan Siew-sin. He urged Chinese women to take part in public life.[6] The forming of the Selangor Wanita MCA was quickly followed by similar state organizations in Perak,[7] Penang,[8] Kedah,[9] Negri Sembilan[10] and Kelantan.[11]

Tan Siew-sin's appointment of Mrs Rosemary Chong as chairperson of the Selangor Wanita MCA led to controversy. Charges were made in the Press that she and her executive committee were an effete lot who took up politics as a hobby; they were labelled a 'tai-tai tuan' or a party of rich wives.[12] The section, though, was led by educated women: of the seven office bearers, two were headmistresses and the others were a secretary to a high commissioner, a teacher, a lecturer at the University of Malaya, a lawyer and a housewife.[13] Mrs Rosemary Chong came from a wealthy family and was English-educated in Hong Kong at St. Mary's College and the University of Hong Kong. She studied classical Chinese (she is fluent in Mandarin, Cantonese, English and Bahasa Malaysia).[14] Reacting to the 'tai-tai tuan' label, she pointed out, 'I think [the charges] are grossly unfair. Look, we've had only two months. Give us more time to prove ourselves before condemning us as an effete lot.... Surely people must know that if we're looking for hobbies we'd find more pleasurable things to do.'[15] Given the MCA women had to travel at their own expense[16] and the MCA drew its leaders from the propertied class, it was not a surprise that the first women leaders would be among the more affluent and better educated.

Though other Wanita MCA sections formed, the Selangor branch remained the major women's section. In March 1973, the section resolved that: 1) academic and other staff employed in institutions of higher learning reflect a racial balance, 2) the Selangor government should open up land to solve the squatters' problem, and 3) city hall (Kuala Lumpur) should provide proper bus station facilities.[17] In April, the section announced it would present a report to Parliament in May on the question of separate tax assessments for working wives.[18] The section further issued a statement to express its concern over the safety of factory girls. (They would work late shifts and were in danger of being waylaid on their way home.) They urged that the factories should provide transportation for their female workers and the police should pay attention to the problem.[19] In April, Kelantanese and Selangor MCA women held a forum. They called on the MCA central leadership to respect the rights of women members and see that they were represented at the annual meeting of the party.[20]

The progress made by the women in the MCA came to a halt with the 1973 party power struggle between the 'old guard', Tan Siew-sin, Deputy Leader Lee San-choon and Secretary-General Kam Wooh-wah, and 'new blood' reformists, Dr Lim Keng-yaik (Minister of Special

Functions in the Malaysian Cabinet) and Michael Chen (Tun Razak's former parliamentary secretary).[21] The outcome was Lim's expulsion from the party. Four, out of a handful of Wanita MCA divisions, pledged support for Lim and Chen.[22] Further, 100 members of the Bidor MCA youth and women's sections burned Tan Siew-sin in effigy as well as a copy of the MCA constitution. This was in protest against the expulsion of Lim.[23] Further, the Selangor Wanita MCA issued a statement in which they supported the reformist faction. Wanita MCA Selangor called on the MCA Central Committee to adopt a liberal attitude and not use high-handed tactics. They asked the Committee to withdraw the expulsion of Lim, to stop the public airing of conflict, and to discuss party differences.[24] The branch also called for the MCA to amend its constitution. That was to prevent the concentration of power in one person's hands (i.e. the party president's). They also appealed to all Chinese women to help the reform movement and so enable the MCA to play a greater role in nation-building.[25]

A two-month suspension of the Wanita MCA by Tan Siew-sin was followed in August by the dissolving of 11 MCA divisions and 30 branches including the Selangor Wanita MCA.[26] Few details on the party crisis are available. Tan Siew-sin remained in control and was re-elected unopposed in August 1973.[27] A 'reformation committee' was, however, set up with Lee San-choon and Michael Chen as co-chairmen.[28] The challenge to Tan Siew-sin had been deflected.

The dissolution of the Selangor Wanita MCA did not preclude women from the section meeting in July to discuss their future objectives. The meeting envisaged an increased role for women within the MCA and agreed:
1) to fight for the representation of women on the Central Committee so that the MCA would not be a party of men only,
2) to make the chairman of the national Wanita a party vice-president,
3) to bring unity to the MCA women and carry out objectives of the MCA as laid out in the MCA constitution,
4) to call for the political awakening of Chinese women and instil in them the correct (i.e. MCA) political ideologies,
5) to bring about social progress (not elaborated upon), and
6) to encourage women to take part in all activities beneficial to party and country.[29]

Aside from this July meeting, MCA women remained inactive until the spring of 1974 when MCA president Tan Siew-sin resigned as Minister of Finance and president of the party.[30] He was succeeded as party leader by Lee San-choon, the previous deputy leader and former youth leader. Lee approved the revitalization of the women's section. MCA women then called for a general meeting for 30 June 1974, to set the stage for renewed political involvement. There were 1,000 women, most in their twenties, who attended. They represented a total of roughly 40,000 MCA women members from 58 divisions and branches. MCA membership figures are generally inflated because the party counted not only dues-paying members but members in arrears and others who had just shown an interest in the party. The women elected a 33-member pro tem committee to work out a structure for a national Wanita MCA. Further, 19 Wanita resolutions were passed that included: 1) full support for Lee San-choon and the party's stand on the National Front, 2) a call on the government to abolish joint taxation for working wives, and 3) more parliamentary and state assembly seats for MCA women.[31]

In October, Lee San-choon announced plans to revamp the women's section. He would appoint a national chairwoman who, in turn, would appoint a treasurer and secretary. It was hoped that the 60 divisions and 200 branches would soon parallel the MCA's 104 divisions and 467 branches.[32]

The pro tem committee met for the first time on 19 October 1974; they launched a campaign to increase the Wanita MCA membership. The pro tem officers, with Mrs Rosemary Chong as chairperson, toured Malaysia, from 23 November 1974 until 1 March 1975. They addressed members and initiated new branches.[33]

The growth of awareness among Chinese women was described by Lee as the most significant event in the MCA during the second half of the 1970s. In one of his most forthright speeches on women, he outlined the basic problem the MCA faced in its attempts to recruit women—the attitudes that before had excluded women from politics:

For too long we have banished womanhood from public view and indulged in a self-perpetuating mystique about this being a man's world and that a woman's place [is] in the kitchen.
We like to delude ourselves into thinking that the emancipation of women will necessarily mean the loss of their feminity or will diminish their role in the family as wives and mothers. It is not my intention to examine how this view was evolved through the centuries. Suffice it to say that it has come to be accepted in traditional society not only among men but also among women.
This is the basic problem in [the] MCA's attempt to modernize thinking about women's role in society. Not only do we have to educate our men, we also have to educate our womenfolk and impress upon them that they can and indeed should play a more 'emancipated' role in society. The weight of history makes this a formidable task but it is not a task we should shy away from. We are seeking to change attitudes, custom and habit. This will take time but we must make a beginning now.[34]

In June 1975, the first MCA woman stood for a seat in parliament. The selection of Mrs Rosemary Chong as a National Front candidate for the Selayang by-election showed that the MCA sought to increase its appeal. Lee San-choon, speaking on Mrs Rosemary Chong's nomination, noted: 'Such an event has long been overdue. The fact it has come to pass represents a radical turning point in the history of the party. We are all committed now to greater involvement by Malaysian Chinese women in politics and public service.'[35]

The selection of Mrs Rosemary Chong by the MCA was indeed long overdue. During its previous 26-year history, the MCA had never chosen a woman to stand for election at the state or federal level. The selection of party candidates was made by the national election committee. The committee was composed solely of men. Mrs Rosemary Chong's efforts to organize MCA women (as well as her support in Selangor) made it hard for the party to ignore her. As was privately stated many times, the party was more or less compelled to select her in order to retain its new image of representing 'the masses'.

The choice of Mrs Rosemary Chong produced full support from all sections of the Wanita MCA. Women members campaigned vigorously for their pro tem chairwoman, and the wives of top MCA leaders, including Datin Lee San-choon, campaigned for her.[36] Mrs Rosemary Chong won handily in a three-sided fight against two men, a Malay running on the DAP ticket and a Malay running as an independent. She polled 19,338 votes against the combined vote of 7,915 for the others.[37] Mrs Rosemary Chong was the first Chinese woman elected to parliament and she won in a mostly Malay constituency.[38] There was now evidence that a Chinese woman could win an election and that Wanita UMNO and UMNO would campaign for her. (Aishah Ghani campaigned for her—UMNO had 45 branches in Selayang.)[39]

The selection of Mrs Rosemary Chong also served to keep the Wanita MCA going. In her victory speech, Mrs Rosemary Chong announced, 'I believe the victory of the National Front has awakened the political consciousness of women. From now on, we will have to work harder.'[40] She then said that the Wanita MCA would launch a series of courses to instil political awareness in its members.[41]

With state level Wanita MCA organizations set up in every state, it was proper that a national Wanita MCA be inaugurated at the first general assembly of MCA women on 7 August 1975. It was the first time that MCA women were able to elect their own leaders; before, the pro tem chairwoman, Mrs Rosemary Chong, had been appointed by the party leader. Mrs Rosemary Chong stood uncontested as the leader of the national section. She, in turn, appointed a secretary and treasurer, the deputy chair, and two vice-chairs. Further, a 6-member committee was elected for a two-year term at the Wanita MCA general assembly.[42]

In her first address to the national Wanita MCA, Mrs Rosemary Chong acknowledged that most Malaysian Chinese women did not care about matters that did not directly concern them. She, though, urged them to become involved in public affairs. The only requirement was a sense of responsibility for the future of their children and their country.[43] She also spoke out in support of monogamy for non-Muslims. She noted that women were 'as much an equal part of society as everyone else. The laws governing society largely promulgated by men must and should be adapted to treat us as equals.'[44]

The assembly delegates passed 13 resolutions. The government was urged to act on a number of issues including declaring 'Women's Day' a public holiday, opening drug rehabilitation centres, guaranteeing that women be allowed to take part at all levels of government and repealing all legislation which treated the sexes as unequals (such as the passage of a non-Muslim marriage reform bill), prohibiting 'yellow' literature and films (for instance 'X-rated'), and putting aside more land for the landless.[45] The women stated the priorities of their section and were quite clear in defining their goals. Each of the points focused on an issue that directly affected women: from urging better educational and employment opportunities to re-assessing traditional views of the status of women.[46]

While the MCA Wanita could pass any number of resolutions, their impact on party decision-making remained minor. This, in part, was due to the newness of the section. It was also due to the structure of the MCA and the party's complete control over its wings. The Wanita structure and its relations with the MCA shows that the section was very much subordinate. This was true even though the section was governed by its own by-laws drawn up by the pro tem committee in 1974. The objectives of the section were clearly stated:

a) to encourage women members to work in partnership and share the responsibility of promoting and carrying out the objectives of the MCA as laid down in the constitution,
b) to awaken and instil political consciousness among women members,
c) to promote social and national progress, and
d) to encourage women members to take part in various activities beneficial to the party and the nation.[47]

Malaysian women of Chinese descent 18 years and older were allowed to join the MCA and thereby become Wanita MCA members. In contrast to UMNO, younger Chinese women were allowed to join the youth section; but there were very few female members who did join.[48] As with the KI UMNO, MCA women joined the party and became members in a Wanita branch. Twenty-five women were needed to organize a branch.[49] The members at their annual meeting elected their branch executive committee (a chair, vice-chair, and from two to four members). The treasurer and secretary were appointed by the chair. Above the branch was a division of at least 100 members. Each branch elected 1 representative for 25 members to attend the annual division assembly. The assembly then elected the division's executive committee (also a chair, vice-chair and from two to four members). Again, the chair appointed the secretary and treasurer plus three committee members.[50] Above the division was the state organization made up of an annual assembly and a state executive committee. Each branch sent 1 representative for 50 members (or fraction thereof) and each division sent 1 delegate for 100 members. At the state level, something else occurred: the state chair was appointed by the national Wanita MCA chairwoman.[51] This prevented the rise of strong rivals and minimized conflict within the organization and between the national and state leaders. The state chair was, in turn, responsible for the secretary, treasurer, auditor and four committee members. The state assembly elected two vice-chairs and five committee members. The committee was filled out by the division chairwomen in the state.

The highest policy-making body of the Wanita MCA was the General Assembly. It met each year prior to the MCA. Delegates, one per hundred members at the division level (at least two from a division), together with any Wanita member who was a member of the MCA Central Committee, an MP or a member of any state assembly were allowed to attend. The powers of the General Assembly included:

1) to regulate its own proceedings, direct, manage and control the affairs of the Wanita MCA;
2) to recommend to the MCA Central Committee to add to, repeal, amend, substitute or alter the Rules as it shall think expedient for the attainment of any of the objects of the Wanita MCA, or for the better management thereof;
3) to delegate ... all or any of its powers ... to the Central Committee or any other committee or sub-committees; and
4) to deal with all matters pertaining to the Wanita MCA not specifically provided for by these Rules.[52]

The assembly also elected certain members to the Wanita Central Committee (the national chairwoman, deputy chair, two vice-chairs plus six committee members). The Central Committee also included all state Wanita chairwomen as well as the secretary-general and treasurer-general. The latter two were appointed by the national Wanita chairwoman. Office bearers served two-year terms.

The rules which governed the Wanita MCA provided for a well organized auxiliary. In 1976 the section was, however, still very much in its infancy. It was dominated by 20 or so 'active' members, the core leadership of the Selangor state organization in particular.[53]

Class barriers troubled the Wanita MCA. In spite of efforts to visit the rural areas where one-third of the Chinese lived, rural women were often wary of the urban, educated leaders. Most women members came from the urban areas where the MCA had recruited its members in the past.

Selangor leaders dominated the section and found it hard to attract rural women. Language differences also posed problems for its members. While many of the Wanita MCA leaders were educated in English-medium schools, many of the rank and file were educated in Chinese-medium schools. A similar problem was faced by the MCA itself. The language gap that often arose posed problems that the Malays did not have to face. Not only were there two languages, Chinese and English, but spoken Chinese included many dialects which could not be understood by others. The result was meetings often conducted in more than one language, for example Mandarin and English,[54] Malay and Mandarin,[55] etc. Written announcements were printed in both Chinese and English. While the language problem could be overcome, the cultural gap and the different value systems remained difficult to resolve. Frequently heard was the same kind of comment from Chinese- and English-educated: 'We just don't think the same....' The Chinese-educated were more chauvinistic in what they believed to be Chinese interests than the English-educated. As more and more younger women were educated in standard curricula (a goal of recent school policies), the language problem decreased. As of 1976, it still posed a problem, though, for the Wanita MCA.

The Wanita MCA also faced the problem that the male leaders tended to reduce the Wanita to mere problem-carriers. As one Wanita MCA worker lamented: 'Sometimes I wonder why we work so hard when we are not given incentive.'[56] MCA spokesman, Lim Heng-kiap, political secretary to the Health Minister, confirmed the gloomy view: 'The MCA does not place a lot of confidence in women voters. Women are being used because they are not forceful enough. A change of heart in the men will not come automatically. The women must bring it about themselves.'[57]

The suspension of the Selangor Wanita in 1973 showed that the President of the MCA had almost unlimited control over the section. Section 16 of the Wanita MCA by-laws, which was in accord with Article 127 of the party constitution, provided for presidential control over the section. The President was empowered to suspend a member or any Wanita branch for acting against the interests of the party.[58] The subordination of the section president, the 'wait and see' attitude of party leaders, and the newness of the Wanita section all prevented women from taking part in the daily affairs of the party. There were no party guarantees that women be represented on the party's branch, division, state or national committees or assemblies; for the most part, the women remained grossly underrepresented. For example, the 1975 MCA General Assembly had only five women out of hundreds of delegates.[59] This was due to delegates being chosen by election at the division assemblies which few women attended. None of the MCA's 104 divisions (as of 1976) were headed by women and only three women headed MCA branches (2 in Perak and 1 in Selangor).[60] The number of women either elected or appointed to serve on MCA policy-making committees was just one—Mrs Rosemary Chong who now sat on the party's Central Committee. (She was one of 25 members in 1976.) A 1976 amendment to the party constitution, though, provided that the national chairpersons of the Youth and Wanita wings would be party vice-presidents.[61]

By 1976, the Wanita had grown to 60,000 members, divided into 57 divisions and 252 branches.[62] The total membership of the MCA was about 268,163 but this included members who were five years in arrears in paying dues. It is still unclear what women were typical Wanita MCA recruits. Though the section conducted cooking, sewing and language classes, it did not emphasize such activities. ('The women already cook all the time.')[63] Meetings focused on topics that ranged from nutrition to MCA policies and the National Front. The greatest efforts of the Wanita MCA had been in lobbying for a non-Muslim marriage and divorce reform bill. This was eventually passed by parliament in 1975. The bill provided for monogamy among non-Muslims and for the end to arbitrary divorce of the wife. The Wanita MCA lobbied MPs, brought the matter to the Press, and supported the bill in its general meetings. In addition, the Wanita MCA added its efforts to those of the NCWO which supported passage of the reform bill. The Wanita MCA also claimed credit for separate taxation of working wives. They brought the issue before the public and once again lobbied for it. It is hard to evaluate their claims to credit, but there is no doubt that their voices added pressure.

The second General Assembly held on 20 August 1976, witnessed a marked increase in the active participation of the delegates. Women from Kedah, Kelantan, Perak, Pahang, Johore and Selangor dominated the meeting. The Central Committee was criticized by a member who noted that while Mrs Rosemary Chong and the Secretary, Lim Sean-lean, were active, little was heard from other members. In contrast to the 1975 assembly where most delegates had come only to listen, in 1976 the Wanita MCA Treasurer-General Kian Sit-har noted that 'They have cast aside their inhibitions and took part rather actively in the debate on the secretary-general's report and the resolutions.'[64] Party president Lee San-choon urged educated Chinese women to come forward and join the party. Mrs Rosemary Chong discussed the Wanita MCA's plans for the next five years. Those plans would aid party efforts in five major projects: 1) the new headquarters building, 2) mass membership drives, 3) the Tunku Abdul Rahman College fund-raising campaign, 4) the multi-purpose corporation (a multi-million dollar corporation to undertake large projects in order to increase the Chinese part in economic growth), and 5) the Chinese cultural centre (a centre designed to allow the 'genuine interaction of the great civilisations in our society'. It also removed culture from the political arena).[65]

By 1976, the Wanita MCA had begun to broaden its activities. Political seminars to inform members of political developments and a Wanita MCA co-operative society called Koperasi Wanijaya were formed. The co-operative, open to all women, was to start by managing the dining hall of the Tunku Abdul Rahman College (the Chinese-medium college). It hoped to branch out into low-cost housing and scholarship loans.[66] These activities, plus the experience Wanita MCA women were gaining in running the affairs of their auxiliary, pointed to the future involvement of the Wanita MCA in the affairs of the MCA itself.

The MIC

The Malaysian Indian Congress (MIC) was the last of the Alliance parties to organize its women's wing on a national scale. This slowness was due to two factors: the failure of the MIC male leaders to see a need to attract women members and the failure of the women to organize or demand a larger role in the party. For the most part, the MIC had been preoccupied with intra-party politics, 1967–73, during which time little effort had been expended to organize women. During 1969–70, no assemblies were held due to the general ban on political activities as a result of the

May 1969 racial riots. Before the riots and from 1971 to 1973, MIC party politics was taken up with the leadership struggle between the then party President, V. T. Sambanthan and his Vice-President, V. Manickavasagam. Prime Minister Tun Abdul Razak was forced to intervene. This led to Manickavasagam's taking over the party presidency and normal party activities resumed. Prior to 1973, only rudimentary women's branches existed in Taiping (Perak),[67] Kelawai (Penang),[68] Loke Yew and Brickfields (Selangor),[69] with state level committees in Perak and Selangor.[70] It was only when Manickavasagam took over the presidency (1973) that the MIC began to woo women members. In March 1973, Manickavasagam called on Indian women to take an active part in politics. At the same time, the deputy leader of the Penang women's branch, Mrs Aisha Dawood, demanded that a woman be appointed national leader of the women's branch.[71] A major step forward was a seminar sponsored by the Selangor Wanita MIC. Over 450 women attended the seminar on the role of women in nation-building. Many of those who attended were Indian women.[72] The response to the seminar was noted and discussed by the major Tamil language paper, *Tamil Nesan*. It called the response to the seminar a turning point in MIC politics.[73]

Still, the push for a strong women's section did not arise in 1973–4. Though the MIC leadership started a youth section in December 1973, no such move was made for women. As late as 1974, the MIC still had no working women's section though it had a number of sub-committees to deal with matters ranging from citizenship to employment.[74] Women neither sat on the MIC Central Working Committee nor served as officers on any of the nine state level committees.[75] They did not serve as MIC members on the Malaysian Alliance National Council, on the Alliance Executive Council, as cabinet members, as senators, MPs or on the state assemblies.[76] Women remained invisible party members, if members at all.

The women's section was finally started in 1975. On 6 July, Manickavasagam appointed Mrs Meenambal Arumugam as head of the MIC Wanita. On 27 August 1975, he named, as deputy leader, Dr G. Krishnaveni who was at that time a member of the MIC Central Working Committee. Two months later, on 12 October 1975, Manickavasagam announced the formation of the first MIC National Women's Council. Besides Mrs Arumugam and Dr Krishnaveni, the Council consisted of Mrs Devaki Krishnan as secretary, and nine other women from the states of Selangor, Malacca, Negri Sembilan, Pahang, Perak and Johore.[77] All members of the Council understood and most spoke English. (Most meetings of the MIC Central Working Committee were conducted in English.) All but two had husbands active in the MIC (though it is not apparent whether the wife was active in the MIC because of the husband or vice versa). Their occupations were diverse: two were doctors, two were teachers, five were housewives, and one each was a social worker, businesswoman, clerk, and one operated a printing press.[78] The upper class nature of the Council was apparent—most women leaders at the branch level were Tamil schoolteachers. The Wanita MIC, like the Wanita MCA (and to some extent the Wanita UMNO), faced communication problems between lower level and state and national level leaders. Such problems existed in the parent parties as well.

Of the women on the Council, two sat on the party's 33-member Central Working Committee: Dr Krishnaveni was appointed while Mrs Arumugam was elected at the 1975 party General Assembly. (She was one of 11 candidates vying for 4 elective seats.) The 1975-6 party report showed that the forming of a women's section did not elevate the position of women in the party. Other than Mrs Arumugam, no women sat on any of the party sub-committees, none took part as MIC members on any committees of the National Front, and none had been put forth by the MIC as electoral candidates.[79]

By December 1975, the National Council had set four general objectives for the Wanita section. All these were vague and had no further elaboration: 1) to upgrade the status of Indian women, 2) to generate political involvement and awareness in Indian women, 3) to encourage unity among all women and 4) to educate women.[80]

The Wanita MIC sought to enlarge its organization numbers. It planned to form executive committees in all states, to increase membership, to increase its involvement in political and social welfare work, to encourage women to implement the Green Book plan (a government plan to increase agricultural output and cut living costs) and the MIC Blue Print, and to raise funds by holding fun-fairs and cultural shows at the state and national levels.[81] This was truly an ambitious programme for so young an organization.

Structurally, the new section remained very much under the control of the party leadership. The Wanita MIC was not regarded as a parallel section of the party. The 1973 constitution[82] made no mention of a women's section. In fact, women's branches functioned only by the largess of the state committee chairman who appointed the MIC Wanita state leader.[83] The president of the party still appointed the national leader.[84] The 1973 constitution did not provide for separate women's branches at the local level; local branches, though, were operating. Women, 18 years and older, joined the general MIC branch[85] and became members upon paying a M$2 joining fee and a M$1 annual membership fee. As of 1976, about one-tenth of the MIC's 120,000 members were women.[86] Of the 12,000 women, the strongest sections appeared to be in Johore (2,500 members) and Perak (3,200). Strong sections also functioned at the state level in Malacca, Negri Sembilan (where 33 of 66 MIC branches had formed women's sections), Pahang (11 of 22 branches) and Selangor (no data though Mrs Nahappan, the Selangor Wanita leader and other sources indicated the section functioned). Trengganu, Kelantan, Kedah and Perlis, all with small Indian populations, had no state level women's sections; the MIC state leaders had yet to appoint women leaders.[87]

The fledgeling women's section had thus far been concerned with non-political and multi-party seminars. They were attended by women from a number of political and non-political groups and dealt with such topics as 'Women in Development'. They also distributed food parcels during Deepavali (the major Hindu holiday), helped members obtain birth and citizenship certificates (a major need for poorly educated estate workers), and conducted family planning, sewing and cookery classes.[88]

Attracting women as party members proved difficult. Few of the women came from the rural areas while the national level women leaders came largely from the educated and propertied class. As a small party, competition for federal or state elective office was fierce. Very rarely would women be given a chance to compete. Thus the hope of holding elective office could not be held as an inducement for women to join the party. Urban, educated women also eschewed membership in favour of other activities outside of the home. Without such members, the section lacked the leadership it needed to be taken seriously by the MIC leaders. Beyond appointing a National Council for Women and conceding that women were important, the MIC had as of 1976 made little effort to bring women in as MIC party members.

The Dewan Muslimat PAS[89]

While recent years have shown the growth and expansion of the Wanita UMNO and MCA, the Dewan Muslimat PAS (DM), in contrast, showed only a limited increase. The DM leaders shared with the Wanita UMNO and MCA leaders a common frustration over what they saw as the limited role for women.

The DM retained a low profile prior to the national campaign of 1969. The section then launched an all-out effort to support party candidates. In one division (Bagan Datok, Perak), the DM and Wanita UMNO clashed head on. Each side tried to organize the Malays in support of their party (60 per cent of the registered voters were Malay women).[90]

The post-election racial riots of 1969 led to a ban on all party activities until September 1970. In February 1971, the DM began to function again. DM leaders continued to push for an enlarged role within PAS. Sakinah Junid replaced Khadijah Sidek as DM leader in 1967. She addressed the 1971 PAS General Assembly and chided the men for ignoring the Dewan Muslimat: 'As Ketua of the Dewan Muslimat, I know the organization of the Muslimat is facing many weaknesses and deficiencies.... However, the attention given to [the] Muslimat by the party especially at the branch level is not all enthusiastic.'[91] Sakinah Junid was the wife of Tan Sri Mohamed Asri, PAS President and past Chief Minister of Kelantan. That comment, together with her long record as a political activist first seen in the MNP, belied the charge that Sakinah Junid was 'just Asri's wife' (a comment heard frequently). Sakinah Junid, in a press interview, described how she saw the DM and the importance of Islam to the auxiliary's role: 'Generally our struggle [is] based on the position and status of women side by side with Islam. In the past, we have at times supported the policy of equal pay for women. We have also encouraged our women to be active in the cooperative movement. Another field we have encouraged women to enter is nursing.'[92]

As of 1971, DM members did not sit on any party committees. In this respect, they were no different from women in other parties. All nine elected members to the party's Central Committee were men. Men also headed all of the party's working bodies and committees except for the DM.[93] Two years later, *Berita PAS*, the party newsletter, announced that the Central Working Committee for 1973–5 would consist of 21 members; one would be a woman (Salmah Sheikh Hussein, the only woman PAS senator).[94]

In July 1972, Sakinah Junid again addressed the PAS General Assembly. She chastized the PAS MPs and state assembly members for not permitting their wives and families to work in the party: 'We do not allow wives to just live in the kitchen. Let our Dewan also build a strong PAS. Let us roll up our sleeves and enter the political arena.'[95]

Two years later, Sakinah Junid's address to the party congress had become even more critical of the women's role in PAS. In her speech, she blamed the men for holding back the DM's progress: 'It is bitter to admit that the men in our party think that Muslim women do not need to come forward within society and that the only place for women is within the home.'[96] She went on to ask if the party thought it would be just as strong without the women. Sakinah Junid warned PAS members that the role of the DM was not a small one. She claimed that it was the DM's efforts which garnered much Malay support for PAS—particularly among Malay women. In addition, she raised the issue of the neglect of DM members to serve as party candidates. In 1969, only one DM woman stood at the parliamentary level (Salmah Sheikh Hussein ran against Fatimah binti Hashim of UMNO and lost 15,145 to 11,595 votes). No PAS women stood at the state level. PAS, meanwhile, had fielded 179 state and 59 parliamentary candidates in 1969.[97]

Sakinah Junid was re-elected as *Ketua* of the DM again and again. She continued her campaign to expand the role of the DM within PAS— pressing PAS members to have their wives join the party. She warned, though, that she would not let the DM become a 'Mak Turut', or 'Yes Woman' organization. She noted that the DM was influential among Malays on matters of Malay unity.[98] After the PAS decision in 1973 to join the National Front, Sakinah Junid urged that a parallel women's organization be formed within the Front. This was to unify the women in the country. The idea was not implemented.[99]

With the adoption of the new party constitution in 1971, the status of the DM *vis-à-vis* PAS changed. The section had been governed by its own by-laws; the DM, Pemuda and Ugama (religious) sections would hence become part and parcel of the party. The party would co-ordinate their activities.[100] Little change occurred in the section's structure or relation to PAS. The DM rules show that the section remained loosely organized at the state and national levels. The section remained under the firm control of the party.[101]

By 1976, the DM had 18,000 members while all PAS numbered 116,000.[102] DM members thus remained a minority. Rural women still comprised most of its membership. Sakinah Junid agreed that the DM (like PAS) lacked support from urban, well-educated women.[103] While sharing a membership base with the Wanita UMNO, the DM differed greatly from the Wanita UMNO. DM Secretary, Hayati Hasman, explained that the DM was first an Islamic organization concerned with Muslim policies, followed by party, then women's policies, in that order. 'The women's policy in the DM is different from that of other parties. The DM policy is in accord with Islam. We are an Islamic party.... The DM is the backbone of the party, (but) the DM is not like the KI. They want everything. The DM only wants what Islam can give them.'[104] Though vague, the statement is significant since it shows that the DM leaders themselves saw the differences between Muslim, party, and women's policies. Of the three, women's policies had the least priority for the section.

DM women, as well as those of the Wanita UMNO, passed a number of resolutions at their annual meetings. In general, these resolutions supported general party policies. In 1974, 100 DM members voted to urge the government to: 1) ban massage parlours and Muslim stores which sell liquor, 2) build hotels for women, and 3) use good judgement to deal with the Singapore government's decision to stop the Muslim morning call to prayers.[105]

Aside from the resolutions, the DM also engaged in sewing, cooking, literacy, and the much more popular, religious classes. One cannot, at this time, evaluate the part of PAS women in the party's electoral fortunes. Party members do mention that DM members were organized to canvass house-to-house and campaign during an election. However, the press coverage of such efforts remained minimal. Given that the DM was a small wing and poorly organized, the electoral role of the DM was far from that of its chief rival, Wanita UMNO. Within the party, they retained a very low profile, playing a peripheral role.

The DAP

In 1965 Singapore withdrew from Malaysia. Two new opposition parties then formed to provide an outlet for non-Malay discontent over the Alliance in general and the MCA and MIC in particular. These were the Democratic Action Party (DAP) and the Gerakan Rakyat Malaysia or, more simply, Gerakan (GRM) (Malaysian People's Movement). The new parties, though, did not alter the minor role that women played within the party system. By 1976, only modest gains had been made by women in the DAP while GRM women remained in the background. In part, this was due to the problem of attracting members that all opposition parties faced. In part, it was a general apathy among party leaders as to the need. While weak, the role of women in the opposition should be examined to gain a balanced view of party politics in Malaysia.

Once Singapore left Malaysia, the PAP was de-registered as a party on the grounds that it was based in a foreign country (Singapore). A new party, the Democratic Action Party (DAP) was then formed under the leadership of C. V. Devan Nair, a Malaysian citizen by birth. The new party was registered with the government in March 1966. Its programme borrowed heavily from the earlier PAP.

The policies of the DAP were set forth in its manifesto, the Setapak Declaration of 29 July 1967. The DAP called for a free, democratic, socialist Malaysia based on racial equality, social and economic justice, and parliamentary democracy. The DAP eschewed any idea of racial hegemony and rejected the 'privileged' position of the Malays in the constitution. Further, the DAP, reflecting severe non-Malay grievances, called for a 'Malaysian Malaysia'—that Chinese (Mandarin), English and Tamil, in addition to Malay, be accepted as official languages.[106] Unlike the Labour Party, the DAP made no direct appeal to women. They ignored the two major issues that were in the public arena: equal pay for equal work and marriage/divorce reform.

At first the DAP remained small. It numbered only 500 members in 1967 with its members concentrated in the large towns of West Malaysia. At that time, there were six party branches: Kuala Lumpur, Petaling Jaya (a suburb of Kuala Lumpur), Ipoh, Malacca, Seremban and Johore Baru. By 1968, the party claimed some 50 branches throughout Malaysia in the major towns and the rural areas near them.[107] Control of the DAP rested with the 10-member Central Executive Committee. Members were divided between cadres and ordinary supporters. As Michael Ong Hung-choon points out, the DAP was an élite party which felt a need, greater than its opponents, to control its members.[108]

Few women were active in the DAP. Efforts to organize women began at the DAP's First National Women's Seminar held in Klang on 9 January 1972. The chairman of the party, Dr Chen Man-hin, presented the women with a mixed message: he encouraged them to enter a 'man's world' but not to lose sight of homemaking.[109] The message did little to clarify the DAP position on women in the party. S. Mary, secretary of the women's branch in Perak argued that the men and women perceived the women's problem differently: men argued that there were no women leaders because none were qualified while women argued that none were qualified because men led the parties. Regardless, she added, 'It is a fact that no sincere effort has been made so far to bring in women members by men leaders'.[110] Closing the seminar on the role of women in politics, the women formed the National Women's Committee of the DAP. Tan Chui-swee (from Johore) was elected chairperson and was to be assisted by a 10-member committee with members from Johore, Selangor and Perak.[111]

The National Women's Council remained the main executive body for women in the DAP. As of 1976, there had been no formal, organization of DAP women. Women's branches existed where there were at least five members. The NWC then had the right to form a state women's section if there were at least three women's branches in a given state. As of 1976, the DAP had 20 women's branches throughout the states of Pahang, Perak, Malacca, Selangor, Johore and Negri Sembilan with about 500 members; the DAP membership was purported to number 10,000.[112] Women, 17 years and older, who joined the DAP, would be members of a women's branch and would elect their own leaders. Women members, according to the Treasurer of the National Women's Council (Au Keng-wah) and other party sources, were rural working women, usually rubber tappers, hawkers, tailors and other labourers. Most, but not all, were Chinese and Chinese-educated. As with the other parties, the DAP had failed to attract urban, better educated women. In part, this was due to working urban women having little time and few child care facilities to free them for such activities. In part, this was also due to the problem of bringing women (as well as men) to an opposition party. Opposition party members had many complaints. They received less press coverage than Alliance/Barisan Nasional parties. Their leaders had, at times, been detained under the Internal Security Act. Their party's stand on certain issues (language, education, etc.) was often equated with a lack of patriotism. As Ganga Nayar, a member of the Labour Party, then the DAP, and still later the GRM explained, many Malaysians of all races viewed the opposition parties with suspicion. The few who did join, though, tended to be zealous and hardworking members. The ordinary members simply failed to join. The DAP also ran into competition in the urban areas with the MCA which was now making a major effort to organize urban Chinese women. The greater size and resources of the MCA allowed it to support activities which appealed to women (lectures, classes, etc.). This attracted women to MCA party membership. The opposition parties, as well as the non-Malay parties in the Alliance/Barisan Nasional, had failed to see the need to bring women into politics. No concerted effort was made to gain their support. In part, this stemmed from the failure of the non-Malay women to see the part they could play. The greater educational and economic opportunities afforded urban women had not yet resulted in a larger political role particularly for non-Malay women. (Most women living in the urban areas were non-Malay.)

As of 1976, the role of women in the opposition party, the DAP, was limited. As Au Keng-wah explained, 'the time isn't right yet for a strong women's section'.[113] DAP women had not formed a strong national section. This, in turn, confirmed their limited role within the DAP. Since its inception, the DAP Central Executive Committee (CEC), the party power centre, remained an all-male preserve. Women had only a small role in any DAP bureau. At a branch and state committee level, women were conspicuous by their absence. Only Au Keng-wah was a chairperson of a DAP branch (Ampang, Selangor) while Noraini Salleh was the treasurer of the Bentong branch and Liew Lai-ching was the assistant secretary of the Gunung Rapat branch. All other officials were men as of 1976.[114]

DAP women, though few in number and loosely organized, did take up a number of causes. Within the party, they urged women be sent as delegates to international conferences. At least two of their members were elected to the CEC because, as Au Keng-wah explained, getting on the CEC was a first step towards equality. 'Currently, men and women stand on different sides and women have to expect to fight for equality. So far, the Wanita DAP has been "sleepy" and the men haven't seen them do much and do not see any reason to include them on the CEC.'[115] (For example, it was common for only 5 to 8 women to attend the party general assembly held every three years.)

Aside from party matters, DAP women leaders spoke out in opposition to: X-rated films,[116] defecting DAP MPs to the MCA,[117] and public smoking.[118] They supported the increased role of women in public life,[119] sought the recognition of Chinese university degrees,[120] protested prostitution,[121] sought to protect the righs of women workers,[122] and publicized the need for a marriage and divorce reform bill for non-Muslims.[123]

Women in the DAP also worked in support of party candidates and, at times, were selected to run. In the 1969 elections, two parliamentary candidates were women: Au Keng-wah and Mrs Kong, both of whom lost. In 1974, four women ran in the parliamentary and state elections. Mrs Ganga Nayar became the first DAP woman MP while three DAP women, Mrs Azharah, Mrs Benny Ghandi and Au Keng-wah, lost at the state level.[124] In general, the role of women in the DAP remained limited.

The Gerakan

In April 1968, another non-communal party was launched. Dr Lim Chong-eu, the leading figure of the United Democratic Party (a largely unsuccessful party), joined with moderate, English-educated members of the Labour Party to form the Gerakan Rakyat Malaysia (GRM) or People's Movement Party.[125] The GRM laid great emphasis both on its non-communal approach and on the special needs of the Malay community. The party supported constitutional and parliamentary democracy; it also called for a just share of the wealth for all segments of the population, public control of the vital means of production, the protection of the trade unions, as well as all citizens, men and women, having an adequate means of support.[126]

Among the founders of the party were three women—two belonged to the 17-member pro tem committee: Ramlah binti Muzir, a clerk from Kuala Lumpur, and Raja Baagaya binti Yaacob, a housewife from Petaling Jaya, Selangor.[127] Ganga Nayar, the third woman in the GRM's early days, became the leader of a women's section.

The Gerakan openly espoused certain issues that were of direct concern to women: legalized abortion and a women's charter.[128] In its constitution, it urged that women receive equal pay for equal work.[129] It was the only party (aside from the Labour Party) to place such an emphasis on equal pay for women. In its 1968 statement of party objectives, the GRM called on the government to establish a Women's Charter to protect the rights of women.[130] The Gerakan, in an appeal to women voters, included in its 1969 election manifesto a promise to 'work to abolish discrimination of every kind and in particular against women and to work for a Women's Charter to this end', and 'to urge the modification of our divorce laws'.[131]

This approach to women was not accompanied by a strong women's section within the party. The party constitution did not provide for a separate women's wing nor were women reserved posts at any level within the party.[132] Women's branches in the GRM functioned only at the local and state level. Within six months of the start of the GRM, women's branches existed in Malacca, Seremban, Penang, Ipoh and Kuala Lumpur.[133] Until 1971, there had been no attempt, however, to organize GRM women at the national level. In April of that year, a national Wanita Gerakan was formed at a seminar for Selangor Gerakan women. Ganga Nayar, by then the GRM Selangor state assemblywoman, called on all women to join the GRM. She urged women to take an active part in politics and not be less active than men.[134] At the same meeting, Ramlah binti Muzir, who became the secretary of the Wanita Gerakan, encouraged the women to make the Wanita a 'powerful, dynamic and progressive women's wing of [the] GRM'. Ramlah binti Muzir went on to urge that the section should not be simply a social organization. She wanted it committed to a new order—to tackle the economic, social and political problems that faced women.[135] The Selangor seminar thus heralded the advent of the national Wanita Gerakan. Mrs Ganga Nayar was elected president while Ramlah binti Muzir became secretary. The fate of the Wanita GRM, though, was left very much in doubt. In June 1971, the GRM had to order its Pemuda and Wanita sections to postpone functions indefinitely; the GRM constitution did not provide for auxiliaries. They could not function until approved by the Registrar of Societies.[136] It is doubtful that the Wanita Gerakan ever got underway. At most, Mrs Ganga Nayar explained, there were 60 women members during the 1968–9 period when the Gerakan was at its peak. Of these few members, most were Chinese and Malay working women; a very few were Indian.[137]

Pekemas

A struggle within the Gerakan in 1971, reminiscent of that in the Socialist Front in 1963, led to the party's split. One faction formed its own party, the Parti Keadilan Masyarakat Malaysia (Pekemas), the Social Justice Party of Malaysia.[138] Pekemas also strove for a non-communal society based on economic and social justice for all. Unlike many Malaysian

parties, the 1971 Pekemas constitution provided for a national women's section and for female members on the party's central committee.[139] The Wanita Pekemas, organized by the party's central committee, was governed by its own regulations. Its main objectives included:
1) to encourage the members to actively participate in politics, racial integration and domestic science, economics, culture, sports, social welfare, women's rights and family planning,
2) to arrange and hold seminars, courses, training programmes, etc. for realization of the above aims and objects, and
3) to work in close co-operation with other bodies established by the central committee of the party.[140]

The Wanita Pekemas was to be organized at the branch, state and national levels. It was launched on 20 August 1972, in Petaling Jaya, Selangor. One month later, Betty Khoo, the secretary of the newly formed section, urged the women to organize in order to meet the social and economic needs of women.[141] The Wanita Pekemas called for a wages council to protect women workers from unscrupulous employers. They cited industries that often paid women a wage of M$1 to M$1.50 a day.[142] Party president, Tan Chee-khoon, was one of the men who called on the government to assess separately the tax on married women.[143]

Details on women in Pekemas remain scarce. Two party annual reports (1973 and 1974) showed that one woman, Norashikin binti Yusof (leader of the Wanita Pekemas and a bus conductress), had sat on the party's Central Executive Committee since it began. Few women, however, had attended the annual general assemblies. For example, only 6 of 117 delegates were women at the first general assembly.[144] The party, in its infancy as of 1976, had yet to develop a strong organization. The annual reports mention little about the Wanita Pekemas whose pro tem committee was elected in 1972. Due to the party's newness and its small size, about 3,500 in 1974,[145] of whom 15 per cent were women,[146] little could be said about either the party or its women's auxiliary.

Other Parties

Information on women in Malaysia's other political parties is sparse. The Labour Party, having decided to boycott the 1969 general elections, was officially defunct by 1972. The PSRM and the PPP remained diminutive.

The Malayan People's Socialist Party, the PSRM (the Malay-based agrarian socialist party), continued to function but its women's section did not develop. As of 1976, there was no national level Wanita Rakyat though a few branch and state level women's sections functioned in Pahang, Kedah and Trengganu. In other states, women joined the party but did not take part in the women's branches. In general, those women's branches that functioned did so only during election campaigns.[147] There was an absence of the sewing and cooking classes used by other parties to attract women members. Of the women in the party, Siti Noor Hamid Tuan, an independent in a 1973 by-election,[148] was recognized as the leader. She replaced the former Wanita Rakyat leader Zaidah Hashim (1963–73). Siti Noor Hamid Tuan sat on the party's central committee; she was one of three women on the major policy-making body of the party.[149] Since the PSRM kept no separate membership figures, one cannot estimate how many of the party's purported 20,000 members were women.[150] Given that the women's section did not develop and that party publications failed to record the activities of PSRM women, it is likely that the role of women in party affairs remained limited.

Finally, the People's Progressive Party, founded by the Seenivasagam brothers, remained confined to one state (Perak). It failed to develop a women's section. Neither did individual women appear to play much of a role in party affairs. While it attained some electoral success (the PPP won 12 state and 4 federal seats in 1969) the party did not field women. A small party, numbering only 591 members in 1975,[151] it had yet to bring women into party affairs.

The Importance of Women as Electoral Candidates and Workers—The General Elections of 1969 and 1974

Though women party members provided much of the labour needed for Malaysia's general elections, there was no change during the elections of 1969 and 1974, of the pattern begun in the 1950s: women would campaign and vote but rarely would they be selected as party candidates.

The 1969 electoral efforts, particularly by the KI, were once more effective in getting women to vote in large numbers. According to one report:

> ... it was the women who dominated the polling at Utan Aji—where they arrived by the hundreds half an hour before the polling station opened and waited rather impatiently.... In Malacca ... most of the voters were housewives who took the opportunity to go to the polls before preparing meals for their families ... also, a large number of supporters, many of them women, helped the Alliance to take voters to the polls in 600 cars....[152]

Housewives with market baskets were among the first voters in Kuala Lumpur. Many of the early voters in Kedah were women and elderly men. In Kedah (as in Johore), most of morning voters were women.[153] Because statistics do not distinguish between the number of male and female voters, it is not possible to measure the importance of women to the fortunes of the parties. What is clear, though, is that women have remained, through election after election, voters. Their numbers were so great as to receive attention from the Press.

The readiness to vote was not rewarded by an increased number of women candidates. Not even UMNO, with 50 per cent women, would nominate a proportionate number of women. Details at the state and federal levels for the 1969 general elections in West Malaysia are shown

TABLE 7.1
State and Federal Electorates by Party, 1969

	State		Federal	
	Male	Female	Male	Female
Alliance	269	12 (all UMNO)	104	3 (all UMNO)
PMIP	185	0	61	1
PSRM	38	0	6	0
PPP	16	0	6	0
DAP	57	1	22	2
GRM	37	1	14	0
UMCO	12	0	3	0
Independent	38	1	4	1
(Uncontested)	19	1 (UMNO)	—	—
Total	662	16	220	7

Sources: Compiled from the *Report on the Parliamentary (Dewan Ra'ayat) and State Legislative Assembly General Elections 1969 of the States of Malaya, Sabah and Sarawak*, Kuala Lumpur, Government Printer, 1965; *BH*, 13 May 1969. All figures apply only to West Malaysia. The UMCO was a minor party that appeared briefly and for our purposes was not significant.

in Table 7.1. For 105 parliamentary seats, 7 women competed as compared to 220 men. Out of 678 candidates for 282 state assembly seats, 16 were women. By party, the breakdown was also shown in the Table.

Of the women who stood, Alliance candidates fared best. At the parliamentary level, three UMNO women were elected; the other four women were defeated. At the state level, seven UMNO women won as did Mrs Ganga Nayar of the Gerakan. In 1969 (as in past elections), successful women candidates were nearly always UMNO members. This was true both because UMNO contested the greatest number of seats and because UMNO put forth the largest number of women. An UMNO label did not, however, guarantee victory: six UMNO women were defeated at the state level. Also, as in previous elections, neither the MCA nor the MIC (the largest parties representing non-Malays) had put forth women candidates. Opposition parties either failed to nominate women or chose to nominate very few.

The 1969 general election results ensured an Alliance victory. It was a set-back, though, in terms of its performance in the largely non-Malay states of Selangor, Penang and Perak. Vasil[154] noted, for example, 'the MCA was almost completely demolished'. Briefly, the results for the Alliance in West Malaysia follow the results from the 1959 and 1964 elections as shown in Table 7.2

Though UMNO incurred losses, it was the MCA which suffered the greatest. In Selangor, for example, UMNO won 12 seats; the MCA and MIC won only 1 seat each. (In 1959, it was: UMNO 14, MCA 8 and MIC 1; and in 1964: UMNO 13, MCA 9 and MIC 3.)[155] This pattern

TABLE 7.2
Results of the Alliance in West Malaysia in the 1959, 1964, 1969 Elections

Parliament		Per Cent of Vote Received
1959	74 out of 104 contested	51.78
1964	89 "	58.37
1969	66 "	48.10
State		
1959	206 of 282 contested	55.52
1964	241 "	57.62
1969	162 "	47.95

Source: R.K. Vasil, *The Malaysian General Election of 1969*, Kuala Lumpur, Oxford University Press, 1972, p. 36.

was repeated in Penang and Perak where the MCA suffered severe losses.[156]

The Alliance losses in 1969 have been detailed elsewhere.[157] For present purposes, though, it was the MCA defeat that led to an attempt to broaden its base of support. This was to include women. Women have been 'discovered' as valuable to a party when there has been a party crisis which threatened the existence of the party—this is borne out by the UMNO and MCA experiences. At first, UMNO had to convince the British that it represented the whole Malay community; in subsequent years, UMNO needed women members for vital election support. The MCA needed women after 1969 to bolster its claim that it was the major spokesparty for Chinese interests. For the MCA which had done little to attract such members, women offered a great potential for party support.

The 1969 election set-back for the Alliance and the racial riots produced an expanded UMNO–MCA–MIC Alliance, the National Front or Barisan Nasional (BN). By the advent of the 1974 general elections, the Front included UMNO, the MCA and the MIC with PAS, the GRM, the PPP and three East Malaysian parties: the Sabah Alliance, the Sarawak Alliance and the Sarawak United People's Party (SUPP). Only the DAP, PSRM, and Pekemas remained in opposition.

The Barisan Nasional scored a major victory in the 1974 general elections,[158] even though the roles of women had not changed. All UMNO women who stood for election were successful; it was the first time. This prompted Aishah Ghani to remark: 'Their overwhelming victories had shown that women politicians have received the trust and support of the voters.'[159] A build up in the Press heralded both the presence of women candidates and their contributions to the campaign. (For example, the women's movement had been elevated from the 'backbone' of UMNO to becoming the 'backbone' of the National Front.)[160] However, only 29 women stood as candidates with only 1, an independent, losing her deposit. At the parliamentary level 7 women competed, 4 UMNO women successfully. One UMNO woman was

TABLE 7.3
Breakdown of Candidates by Party and Sex in the 1974 General Elections

	State		Parliament	
	Male	Female	Male	Female
BN	301	10 (UMNO)	110	4 (UMNO)
DAP	116	4	45	1
PSRM	104	3	20	1
Pekemas	91	2	34	0
Independent	175	1	37	1
Uncontested	43	1 (UMNO)	31	1 (UMNO)
IPPP	6	0	1	0
KITA	9	0	4	0
Total	845	21	282	8

Source: Compiled from *Report on the Parliamentary and State Legislative General Elections 1974 of the States of Malaya and Sarawak*, Kuala Lumpur, Government Printer, 1975. The IPPP and KITA were 'mosquito' parties that formed just prior to the elections.

returned unopposed. The 3 who lost were from the DAP, PSRM and an independent.

At the state level, 20 women competed with 10 UMNO wins and 1 being returned unopposed. All opposition women candidates were defeated: 3 PSRM, 4 DAP, 1 independent and 2 from Pekemas. No women candidates were put forward by the MCA, the MIC or PAS despite repeated complaints by women members. Table 7.3 shows the breakdown of candidates by party and sex.

By 1974, it was clear that despite their protests and electoral efforts, few women would be chosen as party candidates. Excluded from the major decision-making bodies of all the political parties, women were not in a position to demand a greater role. Until more women attended their parties' branch and division assemblies, and were elected to the major decision-making bodies of all the parties, it was unlikely that the role of women would change.

Conclusion

By 1976, all of Malaysia's major parties had tried to organize women's wings (auxiliaries). Of the wings, the Wanita UMNO remained the largest and the best organized. It had only a limited influence in the party, though. The 1970s saw the first major attempt to organize women in the MCA. The first efforts to organize the Wanita MIC only heralded a possible start for Indian women in MIC affairs. For the Dewan Muslimat PAS, the period prior to 1976 had resulted in limited growth. The section remained loosely and poorly organized at the branch and division level as was PAS itself. Repeated complaints by DM leaders as to the section's limited role had wrought little change; the DM remained subordinate to the party, a male preserve. Women active in the opposition (the DAP, PSRM and Pekemas) were poorly organized. In such parties, women tended to take part as individuals, though occasionally they were organized at the branch and state levels.

By the end of the 1970s, it was clear that forming a women's wing increased female membership. These sections, though, were to play only a limited and subordinate role in party affairs. Whether *de jure*, as defined by the constitutions of the MCA, MIC and PAS, or *de facto*, as in UMNO, women did not attend party bodies. Despite the auxiliary, the role played by women stemmed from cultural values about the part women should play. For Malays, the participation of women was accepted as long as it was supportive and did not threaten party unity. For non-Malays, cultural values placed women in the home and barred them from public life. This was slowly changing.

While auxiliaries were useful to a party's fortunes, it remained less clear how well they expressed the interests of their particular members. The passage of resolutions in itself had little meaning beyond expressing a certain view or demand. Unless the resolutions were taken up by the parent bodies, the women's sections had little influence. Auxiliary interests remained clearly subordinate to the interests of the party itself.

1. *ST*, 12 September 1970.
2. MCA, *Constitution of the MCA Approved and Adopted by the Central General Assembly of the Association at an Extraordinary General Meeting held on 11th September 1970*, Kuala Lumpur, MCA.
3. *ST*, 24 July 1972.
4. Judith Strauch, 'Tactical Success and Failure in Grassroots Politics: The MCA and DAP in Rural Malaysia', *Asian Survey*, December 1978, Vol. 18, No. 12, pp. 1280–94.
5. *ST*, 24 July 1972.
6. *ST*, 28 August 1972.
7. *China Press*, 25 August 1972, *D.P.S.*
8. *Sing Pin Jih Pao*, 10 October 1972, *D.P.S.*
9. *Sing Pin Jih Pao*, 14 October 1972, *D.P.S.*
10. *Sing Pin Jih Pao*, 1 December 1972, *D.P.S.*
11. *ST*, 27 August 1972.
12. *Malay Mail*, 24 September 1972.
13. *Malay Mail*, 24 September 1972.
14. *ST*, 1 July 1975. She is also married to a doctor and has four children.
15. *Malay Mail*, 24 September 1972.
16. Interview with Mrs Rosemary Chong on 17 June 1976.
17. *Sin Chew Jit Poh*, 13 March 1973, *D.P.S.*
18. *Malay Mail*, 26 March 1973.
19. *Malayan Thung Pau*, 10 April 1973, *D.P.S.* In response two bus companies agreed to provide special transport services for the night shift factory workers in Petaling Jaya. *Malay Mail*, 19 April 1973.
20. *Nanyang Siang Pau*, 18 April 1973, *D.P.S.*
21. See *Far Eastern Economic Review*, 4 June 1973, Vol. 80, p. 11, for details.

22. *The Star*, 5 June 1973, *D.P.S.*
23. *Nanyang Siang Pau*, 7 June 1973, *D.P.S.*
24. *Sin Chew Jit Poh*, 8 June 1973, *D.P.S.*; *Malay Mail*, 8 June 1973.
25. *Malay Mail*, 8 June 1973.
26. *ST*, 14 August 1973.
27. *Nanyang Siang Pau*, 9 August 1973, *D.P.S.*
28. *Far Eastern Economic Review*, 25 June 1973, Vol. 80, No. 25.
29. *Nanyang Siang Pau*, 16 July 1973, *D.P.S.*
30. *ST*, 9 April 1974.
31. *The Guardian*, 3 July 1974, Vol. 6, No. 7, p. 3; *ST*, 1 July 1974; *Sin Chew Jit Poh*, 1 July 1974, *D.P.S.*
32. *The Guardian*, October 1974, Vol. 6, No. 10, p. 2.
33. Mrs Rosemary Chong, two deputy chairs, the secretary, treasurer and executive secretary.
34. *The Guardian*, 25 March 1975, p. 7.
35. *The Guardian*, 'Selayang Parliamentary By-Election Supplement', 19 June 1975, p. 5.
36. *Suara Wanita*, August 1975, p. 1.
37. *ST*, 16 June 1975.
38. *ST*, 16 June 1975.
39. *ST*, 16 June 1975.
40. *Malay Mail*, 16 June 1975.
41. *Malay Mail*, 16 June 1975.
42. MCA, 'Bye-Laws of the MCA Women's Section', Kuala Lumpur, MCA, n.d., Section 12.4, p. 6.
43. MCA, 'Speech by Sdr Chow Poh-kheng (Mrs Rosemary Chong), National Chairman Wanita MCA, at the National Wanita MCA 1st General Assembly on 7 August 1975', Kuala Lumpur, MCA, mimeograph.
44. Ibid.
45. MCA, 'Resolutions of the 1st General Assembly of the Wanita MCA', Kuala Lumpur, MCA, 1975, mimeograph.
46. 'Declaration and Statement of Objectives of the Wanita MCA, 7 August 1975', Kuala Lumpur, MCA, mimeograph.
47. 'Bye-Laws of the MCA Women's Section', p. 1.
48. Interview with Lim Swee-chin, leader of the Ampang Selangor Youth Section on 21 June 1976.
49. 'Bye-Laws of the MCA Women's Section', Section 5, p. 2.
50. Ibid., Section 6, p. 3.
51. Ibid., Section 8, p. 4.
52. Ibid., Section 10, 1–4, pp. 5–6.
53. Interview with Mrs Rosemary Chong, 17 June 1976.
54. *Suara Wanita*, April 1975, p. 8.
55. *Suara Wanita*, April 1975, p. 9.
56. *ST*, 17 December 1974.
57. *ST*, 17 December 1974.
58. MCA, *Constitution of the MCA Approved and Adopted by the Central General Assembly of the Association at an Extraordinary General Meeting held on 11th September 1970*, Article 127.
59. Interview with Mrs Rosemary Chong, 17 June 1976.
60. Interview with Tan Ken-sing, Chief Executive Secretary of the MCA on 15 June 1976.
61. *The Guardian*, September 1976, Vol. 8, No. 6, p. 3.
62. Interview with Tan Ken-sing, 15 June 1976.
63. Interview with Mrs Rosemary Chong, 17 June 1976.
64. *The Guardian*, September 1976, Vol. 8, No. 6.
65. *The Guardian*, September 1976, Vol. 8, No. 6.

66. *ST*, 10 September 1976.
67. *Tamil Malar*, 14 November 1972, *D.P.S.*
68. *Tamil Nesan*, 28 November 1972, *D.P.S.*
69. *Tamil Malar*, 2 February 1973, *D.P.S.*; *Tamil Nesan*, 9 April 1973, *D.P.S.*
70. *The Star*, 26 January 1973, *D.P.S.*; *Tamil Nesan*, 28 April 1973, *D.P.S.*
71. *The Star*, 3 March 1973, *D.P.S.*
72. *Tamil Nesan*, 3 May 1973, *D.P.S.*
73. *Tamil Nesan*, 8 May 1973.
74. MIC, *MIC Annual Report 1973–4*, Petaling Jaya, Percetakan P.K.S., 1974, pp. 10–18.
75. Ibid., pp. 18–20.
76. Ibid., pp. 6–7.
77. MIC, *MIC Annual Report 1975–6*, Petaling Jaya, Percetakan P.K.S., Section 15, pp. 32–3.
78. Interview with Dr Krishnaveni on 25 February 1976.
79. MIC, *MIC Annual Report*, pp. 2–7.
80. Ibid., p. 34.
81. Ibid.
82. A new party constitution was to be drafted in 1976. It was not, however, available to the author at the time of writing.
83. *Constitution of the Malaysian Indian Congress, Approved and Adopted by the General Assembly of the Congress on 25th August 1973*, Kuala Lumpur, MIC, Article 8, Section 5b.
84. Ibid., Article 9, Section 4b.
85. Ibid., Article 5, Section 1b.
86. Interviews with Dr Krishnaveni, 25 February 1976, and Mr Dorairaj on 22 September 1976.
87. The above data was taken from the *MIC Annual Report 1975–6*, pp. 27–56.
88. Ibid., pp. 37–56.
89. Information on the Dewan Muslimat was difficult to obtain. Despite repeated efforts, the author was unable to interview Datin Sakinah Junid or her husband, Party President Tan Sri Mohamed Asri. Puan Azah Aziz, feature editor of *Utusan Melayu* and founder of Pertama, the Women Journalists Association of Malaysia, confirmed the difficulty of obtaining information on the DM. For example, at the 1975 DM general assembly all reporters were asked to leave thus making press coverage very difficult. Interview with Azah Aziz on 1 September 1976.
90. *BH*, 10 January 1969.
91. *BH*, 19 June 1971.
92. *BH*, 22 June 1971.
93. 'Report on the Political Organization of the PAS Central Committee May 12, 1971', in 'Miscellaneous speeches, press statements and reports on PAS', Kuala Lumpur, NST Library, mimeograph.
94. *Berita PAS*, 10 October 1973, No. 10.
95. *BH*, 29 July 1972.
96. *BH*, 14 June 1974.
97. *BH*, 13 May 1959, 14 June 1974; Federation of Malaysia, *Report on the Parliamentary (Dewan Ra'ayat) and State Legislative Assembly General Elections 1969 of the States of Malaya, Sabah and Sarawak*, Kuala Lumpur, Government Printer, 1972, Appendix B, p. 52; R. K. Vasil, *The Malaysian General Election of 1969*, Kuala Lumpur, Oxford University Press, 1972, Appendix 2, Table 1a, p. 73, and Appendix 2a, p. 85.
98. *BH*, 29 July 1975.
99. *Utusan Melayu*, 29 July 1975, *D.P.S.*; *BH*, 29 July 1975.
100. *ST*, 22 June 1971.
101. PAS, 'Cabutan Perlembagaan PAS mengenai Dewan Muslimat PAS Pusat dan Negri, 1973', Kuala Lumpur, PAS, 1973, mimeograph.
102. Interview with DM Secretary, Hayati Hasman on 5 October 1976.
103. *BH*, 29 July 1972.

104. Interview with Hayati Hasman, 5 October 1976.
105. *BH*, 14 June 1974.
106. *The Setapak Declaration* reprinted in DAP, *DAP: Who Lives if Malaysia Dies? Selection from the Speeches and Writings of DAP Leaders and Basic Documents of DAP Malaysia*, Selangor, DAP, 1969.
107. Michael Ong Hung-choon, 'The Democratic Action Party of Malaysia: the Case for a Malaysian Malaysia Restated', unpublished MA thesis, Melbourne, La Trobe University, 1969, pp. 33-4.
108. Ibid., p. 35.
109. DAP, 'Speech of Dr Chen Man Hin, Chairman of the DAP addressing the First National DAP Women's Seminar', 9 January 1972, Kuala Lumpur, mimeograph.
110. DAP, 'Working Paper on Women and Democratic Socialism', presented by S. Mary, secretary of DAP's Perak's Women's section at the First National Women's Seminar on 9 January 1972, Kuala Lumpur, mimeograph.
111. *Press Release of the DAP*, 9 January 1972.
112. Letters to the author from N. Madhavan Nair, Secretary to the Opposition Leader, 24 February 1976 and 26 April 1976.
113. Interview with Au Keng-wah on 30 September 1976.
114. Letter from N. Madhavan Nair, 26 April 1976.
115. Interview with Au Keng-wah, 30 September 1976.
116. *China Press*, 9 March 1972, *D.P.S.*
117. *Kin Kwok Daily News*, 24 May 1972, *D.P.S.*
118. *Sin Chew Jit Poh*, 14 August 1972, *D.P.S.*
119. *Malayan Thung Pau*, 13 November 1972, *D.P.S.*
120. *Sin Chew Jit Poh*, 11 January 1973, *D.P.S.*
121. *Sin Chew Jit Poh*, 19 April 1973, *D.P.S.*
122. *Sing Pin Jih Pao*, 24 July 1973, *D.P.S.*
123. *Sin Min Daily News*, 6 October 1973, *D.P.S.*
124. Letter from N. Madhavan Nair, 26 February 1976.
125. See Vasil, pp. 16-20 for a discussion of the demise of the LP and the emergence of the GRM and the DAP.
126. GRM, 'April 15, 1968 Statement of Objectives of the Gerakan', Kuala Lumpur, NST Library, mimeograph.
127. Registrar of Societies report on the GRM.
128. *Malay Mail*, 28 March 1969.
129. GRM, *The Constitution and Rules of the GRM, 1973*, Kuala Lumpur, Registrar of Societies, Clause 3.
130. GRM, *Statement of GRM Objectives*, 20 December 1968, point 22, NST Library.
131. GRM, *1969 GRM Election Manifesto*, measures Nos. 19 and 26, NST Library.
132. See the Registrar of Societies file on the GRM.
133. *Malay Mail*, 20 April 1971.
134. *Malay Mail*, 20 April 1971.
135. 'Address by Ramlah Muzir', Secretary of Gerakan Wanita, Reception for Selangor members of the Wanita Gerakan, 17 April 1971, NST Library.
136. GRM, 'Minutes of the Central Committee of the GRM, June 26, 1971', Registrar of Societies file on the GRM.
137. Interview with Mrs Ganga Nayar on 24 May 1976.
138. *Sing Pin Jih Pao*, 6 July 1971, *D.P.S.*; *ST*, 5 July 1971; *Straits Echo*, 6 July 1971, *D.P.S.*
139. Pekemas, *1972 Regulations of the Wanita Pekemas Section*, Kuala Lumpur, Registrar of Societies, Clause 5.2.
140. Pekemas, *1972 Regulations of the Wanita Pekemas Section*, Kuala Lumpur, Registrar of Societies.
141. *The Star*, 3 September 1972, *D.P.S.*
142. *Malay Mail*, 19 September 1972.
143. *Pekemas Newsletter*, January–February 1974, Vol. 11, No. 1.

144. *Pekemas Lapuran Tahunan, 1974*, Kuala Lumpur, NST Library.
145. *Registrar of Societies Report on Pekemas*, n.d.
146. *ST*, 29 May 1973.
147. The party announced it was reorganizing its women's division in preparation for the 1974 elections. *The Star*, 8 May 1974, *D.P.S.*
148. She lost 10,410 to 16,471 votes against the Secretary-General of UMNO, Senu Abdul Rahman. *ST*, 4 August 1974.
149. Interview with A. Razak Khalifah, Selangor State Secretary of the PSRM on 17 October 1976.
150. *Registrar of Societies Report on the PSRM, 1975*, Kuala Lumpur, Registrar of Societies.
151. *Registrar of Societies Report on the PPP*, Kuala Lumpur, n.d., Registrar of Societies.
152. *Malay Mail*, 11 May 1969.
153. *ST*, 10 May 1969.
154. Vasil, op. cit., p. 37.
155. Ibid., p. 37.
156. Ibid.
157. See Vasil, op. cit., as one example.
158. *ST*, 25 and 26 August 1974: The BN won 104 seats in West Malaysia, the DAP won 9 and Pekemas 1. The BN won 61.6 per cent of the vote. Also see, C. Pillay, *The 1974 General Elections in Malaysia*, Singapore, Institute of Southeast Asian Studies, 1974, Occasional Paper No. 25, pp. 4–12, for an analysis of the elections.
159. *ST*, 26 August 1974.
160. *BH*, 12 August 1974.

Part III
Postscript

8 A Quarter Century of Independence Fulfilled, 1976–1983

By 1983, Malaysia had completed a quarter century of independence. During that period, a party system had formed that remained stable and constant, and women's political auxiliaries had formed with varying degrees of success. The end of this period provides an opportunity to re-examine the women's political auxiliaries for signs of continuity and change.

From 1976 to 1983, Malaysia experienced steady economic growth and a lessening of racial tension. Bahasa Malaysia was widely accepted and the explosive issues of language and education no longer threatened society. Clearly, the most evident change was the growing rift within the Malay community sparked by Muslim fundamentalism. Fundamentalism, an outgrowth of Middle Eastern Islamic revival had taken hold among segments of the more traditional Malay community. It had its greatest impact on PAS, the party that represented the interests of this group. As such, Muslim revivalism had yet to challenge the leadership within UMNO or the party's control of the government. It had, though, been the cause of some alarm in party circles. As of 1983, the religious issue had rent PAS, captured the imagination of many young Malays (in form if not substance), caused unease among non-Malays, and become a threat to UMNO's unity and approach to government. The impact of the movement on Malay women was also unclear. Despite the adopting of more conservative clothing by many younger women, there had yet to be much debate on how this religious issue affected women, work and their political role. For non-Malays, the movement sparked private unease but little public comment. The future of fundamentalism and the direction it would take remained unclear.

Party development in this period followed the pattern of the previous decades. UMNO, the MCA and the MIC were still the major spokesmen of the communal groups. Gerakan remained the major non-communal voice within the Barisan Nasional. In the opposition, PAS expressed conservative Malay/Muslim views. It, though, had been split apart over the fundamentalism issue. The DAP also remained in opposition. It represented those whose interests were opposed to the UMNO–MCA–MIC approach to government. As in the past, 'mosquito' parties, i.e. those with little or no electoral impact, had formed but had little popular appeal. Politics remained the province of the main Alliance parties. No new players emerged.

Women made important strides forward. There were in 1983, 2 female cabinet ministers, 4 deputy ministers, 4 senators, 6 members of parliament, and the first federal judge. Increasing numbers of women were also entering the work force. All political parties had increased their numbers of women members. In UMNO, women were 54 per cent of the membership; in the MCA, around 20 per cent and increasing but smaller percentages could be found in most other parties. For UMNO, women now attended party branch meetings whereas they had eschewed such involvement before. They still did not elect their own to party positions of power. In all other parties, the emphasis remained on the task of getting women involved at all levels. For Malay women, PAS in 1982 was split apart by the fundamentalist or '*kafir-mengkafir*' (infidel *v.* faithful) debate. This resulted in a shift towards fundamentalism, a break up of the party, and a much reduced role for Malay women.

In overview, women leaders were aware of the strength of the auxiliaries but awareness was coupled with a restraint borne out of respect for the views of the memberships. Wanita UMNO and Wanita MCA had also seen increased strains between those who urged more definite stands on issues which related to women (for instance, greater female representation in the parties), to society in general (for instance, opposition to the Soviet invasion of Afghanistan) and those who sought a more traditional approach. Signs also occurred which showed that the largest auxiliaries were coming of age and were grappling with the issues that plague any organization: maintaining continuity and yet contending with change. For the other auxiliaries, the issue remained more basic—how to develop.

Wanita UMNO

By 1983, Wanita UMNO remained the largest women's auxiliary in Malaysia. As a major branch of UMNO, the Wanita membership was put at 430,000, or 54 per cent of UMNO's membership in 1982.[1] As such, Wanita UMNO had maintained the steady membership growth that typified its 36-year history. The nature of that membership, however, had changed. Younger women were now put at 60 per cent of the Wanita membership,[2] and the change brought some internal strain. The Wanita, during this time, pressed for legislation on marriage and divorce reform,[3] drug abuse programmes[4] and other traditional concerns by passing resolutions. Increasingly, the Wanita grappled with organizational issues: the change in the nature of its membership, the auxiliary's role in UMNO, its part in the electoral process, and the future direction of the auxiliary. Nowhere were the tensions more evident than in the three-cornered fight for the office of *Ketua* among Aishah Ghani, Zaleha Ismail and Marina Yusof in 1982. At the branch and division levels, the auxiliary's leadership remained the same. It was dominated by older women who had held their positions for years. Over 3,000 of the Wanita's branches were led by elderly women.[5] Aishah Ghani addressed this issue and called for younger women to step forward and assume leadership positions.[6] She created a furore within the section when in July 1980 she announced that most of the state level leaders would be replaced. Most notable were changes in the state leaders of Selangor, Perak, Kedah and Pahang, states in which individual leaders had held office for years. (For example, the incumbent leader in Selangor had held her office for 21 years[7] while that of Perak's 19 years.)[8]

Ironically, the issue of the auxiliary's future came to a head in September 1982 with the election of the Wanita UMNO *Ketua*. In the bitter, three-cornered fight, Aishah Ghani was re-elected after being challenged by her protégé and political secretary, Zaleha Ismail, and an ideological rival, Marina Yusof. Within the Wanita, the style of the three candidates was seen to differ greatly. Aishah Ghani saw the Wanita in terms of KI activities in the 1940s and 1950s. Her firm view held that the Wanita was an arm of UMNO and should first and foremost support the party. In fact, upon her election, she expressed this view: 'Wanita UMNO is not an independent organization.... It is an arm of a political party. As such, its primary objective is the same as UMNO's—to win elections and help hold power for the government.'[9] Such a view was very much in accord with Malay values. That tradition viewed the role of women as supportive to men. In contrast to Aishah Ghani, Zaleha Ismail vowed to fight for women's rights through the constitution and by emphasizing Eastern (e.g. non-Western) values.[10] In essence, Zaleha Ismail urged changes in organization and attitudes: 'I feel that it is time for a change. Women must learn to be more assertive.'[11] Lastly, Marina Yusof, a well-known Kuala Lumpur attorney who had previously alienated much of the Wanita's membership in the 1970s, was seen largely as a rebel. It was felt she would campaign ardently for women's rights. Marina Yusof argued[12] that her campaign for *Ketua* was not a serious attempt to challenge Aishah Ghani. Rather it was an attempt to make the election more democratic by provoking dialogue. Marina Yusof remained one of UMNO's most outspoken members. She was successful in winning a seat to the UMNO Supreme Council in 1981. The effect of Marina Yusof's candidacy for the office of Wanita UMNO *Ketua* was profound. Aishah Ghani won by a narrow margin of only 17 votes:[13]

    Aishah Ghani   154
    Zaleha Ismail   137
    Marina Yusof   69

Not surprisingly, Marina Yusof was accused of taking away votes from Zaleha Ismail.[14] Zaleha Ismail was, in turn, accused of attacking her mentor, Aishah Ghani.[15] Also notable was that Rafidah Aziz, deputy leader (*Naib Ketua*) and long assumed heir to the post of *Ketua*, stayed out of the fight. Instead, she stood for re-election to the post of deputy leader against an unexpected challenge by Rahmah Othman, former Wanita UMNO secretary, senator and MP from Ampang, Kuala Lumpur.

Rafidah Aziz won the election handily 250 to 111[16] but Rahmah Othman's showing was respectable given her late entry in the race. The outcome of the election left much bitterness among the Wanita rank and file. The political future of Zaleha Ismail looked bleak. Neither she nor Marina Yusof could then play an active role in the Wanita UMNO at the state or national level. Both, though, could seek to serve on UMNO's Supreme Council. Aishah Ghani's narrow victory after ten years of service also took its toll. She maintained that 1982 was her last campaign and that she would soon step down. Her most likely successor would be Wanita UMNO *Naib Ketua*, Rafidah Aziz. Rafidah Aziz was one of only two women cabinet ministers, and she alone emerged unscathed from the electoral contest.

While this battle provided much colourful news, Wanita UMNO still pressed the struggle to increase the role of women as electoral candidates—a struggle begun with the auxiliary's inception. Again in 1977, Aishah Ghani urged UMNO to put forward at least one woman in every state assembly; only Selangor and Perak had state assemblywomen at that time.[17] In July of that year, the Wanita UMNO General Assembly once more pressed for at least one-third of UMNO's electoral candidates to be women.[18] As Malaysia readied itself for the 1978 national elections, Aishah Ghani again urged the party to select women as UMNO candidates for state seats in Perlis, Kedah, Kelantan, Penang and Trengganu—states which had no state assemblywomen.[19] Barisan Nasional leaders did offer to consider a woman candidate in Kelantan. When the 24 candidates filed their nomination papers, though, no women were among them.[20] Despite this set-back, Wanita UMNO pledged to go all out to support the BN candidates in Kelantan[21] though they did send letters to each party in the BN urging them to put forward women candidates—at least one state and parliamentary candidate in each state.[22] Limited success was achieved when UMNO president, Datuk Hussein Onn, agreed to one woman state candidate in each state and possibly more women parliamentary candidates.[23] Twelve days later, Wanita UMNO submitted its list of 40 candidates for 10 state assembly seats and 3 candidates for parliament (Rafidah Aziz, Zaleha Ismail and Rahmah Othman). The 9 July 1978 general election saw a clear victory for the Barisan Nasional:[24]

	Parliamentary Seats	Total State Seats
BN	98	240
DAP	15	24
PAS	5	9
Independent	—	2

In the election, the number of female candidates still remained minimal.[25] Wanita UMNO won all 6 federal seats contested (including three incumbents) and 12 out of 13 state seats. Mrs Rosemary Chong won a parliamentary bid for a state seat in Perak. (In that election, voters refused to support all the 'mosquito' parties. In 1978, these included the PSRM, KITA, the new Social Democratic Party, the UDP and the new Workers' Party; the last party was organized by Mrs Ganga Nayar, a long time opposition candidate.)

Three years later, in June 1981, Aishah Ghani stressed that Wanita UMNO was not simply a supportive wing to UMNO, but a full partner.[26] She urged UMNO to give the Wanita the right to contest elections. To emphasize this view, a 20-member Wanita delegation pressed their case before Deputy Prime Minister, Musa Hitam, who concurred with their views. He added though, that only 'suitable' candidates would be considered.[27] The lack of women candidates was not simply a sign of party neglect or omission. The Wanita still faced the problem of drawing suitable lists of candidates from its branches and divisions. In the rural areas, a general UMNO and Wanita UMNO fear has been that the voters would reject a woman candidate on religious grounds—a justified fear given that in 1982 PAS refused to stand any women candidates, arguing that they were not suitable for such positions.[28] Indeed, most Wanita leaders who stood for elections were residents of the towns and cities and won in mixed constituencies. Support from other parties working with UMNO was crucial. Again in 1982, the Wanita pushed for at least one state and one federal woman candidate in every state. Aishah Ghani in a candid interview to the Press, though, admitted that she was not optimistic. The reason she cited was the lack of active decision-making by women in the lower levels of UMNO. She noted that she was the only woman to head an UMNO division in 1982 (she withdrew later that year)[29] and that of 8,000 UMNO branches, no more than 25 were headed by women.[30]

In the April 1982 general elections, 100 per cent of the Barisan Nasional women candidates were elected:[31]

	Parliamentary Seats	Total State Seats
UMNO	7	11
MCA	1	1

As of 1982, state assemblywomen were now elected in Kedah, Selangor, Negri Sembilan, Malacca and Kelantan while Perak, Pahang and Johore each had two. Notably, only UMNO and the MCA fielded women candidates.

The failure of women to increase their numbers as candidates stemmed from two sources:
1) the Wanita sections did not groom women leaders which could be accepted by the parties—a task which they have begun to tackle through leadership training courses, and
2) the exclusion of women from the decision-making process within the parties themselves.

In all parties, the lack of women candidates remained a problem of long duration.

In 1983, no women headed UMNO divisions and fewer than 25 led any of the 8,000 UMNO branches. Neither had the pattern of membership on any of the party committees or bureaus changed—women remained underrepresented. On UMNO's seven bureaus, ranging in subject matter from politics to religion, at most one or two women served. These committees each ranged from 8 to 16 members. On the party's administrative committees (building, discipline, etc.) the numbers were similar.[32] The pattern begun years earlier continued. With rare exception, it was the most prominent of Wanita UMNO women who sat on these committees; Aishah Ghani, Zaleha Ismail, Rafidah Aziz and Rahmah Othman. No woman ever served as officers on these committees.[33] Without doubt, the Supreme Council, Majlis Tertinggi, remained the highest decision-making body within UMNO. It had, at most, three or four women members out of 35. In 1978, Wanita UMNO changed its strategy and decided to run only two women (versus 74 male candidates) for the 20 elective seats on the Council. The theory was that only two women candidates would not split the women's votes. Both Zaleha Ismail and Rafidah Aziz won handily. In fact, Rafidah Aziz obtained the second highest number of votes. Some attributed this to a change in men's attitudes.[34] (They joined Aishah Ghani and Deputy Leader Fatimah binti Abdul Majid on the Supreme Council to bring the total number of women to four.) This policy of only running two candidates to the Supreme Council created a furore in Wanita UMNO, and to a lesser extent in UMNO in 1981. Marina Yusof (Deputy Head of the Wanita in 1972–4) stood for the Supreme Council without the support of Wanita UMNO. She lost. Even with Marina's candidacy, only three candidates were women.

In 1981, fewer than 20 per cent or 200 of the 1,240 delegates to UMNO's General Assembly were women.[35] The UMNO General Assembly elected the Supreme Council. (This included five reserved delegates each from the Wanita and the Pemuda.) UMNO, in response to the Pemuda and Wanita requests for more delegates, altered its by-laws in 1982 so that all Wanita and Pemuda division heads would be delegates to the UMNO General Assembly. This raised the guaranteed number of women to 114. What impact this would have on UMNO policy-making remained unclear. Unless women start to assume more decision-making roles by being elected as delegates, the impact would remain slight.

The six years (1976–83) had seen little real change in the Wanita. The section had grown in membership. All agreed the Wanita had attracted younger members and that many members now attended UMNO branch meetings. Women were still not elected to decision-making positions within the party. This was both because the women did not stand for such positions and because UMNO itself made no effort to promote them. This situation stemmed from a heritage that still saw women in a supportive role. The Wanita's relation to UMNO remained unchanged and was likely to remain so. It was not clear if, and if so how, the Wanita was dealing with the issue of Islamic fundamentalism beyond offering religious classes in the rural areas. While the split within the Muslim community was a major concern of the 1982 UMNO General Assembly,[36] the Wanita did not take a public position. This issue of the conservative younger Malays, including women, seeking to adopt Islamic values for Malaysia as a whole was ignored. Other women were drawn to this issue, for example, ABIM, the Muslim Youth Movement of Malaysia, launched in July 1970 by Anwar Ibrahim and others to reinstate Islam as the way of life in Malaysia. Of its membership of 40,000, 40 per cent were women. Muslim women aged 18 and older were eligible to join. They were organized into their own auxiliary, HELWA (Hal Ehwal Wanita), or, the Ladies Affair Bureau.[37] The issue was fraught with emotional intensity; regardless of what stand Wanita UMNO took, it would only divide the section, as happened in PAS. Religious fundamentalism remained an issue that had profound implications for Malaysia. Instead, however, Wanita UMNO focused its efforts on bringing about marriage and divorce reform for Muslims. Primarily, Wanita UMNO sought to safeguard the welfare of Muslim women. As of 1983, the Wanita had once again reviewed and offered changes in marriage and divorce practices in each state; a slow and, at times, frustrating process.

Wanita MCA

The years 1976 to 1983 were years of consolidation and growth for the Wanita MCA. The organization had its true birth only in 1975. By 1983, its membership totalled about 100,000 members as compared to the party's total of 547,815.[38] Branches and divisions in both the MCA and the Wanita MCA had continued to grow. By October 1982, the party could boast 112 divisions and 1,240 branches while the Wanita followed with 75 divisions and 452 branches.[39] Clearly, the Wanita MCA had grown in numbers. However, had its orientation, leaders or activities changed over the years? The answer is mostly no.

Several factors prevented change. The Wanita MCA in 1983 was still a young and hence insecure organization as compared to the MCA which traced its history to 1949. The auxiliary did not exist as an autonomous body. Further, Malaysian Chinese women still lacked political experience. The experience of the Wanita MCA did not differ greatly from that of Wanita UMNO. Both wings had similar goals and activities and faced similar problems with their role within their parent party. Both women's groups remained first and foremost party wings and only on occasion acted as pressure groups for women.

The Wanita MCA continued to reflect the concerns of its members. While one found fashion and cultural shows, activities were mostly geared to raise funds and support the MCA. One also found repeated efforts to increase the standard of living for some of the section's poorer members. The Wanita MCA multi-purpose training centre in Setapak, Selangor, was launched in 1977 to provide hotel and catering skills for Wanita members.[40] By April 1978, a kindergarten teacher training programme had also been added.[41] Also, a low cost housing project in Selayang (50–100 units) was begun in February 1979.[42]

Together with these efforts, Wanita MCA's resolutions continued to show the orientation of the section. Since 1975, the Wanita MCA had championed issues it saw in the interests of the party as well as of Malaysian Chinese women. The year 1982 saw no change, with the section urging more scholarships for non-Malays, the banning of lurid Chinese comics,[43] the eradication of poverty, the expansion of new villages and guardianship rights over children for women.[44]

As the orientation and forms of activities of the Wanita MCA seemed to parallel those of Wanita UMNO, so did the Wanita MCA seem destined to face the same hurdles, namely, the lack of a role in party decision-making and the failure by the party to select women as electoral candidates. Efforts to overcome these problems began with its inception and have continued through to the present (1983). Only very limited success was achieved in increasing the number of women on party decision-making bodies and as electoral candidates and political appointees (i.e. cabinet posts).[45] As with Wanita UMNO, MCA women had yet to take part in party decision-making bodies beyond those of their own section. Chow Poh-kheng (Mrs Rosemary Chong), the head of the Wanita section, retained her post as one of the six party vice-presidents and also sat on the MCA's Presidential Council (a version of the Central Committee). In 1981, she became the first Malaysian Chinese woman to sit on the Cabinet as Deputy Minister of Culture, Youth and Sports. However, no MCA divisions and only one or two MCA branches were headed by women.[46] As for the five MCA policy bureaus, the MCA did not list these members. It was not likely given the lack of MCA Wanita electoral candidates that women were active in the bureaus. Only two have been selected to stand for office over the years: Mrs Rosemary Chong at the parliamentary level and Wu Lian-hwa at the state level.

Prior to 1983, only one Chinese woman, Mrs Rosemary Chong was mentioned when a Chinese woman politician was named. However, two other women were then making their presence felt in the Wanita MCA. The first was Lim Sean-lean, the Secretary-General of the national Wanita MCA, who in October 1977 became the first woman elected to the party's Central Committee.[47] Four years later, she was re-elected and received the highest number of votes among all the candidates, to the Committee.[48] A second Wanita MCA woman was also gaining some prominence: Wu Lian-hwa, the only MCA Wanita state assemblywoman elected to state legislature. She was elected in the state of Perak (1982).

Despite its youth, the Wanita MCA has experienced the differences that arise between older and newer members. The wing continued to battle its image of 'tai-tai tuan' (wives of the rich with too much spare time). Party insiders have said that the Wanita was underrepresented within the party due to this image. It was said that the Wanita should bring some 'revolutionary change' to all levels of the party. It was also said they should 'polish up' their image,[49] for instance, attract more educated women to the party. This criticism from the party was also mirrored by some of the Wanita members themselves, particularly the leaders at the division level. By July 1981, a number of incumbent Wanita division chairs were being challenged for their positions.[50] While often unsuccessful, the 'new blood' succeeded in electing a new chair (Teng Ah-luan—the national Wanita organizing secretary) and deputy chair[51] in the Federal Territory. The struggle to bring in new, educated and/or English-speaking members continued and had the support of the national Wanita. Mrs Rosemary Chong explained the problems in training and keeping effective leaders. Young women who joined and were then groomed as leaders often left an active party role upon marriage, birth of children or a new job. Many potential leaders were thus lost and the auxiliary still had problems attracting the English-educated who did not understand the meetings conducted in Mandarin. They become frustrated and dropped out—a problem common to both party and auxiliary.

Perhaps nothing shows the relationship between party and auxiliary more clearly than the Wanita MCA expulsions. Since 1976, there have been two major cases:

1) Lim Diw-loon, the chair of the Ayer Puteh, Penang Wanita branch and the Penang Wanita chairwoman, was expelled from the MCA in 1978 for 'serious breach of party discipline'.[52] Lim Diw-loon had, in fact, criticized Party President Lee San-choon's decision to return Lim Kean-siew as Penang MCA chairperson. Accused of causing party disunity she and the youth leader (David Choong) were expelled. This occurred in spite of the full support she had from the Wanita and Youth sections. Following the expulsions, effigies were burnt in protest and 40 Wanita members as well as the Ayer Puteh Wanita committee resigned en mass from the MCA.[53] The national Wanita MCA did not become involved. The expulsion stood.

2) In April 1981, the national Wanita deputy chair, Ng Ah-lan was expelled along with 60 other MCA members. Ng Ah-lan argued that she was not notified as to why she had been expelled only that she had been outspoken. The national Wanita supported the party's decision in this expulsion. In a prepared statement, it argued that the 'party must rid itself of obstacles to its progress'.[54] One test of the auxiliary's strength would be if it could halt the expulsion of a member, for technically there was no appeal from the decision of the party's discipline committee (for example, the president). Such did not happen.

Overall, the Wanita MCA increased in size. It still faced major problems, not the least of which was political apathy among young Chinese women. They did not see what membership in the Wanita MCA could do for them. This problem was faced by all women's political wings.[55] Unless the Wanita addressed very real questions concerning its stands and what young women could contribute, there would be very little change in the direction of the auxiliary.

Wanita MIC

The Wanita MIC from 1976 to 1983 had made little if any headway. The MIC was once again embroiled in a leadership struggle after the death of its president, Tan Sri Manickavasagam in October 1980. In August 1981, Samy Vellu assumed the MIC presidency and later in 1981 he appointed Mrs Nahappan as the leader of the Wanita MIC.

There were no changes in either the MIC constitution or Wanita MIC by-laws that affected the relationship between wing and party. The Wanita MIC leader was still appointed by the party president as were the Wanita deputy leader, treasurer and secretary. State Wanita MIC leaders were still appointed by state MIC leaders. There was no constitutional provision for Wanita MIC branches. Party annual reports (1976–83) show that women remained absent from leadership posts at the national, state and division levels. Only Mrs Nahappan, who became the first Indian woman senator in 1982, sat on the party's Central Working Committee.[56]

Though MIC records showed a party of 178,149 members in December 1982,[57] figures for women were lacking. As of 1980, Wanita MIC Secretary, Mrs R. Kodikaita guessed that women made up 40 per cent of the MIC membership.[58] The figure was confirmed by Mrs Nahappan in 1983.[59] Of this number, there was a 'good mix' of urban and rural women. The activities of the women were the usual fund-raising activities (fun fairs, rummage sales, etc.) and other cultural events which strengthened the Indian community (for example, Deepavali festivities).

Two of the section's major leaders were Mrs Nahappan and Mrs Bhupalan, a well-known teacher, trade unionist and outspoken advocate of 'women's' issues. They hoped that the Wanita would have a greater voice in MIC affairs. To happen, they admitted that Indian women would have to become better educated and make a commitment to the party. This would only come about when the MIC and the Wanita section tackled the basic issue of Indian poverty.[60] In fact, women leaders in the MIC seemed to face many problems in building a role for women: 1) no funding from the MIC headquarters, 2) a cultural background from which women played only a limited and supportive political role, 3) a limited leadership pool due to the concentration of Indian women on estates and the lack of educational and employment opportunities, and lastly 4) the inability of the Wanita MIC to utilize effectively what leaders it did have. Neither Mrs Arumugam nor Dr Krishnaveni (former Wanita MIC leader and deputy leader respectively) remained involved in the Wanita MIC while Mrs Devaki Krishnan, a long time MIC member, headed the Federal Territory's Wanita MIC, but remained underused.

Most likely, the future of the Wanita MIC would remain one of struggle with limited, but continued progress.

The Opposition—PAS and the DAP

As of 1983, only Parti Islam (well known as PAS) and the Democratic Action Party (DAP) remained as opposition parties of significant size. They were the only parties which could challenge the ruling Barisan Nasional (BN). Within the BN itself, only the three parties, UMNO, the MCA and the MIC, had significant female memberships. Other BN members' women's sections, such as the Gerakan and Pekemas, remained unorganized or in an underdeveloped state. It remains premature to comment upon them.

A significant party event of the 1980s was the expulsion of Mohamed Asri from PAS; the party he helped found and which he had led for more than two decades. Challenged by PAS Islamic fundamentalists, he was accused of being too moderate, too secular and 'more of a nationalist than an Islamic fundamentalist'.[61] He was expelled from the party in October 1982. The expulsion shook PAS to its roots with the party splitting between pro- and anti-Asri forces. Resignations were forthcoming from Asri's supporters on the PAS Central Committee, including that of Sakinah Junid, the Dewan Muslimat leader (Asri's wife). Thousands declared their support for Mohamed Asri, while others pledged their support for PAS. Mohamed Asri's response to the furore was immediate: he announced that he would launch a new party, the Hisbul Muslimin (Muslim Front) in March 1983. The Hisbul Muslimin would dedicate itself to: 1) setting up a government and society which would reflect the purity and fairness of Islam and 2) strengthening Muslim brotherhood and forging national unity.[62]

Within PAS, the ouster of Asri and many of his supporters clearly pointed the party towards Islamic fundamentalism. The structure of the party was changed to reflect the new emphasis. The *ulama*, or Islamic theologians, now formed the highest policy-making body in the party, in order to 'instil Islamic awareness in people'.[63] The Dewan Muslimat still functioned but in a weakened form. With Sakinah Junid went many of the DM's central committee as well as many section leaders at the state and local levels.[64] This left a leadership vacuum. The party itself appeared to want the women to perform lesser roles. In a PAS statement issued during the April 1982 general elections, a spokesman for PAS announced that PAS would try not to put up women electoral candidates. It was holding fast to the *hadis* Islamic saying that a community with a woman as a leader could not succeed.[65]

As for the Hisbul Muslimin, the role women would play is unclear. As of 1983, the party had yet to receive approval from the Registrar of Societies. Once received, the Hisbul Muslimin would then be able to draw on the experience of Sakinah Junid and her supporters to organize women members. Over 5,000 Kelantanese women had pledged their support for the new party.[66] Women, however, would not have their own auxiliary. There would be neither women, youth nor religious sections. Instead there would be a movement to encompass the interests of all three.[67] This concept remained vaguely defined. It is far too early to speculate either on the future of the new party or on the role of women within it. What remains clear, though, is that if the Hisbul Muslimin in the future wishes to mount a successful campaign against PAS and UMNO to woo Malay voters, history shows it would do well to attract and organize Malay women as party members.

By 1982, efforts to start a national women's section within the DAP were dead. This failure to organize DAP women stemmed from many DAP weaknesses: 1) the DAP still had problems attracting members to its fold—this was evidenced by the 1982 election results in which the number of DAP parliamentary seats had dropped from 15 in 1978 to 6 in 1982, and 2) educated women eschewed DAP membership which restricted the pool from which women leaders could be drawn. Alarmed by this state of affairs, two dynamic DAP women, Oon Hing-geok[68] and Lok Swee-chin,[69] in early 1983 approached the DAP leaders and urged that a national women's section be formed. In the first months of 1983, a pro tem committee of 20 women was appointed by the DAP central committee to draft a constitution for the future wing. Of that pro tem committee, most were Chinese, only two were bilingual, but only four had received a higher education. The women members that the pro tem committee sought to organize had changed little over the years: most were poorly educated Chinese working women (hawkers, seamstresses and the like). While often dedicated party workers, they lacked the leadership and organizing skills needed for a viable section. The urban, educated women who could provide such skills remained an untapped resource.

As individuals, few women had made any impact on DAP policies or politics by 1983. While the DAP did run two women candidates for state seats in Perak and Pahang in 1982, both lost. No women headed any of the DAP's 114 divisions or held any positions of influence within the party itself.[70]

The history of women's activities within the DAP depended upon the intentions and efforts of a few motivated women leaders. The future of the DAP women's section at best is precarious and at worst will fail to materialize.

Aside from the UMNO, the MCA, the MIC, PAS and the DAP, efforts to organize women have been minimal. For all practical purposes, the history of women and party politics remained encompassed by the activities of women in Malaysia's two largest parties, the UMNO and the MCA, with smaller efforts contributed by the women's sections of the MIC, PAS and the DAP. In all, the efforts of the women were seen by both men and women as supportive of the efforts of the parties. The interests of women came second.

1. *New Straits Times* (*NST*), 22 March 1982.
2. Interview with Aishah Ghani on 13 May 1983.
3. *NST*, 25 February 1980.
4. *NST*, 6 July 1979.
5. *NST*, 22 December 1980.
6. *NST*, 22 December 1980.
7. *NST*, 18 July 1980.
8. *NST*, 23 July 1980.
9. *The Star*, 9 September 1982.
10. *NST*, 6 September 1982.
11. *The Star*, 9 September 1982.
12. Interview with Marina Yusof on 13 May 1983.
13. *The Star*, 10 September 1982.
14. *The Star*, 10 September 1982.
15. *The Star*, 9 September 1982.
16. *The Star*, 10 September 1982.
17. *NST*, 27 March 1977.
18. *NST*, 1 July 1977.
19. *NST*, 2 February 1978.
20. *NST*, 25 February 1978.
21. *NST*, 28 February 1978.
22. *NST*, 12 May 1978.
23. *NST*, 4 June 1978.
24. *NST*, 10 July 1978.
25. *Malay Mail*, 10 July 1978.
26. *NST*, 26 June 1981.
27. *NST*, 4 November 1981.
28. *NST*, 12 April 1982.
29. *The Star*, 15 August 1982.
30. *NST*, 22 March 1982.
31. *NST*, 26 April 1982.
32. UMNO, *UMNO Penyata 1981/82*, Kuala Lumpur, Penerbitan Ibu Pejabat UMNO, 1982, pp. 1–6.
33. Ibid.
34. *Malay Mail*, 17 September 1978.
35. *NST*, 25 June 1981.
36. *Malay Mail*, 9 September 1982.
37. Interview with Sharifah Aminah Alkhared, Secretary of HELWA on 27 April 1983. See also: *Revival of Islam in Malaysia, the Role of ABIM*, ABIM, Kuala Lumpur, Malaysia.
38. Interview with Chow Poh-kheng (Mrs Rosemary Chong) on 5 May 1983.
39. Interview with Mrs Rosemary Chong on 5 May 1983. Also, MCA, *8th Wanita MCA General Assembly Secretary-General's Report*, Kuala Lumpur, MCA, 1982, p. 13.
40. *The Star*, 12 April 1977.
41. *The Star*, 12 April 1978.
42. *NST*, 24 February 1979.
43. *Malay Mail*, 4 October 1982.
44. *Malay Mail*, 19 September 1982.
45. *Malay Mail*, 1 August 1977; *NST*, 20 August 1977; *NST*, 8 September 1979; *Echo*, 21 September 1980; *Echo*, 19 July 1981; *Malay Mail*, 27 April 1981 and *NST*, 27 March 1982.
46. Interview with Mrs Rosemary Chong on 5 May 1983.
47. *NST*, 23 August 1977.
48. *Malay Mail*, 18 September 1981.
49. *Echo*, 19 July 1981.
50. *Echo*, 8 July 1981.
51. *Echo*, 24 August 1981.

52. *Malay Mail*, 18 September 1978.
53. *Echo*, 12 November 1978.
54. *The Star*, 2 April 1981.
55. *NST*, 8 March 1983.
56. MIC, *MIC Annual Report 1982/3*, Petaling Jaya, Percetakan P.K.S., p. 3.
57. Ibid., p. 41.
58. *Malay Mail*, 25 April 1980.
59. Interview with Mrs Nahappan on 20 May 1983.
60. Interview with Rasamma Bhupalan on 20 May 1983.
61. *The Star*, 11 April 1983.
62. *NST*, 25 March 1983.
63. *NST*, 30 April 1983.
64. *The Star*, 10 February 1983.
65. *NST*, 12 April 1982.
66. *NST*, 3 May 1983.
67. *NST*, 12 April 1982.
68. Oon Hing-geok is an English-educated paediatrician.
69. Lok Swee-chin is a teacher who also sat as the 'women's delegate' on the DAP Central Committee.
70. Interview with Oon Hing-geok on 12 May 1983.

9 Conclusions

THIS book sought to examine the roles that women's political auxiliaries (wings) have played within the party system of West Malaysia. Women's auxiliaries, whether part of communal or non-communal parties that functioned up to 1983 were included with the emphasis on the development of auxiliaries prior to 1976. The wings were viewed both in terms of the functions they performed for the political parties and for the auxiliary members themselves. A political history of women in West Malaysia needed for the study of the women's auxiliaries was also included.

For clarity, the conclusions have been divided into three sections: 1) the political mobilization of Malaysian women, which examines who became politically active and why, the conditions under which women's wings formed, and the factors which aided or impeded the growth of such wings; 2) party–auxiliary relations, which looks at the roles and functions that women's wings performed for the political parties and 3) auxiliary–member relations, which looks at the needs served and roles filled by the auxiliary–party for the woman member.

The Political Mobilization of Malaysian Women

In Malaysia, the political mobilization of women took place solely within the party system. There were no cases of individual women or women's groups that sought and won elected office outside of the political parties. Political activities for women were thus largely party activities with women members being placed in their own party wings. The pattern set by the parties themselves, for instance, communal groups, carried over into the women's wings. UMNO, the MCA, the MIC and Parti Islam (all communal) had separate women's wings—wings, which due to their recent advent, rarely interacted with one another. Only these main bodies of communal interests were able to bring women into politics. The non-communal parties, the Labour Party, the DAP, Gerakan and others, all faced major problems. Such difficulties lay both in appealing to the voters and in organizing their parties. They had yet to make a serious attempt to attract women party members. In essence, the history of women in politics remained confined to the members of the UMNO, MCA, MIC and Parti Islam; further, the women's section of UMNO was by far the largest and most influential wing.

By the 1970s, the parties believed the best way to bring women into the party was to form 'women's auxiliaries'. This idea stemmed from the early example set by UMNO and the successful record of its women's wing, the Kaum Ibu/Wanita UMNO. The KI, with its 36 years of organizing women, set the pattern to be followed by the other parties. It was assumed by both men and women that women would be able to do the same for other parties.

The need to place women into separate wings (as dictated by the social norms) was borne out by all examples: Those parties in which women's wings were not formed (the MCA and the MIC before the 1970s), had little appeal for women members. The role of women in those parties remained slight. Data on women's participation in both the internal and public party affairs of the MCA, MIC, DAP, Gerakan and PSRM all confirm this claim. UMNO and Parti Islam both made attempts to organize women members. Both could also point to large female memberships in 1970: 250,000 for UMNO and 18,000 for the PI. Once a women's auxiliary was formed and a serious effort was made by party leaders to interest women, the numbers of women members rapidly grew. This was shown by the growth of the Wanita MCA beginning in 1975.

This increased role of women within the party system by forming women's wings can be explained by the views of the women's place held by men and women of all races. For Malays, men and women socialized separately. Malay women, reluctant to assert themselves before men, needed the 'shelter' that the wing provided. As Puteh Mariah, the first *Ketua* of the KI explained, a women's wing was needed within UMNO because Malay women were shy and uncomfortable before men. They simply would not speak out at meetings attended by men and women. As for Malay men, it was common for them to be uneasy over the expanded role of Malay women. A separate wing provided the women with a way of involving themselves in the affairs of the parties while holding to Islamic customs that separated the public activities of men and women.

Though the women's auxiliary increased the role of women in support of UMNO, the women's auxiliaries of most other parties were not formed until the 1970s. This is in part, explained by the unique way the KI emerged. While AWAS (the women's wing of the Malay Nationalist Party) and later women's wings formed as a result of party directives, the KI UMNO grew from women's patriotic groups that emerged in 1945–8. Although UMNO leaders, particularly Datuk Onn bin Jaafar and Tunku Abdul Rahman, strongly supported the KI, the force to bring these groups together came from the women themselves. The mobilizing of Malay women against the Malayan Union (MU) proposals went hand in hand with that of Malay men. The crisis brought on by the MU proposals provided the catalyst that mobilized the Malays and led to the forming of UMNO. Opposition to the MU plan was led by Malay leaders of that time, for example, aristocratic, bureaucratic and religious leaders. Mobilization flowed through accepted Malay channels of authority from the sultans and national leaders down through the village headmen and religious leaders/teachers. In 1946, involvement was not only patriotic but also socially accepted and even, expected. Women as well as men were moved by the appeals of Malay leaders to oppose the MU proposals.

The political role of Malay women was accepted by Malay society for a number of other reasons as well: 1) The women were led by well respected women, women of the Malay-, Arabic- and English-educated élite as well as women religious teachers at the local level. Women such as Puteh Mariah, Ibu Zain, Khadijah Sidek and Fatimah binti Hashim, were the driving force behind the KI. They had the skills to organize the wing and keep it going. 2) The support given the KI by UMNO leaders provided the new organization with an acceptance by Malay society. This prevented opposition to the expanded activities of women. The support and acceptance by UMNO at large came to depend on the KI's success in getting the Malay electorate behind UMNO (and the Alliance)—an ability the KI used again and again. 3) As Manderson[1] noted, the KI did not break with the traditional roles of Malay women but kept to a tradition in which women pursued their own goals subordinate and complementary to those of men. The KI was subordinate to UMNO in much the same way that Malay women were subordinate to Malay men.

By 1957, UMNO had proved itself as both the party of independence and the major ruling party. However, after 1957 neither UMNO nor the KI had the rallying cry of 'Merdeka' (Independence) with which to attract members. Yet both the party and its wing continued to grow. For the KI, this success largely was due to efforts made to attract members at the local level. Hence literacy, cooking, sewing and religious classes together with fun fairs, etc., attracted village women to UMNO events and then maintained their interest. Always with these events was the message that UMNO represented the Malays and was the party for and defender of the Malay people. Until there is an even greater permeation of the villages by radio, television and the Press, the KI and UMNO will continue to provide Malays, in particular Malay women, not only with social entertainment but with political education as well. These efforts have proved to be a useful technique to increase party membership.

Yet for years, the example set by the KI was not followed by any other party except possibly Parti Islam. (The PI's Dewan Muslimat functioned mostly as an electoral aid to the party. The DM itself remained weak and poorly organized at the local level.) This limited success of the DM in organizing women can be related to many of the same factors which aided the KI; racial tension, rising Malay nationalism, a core of educated women leaders, and being organized within the Malay social structure. Once the PI set up its core supporters among village religious leaders (including women religious teachers), the party could mobilize more conservative Malays, be they male or female, in support of its strongly pro-Malay policies.

In contrast to UMNO and the PI, neither the MCA nor the MIC sought women as a base of support. This was in spite of party electoral failures of crisis proportions. The MCA in particular was rent with intra-party strife. The set-back of 1959 and 1969 and the withdrawal of dissident leaders to form new non-communal parties (for example the Gerakan) all caused the MCA to lose Chinese support. A further problem was the factionalism between the older, entrenched leaders and the 'new blood'. This carried over into the party crisis of 1973, where the very existence of the party was threatened. The MCA then began to appeal to the 'masses'. Women became one segment to be courted. The 1973 party crisis was of such dimension that women were now sought as one source of party strength. This readiness to involve women by the MCA male leaders was aided by the efforts of a few Chinese women. Mrs Rosemary Chong, in particular, helped bring about a greater role for Chinese women in the MCA. The result was the Wanita MCA—a joint effort between the party and a few Chinese women leaders.

The MIC, a party long known for internal disputes and crises, began to seriously court women as members only in 1975–6. Some efforts to organize MIC women in Selangor, though, were made in the 1950s. Women themselves did not start the women's section; the idea came largely from the party's executive council and was strongly supported by Tan Sri Manickavasagam. As with the MCA, party misfortunes and electoral failures had not been enough to compel the leaders to form a women's wing.

Non-Malay women remained unorganized for a number of reasons. Foremost was the 'crisis' experienced by both the Chinese and Indians following World War II—a crisis that was qualitatively different from that of the Malays. For the Chinese, the effect of the communist insurgency and the government's response turned many away from politics. Organized political activity was not only met with indifference but was also avoided by a large segment of the Chinese. For Indians, their political role was impeded by their wartime involvement in the Indian Independence League. (This had been strongly anti-British.) A post-war uncertainty and fear followed the reimposition of colonial rule. The post-war colonial crackdown on trade unionists, mostly Indian, can be cited as a way the Emergency affected the political involvement of the Indians in post-war Malaya. Thus, the effect of the Emergency was perceived as a crisis by all. It led both to a suppression of leftist activities and parties and the growth of conservative parties.[2] Thus not only were the activities of women leaders curtailed but also the parties which did emerge failed to use women to forward their party goals.

Many factors prevented non-Malay post-war involvement in colonial policy: the social climate created by the Emergency, government measures to suppress the insurgency, the British way of consulting only with Malay leaders in setting policies, and nationalist feelings which directed thinking towards China and India. Yet, non-Malay women remained far less active than men. Such factors as language, caste/class and education slowed the mobilizing of non-Malay women, as well as men. Non-Malay women remained inactive even compared to non-Malay men because post-war events failed to create an environment which could expand the women's roles. The Emergency and government crackdown on political parties and trade unions all served to 're-traditionalize' the non-Malays. All public posts continued to be occupied by men and access to the business and merchant communities, from which the non-Malay élites emerged, was denied to women; women were denied public status within their communities. Malays, in contrast, were encouraged to expand their roles. This permitted Malay women access to political positions, albeit subordinate ones. Thus the political roles of Malay women expanded; the roles of non-Malay women did not develop and would not begin to expand so until the 1970s.

All non-communal parties provided for women's wings in their constitutions. One or two of the more prominent women in these parties, like Ganga Nayar and Au Keng-wah, spoke of the need to bring women into the opposition parties. As of 1983, no opposition party had made a directed effort to attract women members. In part, this reflects their opposition status. Three major factors hindered opposition parties in Malaysia: 1) the restrictions placed upon the Press (press licences had to be renewed annually) which limited the extent of press coverage, 2) the threat of arbitrary arrest and detention under the Internal Security Act (during the 1960s, the PSRM, the LP and PI all had several party leaders detained),[3] and 3) since 1971, the constitutional ban on the discussion of 'sensitive issues' (for instance Malay privileges, language, etc.). It has thus been hard to attract members (as distinct from voters) whether male or female.

Opposition parties (besides PAS) while aspiring to be non-communal were composed mostly of non-Malays. Often dissidents from the MCA and the MIC (for example, Dr Lim Chong-eu of the UDP and the Gerakan) challenged the non-Malay leadership of the communal parties. Such dissident leaders sought far-reaching changes in the structure of society—changes which found little support among Malays. Such leaders had problems appealing to non-Malay loyalties and could not mobilize men and women members, as the UMNO had done so well.

Women were not organized within the opposition parties for other reasons as well. Despite the efforts of a few women, there was little attempt by women members to improve their role. For instance, one did not hear of opposition women calling for a drive to attract more women members, or to form a women's wing. Women members, so few in number, lacked the leaders needed to increase their influence within the parties. Further, male leaders had not opened a place for women in the parties. In short, such parties had not yet used any special appeals to attract women—appeals, judging from the UMNO and MCA examples, which were needed to increase female membership.

Once formed, the women's wings shared a number of traits that have affected their development. Foremost was the common problem that members, aside from electoral work, confined their attention to the wing and not to the party itself. Taking part in auxiliary affairs was more comfortable for the women yet it resulted in women being excluded from a role in internal party affairs. This separation resulted from views of the woman's place in society held by both men and women. Women leaders in 1983 viewed this separation as a problem and they have started to educate their members on the need to take part in full party affairs.

Factionalism, a second factor, prevented the wings from acting as cohesive bodies. All of the wings, to one degree or another, were composed of factions. As in the parties themselves, factions in the wings formed along age, educational, economic, and urban/rural cleavages. In all the wings, it was common for the leaders at the division, state and national levels to be better educated, wealthier, and better informed than the members. For the Malay wings (particularly the KI), such differences led to charges that the KI failed to address major problems that faced Malay women. It was charged that they ignored economic impoverishment while they focused on less important matters—banning swim-suit contests and the like. Such a charge is the essence of the problem faced by each organization: how to forge consensus out of the wishes of a diverse group. For the KI, this was between the older, often illiterate KI members and the better educated, more affluent (and often more impatient) women who led them.

In the non-Malay wings (as within the parties), this problem was compounded by language differences as well. In the Wanita MCA, as in the MCA itself, the national level leaders who set the direction of the wing were often English-educated while the rank and file attended Chinese schools. As MCA members admitted, the differences between the English-educated and the Chinese-educated extended to their value systems. Not only were there problems in conducting meetings, issuing publications and communicating directly with some members, but there were also fundamental differences of values and culture. These differences made it difficult to build a strong auxiliary. The Wanita MIC faced the same problem with the English- and the Tamil-educated. The non-communal parties faced an even greater problem in trying to appeal to all three races. The Malaysian government's programme to pursue an educational policy where all schoolchildren used Bahasa Malaysia (Malay) appears to be reducing this problem. For now, communication problems remained a major obstacle to building strong women's wings within the MCA, MIC and the non-communal parties.

A final factor that shaped the course of the women's auxiliaries was an interest in issues of direct concern to women. While the wings passed resolutions on nuclear proliferation treaties, South African apartheid and the like, the late 1960s and 1970s saw an increased focus on issues such as marriage and divorce reform, married women's tax reform, the economic problems of Malay women, and the lack of women jurors. While voicing concern over such matters, the ability of the wings to bring about the changes they sought was limited. If the wing's goal did not coincide with those of the party, the wing had little leverage. One tactic used by the KI over the issue of Muslim marriage and divorce reform, was to raise the issue repeatedly. The UMNO now supports the KI in its efforts to 'encourage' the Malay religious community to effect such reforms. Marriage and divorce reform has been a protracted struggle under unique circumstances—the issue was defined as a religious and not a political one. The main tactic used by the women has been the passage of resolutions at annual assemblies with appeals by women leaders. Given that women seldom sat on decision-making bodies in the parties and rarely attended meetings where decisions were made, their impact on such issues remained slight.

Party–Auxiliary Relations

A women's auxiliary in Malaysia served five major functions for a political party:

1) It targeted a large sub-group of the population, women, to be courted as party members. Efforts, such as lectures on child care, nutrition, cooking, sewing and religious classes, attracted party members to meetings where party activists could explain party goals and the reasons for party membership. Such activities were also used to involve women members whose interest in politics might be minor but who enjoyed the social aspects of the meetings. A related benefit to the party was that such activities gained new and retained old members at little or no expense and effort to the party itself.

2) The forming of a wing simplified the operation of the party by delegating to the wing's own leaders the day-to-day running of the wing. It was the wing which was given the task of educating its members as to party goals and informing its members of party decisions.

3) The wing was also given the task of mobilizing its members for the elections, both as voters and as electoral workers. For UMNO, this mobilizing had been a major function of the KI. Its example was the main reason for the creation of women's wings in other parties.

4) The women's wing with its own hierarchy provided the party with a communications network. This network informed the wing of party policy and brought to the attention of party leaders specific concerns of the wing. For each auxiliary body there was a parallel party body: for example, KI branch and UMNO branch, MCA division and Wanita MCA division. Auxiliary views could be forwarded either to the parallel party body or to the next higher level of the auxiliary. This could proceed until it finally reached the highest national bodies of either the auxiliary or the party.

5) A women's wing provided the party with a steady source of income from both dues and from fund-raising without being a burden on the party.

The KI was the prime example of this function. Additionally, an auxiliary could provide the party with a training ground for future leaders. Promising members could rise to be leaders within the wing and gain political experience in that smaller, often less competitive arena. The youth sections of UMNO, the MCA and PI served this function. Datuk

Hussein Onn, Lee San-choon and Mohamed Asri, were all former leaders of their party youth sections (wings) who later became party presidents and national leaders. In marked contrast, the women's sections did not perform this function. Talented and experienced party women moved to positions of leadership within the section but seldom within the party itself. Thus, forming an auxiliary did not by itself increase the role of the auxiliary's members in intra-party affairs. Within the Malaysian party system, few if any women were present on any of the division, state or national level committees. No women served as party national treasurer, attorney-general, vice-president, or most obviously, as party president. As late as the 1970s, male party leaders still appointed the leaders of the MCA and MIC women's wings. The selection of the DM leader and the composition of the KI National Executive Committee remained subject to PI and UMNO approval, respectively.

A standard attitude held by both men and women (frequently expressed in the Press) helps to explain this phenomenon: women had yet to 'prove themselves' able to handle party affairs and government posts. UMNO leaders emphasized that the KI had not produced leaders acceptable to the (male) UMNO leaders. While the stereotype of the KI member as older and poorly educated was often accurate, the current KI leaders have shown that the KI produced competent leaders in excess of their numbers in party leadership positions. The main obstacle to a larger KI role in party affairs was a feeling held by the women, both leaders and members, that they had to 'prove themselves'. As for other parties, most men and women leaders have adopted a 'wait and see' attitude citing the fact that the advent of women in party affairs was recent and it was too early to give them responsible posts within the parties.

Forming an auxiliary included a degree of risk to the party élite. It selected a sub-group and gave it an identity together with its own leaders. The relationship between UMNO or the MCA and their youth wings was replete with examples of tension and friction. The youth sections often challenged party control and decisions. In UMNO, a recent crisis involved the disciplining of the Pemuda leader, Harun bin Idris. He was accused and convicted of corrupt practices in 1976. In 1973, the unity of the MCA was threatened by a leadership crisis brought on by its youth section. Such events led all parties to adopt strong constitutional measures to control their auxiliaries. UMNO had party representatives on all KI bodies. Further, the auxiliary, as well as each member, was subject to the decisions of the UMNO Supreme Council. No KI member was exempt from party decisions; the expulsion of the third KI *Ketua*, Khadijah Sidek was an example of such party control. The MCA constitution clearly spelled out the authority of the party president over all sections and members. The suspension of the Wanita MCA Selangor in 1973 stemmed from an order of Party President Tan Siew-sin. The Wanita MIC and the DM of Parti Islam had similar constraints: women members were under the control of the party presidents.

In contrast to the youth sections, the women's sections posed little threat to or problems for the parties' élites. While KI and DM leaders were vocal in their discontent over their limited role in party affairs, they have never truly challenged the parties' male leaders over the limited role of KI and DM women. Other women's sections were too recent to evaluate in this way. The women leaders' attitude that their auxiliaries' main function was to support their parent parties, shows that the chance of intra-party tension was slight. This approach adopted by the women's wings reflected the priority they placed on their party; they accepted the view that women perform needed but supportive work in the home and this should carry over into the party. The nature of this parent/child or husband/wife relation is shown by the often used phrase 'Bapa UMNO' (Father of UMNO), to refer to UMNO itself. Women, unlike the 'youths' seldom challenged party élites but rather voiced their dissatisfactions through other channels: the passage of resolutions and personal meetings between women and men party leaders. Such methods were only partly effective.

Auxiliary–Member Relations

For women, a party's women's wing served four functions:

1) It strengthened the political party of their choice by adding to its numbers, financial base and the labour pool. Thus, women who joined UMNO felt that they were helping the Malay cause; women who joined the MCA and MIC in turn felt that they were helping the Chinese and Indian communities respectively.

2) Membership provided activities of interest to women (i.e. sewing and cooking classes, etc.) that provided a social outlet and a break in daily routine. The KI, in particular, provided village women with a change from the humdrum of daily life. The Wanita MIC, in order to grow in size, must appeal to women on the estates and provide the same types of activities to attract Indian women to the MIC. For the Wanita MCA and the non-communal parties which appeal to urban populations, this was more difficult simply because urban women had sources of diversion at hand. Appeals would have to focus on the problems and concerns of urban women, such as daycare for working mothers and job opportunities.

3) Membership provided a forum for women alone in their homes where they could come together to voice and discuss their opinions. This gave them a greater sense of participating in party affairs. For many women, a party auxiliary was often the first chance that they had had to discuss issues and topics with a group of like-minded women.

4) Membership provided women with a chance to become involved in party affairs. It provided a 'safe' arena in which they learned how to run their own group, become familiar with party policies, and learned how to work within the party. In short, it provided a haven in which women became educated in politics.

Membership in an auxiliary affected the average member in one more way: the auxiliaries provided a way to increase co-operation among all women through membership in the National Council of Women's Organizations. Within the NCWO, the women's auxiliaries, and the non-political women's groups came together. Their efforts were focused on matters of direct concern to women. Hence, to evaluate the success of the auxiliaries in terms of meeting their members' needs, one must take into account their role as NCWO members in shaping NCWO policies—a role hard to measure but real. Acting through the NCWO, the auxiliaries gained strength and achieved goals that they could not achieve by themselves. When the NCWO supported the issue of marriage and divorce reform for non-Muslims, all Wanita MCA and MIC members gained. While the number of women in any given auxiliary might be small, a role in the NCWO often yielded great benefit. The NCWO (as the main spokesbody of women) enjoyed respect among all communities and all leaders.

Whether the roles that women's wings perform within Malaysia's party system will expand and develop remains to be seen. It will be of special interest to see if the other parties can achieve the success of the Kaum Ibu/Wanita UMNO.

It is, though, likely that the non-Malay and non-communal women's wings will parallel the structures and functions of the KI: to present their members' views and provide the parties with a dependable source of labour at election time. Until more men and women, of all ethnic groups and party affiliations, broaden their attitudes towards 'suitable' activities for women, it is hard to foresee either a dramatic shift in the orientation of the auxiliaries or a radical change in the auxiliaries' relationship to the parent parties. The role of women in party affairs will likely remain limited.

1. Lenore Manderson, 'The Development of the Pergerakan Kaum Ibu UMNO, 1945–1972', unpublished doctoral dissertation, Australian National University, 1977, p. 268. (Later published as *Women, Politics, and Change: The Kaum Ibu UMNO, Malaysia, 1945–1972*, Kuala Lumpur, Oxford University Press, 1980.)

2. See Mohamed Noordin Sopiee, *From Malayan Union to Singapore Separation, 1945–65*, Kuala Lumpur, University of Malaya Press, 1974, pp. 45–55 for a good discussion regarding the post-war political mobilization of both Malays and non-Malays.

3. Goh Cheng-teik, *The May Thirteenth Incident and Democracy in Malaysia*, Kuala Lumpur, Oxford University Press, 1971, p. 6.

Appendix
Non-political Women's Associations

ASIDE from political wings, Malaysian women have organized and have belonged to a number of organizations whose main focus has been to improve the lives of women. A brief description of each of these follows.

The Malayan Women's Service League

One of the first voluntary associations to be formed in Malaya was the Malayan Women's Service League (MWSL). The MWSL was organized by Lady Gent, wife of the Governor, with other British wives and in conjunction with noted Malayan women: Soo Kim-lan, Hadjjah Fatimah, Mrs Tambidqui, the Tengku Ampuan of Selangor and the wives of the Ruler of Negri Sembilan. Launched on 9 October 1946 to aid in the post-war rehabilitation of Malaya, the League was formed to co-ordinate voluntary services in Malaya. As Mrs Ward, wife of the Resident Commissioner of Selangor put it: 'We women will clear up the mess made by the men of the nations in the aftermath of the War.'[1] Activities ranged from classes on nutrition and child care to sending substitutes for workers who failed to show up at their jobs. While the MWSL was non-communal and appealed to all women, Malay women were often the most numerous.[2]

Malay Women's Welfare Association of Singapore (MWWA)

The Malay Women's Welfare Association of Singapore (MWWA) was set up in October 1947 by a dedicated Malay woman, Zahara binti Mohamed Noor. The MWWA was concerned with all aspects of problems that affected Malay women. Arguing that Malay women were like 'caged birds' hiding behind a curtain, Zahara binti Mohamed Noor became an early and vocal opponent of the system of 'forced marriages' and 'easy divorce'. The MWWA not only raised the question of women's role within marriage, it also tried to reduce the sufferings of widows, promoted the cultural, social, moral and spiritual progress of women, and to help Malay women advocate their rights and claims of equality with men.[3] The MWWA gained public notice when it sponsored a procession to mark the royal wedding of Princess Elizabeth and Philip in November 1947. Immediately, Muslim leaders and six organizations decried the MWWA and opposed the march. It was argued that it would break tradition for women to show themselves in public in such a manner. Opposition to the procession was so severe that it was cancelled. This shows the resistance of segments of the Malay populace to the more public role that Malay women were taking.

The National Association of Women's Institutes in West Malay(si)a

The National Association of Women's Institutes in West Malay(si)a (NAWIM) was begun in September 1952 by Lady Templer, the wife of the High Commissioner. She believed that a women's movement based on village women would play a major part in the future of Malaya.[4] Lady Templer sought to form an organization that would provide rural women with information regarding nutrition, child-bearing, health, hygiene and basic homemaking.[5] Patterned on the National Federation of Women's Institutes of England, NAWIM was to be a national, non-political, self-help movement aimed at rural women.[6]

The first Women's Institute appeared in Penang on 5 November 1952. Thereafter, branches spread throughout Malaya. By the 1970s, about 26,103 women belonged to the WIs.[7] Members were mostly Malay housewives from the rural areas. With meetings conducted in Malay, non-Malays were, in essence, precluded. Leadership in this early period was provided by the English-educated, literate schoolteachers, wives of the district officers and wives of the *penghulu*. Because the WIs sought to enhance the house-keeping skills of the women, NAWIM gained the tacit approval of Malay men who permitted their wives to join. Datuk Onn bin Jaafar, maybe seeing NAWIM as an aid to the forming of his political party, Parti Negara, gave his support to its leaders.[8] Given male approval, the WIs continue to this day seeking to help women to develop habits of thrift, responsibility and co-operation. They also provided women with chances to improve themselves in matters of child care, health, agriculture, and more recently to provide courses on civics and on women's role in development.[9]

The Young Women's Christian Association of Malay(si)a

The Persatuan Wanita Keristian Malaysia, better known as the YWCA, remained a small organization which had only 1,007 members as of 1976.[10] Yet, the YWCA was in the foreground of issues, such as marriage and divorce reform, that directly affected women. The first YWCA was formed in 1875 in Singapore and others followed in Penang (1909), Kuala Lumpur (1913), Malacca (1921), Ipoh (1930), Seremban (1950), Petaling Jaya (1963) and Klang (1964), with the national body forming in 1921.[11] The YWCA branches were first started and run by missionary women but were slowly taken over by Malayan Christian women, mostly English-educated. Malays took little part in the running of the YWCA. In 1976, for example, only 28 Malay women were members; these were well-known women who helped to dispel distrust of an organization seen by some as being greatly influenced by its Anglo-American origins. While formal membership remained low, the activities of the YWCA reached many women. The YWCA was one of the first groups to provide hostels open to women. In 1938, the Penang YWCA ran a crêche for labourers' children, the first in Malaya.[12] While the YWCA has provided self-improvement courses for women (for instance literacy, cooking, etc.), the YWCA has been in the foreground in the fight to improve the political, economic and social status of women in Malaysia.

The Muslim Women's Welfare Council of Malay(si)a

Prior to 1961, no group in Malaya represented the interests of Muslim women of all political persuasions. In May 1961, the first queen of Malaya, Tengku Puan Besar Khursiah, with a number of well-known Malay women (for example, Puteh

Mariah, Aminah Bahaman, Fatimah Musa, Safiah Majeed and Salmah Shamsuddin) formed the Lembaga Kebajikan Perempuan Islam Persekutuan Tanah Melayu, or the Muslim Women's Welfare Council of Malaya. Its main purpose was to improve the lives of poor, old or otherwise unfortunate Muslim women.[13] The Lembaga provided Muslim women with a chance to get together to discuss their problems. Its efforts were centred on holding religious classes for women and on providing a hostel for Muslim girls who came to work and study in Kuala Lumpur. It also strongly lobbied to tighten the marriage and divorce laws for Muslims and to increase educational opportunities for Malay women. A non-political body, the Lembaga's goals show clearly its socio-religious bent:

(1) to raise the status and improve the welfare of Muslim women and children,
(2) to defend the rights of Muslim women,
(3) to improve matters relating to marriage and to help those divorced women, particularly rural women, who are in difficulty,
(4) to contribute to the moral and spiritual needs of young Muslim girls,
(5) to establish a centre for Muslim women who follow the Laws of the Syariah and Muslim religion, and
(6) to co-operate with or aid those organizations, either within or outside of Malaya who have the same goals as those of the Lembaga.[14]

Much like the YWCA, the membership of the Lembaga remained small (4,000 in 1976) though it reached more women through its religious classes. As with the membership of the KI UMNO, many of its members during the 1960s were older women who had few diversions but were interested in Islam. Recently, the Lembaga has attracted younger women, mostly through religious classes in many government departments.[15]

Pertiwi

In November 1967, the Pertubuhan Tindakan Wanita Islam, or the Muslim Women's Action Society (Pertiwi) was launched.[16] Pertiwi was founded by a group of professional Malay women whose members included KI *Ketua*, Aishah Ghani, Azah Aziz (feature editor of *Utusan Melayu*), Rokiah Rashid (librarian), Zaitun Othman (lawyer) and Zakiah Hanun (head librarian of the National Archives). Pertiwi was formed to improve the social and economic status of Malay women through education.[17] Its efforts centred on issuing publications, and conducting seminars and discussions. It focused on matters of concern to the average Malay women (example: explaining their rights within marriage). Pertiwi's most ambitious projects have included setting up three kindergartens and numerous play groups for children. It also was first to compile a bibliography, along the lines of *Who's Who*, of Malaysian women.

Pertiwi remained a small group. Of the 1,976 women members in 1975, 60–70 were core members.[18] Originating in Kuala Lumpur, a second branch formed in Kedah during 1976. Though small in numbers, Pertiwi was a member of the NCWO. Its representatives attended most national and some international conferences that dealt with issues of concern to Muslim women.

1. *Malaya Tribune (MT)*, 9 October 1946.
2. *MT*, 9 October 1946; *MT*, 8 October 1946; *ST*, 10 October 1946; *ST*, 11 October 1946.
3. *MT*, 17 March 1948.
4. Zaibun Nissa Siraj, 'Women and Adult Education: A Case Study of the Women's Institute Movement in Peninsular Malaysia, 1952-1974', unpublished MA thesis, University of Malaya, 1975, p. 45.
5. *ST*, 18 October 1952; *ST*, 28 August 1953. Also see, NAWI, *The National Association of Women's Institutes of Malaya Handbook*, Petaling Jaya, Solai Press, n.d., pp. i–ii for a statement of goals.
6. Zaibun Nissa Siraj, op. cit., p. 181.
7. Ibid., p. 94.
8. Ibid., p. 61.
9. NAWI, *The National Association of Women's Institutes of Malaya Handbook*, pp. i–ii.
10. Interview with Mrs Helen Tan, Honorary Secretary of the YWCA on 3 August 1976.
11. Interview with Mrs Helen Tan, 3 August 1976.
12. YWCA, *Biennial Report 1974–1976*, Kuala Lumpur, YWCA, 1976, p. 27.
13. Interview with Puan Lily Majid on 3 July 1976 and LKPI, *Chenderamata 10 Tahun Lembaga Kebajikan Perempuan Islam Persekutuan Tanah Melayu 1961–1971*, Kuala Lumpur, LKPI, n.d., p. 11.
14. LKPI, *Chenderamata 10 Tahun*.
15. Ibid.
16. *Utusan Melayu*, 31 July 1967, *D.P.S.*; interview with Zakiah Hanun on 20 July 1976.
17. Pertiwi, *Majalah Tahunan Bingkisan Pertiwi, Jilid 4, November 1973*, Kuala Lumpur, Pertiwi, p. 43.
18. Pertiwi, 'Pertiwi Lapuran Tahunan 1975', Kuala Lumpur, Pertiwi, p. 6, mimeograph.

Glossary

Adat: Custom in the widest sense.
Adat perpateh: System of law found primarily in Negri Sembilan and parts of Malacca which assumed kinship principles of matriliny. Now confined to family law and the law relating to land ownership and devolution.
Adat temenggong: Term used to describe any *adat* which is not *adat perpateh*. Implies the existence of a bilateral kinship system.
Anak dara: A virgin or maiden.
Baba: A Straits-born Chinese male.
Bahagian: A district, the intermediate level of political party organization between the branch and state level organizations.
Baju: Traditional Malay blouse or jacket.
Bendahari: Treasurer.
Bilal: Caller to prayer in a mosque.
Bin: Son of; female equivalent is binti.
Bomoh: Malay village healer.
Cawangan: A branch, the lowest level of political party organization. Corresponds to the local level.
Certtu-k-kolu-tal: A temporary union between an unmarried Indian man and woman.
Endogamy and Exogamy: Terms used to mean respectively: a rule of marriage which requires a person to take a spouse from within a kin group; a rule of marriage which requires a person to take a spouse from outside a kin group.
Fasah: Judicial dissolution of a Muslim marriage on the grounds of insanity, impotence or lack of maintenance.
Fatwa: Legal ruling by a Muslim jurist.
Ibu-bapa: 'Mother-father'—head of a lineage or *perut*.
Iddah: Three-month period during which a divorced Muslim woman may not remarry—used to determine paternity.
Imam: Muslim prayer leader.
Janda: Divorced Muslim woman.
Kampong: Malay village.
Kangany: System of Indian labour recruitment whereby passage and expenses to Malaya were paid by an estate foreman in return for a predetermined period of labour by an immigrant.
Kadi: Muslim religious magistrate.
Kebaya: Malay fitted blouse or jacket.
Ketua: Chairman, chief, elder, leader or head of an organization.
Ketua kampong: Village headman.
Khula: Muslim divorce by redemption.
Lembaga: Clan chief in Negri Sembilan and Malacca.

Luak: District in Negri Sembilan or Malacca.
Mas kahwin: Muslim bride price, paid by the groom to the bride.
Mentri Besar: Chief Minister.
Mini telekong: Headwear adopted recently by many Malay women that covers the head and shoulders and fastens under the chin.
Mufti: Muslim legal expert or judge who rules on points of law only.
Mui tsai: Chinese adopted girl servants.
Naib Ketua: Deputy Leader.
Natu-vitu-tali: A second marriage ceremony for a divorced or widowed Indian.
Nusuz: Recalcitrant, refusing to cohabit.
Nyonya: Female *Baba*.
Perut: A lineage, the smallest unit of socio-political organization in Negri Sembilan.
Penghulu: A Malay headman for several villages.
Sawah: Rice land.
Setiausaha: Secretary.
Sim-pu-kia: 'Little daughters-in-law', a type of Chinese girl servant.
Sinkeh: An unpaid Chinese passenger/labourer required to work off the cost of his passage from China to Malaya.
Syariah: Muslim religious court.
Talak: *Cherai biasa* or ordinary divorce—a triple repudiation of the wife by the husband; applies to Muslims.
Ta'alik: Muslim divorce through the breaking of a pre-marital agreement.
T'sai: A Chinese primary wife.
T'sip: A Chinese secondary wife.
Undang: A royal chief in Negri Sembilan or Malacca.
Wali: The male guardian of an unmarried Muslim girl or woman.
Waris: Clan in Negri Sembilan or Malacca.
Yang di-Pertuan Agung: The King of Malaysia.
Yang di-Pertuan Besar: The Ruler of Negri Sembilan.

Select Bibliography

Primary Sources

1. Public Papers and Documentary Sources

Alliance National Council, *Constitution and Rules of the Alliance Party* (as amended 20 May 1958), Kuala Lumpur: Printcraft Ltd., n.d.

──────, *Constitution and Rules of the Alliance Party*, 1967, Kuala Lumpur: Registrar of Societies.

──────, *Alliance (Election) Manifesto 1969*, Kuala Lumpur: New Straits Times (NST) Library.

Angkatan Belia Islam Malaysia (ABIM), or, the Muslim Youth Movement of Malaysia, *Revival of Islam in Malaysia: the Role of ABIM*, Kuala Lumpur: ABIM, n.d. (early 1980s).

Barisan Nasional, *Constitution and Rules of the Barisan Nasional* (approved June 1975), Kuala Lumpur: Registrar of Societies.

Bhupalan, Rasamma, Private Papers, available through Mrs Bhupalan, Kuala Lumpur.

Chander, R., *1970 Population and Housing Census of Malaysia*, Kuala Lumpur: Department of Statistics, 1971.

Choudry, N. S., *Socio-economic Sample Survey of Households, Malaysia, 1967–8, Employment and Unemployment, West Malaysia*, Kuala Lumpur: Department of Statistics, 1970.

Democratic Action Party, *Constitution and Rules of the Democratic Action Party, 1966*, Kuala Lumpur: Registrar of Societies.

──────, *Constitution and Rules of the Democratic Action Party, 1972*, Kuala Lumpur, Registrar of Societies.

──────, 'The DAP and Cultural Democracy', Petaling Jaya: the DAP, n.d. (1975–6).

──────, 'The DAP and Labour Issues', Petaling Jaya: the DAP, 1976.

──────, 'Coalition Politics in Malaysia', Petaling Jaya: the DAP, n.d. (1972–3).

──────, Letters to the author from N. Madhavan Nair, Secretary to the Opposition Leader, 24 February 1976 and 26 April 1976.

──────, *DAP: Who Lives if Malaysia Dies? (Selection from the Speeches and Writings of DAP Leaders and Basic Documents of DAP Malaysia)*, Selangor, Malaysia: the DAP, 1969.

──────, *Report by the CEC Committee to the Third Triennial Delegates Congress*, Ipoh, Perak: March.

──────, 'Speech by Dr Chen Man Hin, Chairman of the DAP Addressing the First National DAP Women's Seminar', mimeograph, Kuala Lumpur, 9 January 1972.

———, 'Working Paper on Women and Democratic Socialism' (by S. Mary), mimeograph, Kuala Lumpur, 9 January 1972.

———, *DAP Women Malaysia: Proposed Statutes* (for the consideration of the first DAP Women National Convention), Kuala Lumpur, n.d. (1975–6).

———, *The 1974 General Elections Manifesto of the DAP*, Kuala Lumpur: the DAP, 1974.

del Tufo, M. V., *Malaya: A Report on the 1947 Census of Population*, Singapore: Government Printer, 1948.

Fenn, W. P. and Wu Teh-yao, 'Chinese Schools and Education of Chinese Malaysians' (Report of a Mission Invited by the Federation Government to Study the Problem of Educating the Chinese in Malaya), England: Department of Education, University of Canterbury, 1951.

Gerakan Rakyat Malaysia (GRM—The People's Movement Party), *The Constitution and Rules of the GRM, 1968*, Kuala Lumpur: Registrar of Societies.

———, *The Constitution and Rules of the GRM, 1973*, Kuala Lumpur: Registrar of Societies.

———, *The 1968 Annual Report of the GRM*, Kuala Lumpur: NST Library.

———, *The 1969 Annual Report of the GRM*, Kuala Lumpur: NST Library.

———, *The 1969 General Elections Manifesto of the GRM*, Kuala Lumpur: NST Library.

———, 'April 15, 1968 Statement of Objectives of the Gerakan', mimeograph, Kuala Lumpur: NST Library.

Hussein Onn, 'Ucapan Y. A. B. Datuk Hussein Onn, Timbalan Perdana Mentri, Ketika Merasmikan Seminar dan Pameran Majlis Kebangsaan Pertubuhan Pertubuhan Wanita Malaysia', mimeograph, Kuala Lumpur, 14 April 1975.

Information Department Malaya Files 1945–1948, Kuala Lumpur: Arkib Negara Malaysia.

Kesatuan Insaf Tanah Ayer (KITA), *The 1974 Constitution of Kesatuan Insaf Tanah Ayer*, Kuala Lumpur: Registrar of Societies.

Labour Party, *Report on the Foundation of the Pan-Malayan Labour Party*, 26 June 1952, Kuala Lumpur: Labour Party, 1952 (Available: NST Library).

———, *The 1959 Annual Report of the Labour Party*, Malaya: the Labour Party, n.d. (Available: NST Library).

———, *The 1961 Annual Report of the Labour Party*, Malaya: the Labour Party, n.d. (Available: NST Library).

———, *Report of the 10th Annual Party Conference, August 18–19, 1962*, Malaya: the Labour Party, n.d. (Available: NST Library).

———, *The 1962 Constitution of the Labour Party*, Kuala Lumpur: Registrar of Societies, n.d.

Lembaga Kebajikan Perempuan Islam, *Laporan Muktamar Pertubohan-Pertubohan Perempuan Islam Malaysia, March 7–9 1975*, Kuala Lumpur: LKPI, 1975.

———, *The First Convention of Muslim Women('s) Organisation(s) 1975*, mimeograph, Kuala Lumpur: LKPI, 1975.

———, *Chenderamata 10 Tahun Lembaga Kebajikan Perempuan Islam Persekutuan Tanah Melayu 1961–1971*, Kuala Lumpur: LKPI, n.d.

Malaya, Federation of, *Files of the Registrar of Societies 1949–1959*, Kuala Lumpur: Government Printer, 1948–59.

———, *Proceedings of the Federal Legislative Council, 1948–1959*, Kuala Lumpur: Government Printer, 1948–59.

―――――, and Federation of Malaysia, *Debates of the Dewan Rakyat, 1959– October 1976*, Kuala Lumpur: Government Printer, 1959–76.
―――――, *1957 Population Census of the Federation of Malaya, Final Report*, Kuala Lumpur: Government Printer, 1960.
―――――, *The Barnes Report on Malay Education*, Kuala Lumpur: Government Printer, 1951.
―――――, *Report of the Education Committee, 1956* (the *Razak Report*), Kuala Lumpur: Government Printer, 1956.
―――――, *Report of the Educational Review Committee, 1960* (the *Talib Report*), Kuala Lumpur: Government Printer, 1960.
―――――, *The Local Authorities (Selangor) Election Regulations 1954 Register of Electors for Port Swettenham Ward, Town Council Klang*, Kuala Lumpur: Election Commission.
―――――, *Report on the Parliamentary and State Elections, 1959*, Kuala Lumpur: Government Printer, 1960.
―――――, and Federation of Malaysia, *Department of Education Annual Reports 1948–76*, selected reports only, Kuala Lumpur: Government Printer, 1949–1976.
―――――, *Department of Labour Annual Reports 1949–1976*, selected reports only, Kuala Lumpur: Government Printer, 1949–76.
―――――, 'The Married Women's Ordinance, 1957, Federation of Malaya, No. 36 of 1957', Malaya: Supplement to the Federation of Malaya, *Government Gazette*, 15 August, No. 18, Vol. X.
―――――, *Hari Wanita: Federation of Malaya Report of Women's Day, August 25, 1962*, Malaya: NCWO, n.d. (1962–3).
―――――, *Second Five Year Plan 1961–65*, Malaya: Government Printer, 1961.
Malayan/Malaysian Chinese Association, *1st Set of Rules of the MCA, passed June 12, 1949*, Private Papers, Tan Cheng-lock, Arkib Negara Malaysia.
―――――, Presidential Address of Annual Meeting of (the) Central General Committee of (the) MCA April 21, 1951, Private Papers, Tan Cheng-lock, Arkib Negara Malaysia.
―――――, 'The First Constitution of the MCA adopted and approved by (the) General Committee of the MCA March 22, 1959', amended 1963 and 1967, mimeograph, Kuala Lumpur: MCA, n.d.
―――――, *Constitution of the MCA approved and adopted by the Central General Assembly of the Association at an Extraordinary General Meeting held on 11th September 1970*, Kuala Lumpur: MCA.
―――――, *Annual Reports of the MCA 1961–1968*, Kuala Lumpur: MCA, 1962–9.
―――――, *Registrar of Societies Report on the MCA*, Kuala Lumpur: Registrar of Societies, 1968.
―――――, 'Position of Membership as of 1963', mimeograph, Kuala Lumpur: MCA, n.d.
―――――, 'Position of Membership as of December 31, 1975', mimeograph, Kuala Lumpur: MCA, n.d.
―――――, *Malayan/Malaysian Chinese Association. Various Published Speeches 1946–1969*, Kuala Lumpur: Faculty of Economics and Administration, University of Malaya, n.d.
―――――, *The MCA 20th Anniversary Souvenir* (booklet), Kuala Lumpur: MCA, 1969.

———, 'Bye-laws of the MCA Women's Section', mimeograph, Kuala Lumpur: MCA, n.d. (1975)

———, 'Presidential Address by Sdr Lee San Choon (Wanita) MCA 1st Annual Assembly, August 7, 1975', mimeograph, Kuala Lumpur: MCA, n.d.

———, 'Declaration and Statement of Objectives of the Wanita MCA, August 7, 1975', mimeograph, Kuala Lumpur: MCA.

———, 'Resolutions of the 1st General Assembly of the Wanita MCA', mimeograph, Kuala Lumpur: MCA, 1975.

———, 'Speech by Sdr Chow Poh-kheng (Mrs Rosemary Chong), National Chairman Wanita MCA, at the National Wanita MCA 1st General Assembly on 7 August 1975', mimeograph, Kuala Lumpur: MCA.

———, 'Proposed Resolutions for the 2nd Delegates Assembly of Wanita MCA, August 20, 1976', mimeograph, Kuala Lumpur: MCA.

———, *Secretary-General's Report 1973–1975, presented 23rd General Assembly of the MCA*, Kuala Lumpur: China Press Bhd., 1975.

———, *Secretary-General's Report, 28th General Assembly of the Malaysian Chinese Association 1980*, Kuala Lumpur: MCA, 1980.

———, *Secretary-General's Report, 29th General Assembly of the Malaysian Chinese Association 1981*, Kuala Lumpur: MCA, 1981.

———, *Secretary-General's Report, 30th General Assembly of the Malaysian Chinese Association, 1982*, Kuala Lumpur: MCA, 1982.

———, *6th Wanita MCA General Assembly Secretary-General's Report*, Kuala Lumpur: MCA, 1980.

———, *7th Wanita MCA General Assembly Secretary-General's Report*, Kuala Lumpur: MCA, 1981.

———, *8th Wanita MCA General Assembly Secretary-General's Report*, Kuala Lumpur: MCA, 1982.

Malayan/Malaysian Indian Congress, Constitution of the Malayan Indian Congress, 1946, Private Papers John Thivy, Kuala Lumpur: University of Malaya Library.

———, *1966 Constitution of the Malaysian Indian Congress*, Kuala Lumpur: Registrar of Societies.

———, *Constitution of the Malaysian Indian Congress, Approved and Adopted by the General Assembly of the Congress on 25th August 1973*, Kuala Lumpur: MIC.

———, *Malaysian Indian Congress Annual Reports 1973–1983*, Petaling Jaya: Percetakan P. K. S., 1973–83.

———, *MIC 18th Annual Report, 1964*, Petaling Jaya: Victory Press.

———, *1967 Report on the MIC*, Kuala Lumpur: Registrar of Societies, 1967.

———, *MIC Ulangtahun Ketiga-puluh 1946–1976 (MIC Thirty Year Yearbook 1946–1976)*, Kuala Lumpur: MIC, n.d.

———, 'MIC Presidential Address by Tan Sri Dato V. Manickavasagam, 24th General Assembly July 31–August 1, 1976', mimeograph, Kuala Lumpur: MIC, n.d.

———, 'History of (the) MIC', mimeograph, Kuala Lumpur: MIC, n.d. (1975)

———, 'MIC Presidential Address by Tan Sri Dato V. Manickavasagam, 23rd General Assembly July 6, 1975', mimeograph, Kuala Lumpur: MIC, n.d.

———, 'MIC Presidential Address by Tan Sri Dato V. Manickavasagam, 21st General Assembly August 24, 1973', mimeograph, Kuala Lumpur: MIC, n.d.

Malayan Union, Government of, *Malayan Union Files, 1946–1948*, Arkib Negara Malaysia.

―――, *Proceedings of the Advisory Council of the Malayan Union, July 1946–48*, Kuala Lumpur: Government Printer, 1948.

―――, *Proceedings of the Advisory Council of the Malayan Union for the Period of January 1947–January 1948*, Kuala Lumpur: Government Printer, 1949.

―――, *Constitutional Proposals for Malaya. Report of the Consultative Committee together with Proceedings of Six Public Meetings. A Summary of Representations made and Letters and Memoranda considered by the Committee*, Kuala Lumpur: Government Printer, 1947.

Malaysia, Federation of, Department of Education, *Educational Statistics, 1938–1967*, Kuala Lumpur: Ministry of Education, 1968.

―――, *Educational Statistics of Malaysia 1972*, Kuala Lumpur: Ministry of Education, 1975.

―――, Election Commission, *Report on the Parliamentary (Dewan Ra'ayat) and State Legislative Assembly General Elections 1964 of the States of Malaya*, Kuala Lumpur: Government Printer, 1965.

―――, *Report on the Parliamentary (Dewan Ra'ayat) and State Legislative Assembly General Elections 1969 of the States of Malaya, Sabah and Sarawak*, Kuala Lumpur: Government Printer, 1972.

―――, *Report on the Parliamentary (Dewan Ra'ayat) and State Legislative Assembly General Elections 1974 of the States of Malaya and Sarawak*, Kuala Lumpur: Government Printer, 1975.

―――, *Report on the General Elections to the House of Representatives and the State Legislative Assemblies other than the State Legislative Assemblies of Kelantan, Sabah and Sarawak 1978*, Kuala Lumpur: Government Printer, 1980.

―――, *Files of the Registrar of Societies 1960–1976*, Kuala Lumpur: Registrar of Societies.

―――, *Malaysia: Civil Marriage Ordinance 1952 (F.M. 44 of 1952) Together with Subsidiary Legislation made there under*, Kuala Lumpur: Government Printer, 1970.

―――, *First Malaysia Plan 1966–1970*, Kuala Lumpur: Government Printer, 1965.

―――, *Second Malaysia Plan 1971–1975*, Kuala Lumpur: Government Printer, 1971.

―――, *Third Malaysia Plan 1976–1980*, Kuala Lumpur: Government Printer, 1976.

―――, *Married Women and Children (Enforcement of Maintenance) Act, 1968. Act of Parliament No. 8 of 68. Malaysia: Acts of Parliament Nos. 1–40*, Kuala Lumpur: Government Printer, 1968.

―――, *Report of the Royal Commission on Non-Muslim Marriage and Divorce Laws*, Kuala Lumpur: Government Printer, 1972.

―――, *Laws of Malaysia, Act 164. Law Reform (Marriage and Divorce) Act, 1976*, Kuala Lumpur: Pemangku Ketua Percetakan dan Diterbitkan, 1976.

―――, *Malaysia: Penal Code* (F.M.S. Cap. 45), Kuala Lumpur: Government Printer, 1971.

―――, *Laws of Malaysia, Act 106, Women and Girls Protection Act, 1973*, Kuala Lumpur: Government Printer, 1973.

―――, *Laws of Malaysia Act A227, Income Tax (Amendment) (No. 3) Act,*

1974, Kuala Lumpur: Government Printer, 1974.

―――――, *Laws of Malaysia Act A273, Income Tax (Amendment) Act 1975*, Kuala Lumpur: Government Printer, 1975.

―――――, 'Lapuran Penyelidekan Mengenai Perceraian dan Kes-kes Tuntutan Nafkah di Kalangan Orang-orang Islam di Negeri-negeri di Malaysia Barat bagi tahun 1974', mimeograph, Kuala Lumpur: Ministry of Social Welfare, 1975.

―――――, *Social Welfare Services in Malaysia*, Kuala Lumpur: Ministry of Welfare Services, Government Printer, 1970.

Malaysia 1984, Official Year Book, Kuala Lumpur: Ministry of Information, Vol. 22, n.d.

Nathan, J. E., *The Census of British Malaya*, London: Waterlow and Sons, 1922.

National Council of Women's Organizations, *Miscellaneous Papers 1962–1983*, Kuala Lumpur: NCWO office.

―――――, *Buku Panduan—An Organizational Handbook by the NCWO*, Kuala Lumpur: NCWO, 1972.

―――――, *Laporan Hari Wanita Persekutuan Tanah Melayu 25 Ogos 1962*, Kuala Lumpur: Economy Printers, 1963.

―――――, *The NCWO Malaya: Rules and Constitution*, Kuala Lumpur: NCWO, n.d.

―――――, 'National Council of Women's Organizations' Report on the Study of a Women's Bureau August 22–25, 1965', mimeograph, Kuala Lumpur: NCWO, 1965.

―――――, *Lapuran Kegiatan-kegiatan dan Kejayaan M.K.P.W. 1972–74*, Kuala Lumpur: Union Press, 1974.

―――――, *Lapuran Kegiatan-kegiatan dan Kejayaan M.K.P.W. 1974–76*, Kuala Lumpur: Union Press, 1976.

―――――, *Lapuran Kegiatan-kegiatan dan Kejayaan M.K.P.W. 1976–1979*, Kuala Lumpur: NCWO, n.d.

―――――, *Lapuran Kegiatan-kegiatan dan Kejayaan M.K.P.W. 1979–1981*, Kuala Lumpur: NCWO, n.d.

National Family Planning Board Annual Report, 1966–70, Kuala Lumpur: NFPB, 1971.

Nayar, Ganga, Private Papers, available through Ganga Nayar, Kuala Lumpur, Malaysia.

Parti Bebas Progresif Rakyat (Independent Peoples' Progressive Party), *Parti Bebas Progresif Rakyat Rules, 1974*, Kuala Lumpur: Registrar of Societies.

Parti Islam Sa-Malaysia (PAS—Islamic Party of Malaysia, previously known as the PMIP—Pan-Malayan Islamic Party and currently often referred to as the PI—Parti Islam), *Undang-undang Tuboh Persatuan Islam Sa-Tanah Melayu, 1966*, Kuala Lumpur: Registrar of Societies.

―――――, *Peratoran Dewan Muslimat PAS, 1966*, Kuala Lumpur: Registrar of Societies.

―――――, *Undang-undang Tuboh Persatuan Islam Sa-Tanah Melayu, 1967*, Kuala Lumpur: Registrar of Societies.

―――――, *Undang-undang Tuboh Persatuan Islam Sa-Tanah Melayu, 1971*, Kuala Lumpur: Registrar of Societies.

―――――, *Undang-undang Tuboh Persatuan Islam Sa-Tanah Melayu, 1973*, Kuala Lumpur: Registrar of Societies.

―――――, 'Cabutan Perlembagaan PAS mengenai Dewan Muslimat PAS Pusat dan Negri, 1973', mimeograph, Kuala Lumpur: PAS, 1973.

———, 'PAS Usul-usul Dewan Muslimat PAS' (approved by the 22nd Annual Assembly of the Dewan Muslimat, 5 August 1976), mimeograph, Kuala Lumpur: PAS.

———, 'Peratoran Dewan Muslimat PAS 1973', mimeograph, Kuala Lumpur: PAS.

———, 'Miscellaneous speeches, press statements and reports on PAS', Kuala Lumpur: NST Library.

Parti Keadilan Masyarakat Malaysia (Pekemas—the Social Justice Party of Malaysia), *1971 Constitution of the Social Justice Party*, Kuala Lumpur: Registrar of Societies.

———, *1972 Regulations of the Wanita Pekemas Section*, Kuala Lumpur: Registrar of Societies.

———, *1974 Pekemas Resolutions*, Kuala Lumpur: NST Library.

———, *1st Annual Report of Pekemas, 1973*, Kuala Lumpur: NST Library.

———, *Pekemas Lapuran Tahunan, 1974*, Kuala Lumpur: NST Library.

———, 'Miscellaneous speeches and press releases on Pekemas', Kuala Lumpur: NST Library.

Parti Negara (PN—the National Party), 23 May 1954, 'Statement of Party Negara Policy and Objectives', mimeograph, Kuala Lumpur: NST Library.

———, '1954 Official Rules of Party Negara', mimeograph, Kuala Lumpur: NST Library.

———, *1955 Election Manifesto of Party Negara*, Kuala Lumpur: PN, n.d.

Parti Sosialis Rakyat Malaya (PSRM—Malayan People's Socialist Party), *Malayan People's Socialist Party 1969 Constitution* (adopted 26 December 1969).

———, 'Perlembagaan Parti Sosialis Rakyat Malaya, 1974', mimeograph, Kuala Lumpur: PSRM.

———, *PSRM 1969 Election Manifesto*, Kuala Lumpur: PSRM.

———, 'Miscellaneous speeches and press releases', Kuala Lumpur: NST Library.

Party Election Manifestos, *1964 State and Parliamentary Election Party Manifestos* (contains Alliance, PAP, PMIP, PPP, UDP, SF and PN manifestos), Kuala Lumpur: Jabatan Penerangan Malaysia, April 1964.

———, *1969 State and Parliamentary Election Party Manifestos* (contains Alliance, DAP, GRM, PPP, PSRM and United Malaysian Chinese Association Manifestos), Kuala Lumpur: Jabatan Penerangan Malaysia, 1969.

Peoples' Progressive Party, *1956 Constitution of the Peoples' Progressive Party*, Kuala Lumpur: Registrar of Societies.

———, *1966 Rules of the Peoples' Progressive Party*, Kuala Lumpur: Registrar of Societies.

———, *1975 Constitution of the Peoples' Progressive Party*, Kuala Lumpur: Registrar of Societies.

———, *Registrar of Societies Reports on the PPP, 1963–1976*, Kuala Lumpur: Registrar of Societies.

———, 'Miscellaneous speeches and press releases of the PPP', Kuala Lumpur: NST Library.

Pertiwi, *Bingkisan Pertiwi Majalah Tahunan Jilid 3, Julai 1972*, Kuala Lumpur: Utusan Melayu Bhd., n.d.

———, *Majalah Tahunan Bingkisan Pertiwi, Jilid 4, November 1973*, Kuala Lumpur: Pertiwi.

———, 'Pertiwi Lapuran Tahunan 1975', mimeograph, Kuala Lumpur: Pertiwi.

Pountney, A. M., *The Census of the Federated Malay States 1911*, London: Darling and Son, 1911.

Ragunathan, A., *Who's Who in the Labour Movement*, Kuala Lumpur: Institut Malaysia Sdn. Bhd., 1975.

Smith, T. E., *Official Report on the 1st Election of Members to the Legislative Council of the Federation of Malaya*, Kuala Lumpur: Government Printer, 1955.

Socialist Front Party (SF), *1958 Constitution of the Socialist Front*, Kuala Lumpur: Registrar of Societies.

———, *1962–3 Annual Report of the Socialist Front National Executive Council*, Kuala Lumpur: NST Library.

———, *Report of the 10th Annual Party Conference August 18–19 1962*, Kuala Lumpur: NST Library.

———, 'Miscellaneous speeches and press releases on the SF', Kuala Lumpur: NST Library.

Thivy, John, *Collected Papers 1938–1948*, Kuala Lumpur: University of Malaya Library.

United Democratic Party (UDP—Parti Demokratik Bersatu), *UDP Constitution 1962*, Kuala Lumpur: Registrar of Societies.

———, 'Miscellaneous speeches and press releases of the UDP', Kuala Lumpur: NST Library.

———, *Report of the UDP to the Registrar of Societies*, Kuala Lumpur: Registrar of Societies, 1962.

United Malays National Organization (UMNO—Pertubohan Kebangsaan Melayu Bersatu), *Private Papers of the United Malays National Organization: Files of the Setiausaha Agung, 1946–1961; Files, UMNO Pelbagai, 1947–1962; Files, Setiausaha Agung UMNO tidak bernombor, 1949, 1953–1962; UMNO Files, Senarai-senarai Fail-fail, Kuala Lumpur, 1949–50, 1955–62*, Kuala Lumpur: Arkib Negara Malaysia.

———, *Peratoran Pergerakan Kaum Ibu UMNO 1956*, Kuala Lumpur: UMNO, 1956.

———, *Peratoran Pergerakan Pemuda dan Kaum Ibu UMNO* (approved by the UMNO Supreme Council, 13 March 1961), Kuala Lumpur: UMNO, 1961.

———, *Undang-undang Tuboh* (passed by the 13th UMNO General Assembly), 16–17 April 1960, Kuala Lumpur: UMNO, 1960.

———, *Perlembagaan UMNO* (approved 6–7 September, 1964 at the 17th General Assembly), Kuala Lumpur: UMNO.

———, *Perlembagaan UMNO (UMNO Constitution)* (passed by UMNO Special Assembly), 8–9 May 1971, Kuala Lumpur: Utusan Melayu Bhd., 1971.

———, *Perlembagaan UMNO* (passed by UMNO Special Assembly), 12 September 1982, Kuala Lumpur: UMNO, 1983.

———, *Peraturan Pergerakan Wanita (Rules of the Women's Section) (approved UMNO Supreme Council), January 15, 1972*, Kuala Lumpur: Utusan Melayu Bhd., 1972.

———, *Annual Reports 1954/5–82*, Kuala Lumpur: UMNO, 1955–82.

———, *Annual Reports of the Pergerakan Kaum Ibu UMNO, 1954/5–1976*, Kuala Lumpur: UMNO, 1955–76. (After 1976, included in the UMNO Annual Report.)

———, *Buku Cenderamata Jubli Perak Wanita UMNO Malaysia pada 25hb*

Ogos 1974, Kuala Lumpur: Utusan Melayu Berhad, 1974.

———, *UMNO Duapuluh Tahun*, Kuala Lumpur: UMNO, 1966.

———, 'Miscellaneous: Budget and Resolutions from the 1976 Wanita UMNO General Assembly', mimeograph, Kuala Lumpur: UMNO, 1976.

———, 'Miscellaneous speeches, press releases and reports of the Kaum Ibu/Wanita UMNO', Kuala Lumpur: NST Library.

United Nations, *Commission on the Status of Women, Twenty-second Session*, Background Paper No. 1 (II), 20 November 1968.

Vlieland, C. A., *British Malaya: A Report on the 1931 Census*, London: Government Printer, 1932.

Women's Institutes, National Association of, *The National Association of Women's Institutes of Malaya Handbook*, Petaling Jaya: NAWI, n.d.

Young Women's Christian Association of Malaysia (YWCA—Persatuan Wanita Keristian Malaysia), *Annual Report of the YWCA of Kuala Lumpur, presented at the Association's Annual General Meeting on 26th June, 1961*, Kuala Lumpur: YWCA, n.d.

———, *YWCA of Malaya Biennial Conference Report, 1960*, Kuala Lumpur: YWCA, n.d.

———, 'Constitution of the YWCA amended 1963', mimeograph, Kuala Lumpur: YWCA, n.d.

———, *Constitution of the YWCA amended 1976*, Kuala Lumpur: YWCA, 1976.

———, *YWCA Biennial Report 1974–1976*, Kuala Lumpur: YWCA, 1976.

Zain binti Suleiman, *Wawancara Ibu Zain, 1974* (transcript of interviews conducted with Ibu Zain), Kuala Lumpur: Arkib Negara Malaysia.

2. *Periodicals and Newspapers*
   (All published in Malaysia unless otherwise indicated)

Banteng (official organ of Parti Sosialis Rakyat Malaysia), 1965–9, intermittent publication.

Berita Harian, 1963–83 (Newspaper, Malay daily, member of the New Straits Times publishing group), select issues only.

Berita PAS (official organ of Parti Islam Sa-Malaya), 1973, 1974 and 1976, intermittent publication.

British Malaya (magazine/journal), Vol. 20 (1945–6), Vol. 21 (1946–7), Vol. 24 (1949) and Vol. 25 (1950).

Daily Highlights of the Malay, Chinese and Tamil Press, September 1952–December 1957, Singapore: Government Printer.

Far Eastern Economic Review 1973–83, Hong Kong.

Federation of Malaya Daily Press Summary, January 1958–December 1964 (Ministry of Information).

Female, 1975–6 (monthly magazine, Singapore).

The Guardian, 1966–76 (official organ of the Malaysian Chinese Association), intermittent publication. Not published in the 1980s.

Intisari Akhbar Harian (Daily Press Digest), 1965–76 (Ministry of Information). Miscellaneous copies, 1977–83.

Malay Mail, Sunday Mail, 1945–83 (independent newspaper), select issues only.

Malaya Merdeka (official organ of the United Malays National Organization), 1958–9, 1968.

Malayan Mirror (official organ of the Malaysian Chinese Association), 1952–6, intermittent publication.

Malaya Tribune, 1946–9 (independent daily newspaper).
Mimbar Sosialis (official organ of Parti Sosialis Rakyat Malaysia), 1972–3, 1976, intermittent publication.
Negara (official organ of Parti Negara), 1955.
Pekemas (official organ of Parti Keadilan Masharakat Malaysia), January–February 1974 (monthly).
Pelopor (official organ of UMNO), 1967–8, 1972–6 (monthly).
The Rocket (official organ of the Democratic Action Party), 1972–6, intermittent publication.
Straits Times, Sunday Times (from 1972 known as the *New Straits Times*), 1945–83 (independent daily newspaper).
Suara Merdeka (official organ of UMNO), 1955, 1958–60 and 1962, intermittent publication.
Suara UMNO (official organ of UMNO), 1951–4, intermittent publication.
Suara Wanita (Wanita MCA newsletter), 1975–6, intermittent publication.
Wanita, 1975–6 (monthly magazine).

3. Selected Interviews

A. Razak Khalifah, State Secretary Selangor PSRM; 17 October 1976.
Aishah binti Haji Abdul Ghani, Minister of Welfare Services, Senator and fifth *Ketua* Wanita UMNO; 1 March 1976 and 13 May 1983.
Au Keng-wah, leader of the DAP Ampang branch and prominent DAP member; 30 September 1976.
Azah Aziz, Feature Editor of Utusan Melayu group and founder of Pertama (Malaysian Women Journalists Association); 1 September 1976.
Chong Eu-ngoh, Director of Planning, Research and Evaluation, Ministry of Welfare; 14 July 1976.
Chong, Richard, reference librarian and historian of the MCA; 21 June 1976.
Chong, Rosemary (Chow Poh-kheng), MP and leader of the Wanita MCA; 12 January 1976, 17 June 1976, and 5 May 1983.
Dorairaj (Mr), Executive Secretary of the MIC; 22 September 1976.
Fatimah binti Haji Abdul Majid, MP and long-time member of the Wanita UMNO; 9 December 1975.
Fatimah binti Hamid Don, lecturer, Deputy Dean of Education Faculty, University of Malaya; 30 September 1976.
Fatimah binti Haji Hashim, former Minister of Welfare, fourth *Ketua* of the Wanita UMNO and President of the NCWO; 9 October 1976 and 5 May 1983.
Gunn Chit-wha, lawyer and early MCA member; 24 September 1976.
Gurusamy, Ramani, teacher and prominent trade union activist; 29 June 1976 and 4 May 1983.
Habshah binti Haji Osman, Wanita UMNO's Secretary; 20 April 1983.
Halimahton binti Abdul Majid, first woman elected to the Federal Legislative Council and prominent Wanita UMNO member; 16 September 1976.
Hayati Hasman, Secretary of the Dewan Muslimat PAS; 5 October 1976.
Hendon binti Haji Din, National Head of the Girl Guides and Principal of Datuk Abu Bakar English School; 25 February 1976.

Hu Se Pang (Mr), President of a DAP branch in Negri Sembilan; 30 September 1976.
Khadijah Sidek, MP, third *Ketua* of Wanita UMNO and third *Ketua* of the Dewan Muslimat PAS; 14/15 July and 26 July 1976.
Krishnan, Devaki, first elected woman in Malaya and co-founder of the Wanita MIC; 6 July and 23 September 1976 and 4 May 1983.
Krishnaveni (Dr), doctor and Vice-President of the Wanita MIC; 25 February 1976.
Liew, C.H., lawyer and President of the Federation of Women Lawyers; 9 September 1976.
Lily Majid, founder member of the Muslim Women's Welfare Board; 3 July 1976.
Lim Swee-chin, woman member of the MCA youth section; 21 June 1976.
Mariam binti Abdul Kadir, Ketua Bahagian Bibliographia Negara; 18 June 1976.
Marina binti Yusof, lawyer and political activist; 13 May 1983.
Nahappan, Janaky Thevar, prominent member of the Rani of Jhansi Brigade, MIC Wanita Selangor leader and businesswoman; 16 September 1976, 23 September 1976 and 20 May 1983.
Nayar, Ganga, Opposition MP and active member of the Labour Party, the DAP and the Gerakan; 24 May and 8 July 1976 and 18 May 1983.
Noor Asiah binti Tengku Ahmad, MP and active Wanita UMNO member in Kelantan; 10 December 1975.
Oon Hing-geok, paediatrician and DAP activist; 12 May 1983.
Puteh Mariah binti Ibrahim Rashid, first Malay woman Federal Councillor, first *Ketua* of the Wanita UMNO and long-time supporter of women's rights; 30 August 1976.
Rafidah Aziz, fourth woman to be appointed to the Senate, economics lecturer at the University of Malaya and prominent Wanita UMNO member; 22 July 1976 and 17 May 1983.
Rahmah Othman, Secretary of the Wanita UMNO; 16 February 1976, 22 and 23 April 1976 and 27 April 1983.
Ramachandran, E., former President of the Selangor Indian Women's Association and co-founder of the Selangor Indian Association; 15 July 1976.
Rasamma Bhupalan, Founder President of the Women's Teachers Union and Secretary of the NCWO; 9 July and 13 July 1976 and 20 May 1983.
Sharifah binti Abdullah, Deputy Director-General of the Ministry of Manpower; 17 August 1976.
Sharifah Aminah Alkhared, Secretary of HELWA (auxiliary of ABIM); 27 April 1983.
Soo Kim-lan, first woman on the MU Advisory Council; 12 July 1976.
Suhaila Hussein, wife of former Prime Minister Hussein Onn and active member of various social welfare organizations; 1 July 1976.
Tan Chang-soong, Executive Secretary in charge of research; 12 May 1983.
Tan, Helen, Honorary Secretary of the YWCA; 3 August 1976.
Tan Ken-sing (Mr), Chief Executive Secretary of the MCA: 15 June 1976.
Tan Siew-sin, Catherine, dietician and domestic science teacher (wife of Tan Siew-sin); 4 October 1976.

Teng (Miss), executive secretary and historian of Wanita MCA; 27 January 1976.
Wan Mohd. Muhyiddin, research librarian (UMNO); 17 September 1976.
Wan Zainab binti M. A. Bakar, MP and long-time Wanita UMNO member; 2 December 1975.
Zain binti Suleiman, third *Ketua* of Wanita UMNO, teacher and union organizer, long-time advocate for greater marital rights for Malay women; 19 October 1976.
Zakiah Hanum, President of Pertiwi; 20 July 1976.
Zaleha binti Ismail, first woman parliamentary secretary and active Wanita UMNO member; 14 July 1976.

Secondary Sources

4. Books

Abbott, D. W. and E. T. Rogowsky, *Political Parties: Leadership, Organization and Linkage*, Chicago: Rand McNally and Co., 1971.

Abdul Latif, Syed (trans.), *Al-Quran Rendered into English*, Hyderabad, India: The Academy of Islamic Studies, 1969.

Abdul Majied Mohamed Mackeen, *Contemporary Islamic Legal Organization in Malaya*, Southeast Asian Studies Monograph Series No. 13, New Haven: Yale University, 1969.

Ahmad Boestamam, *Merintis Jalan Ke Punchak (Shortcut to the Top)*, Kuala Lumpur: Penerbitan Pustaka Kejora, 1972.

Ahmad Ibrahim, *Islamic Law in Malaysia*, Shirle Gordon (ed.), Singapore: Malaysian Sociological Research Institute Ltd., 1965.

———, 'Family Law in Malaysia and Singapore', Kuala Lumpur: pre-publication copy, Faculty of Law, University of Malaya, 1973. (Later published under same title, Singapore: *Malayan Law Journal*, 1978.)

Aiyer, Neelakandha, *Indian Problems in Malaya*, Kuala Lumpur: The Indian Officer, 1938.

Aiyer, S. A., *Selected Speeches of Subhas Chandra Bose*, India: Indian Ministry of Information and Broadcasting, Publications Division, 1965.

Alisjahbana, S. Takdir, Wayagam, X. T. and Wang Gung-wu, *The Cultural Problems of Malaysia in the Context of Southeast Asia*, Kuala Lumpur: University of Malaya Press, 1965.

Allen, James de V., *The Malayan Union*, Southeast Asian Studies Monograph Series No. 10, New Haven: Yale University Press, 1967.

Almond, G. A. and J. S. Coleman, *The Politics of the Developing Areas*, Princeton: Princeton University Press, 1960.

Altekar, A. S., *The Position of Women in Hindu Civilization*, Delhi: Motilab Banarsidass, 1962.

Amyot, Jacques, *The Chinese and National Integration in Southeast Asia*, Institute of Asian Studies Monograph No. 2, Bangkok: Chulalongkorn University, 1972.

Anwar Abdullah, *Biografi Dato Onn*, Kuala Lumpur: Pustaka Nusantara, 1971.

Arasaratnam, Sinnappah, *Indians in Malaysia and Singapore*, Kuala Lumpur: Oxford University Press, 1970.

Banerjee, Bejoy, *The Indian War of Independence with Special Reference to the INA*, Calcutta: Oriental Agency, 1946.
Barber, Noel, *The War of the Running Dogs*, London: Collins, 1971.
Bastin, John and H. Benda, *A History of Modern Southeast Asia*, Englewood Cliffs, N.J.: Prentice-Hall Inc., 1968.
Bastin, J. and R.W. Winks, *Malaysia: Selected Historical Readings*, Kuala Lumpur: Oxford University Press, 1966.
Beard, Mary R., *Woman as Force in History*, New York: Collier Books, 1946.
Bienen, H., *Tanzania: Party Integration and Economic Development*, Princeton: Princeton University Press, 1966.
Brown, C.C. (trans.), *Sejarah Melayu (Malay Annals)*, Kuala Lumpur: Oxford University Press, 1970.
Buckley, C.B., *An Ancedotal History of Old Times in Singapore, 1819–1867*, Kuala Lumpur: University of Malaya Press, 1965.
Burling, Robbins, *Hill Farms and Padi Fields*, Englewood Cliffs, N.J.: Prentice-Hall Inc., 1965.
Campbell, P.C., *Chinese Coolie Emigration*, London: P.S. King and Son, Ltd., 1923.
Chambers, W.N. and W.D. Burham, *The American Party System*, New York: Oxford University Press, 1967.
Chan Heng-chee, *Notes on the Mobilization of Women into the Economy and Politics of Singapore*, Monograph on Political and Social Change in Singapore, No. 3, Singapore: Institute of Southeast Asian Studies, November 1975.
Chang, Queeny, *Memories of a Nyonya*, Singapore: Eastern Universities Press, 1981.
Chin Kee-onn, *Malaya Upside Down*, Singapore: Jitts and Co., 1946.
Coleman, J.S., *Political Parties and National Integration in Tropical Africa*, Berkeley: University of California Press, 1964.
Crotty, W.J., *Approaches to the Study of Party Organization*, Boston: Allyn and Brown Inc., 1968.
_____, *Political Parties and Political Behavior*, Boston: Allyn and Brown Inc., 1971.
Dahl, Robert A. (ed.), *Political Opposition in Western Democracies*, New Haven: Yale University Press, 1966.
De Josselin De Jong, P.E., *Minangkabau and Negri Sembilan*, Djakarta: publisher unknown, 1960.
Devapoopathy, Nadarajah, *Women in Tamil Society, the Classical Period*, Kuala Lumpur: University of Malaya Press, 1969.
Djamour, Judith, *The Muslim Matrimonial Court in Singapore*, London School of Economics Monograph No. 31, London: Athlone Press, 1966.
_____, *Malay Kinship and Marriage in Singapore*, London School of Economics Monograph No. 21, London: Athlone Press, 1965.
Dulcos, Ronnie (ed.), *Information Malaysia 1975/76*, Kuala Lumpur: Berita Publishing Sdn. Bhd., 1976.
Duverger, Maurice, *Party Politics and Pressure Groups*, London: Thomas Nelson and Sons Ltd., 1972.
_____, *Political Parties*, London: Methuen and Co. Ltd., 1954.
_____, *The Participation of Women in Political Life*, UNESCO, 1955.
Eldersveld, S., *Political Parties: A Behavioral Approach*, Chicago: Rand McNally and Co., 1964.
Elliot, Alan, *Chinese Medium Cults in Singapore*, Monograph on Social Anthro-

pology No. 14, London: London School of Economics, Department of Anthropology, n.d.

Emerson, Rupert, *Malaysia: A Study in Direct and Indirect Rule*, Kuala Lumpur: University of Malaya Press, 1970.

Finkle, Jason and R. W. Gable (eds.), *Political Development and Social Change*, New York: John Wiley and Sons Inc., 1966.

Firth, Raymond, *Malay Fishermen: Their Peasant Economy*, London: Kegan Paul, Trench, Trubner and Co., 1946.

Firth, Rosemary, *Housekeeping among Malay Peasants*, London: Athlone Press, 1966.

Freedman, Maurice, *The Chinese Family in Singapore*, London: Colonial Officer Research Studies No. 20, 1957.

Funston, N. J., *Malay Politics in Malaysia*, Kuala Lumpur: Heinemann Educational Books, 1980.

Gamba, Charles, *The Origins of Trade Unionism in Malaya*, Singapore: Eastern Universities Press, 1962.

Gangulee, N., *Indians in the Empire Overseas*, London: The New India Publishing House Ltd., 1947.

Geertz, C., *Old Societies and New States*, New York: The Free Press, 1963.

Geertz, Hildred, *The Javanese Family*, New York: The Free Press of Glencoe, 1961.

Ghosh, K. K., *The Indian National Army*, Meerut India: Meenakshi Prakashan, 1969.

Ginsburg, N. and C. Roberts, *Malaya*, Seattle: University of Washington, 1958.

Goh Cheng-teik, *The May Thirteenth Incident and Democracy in Malaysia*, Kuala Lumpur: Oxford University Press, 1971.

Gullick, J. M., *Indigenous Political Systems in Western Malaysia*, London: Athlone Press, 1965.

Gupta, Sri Sankar Sen, *Women in Indian Folklore*, Calcutta: India Publications, 1969.

Gurko, Miriam, *The Ladies of Seneca Falls*, New York: Schocken Books, 1976.

Hall, D. G. E., *A History of Southeast Asia*, London: Macmillan and Co. Ltd., 1964.

Hanrahan, G. Z., *The Communist Struggle in Malaya*, Kuala Lumpur: University of Malaya Press, 1971.

Hindley, Donald, *The Communist Party of Indonesia, 1951–63*, Berkeley: University of California Press, 1964.

Ho, Ruth, *Rainbow Around My Shoulder*, Kuala Lumpur: Eastern Universities Press, 1975.

Holland, W. L. (ed.), *Asian Nationalism and the West*, New York: Octagon Books, 1973.

Hooker, M. B., *Adat Laws in Modern Malaya*, Kuala Lumpur: Oxford University Press, 1972.

————, *The Personal Laws of Malaysia*, Kuala Lumpur: Oxford University Press, 1976.

———— (ed.), *Readings in Malay Adat Laws*, Singapore: Singapore University Press, 1970.

Husin Ali, Syed, *Malay Peasant Society and Leadership*, Kuala Lumpur: Oxford University Press, 1975.

————, *Social Stratification in Kampong Bagan: A Study of Class, Status,*

Conflict and Mobility in a Rural Malay Community, Singapore: Malayan Branch of the Royal Asiatic Society, 1964.
_____ and Sheridan, L. A., *The Federation of Malaya Constitution*, Singapore: University of Malaya Press, 1961.
Jackson, R. N., *Immigrant Labour and the Development of Malaya 1786–1920*, Federation of Malaya: Government Printer, 1961.
Jain, Ravindra, *South Indians on the Plantation Frontier in Malaya*, Kuala Lumpur: University of Malaya Press, 1970.
Kahin, George M., *Governments and Politics of Southeast Asia*, Ithaca, N. Y.: Cornell University Press, 1969.
Kapadia, K. M., *Marriage and Family in India*, Oxford University Press, 1955.
Key, V. O., *Politics, Parties and Pressure Groups*, N.Y.: Thomas Y. Crowell Co., 1942.
Kondapi, C., *Indians Overseas 1838–1949*, Bombay: Oxford University Press, 1951.
La Palombara, J. and M. Weiner (eds.), *Political Parties and Political Development*, Princeton: Princeton University Press, 1966.
Lang, Olga, *Chinese Family and Society*, New Haven: Yale University Press, 1946.
Levy, M., *The Family Revolution in Modern China*, Cambridge, Mass.: Harvard University Press, 1949.
Levy, Reuben, *The Social Structure of Islam*, Cambridge: Cambridge University Press, 1969.
Lim, David, *Economic Growth and Development in West Malaysia 1947–1970*, Kuala Lumpur: Oxford University Press, 1973.
Macridis, R. C. (ed.), *Political Parties, Contemporary Trends and Ideas*, N. Y.: Harper and Row, 1967.
MacNair, H. F., *The Chinese Abroad*, Shanghai: The Commercial Press, Ltd., 1933.
Madron, T. W. and C. P. Chelf, *Political Parties in the United States*, Boston: Holbrook Press Inc., 1974.
Mahajani, Usha, *The Role of Indian Minorities in Burma and Malaya*, Connecticut: Greenwood Press, 1960.
Mahathir bin Mohamad, *The Malay Dilemma*, Singapore: Donald Moore for Asia Pacific Press, 1970.
Manderson, Lenore, *Women, Politics, and Change: The Kaum Ibu UMNO, Malaysia, 1945–1972*, Kuala Lumpur: Oxford University Press, 1980.
Martin, Mary E. (trans.), *Women in Ancient India*, Varanasi: Vidya Vilas Press, 1964.
Mauzy, Diane K., *Barisan Nasional: Coalition Government in Malaysia*, Kuala Lumpur, Marican & Sons, 1983.
Means, Gordon, *Malaysian Politics*, London: University of London Press, 1970.
McGuigan, Dorothy, *New Research on Women and Sex Roles*, Ann Arbor: University of Michigan Press, 1976.
Miller, Harry, *Prince and Premier*, Singapore: Donald Moore Ltd., 1959.
Miller, Henry, *Menace in Malaya*, London: George G. Haup and Co., 1954.
Milne, R. S., *Government and Politics in Malaysia*, Boston: Houghton Mifflin Co., 1967.
Mohamed Noordin Sopiee, *From Malayan Union to Singapore Separation, 1945–65*, Kuala Lumpur: University of Malaya Press, 1974.

Mohamed Suffian bin Hashim, *An Introduction to the Constitution of Malaysia*, Kuala Lumpur: Government Printer, 1976.

Mohammad A. Siddiqi, *Women in Islam*, Lahore, Pakistan: Institute of Islamic Culture, 1972.

Morais, Victor (ed.), *Who's Who in Malaysia 1957–76, 1982*, Kuala Lumpur: J. Victor Morais S.B.ST.J., 1957–76.

_____, *Strategy for Action: The Selected Speeches of Tun Haji Abdul Razak b. Dato Hussein al-Haj*, Kuala Lumpur: Malaysia Centre for Development Studies, Prime Minister's Department, 1969.

Morgentheau, Ruth, *Political Parties in French Speaking West Africa*, Oxford: Clarendon Press, 1964.

Muller, *The Sacred Books of the East (The Laws of Manu)*, Vol. 25, Delhi: Motilal Banarsidas Reprint, 1964.

Musolf, Lloyd D. and J. Frederick, *Malaysia's Parliamentary System: Representative Politics and Policymaking in a Divided Society*, Boulder, Colorado: Westview Press, 1979.

Naguib al-attas, Syed, *Some Aspects of Sufism as Understood and Practiced among the Malays*, Singapore: Malaysian Sociological Research Institute Ltd., 1963.

Nanda, B. R. (ed.), *Indian Women: From Purdah to Modernity*, New Delhi: Vikas Publishing House, 1976.

Netto, George, *Indians in Malaya: Historical Facts and Figures*, Singapore: Netto, George, 1961.

Nyce, Kay, *Chinese New Villages in Malaya: A Community Study*, Kuala Lumpur: Malaysian Sociological Research Institute Ltd., 1973.

Pillay, Chandrasekaran, *The 1974 General Elections in Malaysia*, Singapore: Institute of South-East Asian Studies, Occasional Paper No. 25, November 1974.

Powell, John D., *Political Mobilization of the Venezuelan Peasant*, Cambridge, Mass.: Harvard University Press, 1971.

Purcell, Victor, *The Chinese in Southeast Asia*, London: Oxford University Press, 1951.

_____, *The Chinese in Malaya*, London: Oxford University Press, 1948.

_____, *Malaya, Communist or Free?*, Stanford: Stanford University Press, 1954.

Pye, Lucian, *Guerrilla Communism in Malaya*, Princeton, N.J.: Princeton University Press, 1956.

_____, *Southeast Asia's Political Systems*, Englewood Cliffs, N.J.: Prentice-Hall Inc., 1967.

Rajkumar, N.V., *Indians Overseas*, New Delhi: Foreign Department of the Indian National Congress, 1951.

Ratnam, K.J., *Communalism and the Political Process in Malaya*, Singapore: University of Malaya Press, 1965.

_____ and Milne, R.S., *The Malayan Parliamentary Election of 1964*, Kuala Lumpur: University of Malaya Press, 1969.

Rauf, M.A., *A Brief History of Islam with Special Reference to Malaya*, Kuala Lumpur: Oxford University Press, 1964.

Roff, W.R. (ed.), *Kelantan's Religions, Society and Politics in a Malay State*, Kuala Lumpur: Oxford University Press, 1974.

_____, *The Origins of Malay Nationalism*, Kuala Lumpur: University of Malaya Press, 1974.

Rosaldo, M. Z. and L. Lampere (eds.), *Woman, Culture and Society*, Stanford: Stanford University Press, 1974.
Rustow, Dankwart, *A World of Nations: Problems of Political Modernization*, Washington, D. C.: Brookings Institution, 1967.
Ryan, N. J., *The Cultural Heritage of Malaya*, Kuala Lumpur: Longman Malaysia Sdn. Bhd., 1971.
Sandhu, Kernial Singh, *Indians in Malaya, Some Aspects of their Immigration and Settlement (1786–1957)*, Cambridge: Cambridge University Press, 1969.
Scott, James C., *Political Ideology in Malaysia: Reality and the Beliefs of an Elite*, Kuala Lumpur: University of Malaya Press, 1968.
Short, Anthony, *The Communist Insurrection in Malaya 1948–60*, London: Frederick Muller Ltd., 1975.
Smith, T. E., *Population Growth in Malaya*, London: Royal Institute of International Affairs, 1952.
Song Ong-siang, *One Hundred Years' History of the Chinese in Singapore*, Singapore: University of Malaya Press, 1967.
Sopan, Netaji, *Subash Chandra Bose: His Life and Work*, Bombay: Azad Bhandar, 1946.
Sorauf, Frank J., *Party Politics in America*, Boston: Little, Brown and Co., 1968.
Stenson, M. R., *Industrial Conflict in Malaya*, London: Oxford University Press, 1970.
Swettenham, Frank, *Malay Sketches*, London: John Lane, 1895.
―――, *British Malaya*, London: George Allen and Unwin Ltd., 1906 (revised 1948).
Swift, M. G., *Malay Peasant Society in Jelebu*, London School of Economics Monograph on Social Anthropology No. 29, London: Athlone Press, 1965.
Ta Chen, *Emigrant Communities in South China*, New York: Secretariat Institute of Pacific Relations, 1940.
Thompson, Virginia and R. Adloff, *The Leftwing in Southeast Asia*, N. Y.: William Sloane Associates, 1950.
Tilman, Robert (ed.), *Man, State and Society in Contemporary Southeast Asia*, London: Pall Mall Press, 1969.
van der Kroef, J. M., *The Communist Party of Indonesia*, Vancouver, B. C.: University of British Columbia Publishing Center, 1965.
―――, *Communism in Malaysia and Singapore*, The Hague: Martinus Nijhoff, 1967.
Vasil, R. K., *Politics in a Plural Society*, Kuala Lumpur: Oxford University Press, 1971.
―――, *The Malaysian General Election of 1969*, Kuala Lumpur: Oxford University Press, 1972.
Von Vorys, K., *Democracy Without Consensus*, Princeton, N. J.: Princeton University Press, 1975.
Wang Gungwu (ed.), *Malaysia: A Survey*, New York: Frederick A. Praeger, 1965.
Ward, Barbara E. (ed.), *Women in the New Asia*, Netherlands: UNESCO, 1963.
Wilkinson, R. J., *Papers on Malay Subjects (1907–1916)*, Kuala Lumpur: Oxford University Press, 1971.
Wilson, Peter J., *A Malay Village and Malaysia*, New Haven: HRAF Press, 1968.
Winstedt, Richard, *A History of Classical Malay Literature*, Kuala Lumpur: Oxford University Press, 1972.

_____, *Malaya and Its History*, London: Hutchinson Ltd., 1948.

_____, *The Malays: A Cultural History*, London: Routledge and Kegan Paul Ltd., 1950.

Wolf, Margery, *Women and the Family in Rural Taiwan*, Stanford: Stanford University Press, 1972.

Wong, Aline K., *Women in Modern Singapore*, Singapore: University Education Press, 1975.

Wong Hoy-kee (Francis) and Gwee Yee-hean, *Perspectives: The Development of Education in Malaysia and Singapore*, Kuala Lumpur: Heinemann Educational Books (Asia) Ltd., 1972.

Wu Min-aun, *An Introduction to the Malaysian Legal System*, Kuala Lumpur: Heinemann Educational Books (Asia) Ltd., 1975.

Yang, C. K., *Chinese Communist Society: The Family and the Village*, Cambridge, Mass.: M.I.T. Press, 1969.

Yip Yat-hoong, *The Development of the Tin Mining Industry of Malaya*, Kuala Lumpur: University of Malaya Press, 1969.

Yong Mun-cheong (ed.), *Trends in Malaysia II*, Institute of South-East Asian Studies, Proceedings and Background Paper, Singapore: Singapore University Press, 1974.

5. Articles

Ardjasni (Khadijah binti Mohamed Sidek), Part I, 'Riwayat Hidup Saya: My Life', *Eastern Horizon*, Vol. 2, No. 1, January 1962, pp. 11–17.

_____, Part II, 'Fight for Merdeka', *Eastern Horizon*, Vol. 2, No. 2, February 1962, pp. 16–23.

_____, Part III, 'Collective Strength', *Eastern Horizon*, Vol. 2, No. 3, March 1962, pp. 39–50.

_____, Part IV, 'We are One People', *Eastern Horizon*, Vol. 2, No. 4, April 1962, pp. 37–46.

_____, Part V, 'Life in Prison', *Eastern Horizon*, Vol. 2, No. 5, May 1962, pp. 47–52.

_____, Part VI, 'Merdeka Restaurant', *Eastern Horizon*, Vol. 2, No. 6, June 1962, pp. 39–48.

_____, Part VII, 'Communalism in Malaya', *Eastern Horizon*, Vol. 2, No. 7, July 1962, pp. 49–58.

_____, Part VIII, 'Malayan Women and Merdeka', *Eastern Horizon*, Vol. 2, No. 8, August 1962, pp. 47–52.

Bamberger, Joan, 'The Myth of Matriarchy: Why Men Rule in Primitive Society', in M. Z. Rosaldo and L. Lampere (eds.), *Women, Culture and Society*, Stanford: Stanford University Press, 1974, pp. 263–80.

Bernard, Jessie, 'The Status of Women in Modern Patterns of Culture', *American Political Science Review (APSR)*, Vol. 375, January 1968, pp. 3–14.

Blythe, W. L., 'A Historical Sketch of Chinese Labour in Malaya', *Journal of the Malayan Branch of the Royal Asiatic Society (JMBRAS)*, Vol. 20, Part 1, June 1947, pp. 64–114.

Cheng Siok-hwa, 'Singapore Women: Legal Status, Educational Attainment and Employment Patterns', *Asian Survey*, Vol. 17, No. 4, April 1977, pp. 358–74.

Chung, Betty, 'Some Thoughts on the Status of Women in Southeast Asia: 1975 the International Women's Year', in *Southeast Asian Affairs, 1976*, Singapore: Institute of Southeast Asian Studies.

Deutsch, Karl, 'Social Mobilization and Political Development', *APSR*, Vol. 55, No. 3, September 1961, pp. 493-514.

Emerson, Rupert, 'Nationalism and Political Development', *Journal of Politics*, Vol. 22, February 1960, pp. 3-28.

Fisher, Marguerite J., 'Women in the Political Parties', *APSR*, Vol. 251, May 1947, pp. 87-93.

——, 'Higher Education of Women and National Development in Asia', *Asian Survey*, Vol. 8, No. 4, April 1968, pp. 263-9.

Gordon, Shirle, 'Marriage/Divorce in the Eleven States of Malaya and Singapore', *Intisari*, Vol. 2, No. 2, 1964, pp. 23-32.

Grant, Zalin, 'Mobilization of Women in Vietnam', *New Republic*, 1 June 1968, pp. 11-13.

Hashinah Roose, 'Changes in the Position of Malay Women', in Barbara Ward (ed.), *Women in the New Asia, the Changing Social Roles of Men and Women in South and South-East Asia*, Netherlands: UNESCO, 1963, pp. 287-95.

Hawkins, Gerald, 'Reactions to the Malayan Union', *Pacific Affairs*, Vol. 19, No. 3, September 1946, pp. 279-85.

Hirschman, C. and Aghjanian, A., 'Women's Labour Force Participation and Socio-economic Development in Peninsular Malaysia, 1957-70', *JSEAH*, Vol. 11, March 1980, pp. 30-49.

Ishak bin Tadin, 'Dato Onn and Malay Nationalism, 1946-1951', *Journal of Southeast Asian History*, Vol. 1, No. 1, March 1960, pp. 65-92.

Itagaki, Yoighi, 'Some Aspects of the Japanese Policy for Malaya under the Occupation, with Special Reference to Nationalism', in K. G. Tregonning (ed.), *Papers on Malayan History*, Singapore: Journal of Southeast Asian History, 1962, pp. 256-67.

Kessler, Clive S., 'Islam, Society and Political Behaviour: Some Comparative Implications of the Malay Case', *British Journal of Sociology*, Vol. 23, No. 1, March 1972, pp. 33-47.

Leis, Nancy, 'Women in Groups: Ijaw Women's Associations', in M. Z. Rosaldo and L. Lampere (eds.), *Women, Culture and Society*, Stanford: Stanford University Press, 1974, pp. 223-42.

MacAndrews, C., 'The Politics of Planning: Malaysia and the New Third Malaysia Plan (1976-80)', *Asian Survey*, Vol. 17, No. 3, March 1977, pp. 293-308.

Means, G. P., 'The Role of Islam in the Political Development of Malaysia', *Comparative Politics*, Vol. 1, No. 2, January 1969, pp. 264-84.

Menon, Lakshmi, 'From Constitutional Recognition to Public Office', *APSR*, Vol. 375, January 1968, pp. 34-43.

Mohamed Din bin Ali, 'Malay Customary Law and the Family', *Intisari*, Vol. 2, No. 1, 1965, pp. 34-41.

Png Poh-seng, 'The Kuomintang in Malaya', *Journal of Southeast Asian History*, Vol. 2, No. 1, March 1961, pp. 4-35.

Radin Soenaro, 'Malay Nationalism, 1900-1945', *Journal of Southeast Asian History*, Vol. 1, No. 1, March 1960, pp. 1-28.

Raksasataya, Asmara, 'The Political Roles of Women in Southeast Asia', *APSR*, Vol. 375, January 1968, pp. 86–90.

Rauf, M. A., 'Islamic Education in Malaya', *Intisari*, Vol. 2, No. 1, 1965.

Ridley, Jeanne C., 'Demographic Change and the Roles and Status of Women', *APSR*, Vol. 375, January 1968, pp. 15–25.

Roff, Margaret, 'The Malayan Chinese Association, 1948–65', *JSEAH*, Vol. 6, No. 2, September 1965, pp. 40–53.

Roff, W. R., 'The Persatuan Melayu Selangor: An Early Malay Political Association', *JSEAH*, Vol. 9, No. 1, March 1968, pp. 117–46.

―――, 'The Kaum Muda–Kaum Tua: Innovation and Reaction Amongst the Malays, 1900–1941', in K. G. Tregonning (ed.), *Papers on Malayan History*, Singapore: Journal of Southeast Asian History, 1962, pp. 162–92.

Rogers, Marvin L., 'Patterns of Change in a Rural Malay Community: Sungai Raya Revisited', *Asian Survey*, Vol. 22, No. 8, August 1982, pp. 757–76.

―――, 'Electoral Organization and Political Mobilization in Rural Malaysia', *Manusia dan Masyarakat*, New Series, Vol. 4, 1983, pp. 13–23.

Rosaldo, M. Z., 'Woman, Culture and Society: A Theoretical Overview', in M. Z. Rosaldo and L. Lampere (eds.), *Woman, Culture and Society*, Stanford: Stanford University Press, 1974, pp. 17–42.

Short, Anthony, 'Communism in Malaya', in Wang Gung-wu (ed.), *Malaysia: A Survey*, New York: Frederick A. Praeger, 1965, Chapter 10.

Silcock, T. H. and Ungku Abdul Aziz, 'Nationalism in Malaya', in William L. Holland (ed.), *Asian Nationalism and the West*, New York: Macmillan, 1953, pp. 267–345.

Siraj, M., 'Status Muslim Women/Family Law, Singapore', *Intisari*, Vol. 2, No. 2, 1964, pp. 9–17.

Soh Eng-lim, 'Tan Cheng Lock: His Leadership of the Malayan Chinese', *JSEAH*, Vol. 1, No. 1, May 1960, pp. 34–61.

Strauch, Judith, 'Tactical Success and Failure in Grassroots Politics: The MCA and DAP in Rural Malaysia', *Asian Survey*, Vol. 18, No. 12, December 1978, pp. 1280–94.

Swift, M., 'Men and Women in Malay Society', in Barbara Ward (ed.), *Women in the New Asia, the Changing Social Roles of Men and Women in South and South-East Asia*, Netherlands: UNESCO, 1963, pp. 268–86.

Tanner, N., 'Matrifocality in Indonesia and Africa and among Black Americans', in M. Z. Rosaldo and L. Lampere (eds.), *Woman, Culture and Society*, Stanford: Stanford University Press, 1974, pp. 129–56.

Topley, Marjorie, 'Chinese Women's Vegetarian Houses in Singapore', *JMBRAS*, Vol. 27, Part I, May 1954.

Tsubouchi, Yoshiro, 'Marriage and Divorce among Malay Peasants in Kelantan', *JSEAS*, Vol. 6, No. 2, September 1975, pp. 135–50.

von der Mehden, Fred, 'Communalism, Industrial Policy and Income Distribution in Malaysia', *Asian Survey*, Vol. 15, No. 3, March 1975, pp. 248.

Wang Gungwu, 'Chinese Politics in Malaya', *China Quarterly*, Vol. 43, July–September 1970, pp. 1–30.

Wee, Ann E., 'Some Aspects of the Status of Chinese Women in Malaya', in A. Appadori, *Status of Women in South Asia*, Bombay: Orient Longmans Ltd., 1954.

Wolf, Margery, 'Chinese Women: Old Skills in a New Context', in M. Z. Rosaldo and L. Lampere (eds.), *Woman, Culture and Society*, Stanford: Stanford University Press, 1974, pp. 157–72.

6. Unpublished Dissertations, Theses and Academic Exercises

Abdul Hamid bin Ahmad Khan, 'An Analysis of the UMNO Kaum Ibu as a Women's Political Organization', B.Ec. (Hons.), Graduation Exercise, University of Malaya, 1969.

Abdul Latib b. Omar, 'The Penghulu and Rural Development', BA Graduation Exercise, University of Malaya, 1970.

Abdul Latiff bin Sahan, 'Political Attitudes of the Malays, 1945–1953', BA (Hons.), Graduation Exercise, University of Malaya, 1959.

Amarjit Kaur, 'North Indians in Malaya: A Study of their Economic, Social and Political Activities with Special Reference to Selangor, 1870s–1940s', MA thesis, University of Malaya, 1973.

Ampalavanar, Rajeswary, 'Social and Political Developments in the Indian Community of Malaya 1920–41', MA thesis, University of Malaya, 1969.

Asiah binti Abu Samah, 'Emancipation of Malay Women, 1945–1957', BA (Hons.), Graduation Exercise, University of Malaya, 1960.

Chan Heng-chee, 'The Malayan Chinese Association', MA thesis, University of Singapore, 1965.

Chew Kee-moi, 'Some Aspects of Women in Employment in West Malaysia with Particular Reference to the Government and Estate Sectors', BA Graduation Exercise, University of Malaya, 1970.

Clark, Margaret, 'The Malayan Alliance and its Accommodation of Communal Pressures, 1952–63', MA thesis, University of Malaya, 1964.

Enloe, Cynthia, 'Multi-Ethnic Politics: The Case of Malaysia', Ph.D. dissertation, University of California, Berkeley, 1967.

Gerhold, Caroline R., 'Factors Relating to Educational Opportunities for Women Residents of the Malay Peninsula', Ph.D. dissertation, Cornell University, Ithaca, N.Y., 1971.

Halinah Bamadhaj, 'The Impact of the Japanese Occupation of Malaya on Malay Society and Politics 1941–45', MA thesis, University of Auckland, 1975.

Jesudason, Rosemary, 'The Causes and Significance of the Hertogh Riots', Long Essay, History Department, University of Malaya, 1969.

Khalidah Adibah binti Haji Amin, 'Ahmad Luthfi on the Education and Freedom of Women', BA (Hons.), Graduation Exercise, University of Malaya, 1971.

Lim Hong-hai, 'The Democratic Action Party in Perak', BA Graduation Exercise, University of Malaya, 1971.

Manderson, Lenore, 'The Development of the Pergerakan Kaum Ibu UMNO, 1945–1972', Ph.D. dissertation, Australian National University, 1977. (Later published as *Women, Politics, and Change: The Kaum Ibu UMNO, Malaysia, 1945–1972*, Kuala Lumpur, Oxford University Press, 1980.)

Mohamed Rosnan bin Sulaiman, 'Organization of the Council of Religion and the Department of Religious Affairs, Malacca', BA Graduation Exercise, University of Malaya, 1971.

Moore, Daniel E., 'The UMNO and the 1959 Malayan Elections: A Study of a Political Party in Action in a Newly Independent, Plural Society', Ph.D. dissertation, University of California, Berkeley, 1960.

Narendran, Vasantha M., 'The Women of Perupuk—An Economic Study', MA thesis, Universiti Sains Malaysia, 1975.

Ng Shui-meng, 'Legal Status of Women in Malaysia and the Philippines', unpublished paper, Institute of Southeast Asian Studies, Singapore, 1976.

Neuman, S. G., 'The Malay Political Elite: An Analysis of 134 Malay Legislators', Ph.D. dissertation, New York University, 1971.

Ong Hung-choon, Michael, 'The Democratic Action Party of Malaysia: The Case for a Malaysian Malaysia Restated', MA thesis, La Trobe University, Melbourne, 1969.

Pillay, Chandrasekaran, 'Protection of the Malay Community: A Case Study of UMNO's Position and Opposition Attitudes', MA thesis, Universiti Sains Malaysia, 1974.

Ramachandra, G. P., 'The Indian Independence Movement in Malaya', MA thesis, University of Malaya, 1970.

Rogers, Marvin L., 'Political Involvement in a Rural Malay Community', Ph.D. dissertation, University of California, Berkeley, 1968.

Sarojini, Devi A., 'Socio-Economic Aspects of Women Plantation Workers: A Case Study of the Indian Women Workers of Ladang Tengah', BA Graduation Exercise, University of Malaya, 1971.

Shaikha Zakaria, 'Muslim Women and the Law of Islam in West Malaysia', MA thesis, University of Kent, Canterbury, 1973.

Shamsul Bahrin, Tunku, 'The Indonesians in Malaya', MA thesis, University of Sheffield, 1964.

Siraj, Zaibun Nissa, 'Women and Adult Education: A Case Study of the Women's Institute Movement in Peninsular Malaysia, 1952–1974', MA thesis, University of Malaya, 1975.

Sonnadurai, Kathugamanathan, 'The Emergence of Gerakan Rakyat Malaysia—A Study of Non-Communalism', BS Hons., University of Malaya, 1970.

Index

ABDUL AZIZ BIN ISHAK, 138
Abdul Hamid bin Ahmad Khan, 164–5
A. Karim Rashid, 25
Abdul Rahman bin Haji Maulana, 110
Abdul Rahman, Tunku: Chief Minister, xviii; founder of Saberkas, 25; and IMP, 106; and KI, 96–8, 114, 170, 172, 226
Abdul Razak bin Dato Hussein, Tun, xviii–xix, 135, 161, 190
Abdullah Zawawi, 135
ABIM, 217
Abu Hassan Ashaari, Dato Haji, 162
Adams, Sir Theodore, 85–6
Adat perpateh, 4–8
Adat temenggong, 8–12
Ahmad Boestamam, 86, 105, 136, 143
Aisha Dawood, 190
Aishah Ghani: AWAS president, 86–7; biographical details, 173; in elections, 143, 173; KI positions, 158, 160, 168–9, 172–7, 212–14; and Malay women, 158–9, 174–5; and marriage and divorce reform, 160–1, 174; Minister of Welfare, 163, 173; Pertiwi founder, 237; Senator, 173; support for MCA, 185; UMNO positions, 126–7, 156, 173, 216; and women politicians, 111, 155, 202, 214–15
Aishahton binti Mohd. Fadhullah Suhaimi, 158
Alien's Ordinance, 1933, 49
All Indonesian Women's Association, 96
All-Malaya Council for Joint Action (AMCJA), 91, 101, 104
Alliance Party, xvii–xix, 98, 104, 111–12, 142–3, 146
Aminah Baharin, 237
Ampalavanar, Rajeswary, 61
Angkatan Wanita Sedar (AWAS), 86–7, 173, 226
Anti-Imperialist League, 51
Anwar Ibrahim, 217
Arumugam, Meenambal, 190–1, 220
Asiah binti Abu Samah, 26, 111
Au Keng-wah, 196–7, 229

Azah Aziz, 237
Azharah, 197
Azizah binti Jaafar, 93
Azizah binti Tengku Petra, Tengku, 93

BAAGAYA BINTI YAACOB, RAJA, 197
Banerjee, Bejoy, 74
Barisan Nasional (BN), xix
Beard, Mary R., xiii
Bhupalan, Rasamma, 139–40, 220
Bibi Aishah binti Hamid Don, 110
Blythe, W. L., 49
Bose, Ras Behari, 71–2
Bose, Subhas Chandra, 72–4
British in Malaya, 4, 84–6, 90
Budariah, Tengku, 96
Bulan Melayu, 26, 170
Burhanuddin, 86, 133, 173

CENTRAL INDIAN ASSOCIATION OF MALAYA (CIAM), 69–70
Chan Sow-ying, 138
Che Bee Noor, 98
Cheah Inn-kiong, 92
Chen Man-hin, 195
Chen, Michael, 183
Chia, S. E., 107
Chinese, xv–xvii, 33–6
Chinese Chambers of Commerce, 101
Chinese Ladies Association of Singapore, 49
Chinese Marriage Committee, 48
Chinese women: and associations, 49–52, 100–3, 108–10, 114–15; and education for girls, 36, 41–2, 100; and Japanese Occupation, 51–2; and Malayan Union, 101; and marriage and divorce, 42–8, 188–9; migration to Malaya, 33–9, 49; role in economy, 40–2
Chong, Rosemary, 181–2, 184–5, 188–9, 214, 218, 228
Choong, David, 219
Chow Poh-kheng, *see* Chong, Rosemary

Constitution, 112-13
Consultative Committee on the Constitutional Proposals (CCC), 91-2
Council of Ulamas, 96

DASIMAH DASIR, 159, 168
Daughters of Islam, *see* Pemudi Islam
Daughters of the Country, *see* Putri Negara
De Josselin de Jong, P. E., 4
Democratic Action Party (DAP), xvii, xix, 139, 194-6, 211, 221; women in, 194-7, 222, 225-6
Devi, N. Saraswathi, 146
Dewan Muslimat, 99, 105, 133-5, 171, 192-4, 221, 227
Divorce, *see* Marriage and divorce
Djamour, Judith, 9-11, 16-17
Duverger, Maurice, xiii

ELECTIONS, xvi-xix, 102, 109-10, 142-6, 200-3
Elliot, Alan, 46-7
Emergency, xvi, 101, 228-9
Emerson, Rupert, 113
Eu, Mrs Robert, 110

FAJAR ASIA, 27
Fatimah binti Abdul Majid, 145, 216
Fatimah binti Haji Yunos, 110
Fatimah binti Musa, 89, 237
Fatimah binti Sulaiman, 159
Fatimah Harun, 27
Fatimah Hashim, on Alliance committee, 126; biographical details, 171-2; in Dewan Rakyat, 143, 145, 193; KI positions, 99, 126, 158-9, 168, 171-2, 176, 227; and Malay women, 175; and marriage and divorce reform, 172; NCWO founder, 140; and women politicians, 141
Federation of Malaya Agreement 1948, xvi, xviii, 90-2, 169
Fernandez, Mrs, 133
Firth, Raymond, 10, 21
Firth, Rosemary, 10, 18, 21
Freedman, Maurice, 41, 46-8

GAMMONS, L. D., 85-6
Gent, Governor, 91, 169
Gent, Lady, 235
Gerakan Rakyat Malaysia (GRM), xvii, xix, 139, 197-8, 211; women in, 197-8, 225-6
Ghandi, Benny, 197
Ghosh, K. K., 73-4
Goh Cheng-teik, xvii
Gunn Chit-wha, 103
Guru, 170

HALIMAHTON BINTI ABDUL MAJID, 88, 92-3, 97, 110-11, 114, 126, 141
Halinah Bamadhaj, 26-7
Hamid Tuah, 135
Harun bin Idrus, 232
Hasan Manan, 25
Hashinah Roose, 9
Hasnah binti Ahmad, 146
Hayati Hasman, 194
Hisbul Muslimin, 221-2
Holland, W. L., 73
Hussein Noordin, 144
Hussein Onn, Datuk, 161, 163, 214, 232

IBRAHIM BIN YAACOB, 25
Ibu Zain, *see* Zain binti Haji Suleiman, Hajjah
Idris, Raja (Sultan of Perak), 12
Independence, xviii, 112
Independence of Malaya Party (IMP), xvi-xvii, 104, 106-7, 109, 170
Indian Association of Taiping, 69
Indian Independence League (IIL), 52, 69, 71-4, 228
Indian Muslims, 67
Indian Nationalist Army (INA), 71-5
Indian women: and associations, 69-70, 103-5, 107-10, 115; education, 66-7; and Japanese Occupation, 70-5; migration, 56-60; marriage and divorce, 60-4; non-Hindus, 67-9; in public office, 105, 109-10; role in economy, 64-7
Indian Women's Association of Negri Sembilan, 104
Indians, xv-xvii, 56-60
Isa Mohammed, 25
Ismail, Tun, 159
Isteri Milap, 104
Isteri Sat Sangh Sabha Sentul, 69, 103-4
Isteri Sansar, 104

JAIN, RAVINDRA, 63
Japanese Occupation of Malaya, xvi, xx, 27, 51-2, 70-5
Jayaraj, Mrs, 133
Johore Malay Women's Association, 93
Joseph, Amy, 110

KAM WOOH-WAH, 131, 182
Kaum Ibu UMNO, xx, 225-7; 1947-57, 86-100, 113-14; 1957-69, 122-30, 146-7; 1969-76, 153-77; 1976-83, 212-17; co-operative, 158; education for girls, 95, 99; and elections, 95-6, 98, 111, 141-3, 161-2, 214-15; formation of, 87-94; and fundamentalism, 216-17; goals of, 154, 170, 174; leaders, 165-75;

marriage and divorce, 90, 95, 128–9, 160–1, 217, 230–1; members, 99–100, 159, 164–5, 212–13; status of women, 129, 140, 162–3; structure of, 94, 123–8, 154–5; and UMNO, 96–8, 114, 123–9, 144, 154–6, 227, 232; women's foundation, 158
Kelsom Lateh, Raja Perempuan, 86
Kesatuan Insaf Tanah Ayer (KITA), 215
Kesatuan Melayu Muda (KMM), 25
Kesatuan Melayu Singapura (KMS), 24
Kesatuan Raayat Indonesia Semenanjong (KRIS), 25
Khadijah Sidek: biographical details, 96–7; DM leader, 99, 133–4; in elections, 143, 145–6; KI positions, 96–7, 114, 170–1, 227; and UMNO, 97–9, 232
Khalsa Diwan Selangor, 69
Khoo, Betty, 199
Khoo Teck-ee, 106
Khursiah, Tengku Puan Besar, 236
Kian Sit-har, 189
Kodikaita, Mrs R., 220
Kong, Mrs, 197
Koperasi Dermajaya Wanita, 158
Koperasi Wanijaya, 189
Koruthi, Mrs, 105
Krishnan, Devaki, 105, 109–10, 113, 132–3, 143, 190, 220
Krishnaveni, G., 190–1, 220
Kumpulan Ibu Sepakat, 88–9, 170
Kuomintang (KMT), xv, 50–1, 102

Labour Party (LP), xvii, 107–8; women in, 107–8, 136–8, 146, 225–6
Laycock, Amy, 110
Lee Choo-lan, 131
Lee Chou-neo, 36
Lee Hau-shik, Datuk Sir Henry, 102
Lee Kiu, 100
Lee San-choon, 131, 182–4, 189, 219, 232
Lembaga Kebajikan Perempuan Islam Persekutuan Tanah Melayu, *see* Muslim Women's Welfare Council of Malaya
Lew Siat-yee, 143
Liew Lai-ching, 196
Light, Francis, 33, 56
Lim Chong-eu, 102, 111, 130, 138–9, 197, 229
Lim Chong-eu, Mrs, 139
Lim Diw-loon, 219
Lim Heng-kiap, 188
Lim Keng-yaik, 182–3
Lim, P. G., 137, 146
Lim Sean-lean, 189, 218
Lim Swee-sim, 103, 131
Lobo, Mrs, 104

Lok Swee-chin, 222
Loke Soh-lip, 107, 109

MacMichael, Sir Harold, 85–6
Malay Mail, 162
Malay Nationalist Party (MNP), xvi, 86–7, 91, 101, 173
Malay Rulers, 84–5, 90–2, 112
Malay women: and associations, 86–100, 105–15; and class, 18–20; and education, 22–3, 25–7; and Federation Agreement, 92; and Islam, 6, 9, 12–18; and Japanese Occupation, 27–8; in Kelantan, 10, 21; and Malayan Union, 85–6, 92, 226–7; and marriage and divorce, 7–18; in Negri Sembilan, 5–8; position in family, 10–12; role in economy, 20–3
Malay Women's Association of Kelantan, 88
Malay Women's Association of Lower Perak, 88
Malay Women's Progressive Party, *see* Persekutuan Wanita Melayu Progresif
Malay Women's Training College (MWTC), 26
Malay Women's Welfare Association of Singapore, 235
Malayan Communist Party (MCP), xx, 50–1, 101
Malayan Democratic Union, 91
Malayan Indian Association, 69
Malayan Labour Ordinance of 1923, 60
Malayan People's Anti-Japanese Army (MPAJA), 52, 83
Malayan People's Anti-Japanese Ex-Servicemen's Association, 101
Malayan People's Anti-Japanese Union (MPAJU), 52
Malayan Union (MU), xvi–xvii, 84–6, 89–90
Malayan Women's Service League, 235
Malays, xiv–xvii, 3–4; nationalism, 83; privileges of, 112–13; traditional political system, 18–19
Malay(si)an Chinese Association (MCA), xvi, 102–3, 130, 211, 232; in Alliance Party, xvii–xix; and IMP, 106; and UMNO, xviii, 102–3, 109; women in, xx, 102–3, 130–2, 181–9, 225–8
Malay(si)an Indian Congress (MIC): in Alliance, xvii–xix, 104; in AMCJA, 91, 104; formation, xvi, 104; and IMP, 104, 106; women in, xx, 104–5, 132–3, 225–8
Malaysian People's Movement Party, *see* Gerakan Rakyat Malaysia (GRM)
Malaysian Social Justice Party, *see* Parti

Keadilan Masyarakat Malaysia
Manderson, Lenore, 25, 129, 165–6, 168, 227
Manickavasagam, Tan Sri V., 115, 190, 220, 228
Marina Yusof, 158, 160, 168, 172, 212–14, 216
Marriage and divorce: Chinese, 42–8; Indians, 60–4; Malays, 7–18
Mary, S., 195
Matahari Memanchar, 27
Milap, 104
Milne, R. S., 111, 143
Minangkabau, 4–8
Mohamed Asri, Tan Sri, 192, 221, 232
Mohammad Eunos bin Abdullah, 24
Murugesu, S. S., 132
Musa Hitam, 215
Muslim Women's Council, *see* Dewan Muslimat
Muslim Women's Welfare Council of Malaysia, 236–7

NAHAPPAN, JANAKY THEVAR, 74, 104, 220
Nair, C. V. Devan, 195
Nair, Mrs, 107
Narayanan, P. P., 106
Narendran, Vasantha M., 21
Nathan, J. E., 10, 38, 42–3, 46, 61
Nathan, Mrs James, 105
National Association of Women's Institutes in West Malaya, 236
National Convention Party, 138
National Council of Women's Organizations (NCWO), 122, 139–41, 146, 173, 234
National Front, *see* Barisan Nasional (BN)
National Islamic Council, 160
National Operations Council, xviii, 154
National Party, *see* Parti Negara
Nayar, Ganga, 137, 196–8, 201, 215, 229
Netto, George, 56
New Democratic Youth League, 101
Ng Ah-lan, 219
Noraini Salleh, 196
Norashikin binti Yusof, 199
Normah binti Kamaruddin, 110, 160

OEI SOIE-NIO, 111
Ong Hung-choon, Michael, 195
Onn bin Jaafar, Datuk: in Dewan Rakyat, 139; founder of IMP, 106; founder of PMS, 85, 89, 170; founder of PN, 107; founder of UMNO, 85; and KI, 89, 94–5, 114, 169, 226; and votes for women, 92; and Women's Institute, 236
Oon, B. H., 93, 108, 143
Oon Hing-geok, 222

PAN-MALAYAN FEDERATION OF TRADE UNIONS, 91
Pan-Malayan Islamic Party (PMIP), *see* Parti Islam sa-Malaya
Pan-Malayan Labour Party (PMLP), *see* Labour Party (LP)
Pan-Malayan Malay Congress, 89
Parti Demokratik Bersatu, 138–9, 146, 215
Parti Islam sa-Malaya, xvi, xix, 105, 211–12, 221, 225
Parti Keadilan Masyarakat Malaysia, xvii, xix, 198–9
Parti Negara, xvii, 107, 139, 142
Parti Sosialis Rakyat Malaysia (PSRM), xvi, 105–6, 135–6, 138, 215
Pekemas, *see* Parti Keadilan Masyarakat Malaysia
Pemanas, 89
Pemudi Islam, 27
Penang Women's Association, 100
Peninsular Indonesia People's Union, *see* Kesatuan Raayat Indonesia Semenanjong
People's Progressive Party (PPP), xix, 139, 200
People's Socialist Party of Malaysia, *see* Parti Sosialis Rakyat Malaysia (PSRM)
Perak Chinese Women's League, 100
Perak Progressive Party, 108
Pergerakan Kaum Ibu, *see* Kaum Ibu UMNO
Pergerakan Melayu Semenanjong Johor (PMS), 85–6, 89, 170
Persatuan Kaum Ibu Selangor, 88–9
Persatuan Melayu Perak, 88–9, 169
Persatuan Melayu Seberang Prai, 89
Persatuan Melayu Selangor (PMS), 24, 89
Persekutuan Guru-Guru Perempuan Johor (PGGPJ), 26–7
Persekutuan Wanita Melayu Progresif, 89
Pertiwi, 237
Pillai, Malathi, 109
Pires, Tomé, 20
Progressive Malay Women's Corps, *see* Angkatan Wanita Sedar (AWAS)
Prostitution, 17, 37–8
Province Wellesley Labour Party, 93, 108
Purcell, Victor, 33, 50
Puteh Mariah binti Ibrahim Rashid, Datin: biographical details, 169; in Federal Legislative Council, 93, 169; founder of Muslim Women's Welfare Council,

236-7; in IMP, 106-7; KI head, 89-90, 93, 95, 114, 169, 226-7; in Perak State Council, 93, 169; in Persatuan Melayu Perak, 88-9, 169; and votes for women, 92
Putri Negara, 107

RACIAL VIOLENCE, xviii, 153-4
Raffles, Sir Thomas Stamford, 33, 37
Rafidah Aziz: in Dewan Rakyat, 214; and *ketua kampong*, 162-3; KI positions, 160, 168, 172, 213-14; and Malay women, 175; parliamentary secretary, 163; on UMNO Supreme Council, 216
Rahimah binti Abdul Rahman, 142, 145, 170
Rahmah binti Salleh, 107
Rahmah Othman: in Dewan Rakyat, 214; KI positions, 213-14, 216; on women in UMNO, 155, 159, 175
Ramachandra, G. P., 73-4
Ramachandran, E., 69, 107, 109
Ramachandran, M. K., 69
Ramani, R., 106
Ramlah binti Dahlan, 111
Ramlah binti Muzir, 197-8
Rani of Jhansi Brigade, 73-5, 103
Ratnam, K. J., 83, 111, 143
Roff, W. R., 24
Rogers, Marvin L., 155, 164-5
Rokiah Rashid, 237
Rosaldo, M. Z., xx, 76

SAADIAH SARDON, 158
Sabah Alliance, xix
Saberkas, 25
Safiah Majeed, 237
Sakinah Junid, 87, 133, 135, 192-4, 221
Saleha binti Mohamed Ali, 88-9, 94, 106-7
Salmah Shamsuddin, 237
Salmah Sheikh Hussein, 134, 146, 163, 193
Sambanthan, V. T., 132, 190
Samsuddin bin Harun, 139
Sandhu, K. S., 56-8
Sarawak Alliance, xix
Sarawak National Party, xix
Sarawak United People's Party, xix
Sarojini, Devi A., 63, 66
Secretary of Chinese Affairs, 37, 48
Seenivasagam brothers, 108, 139
Selangor Indian Association (SIA), 69
Selangor Ladies Association (SLA), 92, 100
Selangor Malay Union, *see* Persatuan Melayu Selangor (PMS)
Selangor Women's Association, *see* Persatuan Kaum Ibu Selangor
Selangor Women's Relief Association, 100
Semangat Asia, 27
Senu Abdul Rahman, 98
Shamsiah Fakir, 87
Sharifah Alwijah, Tengku, 89
Sharifah Mahani binti Syed Hamzah, 135
Sharikat Sendikit Sri Wanita, 158
Sikhs, xv, 68-9, 104
Singapore Malay Union, *see* Kesatuan Melayu Singapura (KMS)
Singapore Malay Women's Association, 96
Singh, Mohan, 71
Singh, Sardar Budh, 115
Siow See-lian, 138
Siti Noor Hamid Tuan, 199-200
Siti Nurani Janain, 27
Smith, T. E., 111
Socialist Front (SF), 137-8, 146
Sofiah binti Abdullah, 23
Somasundram, L. C., 109
Soo Kim-lan, 92-3, 235
Soosay, A. M., 70
Star, 162
Status of women, 129, 140-1
Straits Chinese British Association, 101
Suhaila Hussein, 167
Suit Sai-mooi, 131
Swaminathan, Lakshmi, 72
Swettenham, Frank, 8, 19-20
Swift, M. G., 4, 6, 11
Syarikat Dermajaya, 158

TAMBIDQUI, MRS, 235
Tamil Nesan, 190
Tan Ah-gogh, 145-6
Tan Chee-khoon, 199
Tan Cheng-lock, Sir, 102-3, 106-7, 130
Tan Chui-swee, 195
Tan Siew-eng, 137-8
Tan Siew-sin, 102, 130-1, 181-3, 232
Templer, Lady, 236
Ten Yoon-fong, 103
Teng Ah-luan, 219
Thaver, G. V., 69
Thaver, K. V., 107
Thaver, M. S., 74
Thevar, S. M., 104
Thivy, John A., 74, 104, 115
Thompson, V., 101
Tsubouchi, Yoshiro, 17-18

UMI KALTHUM AHMAD, 136
Union of Johore Women Teachers, *see* Persekutuan Guru-Guru Perempuan Johor
Union of Malay Youths, *see* Kesatuan

Melayu Muda (KMM)
United Democratic Party, *see* Parti Demokratik Bersatu
United Malays National Organization (UMNO): in Alliance Party, xvii-xix; and elections, xvi-xvii, 109–10; and Federation Agreement, 91; formation, xvi, 85, 89; and IMP, 106; and KI, 96–8, 114, 123–9, 144, 154–6, 227, 232; and MCA, 102–3
United Women's Association, *see* Kumpulan Ibu Sepakat

VASIL, R. K., 108, 201
Vellu, Samy, 220
Vlieland, C. A., 42–3

WAN AMINAH BINTI YUSOFF, 134
Wan Teh Aminah binti Wan Yusof, 163
Wang Gungwu, 51
Wanita MCA: activities, 189; formation, 181–5, 228–30; goals, 183, 185–6; growth of, 188; language problems, 230; period 1976–83, 217–19; structure, 186–7
Wanita MIC, 104–5, 189–92, 220, 232–3
Wanita Pekemas, 199
Wanita Rakyat, 105–6, 135–6, 199–200
Wanita UMNO, *see* Kaum Ibu UMNO
Ward, Mrs, 235
Wilkinson, R. J., 4
Williams, Mrs Lloyd, 107
Wilson, P. J., 9–11
Winstedt, Richard, 12

Women's Bureau, 140–1
Women's Federation, 91, 100–1
Women's Institute, 113
Women's International Democratic Federation, 100–1
Wong Chin, 92, 100
Workers' Party, 215
Working Committee, 91, 169
Wu Lian-hwa, 218

YOUNG MEN'S INDIAN ASSOCIATION (YMIA), 69
YWCA, 113, 139, 236

ZAHARA BINTI MOHAMED NOOR, 96, 235
Zahara binti Mohamed Talib, 110
Zaharah binti Abdul Majid, 156
Zaharah Othman, 133–4
Zahariah binti Abdullah Kuang, 89
Zahrah binti Abdullah, 86
Zaidah binti Hashim, 135, 200
Zain binti Haji Suleiman, Hajjah: biographical details, 23, 170; in Dewan Rakyat, 143; in Johore State Council, 93; KI president, 96, 99, 114, 227; KIS founder, 88–9, 170; PGGPJ founder, 26–7, 170; and women in UMNO, 96
Zainab binti Ahmad, 106, 135
Zaitun Othman, 237
Zakiah Hanun, 237
Zaleha Ismail, 156, 168, 175, 212–14, 216
Zubaidah binti Haji Ali, 105, 133–4
Zulkifli Mohammed, 135

WITHDRAWN
From Bertrand Library